Knowing God
The Journey of the Dialectic

Related titles by Anthony Mansueto

Knowing God series:

Restoring Reason in an Age of Doubt, Volume 1 (Ashgate 2002)

The Ultimate Meaningfulness of the Universe, Volume 2
(forthcoming 2011)

Doing Justice, Volume 4 (forthcoming 2010)

Forthcoming in the Theopolitical Visions series
(Cascade Books):

The Death of Secular Messianism:
Religion and Politics in an Age of Civilizational Crisis

Knowing God
The Journey of the Dialectic

VOLUME 3

A̲N̲T̲H̲O̲N̲Y̲ E. M̲A̲N̲S̲U̲E̲T̲O̲

◆PICKWICK *Publications* • Eugene, Oregon

THE JOURNEY OF THE DIALECTIC: KNOWING GOD, VOLUME 3

Copyright © 2010 Anthony E. Mansueto. All rights reserved. Except for brief quotations in critical publications or reviews, no part of this book may be reproduced in any manner without prior written permission from the publisher. Write: Permissions, Wipf and Stock Publishers, 199 W. 8th Ave., Suite 3, Eugene, OR 97401.

Pickwick Publications
An Imprint of Wipf and Stock Publishers
199 W. 8th Ave., Suite 3
Eugene, OR 97401

www.wipfandstock.com

ISBN 13: 978-1-55635-987-3

Cataloguing-in-Publication data:

Mansueto, Anthony E.

    Knowing God / Anthony E. Mansueto.

    xxiv + 378 p. ; 23 cm. Includes bibliographical references.

    Contents: 1. Restoring Reason in an Age of Doubt—3. The Journey of the Dialectic.

    ISBN 13: 978-0-75460-853-0 (v. 1)
    ISBN 13: 978-1-55635-987-3 (v. 3)

    1. Metaphysics. 2. Philosophy — Modern. I. Title.

BT50 .M265 2002

Manufactured in the U.S.A.

Contents

Introduction / vii

1 Before Metaphysics / 1

2 The Axial Age / 22

3 The Great Age of Metaphysics / 76

4 Modernity and Metaphysics / 220

5 Towards a New Dialectical Metaphysics / 312

Bibliography / 365

Introduction

STATEMENT OF THE PROBLEM

THE PURSUIT OF WISDOM—of some first principle in terms of which the universe can be explained and human action and human society ordered—is the leading factor in all human development and civilizational progress. Wisdom is, on the one hand, the very substance of spirituality: it is nothing more or less than knowledge of God—or, if one of concludes that there is no God, of how to live meaningfully with that truth. But it is, at the same time, the beginning and rule of all practical rationality. Without knowledge of the end or *telos*, neither *techne* (excellence in making) nor *phronesis* (excellence in judging the means to the ends of human action) are possible. It is wisdom which gives us a vision of the Good we strive to create, which reveals to us the transcendental principles of value which properly govern social life, and which points us towards our final end or purpose.

There are, to be sure, many paths to wisdom. The simplest and most fundamental of these—that of right action—is, in principle at least, open to all human beings, regardless of their social condition or context. By doing justice we gain an immediate, preconceptual and connatural knowledge of the Good and thus of God. This is the ordinary way of wisdom that makes the scientific classification of our species as *homo sapiens* (and not, for example, merely *homo faber* or *homo sciens*) so apt. It is also the way of the great mystics who, having mastered all of the intellectual and practical disciplines, exoteric and esoteric, arrive at long last at the simplicity of the divine.

But in order to do the Good we must know the Good—or at least be under the guidance of someone who can set us on the right path. And herein lies the dilemma. How do we know the Good, or know who is a reliable guide to the Good? In a just social order people are habituated from birth to right action and thus set on the road towards the cultivation of the moral virtues and of connatural knowledge of God. But what if the society we live in is not just, and cultivates not virtue but vice? So long as the injustice is straightforward and transparent—a question of warlords extracting rents, taxes, and forced labor from dependent peasant communities, which themselves remain intact, it may be enough for prophets and sages to point out that the end to which the society as a whole is ordered has become distorted—that rather than seeking the good of the people the rulers exploit them and live a life of luxury and violence. This is the sort of wisdom represented by the ancient Chinese *ru* (sages), intellectual ancestors of the Confucian tradition, who exposed the rapacious and violent character of the Shang dynasty and set the stage for the Chou revolution (Yao 2000: 16–30). It is also the sort of wisdom represented by the "judges" or *shophetim* of earliest Israel, who rallied the people against their Canaanite oppressors and set the stage for the development of a tradition which met God in the struggle for a just social order (Gottwald 1979).

Things change, however, with the advent of petty commodity production—of a society in which decisions regarding resource allocation are driven by supply and demand—around 800 BCE. On the one hand, this opens up new opportunities for those who historically lacked the resources or lineage to participate actively in the public arena (which, we must remember, was also the cultic arena, the arena of meaning and value *par excellence*). And trade brings people who historically upheld different meanings and different values into contact with each other. But petty commodity production also tends increasingly to dissolve village communities and to make all human interactions simply a means of advancing individual consumption interests. People in a market society experience the world as a system of only externally related individuals—atoms—without *arche* or *telos* or else as a structured but ultimately meaningless system of quantities (prices). This undermines the basis in experience for knowing the Good and thus for the development of a connatural knowledge of God. Thus it is not surprising that it is just precisely around this time that we see the first assault on wisdom as such, and the emergence, in all of the principal civilizational centers, of emerging petty commodity production, of nihilistic ideological trends: Hellenic Atomism and Sophism, the Indian *Caravka* and *Ajivika* schools, and just a little bit later Chinese Legalism (Collins 1998). Meaning, in other words, becomes contested and problematic.

Introduction

It is also at just precisely this same moment that we witness the advent of a new way of wisdom—rational metaphysics or the *via dialectica*[1]—which attempts to ascend by means of rational argument to the principle which before human beings knew by means of an experiential and preconceptual knowledge. Between roughly 800 and 200 BCE we witness the development of something like a rational metaphysics in all those centers of civilizational development undergoing a transition to petty commodity production: the Mediterranean Basin (Socrates, Plato, and Aristotle), India (Upanishadic Brahminism, Jainism, and Buddhism), and China (Taoism, Confucianism, and Mohism). And it is under *generalized* commodity production (capitalism), in which labor and capital as well as goods and services have become commodities, that dialectics achieves its most ambitious expression in the philosophical system of Hegel and in the political movement towards socialism.

This new way of wisdom is not just a response to skeptical critiques. It represents real progress. It is a good thing to learn right action under the leadership of a wise guide; it is better to choose one's own guide from among many possibilities, and better still to decide rationally and autonomously the fundamental questions of meaning and value that define human life.

It is, however, just precisely this way to wisdom which has come increasingly under attack from the most diverse quarters, so that the "end of metaphysics" is all but taken for granted among most scholars in the West. Indeed, there is no discipline that has been more uniformly derided for a longer period than rational metaphysics. Of the ancient and medieval sciences that have now fallen into disrepute, even astrology and alchemy get better press. Declared impossible (at least as it had traditionally been understood) by Kant (Kant 1781/1969), its assertions were determined to be logically meaningless by Ayer (Ayer 1937). Even the materialist wing of the dialectical tradition has turned against metaphysics, arguing that the universe can be explained adequately in terms of purely material principles (Engels 1880/1940), while others argue that "modern science"

---

1. By "dialectics" in this context we mean any attempt to rise to a first principle by means of rational argument—as opposed to direct experience or revelation. We will argue over the course of this work for the underlying unity of Western dialectics from Socrates, Plato, and Aristotle through their Arab and Latin interpreters, up to Hegel, Marx, Engels, and modern dialectical materialism and idealism. We will also show that Indian and Chinese metaphysics are dependent on cognate disciplines.

has determined the universe to be ultimately meaningless (Krause 1999). Earlier books (Mansueto 2002b, Mansueto and Mansueto 2005) have been devoted to answering these epistemological and cosmological critiques of metaphysics. In this book we turn to what we will call the "political-theological critique": the claim, which has come from diverse philosophical perspectives and divergent positions along the political spectrum (Kierkegaard 1848, Nietzsche 1889, Heidegger 1928/1968, Arendt 1958, Levinas 1965, Derrida 1967/1978), that metaphysics,[2] quite apart from whether one believes it to be epistemologically possible or impossible, scientifically founded or not is, in fact, at the very root of a plethora of social evils, from technological domination through patriarchy, imperialism, and totalitarianism to atheism and despair. It is not only, or not so much, that we no longer *can* do metaphysics as that we *ought* never to have tried in the first place.

The political-theological critique of metaphysics is a complex and diverse ideological phenomenon. Before we can analyze either its social basis and political valence or its substantive claims and internal logic we need to define better its principal characteristics. Broadly speaking the main elements of the political-theological critique of metaphysics include:

---

2. The terminology here is tricky. Most of the critics of a rational ascent to first principles of explanation and action have, at least since Heidegger, called the discipline they criticize "metaphysics" or "ontotheology," and used another term for their own doctrine of the self-disclosure of Being, the laws of motion of matter, etc. (ontology, dialectics). A few, however, (e.g., Levinas) call the discipline that they criticize it by some other name (e.g., ontology), and reserve the term metaphysics for their own doctrine. The Marxist tradition presents particularly difficult terminological problems. Some Soviet philosophy, for example, explicitly rejects metaphysics on the grounds of one or another version of the cosmological critique, but advances just precisely the sort of universal explanatory-causal theory which Heideggerian critics call metaphysical. This is especially true of Bogdanov and Deborin who, as we will see, actually tended to a materialist pantheism. Other Marxists, (e.g., Bhaskar) use the term metaphysics in the disciplinary sense to describe a general inquiring into being, while eschewing the incipient materialist pantheism of the Soviets for an ontology centered on negativity, contradiction, and absence (Bhaskar 1993). Still others reject the term entirely, counterpoising it dialectics (Mao 1937a/1971, Amin 1988/1989, 1999).

For the purposes of this book "ontotheology" means any attempt to ascend rationally to a first principle of explanation and action. Metaphysics means any treatment of being in general, whether or not it concludes to such a first principle.

Introduction

1. a common definition of metaphysics as a universal causal theory which attempts to rise rationally to a first principle in terms of which the universe can be explained and human action ordered;

2. an historical analysis centered on philosophy's lapse into "ontotheology,"[3] so that history is either divided between a pre-ontotheological golden age and later periods of metaphysical/political/technological domination, or else between two historical streams identified variously with Athens and Jerusalem, Center and Periphery, the Same and the Other; and

3. an ideological analysis which links ontotheology with making or *telos*, and which charges it with legitimating patriarchy, tributary empires (Amin 1988/1989), and/or modern "technological" and totalitarian domination, both capitalist and socialist, as well as, in its religious forms, humanity's rebellion against God.

In some cases the aim of this critique is straightforwardly nihilistic in the sense of rejecting a global meaning (Nietzsche and the early Derrida); in others it is mounted in defense of a specifically anti-rationalist spirituality (Kierkegaard, Levinas); in other cases still (Heidegger) it hovers in between.

This situation has, more recently, been altered by two developments. On the one hand, we have witnessed attempts from within the dialectical materialist tradition to come to terms with postmodernism and reground an emancipatory politics. This has involved what we might call a partial re-instatement of metaphysics, albeit one which scrupulously avoids anything which looks like ontotheology. Among the most important examples of this trend we would cite the dialectical critical realism of Roy Bhaskar (Bhaskar 1989, 1993) and the democratic materialism of Alain Badiou (Badiou 1988, 2006). On the other hand, thinkers from within the postmodernist tradition have re-engaged reli-

---

3. The precise historical location of this lapse is constantly shifting. For the early Heidegger (Heidegger 1928) it was in the birth of dialectics itself, in Socrates, Plato, and Aristotle. For the later Heidegger (Heidegger 1941) the lapse took place later with the translation of the Hellenic "unconcealment" of Being into Latin, the language of road builders and empire makers, a crystallization which is completed in the Middle Ages when Being is identified with the supreme maker, the Christian Creator God. More recently John Milbank has located the lapse variously in the Scotist option for a univocal doctrine of Being (Milbank 1989) or in the growing influence of Islamic philosophy in the West (Milbank 2006b).

gious questions, something which has resulted in a broad spectrum of approaches, from the late Derrida's "acts of religion" (Derrida 2001), through John Caputo's "weak theology," (Caputo 2006), to the Radical Orthodoxy of John Milbank and his associates (Milbank 1989, 1999, 2006b). In his later work, at least, Milbank seems to be proposing a re-engagement with metaphysical questions, albeit a limited one intended, like that of the postmodern dialectical materialists, to avoid the pitfalls of ontotheology.

STATE OF THE QUESTION

There have been many defenses of metaphysics during the course of the past 200 years. The work of Hegel was first and foremost an attempt to answer the epistemological questions raised by Kant. The same is true of Neo-Thomists such as Maritain and Garrigou-Lagrange. Objective idealists (Schelling and Soloviev), transcendental idealists (Rahner), process thinkers (Whitehead and Hartshorne), and phenomenological realists (Scheler and Wojtyla) have taken paths around, rather than through, the Kantian critique, but have nonetheless arrived at something like a rational metaphysics. Hegelian philosophers such as Errol Harris have, meanwhile, joined to their defense of dialectical reason a penetrating answer to the cosmological critique, arguing that the foundations of metaphysics are, in fact, to be found in science and that even modern, mathematical physics points clearly towards transcendental principles of meaning and value. Even Marxists, their historic allergy to the term metaphysics and to the idea of transcendental first principles notwithstanding, have increasingly come to recognize that Marx himself was an Aristotelian essentialist (Meikle 1985) and that Marxist ethics is in fact an historicized form of natural law ethics (Daly 2000), something which ultimately depends on metaphysical foundations.

There has, however, to my knowledge, been no attempt to answer what I have called the "political-theological critique," no explicit defense of *ontotheology*. More specifically, there has been no attempt to evaluate empirically the claim that "ontotheology" understood in the Heideggerian sense is at the root of modern nihilism and state terror—and this in spite of the emergence of a comparative historical sociology of philosophy.[4]

---

4. Randall Collins's monumental *The Sociology of Philosophies* (Collins 1998), while an extraordinary scholarly synthesis on which this work in many ways builds, adopts a microsociological perspective in which such questions are not even asked.

Introduction

The reason for this failure is simple: ontotheology lacks an autonomous material base in the modern world. Philosophy generally, where it has not been displaced entirely by the sciences on the one hand and the hermeneutic disciplines on the other (Mansueto 2006), has been forced to perform what Roy Bhaskar (Bhaskar 1993) calls "underlaboring" for these disciplines, for the revolutionary left, or for religious institutions. The result has been that even where an attempt has been made to argue for the necessity of a metaphysics of some kind (Bhaskar 1993, Badiou 1988, 2006, Milbank 2006b), the defenders of metaphysics have carefully avoided making a case for its autonomy, and specifically for the ability of reason to rise unaided to knowledge of first principles.

This said, there are some resources available for our project. Max Weber's *Economy and Society* (Weber 1921/1968) and his comparative historical studies of religion treat the birth of metaphysics as part of a larger process of religious rationalization which he regards as issuing ultimately (but only in the special case of Calvinism) from the instrumental rationality which defines the modern West, a claim which, if sustained, would at least partly second the postmodernist position. Karl Jaspers' (Jaspers 1953) theory of an "axial age" is, in effect, an extension of Weber's theory and attempts to explain the later development of humanity's principal civilizational traditions in terms of an initial "breakthrough" during the period between 800 and 200 BCE, which included, among other things, a turn towards more abstract religious language—in effect the birth of metaphysics—and an associated concern for questions of ethics generally and social justice in particular. Jaspers differs from Weber in taking a somewhat less Eurocentrist approach and in emphasizing the contribution of metaphysics to the larger historical movement towards freedom and social justice. Weber and Jaspers make a powerful case for the essentially progressive character of rational metaphysics; they fail to explain why it emerged when and where it did and not elsewhere, and thus fail to offer a really complete and rigorous analysis of its social basis and political valence. Jaspers also fails to extend his analysis of the impact of "axial age" ideologies into the long period between 200 BCE and 1500 CE—the Silk Road Era—a period which will be critical for our argument, while Weber does so only to demonstrate the "incomplete" character of all attempts at religious rationalization before the advent of Calvinism.

Three texts from the historical materialist tradition attempt to rectify these difficulties, though they often, I will argue, go in exactly the wrong direction. Ellen Meikins Wood's *Class Struggle and Ancient Political Theory* (Wood 1979) argues that rational metaphysics developed as a defense of the slave mode of production against the popular forces represented in philosophy by the Sophists. I will show that, in point of fact, Sophism was an attempt to legitimate the injustices generated by petty commodity production and dialectics an attempt to ground a critique thereof.

Samir Amin's *Eurocentrism* (Amin 1988/1989) argues, as we have noted, that metaphysics helped legitimate the great empires of the Silk Road Era (which he understands as tributary rather than petty commodity societies, and thus as founded on the coercive extraction of surplus from dependent peasant communities rather than trade). What he does not consider is the possibility that it also helped to transform these empires, encouraging the allocation of at least part of the surplus product in ways which promoted the development of human capacities, even as it legitimated the rule of kings who were very far from being sages or philosophers. That it did will be one of the principal claims of this work.

Another resource comes from a much (and unjustly) maligned text in the historical materialist tradition: Georg Lukacs *The Destruction of Reason* (Lukacs 1953/1980). Lukacs suggests that the bourgeoisie has, historically, used two distinct ideological strategies. During the period of its rise, when it could still present itself as a force for progress vis-à-vis the old feudal classes, and during periods of economic stabilization since then, it has employed a direct apologetic, arguing that capitalism is, in fact, a force for the development of human capacities. After about 1848, however, the developing contradictions of capitalism and the emergence of the workers movement puts the bourgeoisie on the defensive. It became increasingly difficult to legitimate capitalism as a force for social progress, which was being constrained both by ever-deeper economic crises and by bourgeois resistance to the economic and political demands of the working class. The result was the elaboration of an "indirect apologetic," which argued not so much that capitalism was just as that a just society is impossible—and that socialism was therefore an empty dream. By the end of the century, this indirect apologetic had taken on the additional task of legitimating imperialist war and expansion—something deeply in conflict with the ideals of the democratic revolutions, but also the only way a capitalist society could resolve its internal contradictions (Lukacs 1953/1980).

Introduction

The indirect apologetic was advanced along a number of fronts. At the epistemological level it became increasingly common to claim that it is impossible to make objective, rational judgments of value and that all knowledge is, in a certain sense, interpretive and perspectival. Physics, biology, sociology, and psychology, meanwhile, arrived at a series of results all of which called into question the ultimate meaningfulness of the universe and the Enlightenment doctrine of progress, results such as the Poincaré Recurrence Theory, the Second Law of Thermodynamics, Darwinian Evolution, Malthusian demographics, Weber's view of history as a kind of war of the gods, and Freud's reduction of human nature to sexual desire and aggression. This line of reasoning culminated ultimately in Nietzsche's doctrine of the "will to power."

What Lukacs misses is the fact that the lineage of the indirect apologetic, which runs from Kierkegaard through Nietzsche to Heidegger, is *also* the critique of ontotheology and that his critique of the indirect apologetic makes sense only as a defense of ontotheology. This is because he himself is firmly situated within a tradition that is nervous about any metaphysics which points towards transcendental principles of meaning and value.

An important contribution to the discussion has, finally, been made by one of the Radical Orthodox critics of autonomous metaphysics— John Milbank—who has argued that modernity is a product not so much of metaphysics generally but of the univocal metaphysics which emerged in the late Middle Ages. Following Joseph Ratzinger, he attributes this turn to Islamic influence and dates to roughly 1300. We will argue that it was, in fact, a reflex of the emergence of the modern nation state and has much older roots, reaching back into the Augustinian tradition which is so important to Milbank. The underlying insight, however, is critical to our argument.

What we need, then, is a comprehensive defense of ontotheology against the political-theological critique, one which understands and criticizes postmodern irrationalism as an attack not only on *reason* but also on meaning, and which not only reveals the social basis and political valence of that attack, but actually refutes it.

Introduction

THESIS, METHOD, AND OUTLINE

Thesis

The *Journey of the Dialectic* is intended to do precisely that. As such, it advances both socio-historical and philosophical theses.

1. On the sociohistorical front, I will argue that:

    1.1 Dialectics and rational metaphysics form part of a larger process of religious rationalization and democratization set in motion by the emergence of petty commodity production, which undermines the basis in experience for the spontaneous development of a preconceptual, experiential, and connatural knowledge of God and renders meaning problematic. This process took place in three phases:

    1.1.1. A series of initial breakthroughs, which took place during what Karl Jaspers called the Axial Age (800–200 BCE) and which accompanied the initial emergence of petty commodity production in the Mediterranean Basin, India, and China;

    1.1.2. A period of systematic elaboration and synthesis (corresponding to the great Silk Road Era (200 BCE–1800 CE) with higher prophetic and mystical wisdoms, which constituted ontotheology in the West and comparable systems in India and China; and

    1.1.3. A (largely aborted) movement towards the democratization of the ideal of the philosopher which was cut short by the Asharite and Augustinian reactions in the West, with only limited parallel developments in India and China.

    Dialectics and, when it emerged, ontotheology, at once helped reground meaning and value where it had been called into question, opened up participation in deliberation around fundamental questions of meaning and value to those outside the traditional hereditary priesthoods, and—far from legitimating either the slave mode of production, or the great tributary empires of the great Silk Road Era—in fact served to transform them, restricting exploitation and redirecting surplus towards activities which promote human development and civilizational progress. And as a global, or at least pan-Afro-Eurasian movement, dialectics and ontotheology, cannot be regarded as in any sense "Eurocentric."

1.2. Contrary to the claims of Heidegger and the postmodernists, ontotheology is innocent of the charge that it lies at the root of the modern nihilism and state terror. Modernity, rather, emerges out of a very specific univocal metaphysics, which developed in both Christendom and *Dar-al-Islam* at the end of the Middle Ages as a reflex of and support for the emergence of sovereign nation states.[5] By a univocal metaphysics we mean one in which all things—including God, if one believes in God—are understood to exist in the same way, with only quantitative differences between them. Under a univocal metaphysics the debate about God is a debate about whether or not there is an infinitely powerful being. If there is, then one must submit to Him. If there is not, then one is free to try to approach divinity by scientific and technological means. An analogical metaphysics, by contrast, understands God as *Esse*, the power of Being as such, and everything as a contingent beings which share in but do not possess that power. This means, on the one hand, that the gulf between God and humanity is qualitative and cannot be breached, but also, on the other hand, that the proper response to God is not submission but rather participation. The nontheistic metaphysics which develops in Mahayana Buddhism offers, we will see, a similar formulation.

    1.2.1. This initially takes the form of a spirituality of authority and submission centered on the doctrine of the sovereignty of God, something shared by both

---

5. This insight regarding the connection between modernity and a univocal metaphysics is due to John Milbank (Milbank 1990). I differ from Milbank, however, in seeing the roots of the univocal metaphysics of modernity in the whole Augustinian trend of the Christian Middle Ages, rather than only in its latest manifestations (e.g., Duns Scotus) and in locating the social basis of this trend in the Germanic warlord class which gradually established sovereign nation states in Europe. A parallel development can be seen in the Islamic world with the rise of Asharite *kalam* and its consolidation under the Turks, and the consequent attack on Aristotelian *falasafa*.

Augustinian Christianity (Catholic and Protestant) and the Asharite strain in Islam which became dominant after the fall of the Abbasid Caliphate.

1.2.2. Eventually, however, this "early modern" ideal yielded, by way of the scientific revolution, to the high modern ideal which seeks to actually *build* god by means of scientific and technological progress—something which is possible if the distance between creature and creator is merely quantitative. The critique of ontotheology is, in effect, a cover for this secret religion of high modernity and for the univocal metaphysics which is the precondition for "liberating" both the market and the state from transcendental principles of meaning and value and from the sapiential authorities, religious or philosophical, who are the guardians of those principles.

1.2.3. There is, to be sure, an alternative critical-humanistic stream of modernity which retains the analogical metaphysics of *Esse* characteristic of medieval Christendom and *Dar-al-Islam*, but which, rather than using this metaphysics to ground higher theological and mystical wisdoms, proposes instead an innerworldly strategy for divinization by means of purely philosophical wisdom and revolutionary political practice. This stream of modernity is the product of an Averroist counter-reaction to the Augustinian and Asharite rejection of reason and ontotheology and is reflected in the tradition of the Latin Averroists, Spinoza, Hegel, (the young) Marx, and their interpreters. While this strain of dialectics does invest philosophical wisdom and revolutionary political practice with tasks they cannot fulfill and represents a kind of sectarian, innerworldly Gnosticism, it cannot be held responsible for modern nihilism and state terror either. Indeed, most proponents of this tradition (e.g., Lukacs, Fromm, and the Frankfort School) have been powerful critics of totalitarianism whether capitalist and fascistic or socialist.

2. At the substantive philosophical level:

   2.1 I will resume the dialogue which was made both possible and necessary by the completion of the Silk Road but which Europe abandoned beginning in the fourteenth century in favor of warfare and conquest, showing how the *via dialectica* was already, during the Silk Road Era, approaching something like a consensus regarding the nature of the first principle. I will extend that dialogue, attempting a higher synthesis which reconciles the Western metaphysics of *Esse* with the sophisticated Buddhist metaphysics of the Tien Tai and Hua-yen traditions, which I will argue represents the completion of a long process of evolution within Buddhism away from metaphysical skepticism and towards a coherent doctrine of the first principle. The result will look surprisingly similar to the metaphysics of the Chinese *dao xue* (Neo-Confucianism) of the Song Dynasty. I will show how the resulting dialectical metaphysics can ground a revitalized and radically historicized natural law ethics and a new spirituality which will, at long last, carry humanity beyond modernity.

   2.2 I will show how it is possible to both defend the autonomy of metaphysics and of ontotheology *and* be respectful towards higher prophetic and mystical wisdoms, thus correcting the error made by Radical Aristotelianism and modern dialectics.

Method

Making this sort of argument is an extraordinarily complex task. It requires situating metaphysics socially and historically with respect to the social contexts out of which it emerged and in which it developed and both substantively and sociohistorically with respect to other wisdoms and *their* social contexts. And this in turn requires a substantial engagement with key questions of history and social theory. If part of what is at issue is the political valence of rational metaphysics and its impact on human development and human civilization, then it will be necessary to address historic debates in social theory regarding the relationship between the material basis of human society, social structure (including technology, economics, and politics), and ideology. Indeed, my defense of dialectics includes a significant revision of Marx's dialectical sociology which "civilizational ideal," the transcendental end to a society is ordered, as against the structural factors (technology, economics, politics, and ideology understood as the way we organize our experience of the universe), the importance of which Marx and his followers tended overestimate.[6]

Demonstrating my thesis will also require engagement with a wide variety of more specific historical questions. The first of these concerns the claim, first advanced in the nineteenth century, that some or all human societies were matriarchal or at least characterized by relative gender equality. This debate is important to our argument because of the close historical association, which we will demonstrate, between Socratic philosophy and various Mediterranean goddess cults. The association between philosophy and the cult of the goddess affects our judgment regarding the political valence of the philosophical tradition, and the debate around primary matriarchy in turn affects our judgment regarding the political valence of the goddess cults. We will defend a modified form of the primary matriarchy thesis and argue that feminist philosophers are not without cause in claiming a feminine origin for dialectics and in arguing for a patriarchal deformation of the tradition, though I will differ in some particulars from Mary Daly's treatment of this question.

Second, it will be necessary to engage the debate around the relative importance of trade, conquest, and religion in the transition from what are generally called "Neolithic" societies and the development of complex urban centers. This debate is important because it bears on the role of wisdom generally in human civilizational progress. I will argue for what I call an "archaic" mode of social organization in which villages are grouped around a temple complex which serves as a center of meaning, which noncoercively centralizes surplus and invests in activities which promote human development and civilizational progress: botanical and astronomical research for example, and religious speculation. I use the term "archaic," partly after Mary Daly (Daly 1998), because the mode of social organization in question involved ordering to an *arche*. These archaic centers also, often, became centers for trade and objects of conquest,

---

6. For a systematic treatment of this question, see Mansueto 2002a.

creating pathways of transition to petty commodity and tributary social structures. It is also possible that in some cases the priestly rulers of these centers themselves became corrupt and coercive, leading to a transition to tributary structures by another means.

Third, it will be necessary to engage the debate around the so-called "axial age," the period between 800 and 200 BCE first identified by Karl Jaspers in which societies throughout Eurasia seemed to have arrived at or received new insights into transcendental principles of value. This was the period of the great Hebrew prophets, of Socrates, Plato, and Aristotle, of Mahavira and Buddha and the Upanishads, and of Confucius and Lao Tzu and Mo Tzi. Jaspers' insight is intriguing, but I will argue that we are, in fact, dealing with three distinct developments. The first is a collapse of the sacral monarchies of the late Bronze Age under the pressure of both peasant and aristocratic revolts, something which issues in the emergence of Israel and primordial Judaism and which produces the literature of Archaic[7] Greece, the Vedas, and the Chou Revolution in China. The wisdom texts of this period reflect a new insight into the first principle—or rather into the failure of human rulers to live up to their sacral claims—but remains essentially mythological, in the sense that it uses image and story to convey meaning. Later, beginning around 700 or 600, with the advent of petty commodity production, which is also a period of political fragmentation throughout much of Eurasia, we see a gradual process of rationalization which involves both the development of an abstract mathematics, an increasing abstract characterization of first principles, and the gradual development of a rational dialectics—but not the widespread development of complete metaphysical systems. (Aristotle is an exception or perhaps rather a transitional figure in this regard.) Finally, around 200 BCE we see the completion of the Silk Road, the emergence of a new complex of empires based on petty commodity production rather than archaic or tributary surplus centralization, and an essentially scholastic effort to elaborate and systematize the metaphysical implications of the teachings of the prophets and sages of the two preceding epochs. This opens the real "medieval" era, which then lasts until 1800 or later when in-

---

7. The term archaic with a lower case "a" refers to archaic social structure as defined above. When I use the term win an initial capital "A" I am using it in the ordinary sense to refer to the period of Greek history between roughly 800 and 500 BCE. As it turns out, early Archaic Greece did, in fact, have an archaic social structure, though it rapidly made the transition to petty commodity production.

dustrial capitalism authentically comes into its own. Even this periodization is fuzzy, of course. Prophecy and epic, for example, continue: witness Jesus and Mohammed on the one hand and Beowulf on the other, and one of the main themes of the medieval epoch—specially in Europe and the Islamic world is the relationship between prophecy and dialectics.

Fourth, it will be necessary to engage the debate around the capitalist transition which, with the recent work of Andre Gunder Frank (Frank and Gillis 1992, 1993, Frank 1998), has become a debate around whether or not the concept of capitalism itself is really meaningful. While I will draw extensively on his work, much of which I find brilliant, I will argue that there is a change in social structure which marks off the modern capitalist era from the long "middle age" of petty commodity production. I support the claim of the dependency/world-systems school that the rise of Europe is due not to unique features of European culture, but rather to the European conquests of Africa, the Americas, and eventually much of Asia. I will, however, show that these conquests were themselves the result of internal contradictions in European society and of the rise of an aggressive, intolerant Augustinian form of Christianity after the middle of the thirteenth century. This transition involved a war on metaphysics and more specifically a war on Aristotle which undermined the metaphysical foundations of natural law ethics and thus the moral check on economic rapacity.

Finally, I will need to engage the debate around the historic significance of socialism, the reasons for the collapse of the Soviet bloc, the likely future of socialism elsewhere, and the next steps in the human civilizational project. Socialism is the response of the dialectical tradition to generalized commodity production, just as institutions such as the *zakat* and the guild system were the response of dialectics to petty commodity production. All are an attempt to subject resource allocation to substantive ethical norms. But socialism has stood in a profoundly ambiguous relationship to modernity. It has, at once, been a movement of peasants and artisans resisting capitalist modernization, of scientifically minded intellectuals frustrated with capitalism's failure to generate a technological utopia, and of humanistic intellectuals frustrated with its failure to promote rational autonomy and democratic citizenship. And its crisis is at once civilizational—part of a larger crisis of modernity—and structural—the result of its own, distinctive internal contradictions, economic, political, and cultural. Our defense of dialectics and thus of rational metaphysics will thus be a *partial* defense of socialism against the charge that it is inherently totalitarian, for example, but will also treat socialism as an historically specific, limited form of civilization and point it towards new ways of subordinating resource allocation to substantive moral norms.

This is a complex, multidimensional, and interdisciplinary book. My method will consist principally in an analysis of the social basis, principal doctrines and arguments, and political valence of dialectics and rational metaphysics from its points of origin in classical Greece, India, and China up until the present, including a discussion of its complex interactions with other wisdoms. The structure of my argument thus depends on situating various developments in philosophy in the social contexts out of which they emerged and which they in turn affected. Since neither I nor any one else, to my knowledge, possesses specialist knowledge of each and every epoch of human history, I have had to rely extensively on the work of other scholars who have devoted their lives to the understanding of particular epochs.[8] Sources important for the analysis of particular historical periods but not for the overall argument of the book are indicated in the relevant chapters and in the bibliography. A few works, however, stand out for having contributed key conclusions which are essential to my overall argument, because they argue theses so diametrically opposed to my own that my entire work is shaped in some significant degree by argument with them, or because they have contributed significantly to my overall understanding of the shape of human history, and thus the larger context in which my argument unfolds. I have already mentioned above those thinkers who contributed most directly to the argument of this work: Weber, Jaspers, Meiksins Woods, Amin, and Lukacs. Works which shaped my overall understanding of either the outlines of human history generally or key periods thereof include Geoffrey de Ste. Croix's *The Class Struggle in the Ancient Greek World* (de Ste. Croix 1980), Perry Anderson's *Passages from Antiquity to Feudalism* and *Lineages of the Absolutist State* (Anderson 1974a and b), Samir Amin's *Class and Nation, Historically and in the Current Crisis* (Amin 1979/1980), Barrington Moore's *Social Origins of Dictatorship and Democracy* (Moore 1966), Theda Skocpol's *States and Social Revolutions* (Skocpol 1979), Andre Gunder Frank's *ReOrient* (Frank 1998), and other works from the world-systems trend. I often disagree

8. See Andre Gunder Frank's excellent defense of the use of secondary analysis in the introduction to *ReOrient* for an extended treatment of this problem (Frank 1998).

with these authors, and make it clear where I do so and why, but am substantially dependent on their mastery of the primary sources and their pioneering work in the development of *longue durée* and comparative historical analyses. Randall Collins's *The Sociology of Philosophies* (Collins 1998), despite theoretical differences so great that we rarely even ask the same questions, provided an inspiring model for how to write a comparative historical sociology of philosophy.

I have, of course, turned to the primary sources when necessary in order to document my claims or substantiate a particular interpretation. This has most often been true with respect to my reading of key texts in the philosophical tradition.

My argument proceeds chronologically. The first chapter addresses the role of wisdom in human societies prior to the emergence of petty commodity production. The second chapter analyzes the initial response to the emergence of markets and situates Socratic dialectics in this context, looking at it side by side with the Upanishads, Jainism, early Buddhism, and early Taoism, Confucianism, and Mohism. The third chapter looks at the long Middle Ages—the Silk Road Era—and shows how rational metaphysics generally and dialectics in particular helped to regulate petty commodity production. The chapter also makes an argument for the gradual convergence of humanity's principal metaphysical traditions. Chapter 4 looks at the complex relationship between metaphysics and modernity, both capitalist and socialist. Chapter 5 outlines the new dialectical metaphysics we have been arguing towards throughout the course of the book and shows how it can help address the current crisis and chart the next steps in the human civilizational project.

1

Before Metaphysics

ANY ASSESSMENT OF THE social basis and political valence of metaphysics must, of necessity, be comparative. We must look at the emergence and development of metaphysics, in other words, against the background not only of its immediate social contexts, but also against the background of the other wisdoms which preceded it and which persist alongside it, and *their* social contexts.

Now prior to the emergence of metaphysics, humanity had at its disposal two principal "ways of wisdom": direct, "ecstatic" experience and the form of imaginative discourse we call myth.[1] These two ways are, furthermore, directly related to each other. Emile Durkheim taught us that the religious symbols embodied in myth constituted a kind of "collective representation" of social structure. This collective representation is generated in the context of what he called "collective effervescence." Collective effervescence is a heightened state of social interaction that occurs primordially in those moments of revolutionary upheaval that constitute a society.

> In such moments of collective ferment are born the great ideals upon which civilizations rest. These periods of creation or renewal occur when men for various reasons are led into a closer relationship with each other, when reunions and assemblies are most frequent, relationship better maintained, and the exchange of ideas most active ... At such moments this higher form of life is lived with such intensity and exclusiveness that it monopolizes

---

1. By imaginative discourse we mean any discourse which approaches fundamental questions of meaning and value by means of images and stories. Imaginative discourse includes myth and literature. Myth is a spontaneous and collective product and reflects shared meanings which are given and unproblematic; literature is the product of an identifiable author or authors and reflects an intervention into an ongoing debate around meaning which has become problematic.

all minds to the more or less complete exclusion of egoism and the commonplace. At such times the ideal tends to become one with the real, and men have the impression that the time is close when the ideal will in fact be realized and the Kingdom of God established on earth. (Durkheim in Bellah 1973: l)

This state is reproduced in ritual, including both the individual rituals followed by shamans and similar religious virtuosos, and the great collective rituals that reproduce the social bond and reorient the people towards the ideals to which their civilization is ordered. Myth is, as it were, the crystallized form of this collective effervescence—and the only form in which we have access to it.

Recent—i.e., postmodern—thought has tended to prefer myth to philosophy, when it considers the possibility of wisdom at all. This is true for two principal reasons. First, it is claimed, myth is open to plural interpretations and is thus less susceptible to manipulation as a strategy for power (Hatab 1990). Second, it is accessible to broader layers of the population, which can not only understand it without special formal preparation, but also participate in creating and transforming it. No one, of course, really believes that we can or should restore myth to its dominant place in the cultural sphere. But the postmodern preference for myth has led to the emergence of narrative strategies in such core sapiential disciplines as theology and ethics. Prime examples of this include the narrative theology of Stanley Hauerwas (Hauerwas 1981) and Alasdair MacIntyre's effort to restore a virtue ethics without its historic metaphysical underpinnings (MacIntyre 1981).

This section will argue that while myth can mediate real wisdom—i.e., authentic knowledge of first principles—societies in which a mythic discourse dominates are, in fact, *less* pluralistic than those in which myth has at least partly given way to philosophy. What distinguishes myth from other forms of imaginative discourse, such as literature, is just precisely the fact that it is a *shared* story and a *shared* complex of images. The pluralism which Hatab and the other postmodern defenders of myth so value emerges only as a part of the Axial Age process of religious rationalization and democratization which took place between 800 and 200 BCE.

Access to myth and its creation and interpretation is, furthermore, quite restricted even in societies that appear to be egalitarian from an economic point of view. This is because even in horticultural, communitarian societies wisdom is the preserve of priestly elites which are, quite often, closed and hereditary. And by the time philosophy emerged, these priestly elites were also very much allied with the warlord ruling classes. Philosophy, along with literature and other new ways of wisdom, which emerge during the Axial Age, represent a relative opening up of access to the sacred by comparison with myth and ritual. Philosophy may require both certain aptitudes and certain training, but it is at least open to those who have these regardless of birth.

Finally, we will argue, even if myth does function in some contexts in a way that is pluralistic and open, it has the disadvantage of not being able to *demonstrate*. This means, on the one hand, that the organization of a society around certain principles and values is a matter of power rather than rational persuasion and, on the other hand, that in a context in which meaning has become problematic, claims on behalf of certain meanings remain ungrounded.

Our basic strategy will be simple. We need to begin by reiterating our definition of wisdom. Following Aristotle, we have defined wisdom as knowledge of some first principle in terms of which the universe can be explained and human action and human society ordered. To put this in another way, the search for wisdom is a search for meaning and value, an attempt to situate ourselves in the universe and in whatever, if anything, lies beyond it, and to determine, on the basis of that knowledge, what is worth doing. We will need to examine the various forms of mythic discourse in order to ascertain whether or not they meet this definition.

Second, we will need to look at the way in which mythic discourse functioned and continues to function in its social contexts, in order to determine whether or not it allowed plural meanings and popular participation in its creation and interpretation. Mythic discourse as we have defined it is dominant in the following types of social formations:

- the hunter-gatherer/tribal societies of the Paleolithic, as well as most surviving societies of this type,
- the horticultural/communitarian societies of the Neolithic, as well as most surviving societies of this type,
- pastoral and raiding/tribal societies, which also emerged during the Neolithic, as well as most surviving societies of this type,
- archaic societies in which clusters of villages are organized around ritual centers, and
- the agrarian/tributary societies of the Bronze Age.

Finally, we will need to assess, in the context of each society, whether or not the fact that mythic discourse does not permit *demonstration* represents a real deficit.

THE TOTEMIC WISDOM OF HUNTER-GATHER/ TRIBAL SOCIETIES

There continues to be considerable debate regarding the religious life of the earliest human societies. At stake in this debate is not so much what people in the earliest human societies worshiped (animal, plant, and mineral forms predominate), but rather why and how. Those who regard the earliest religions as animistic or nature-oriented understand religion as a kind of primitive science and technology: human beings venerate the natural processes on which they are dependent or the spirits they imagine are behind those processes, which they cannot understand. Those who have emphasized totemism, on the other hand, understand religion as primarily a social reality. For Durkheim the natural objects which serve as totems are symbols of various social groups, and the religious system as a whole a way of representing and reinforcing the social structure—an interpretation that is even more compelling in societies that worship real or fictive ancestors. The contemporary focus on shamanism, finally, focuses on religion as a reality *sui generis*, focused on accessing a spirit world by means of various ecstatic processes.

I continue to find Durkheim's argument for the primacy of totemism in hunter-gatherer/tribal societies and his analysis of totemism as a system of collective representations which reflects the kinship structure of these societies most convincing, for the simple reason that they alone actually *explain* the emergence of a conceptual framework in the context of which human beings could begin to think about the origin and structure of the natural world, about the soul, about their relationships with their ancestors, etc. While it is impossible to make definitive inferences regarding the nature of Paleolithic religion, the preponderance of animal images suggests a similar totemic pattern in these societies.

Totemism provides a complex of symbols, which more or less clearly represents to the people the structure of their own society while, at the same time, serving as a means of making sense out of the universe itself. Thus the indigenous peoples of Australia are organized in tribes composed of half-tribes or moieties and clans. Each clan has its own totem—

a mineral, plant, or animal, which serves as its emblem or symbol—as does each individual. Clan solidarity is conserved and reproduced in communion feasts in which the totemic object, taboo during the rest of the year, is eaten in a great feast. These feasts are occasions for the collective effervescence which we discussed earlier—that particularly intense state of social interaction in which individuals are at once brought into a higher degree of interaction with each other and discover or rediscover the principles and values on which their collective life is founded. This system of totems also functions as a kind of universal taxonomy. Members of a clan really *are* their totem. Thus some people are wallabies and others witchity grubs, as are certain kinds of rocks, rivers, and so on. The existence of a scheme of social classification provides a basis in experience for the act of classification. To put the matter in Thomistic terminology, it creates a connatural knowledge of *taxis*,[2] and thus the capacity to produce a taxonomy. There is, furthermore, a kind of "category of totality," the existence of which Durkheim attributes to the experience of inter-tribal relationships, which is represented in a kind of vague and remote "Great Spirit" (Durkheim 1911/1965).

Shamanism, which involves a kind of direct experience of the sacred, may seem to be different from this and we might be tempted to amalgamate it to other types of direct experiential knowledge of first principles—the kind associated, for example, with yogic practice or infused contemplation. These latter forms of knowledge are, however, nonimaginative and nonconceptual. Shamanic experience, on the contrary, makes rich use of images—generally the same images as are important in the larger totemic system. In all probability, therefore, it makes sense to treat shamanism as the "virtuoso" form of the same type of religious knowledge generated at an ordinary level by the totemic system.

Given this analysis, it is apparent, first of all, that totemism really is a kind of rudimentary wisdom. It allows both individuals and communities to orient themselves in the world, finding their place in it, and deriving from this knowledge a sense of what they must do. This said, there are real limitations. There are, for example, rarely coherent myths of origin, and the question of origin and thus of Being is thus not sharply posed. Totemism represents a beginning of wisdom, but no more.

2. *Taxis* is a Greek word for order. It connotes an arranging in accord with a principle or rule, much as a general might order his troops for battle—thus the word "tactics" which is derived from the same root.

The reason for this, we would like to suggest, is that the structure of hunter-gatherer societies, while it provides a basis in experience for *taxis* or classification, does not really provide a basis in experience for the concept of "ordering to an end." Individuals, to be sure, have aims or purposes, but these are, for the most part, all the same, as are the ways in which they realize those purposes. But there is no sense of being part of a larger organic whole in which each part serves an end higher than itself, to which it is ordered, and serves it in a way that is different from the other parts. That experience, and the sort of wisdom it engendered, would have to await the advent of horticulture and of the village community.

Second, it should be clear that there is very little room for pluralism in totemic systems. This is because, in order for the system to work, it must be *shared*. If an interpretation of the system were developed that set its interpreters too far outside the norm, they would set themselves outside the society as well. This may well happen, leading to the formation of new communities, but it is not the same thing as pluralism.

Similarly, while it may be possible to participate in many rituals without formalized training, there is in most hunter-gatherer/tribal societies a distinction between the ordinary member of the society and the *shaman* or religious virtuoso. It is to the latter that higher-order creativity is delegated.

Finally, we must note that totemic systems offer no opportunity for demonstration or debate. This is not a limitation only because meanings are not contested—because there is, in other words, no pluralism. Pluralism and religious rationalization, we will see, go hand in hand.

THE MYTHIC CYCLES OF NEOLITHIC AND SURVIVING HORTICULTURAL/COMMUNITARIAN AND PASTORAL-RAIDING TRIBAL SOCIETIES

Horticultural/Communitarian and Pastoral-Raiding/Tribal societies present us with a very different picture, one which, at first glance, seems to present the best case for the postmodern advocates of myth. By Horticultural/Communitarian societies we mean those which have domesticated plants and animals, but have not developed the plow and which have permanent settlements, but not cities or state structures. Generally speaking the land is owned either by the village or by the clan and is periodically redistributed to families for cultivation (Mandel 1968: 32–36). Political authority in horticultural societies was diffuse and only relatively undeveloped and undifferentiated. Kinship structures still play a very significant role, with villages composed of a variety of clans, each of which has its own elders and its clan rituals. There are, however, cross-cutting religious societies which include members of different clans and often a formal priesthood which integrates clan rituals into a single system. Thus the Zuni of New Mexico maintain to this day a six-fold priesthood, with separate priesthoods corresponding to each of the directions (including the zenith and nadir), organized under the authority of the Pekwin (zenith or sun) priest, with the nadir priests functioning as war leaders. Other Puebloan groups maintain similar systems, with a *cacique* or "inside chief" responsible for organizing religious life and settling internal disputes and a war chief or outside chief, generally ranked lower and assisted by a team of "bow priests," who is responsible for external relations, including warfare.

There is considerable evidence that the horticultural/communitarian societies of the Neolithic were matriarchal and that surviving horticultural/communitarian societies may also have been until shortly before or after their encounter with the West (Engels 1880/1940, Giambutas 1974, Stone 1976), though this point is still very much contested (Hayden 1986).

What about the mythic structures of these societies? It is clear, first of all, that they represent a higher degree of wisdom than the totemic systems of hunter-gatherer/tribal peoples. Specifically, the question of origin is clearly posed, even if that of Being is not. We find authentic (indeed often multiple) myths of origin, including many which are highly rationalized, such as the stories surrounding the wisdom goddess of the Western Puebloans, (Sussistinako or "thinking woman" in the Keres and Huruing Wuhti or "hard beings woman" in Hopi), in which the goddess thinks the world outward, and the competing myth around a male creator or sun god.

The reasons for this are fairly straightforward. Life in the village community provides a basis in experience for the idea of the universe as an organized totality ordered to an end—an idea we see reflected imaginatively in the image of the great goddess who, to be sure, gives birth to the universe, but does so not as the result of some unconscious biological process, but rather as an expression of her wisdom. Understanding the principles of things and their ends, she is able to cultivate and nurture them. Human beings are at once her children and her students. Learning the arts of civilization, we gradually develop to the point that we become her partners, nurturing being, participating actively in the cosmohistorical evolutionary process.

What this represents is, in effect, an emergent capacity for what we have called (Mansueto 2002a) *transcendental abstraction*—the ability to abstract from concrete things to not only a general *taxon* to which they belong, but also to the end to which they are ordered. In this sense the myths of Neolithic societies involve an authentic reasoning regarding purposes and thus an authentic wisdom in the sense of being an attempt to wrestle with fundamental questions of meaning and value.

Pastoral-raiding/tribal peoples, on the other hand, emerged in more difficult ecosystems, which did not permit the generation of a surplus by means of horticulture. Instead they roamed the steppes with their herds and raided the settlements of horticultural communitarian societies. Kinship relations remained dominant, with clans speaking similar languages grouped loosely into tribes. Where raiding and warfare supplemented pastoralism, kinship relations were overlaid with the relationship between warlords and their retainers. Warlords were chosen for their military prowess. Initially this meant strength; gradually, as warfare became more complex, it came to mean the capacity for strategic leadership. Warriors pledged fealty to their lord in return for the promise of gifts should the raid be successful. This sort of warrior's democracy is attested both among the Germans and among the Aryans of Northern India, who even after they settled often preferred what they called *gana sanghas* to full-fledged kingship (Thapar 2002).

In some places a priestly stratum developed and was able to successfully best the warriors for social predominance. This is related to the centrality of *sacrifice* in the religious life of these peoples, a phenomenon that derives from the fact that they live by raising—and killing—animals. Sacrifice is the priestly act *par excellence*. Initially, who presided at the sacrifice may simply have been a function of whose animal was being slaughtered, or it many have been the province of those who had special knowledge associated with this function. We know, for example, that many Indo-European peoples "read" the entrails of the slaughtered animal, either by examining them or viewing them, as a form of divination. In either case, presiding at this function, which was the source of life for the community, would naturally have conferred leadership.

Gradually, however, raiding and warfare become more central to the economic strategy of the people, and the political weight of the warriors and above all of the chiefs increases accordingly. Among some groups this led to the gradual atrophying of the priestly function, so that priests either never developed into a full-time class, or ceased to be one. This seems to have been the case among the Germans. Among other groups—the Aryans and the Celts, for example—the priests were able to fight back, developing rituals which legitimated the rule of the war leader and made him less dependent on his fellow warriors. Thus the development of the elaborate ritual of the horse sacrifice among the Aryans. A horse would be set free and allowed to roam for a year, after which it would be ritually slaughtered. The horse's cries of pain were regarded as a re-enactment of the primal scream of the sacrificed First Man, Purusha, whose death brought the universe into being; the territory covered by the horse became the king's realm, which he was obliged to defend. The Celtic pattern seems to have been different. While the Celts certainly conserved a raiding and warrior tradition, they also seem to have adopted settled agriculture and to have merged in a significant degree with the indigenous peoples of the regions they conquered. There the role of the Druidic priesthood may well have been related to the greater social weight of certain types of knowledge—astronomy, botany, etc.—in an agrarian society.[3]

Here, as in horticultural/communitarian societies, we see real myths of origin, though they are often of a very different character. Thus the Vedas attribute the origin of the world to the primordial sacrifice of Purusha and the Aztecs to a series of primordial acts of self-immolation on the part of various gods, each of whom becomes the Sun of his era. We also see the first steps towards the emergence of the high gods, which become the object of the process of religious rationalization during the Axial Age: the generic Aryan Dyaus Pater, for example, or the Turkic Tengri.

What is it about both horticultural/communitarian and pastoral-raiding/tribal societies that seems to give credence to the postmodern claims regarding the pluralistic and participatory character of mythic discourse? First, political-theological authority at least seems to be diffused. The *cacique* or inside chief is not a king, but more of a ritual coordinator, and each priesthood, each religious society, and each clan has its own myths and rituals. The Aryan *raja*, similarly, initially depended

3. For a more detailed consideration of this debate, see Dumenzil 1952, Lincoln 1981, 1986, 1991; Mallory 1989.

on ritual sanction of the priests, the allegiance of his fellow warriors, and the gifts of the ordinary producers. The result is that what amounts to *conflicting* stories are shared widely throughout the society as a whole. We have already noted, for example, the plural origin myths of the Western Puebloans. This would seem to suggest precisely the kind of pluralism that the postmodernists ascribe to myth. Similarly, in a pastoral raiding/tribal society like the Indo-Aryans, we see competition between various deities, some associated with priestly and royal functions (Mitra and Varuna) and others associated with warfare (Indra) or even productivity (the *Asvins*), for the role of high God.

Similarly, the collective nature of priesthoods and the role of religious societies suggests broad participation in the creation and interpretation of myth. With so many religious leaders and no single, centralized authority, surely ordinary people have room to contribute to the creation and transformation of meaning! Indeed, in some pastoral-raiding/tribal societies such as the early Greeks and Germans, *anyone* could perform a sacrifice.

The reality, however, is rather different, as I discovered during five years teaching philosophy, religious studies, and civilization studies and organizing inter-religious dialogues among the A:shiwi (Zuni) and Diné (Navajo). Three caveats are in order here. First, while the Zuni are, in many ways a classic horticultural/communitarian society, and one which has preserved more of its social structure than other Puebloan groups, largely due to its isolation, the Diné are not fully typical pastoral-raiders. They were primarily desert hunter-gatherers who began raiding the Puebloan communities when they moved into the Four Corners area not too long before the Spanish arrived. From the Spanish they acquired sheep, which became their principal source of subsistence, and horses, which, of course, vastly improved their ability to conduct raids. But much of their religion is borrowed from the Puebloan groups they raided. Second, it is possible that some of what I observed represents a reaction against the encroachments of the West. And third, my observations are not the result of a formal study but rather more a report on an organizing effort and thus partake of all of the risks of participant observation methods and more. This said, everything that follows is based on the direct testimony of members of the Zuni and Diné communities themselves.

What I found were not open, egalitarian societies characterized by plural meanings and centers of power. Rather, the Zuni are a rigid hierocracy in which the people live in constant fear of the religious leaders who possess a wisdom they are not even permitted to share, much less contest. Indeed, many (those who do not have Zuni mothers, a large number given mixing with other indigenous groups) are excluded from participation in the cult (though not from the obligation to give "gifts" to the religious leaders) entirely. There is no pluralism, no public arena, and no sharing of leadership. Wisdom is, in effect, an affair of hereditary priesthood. Everyone else simply grows food. And resisting demands for food from the village priests can have disastrous effects.

The following example will help to illustrate this. One term I was teaching Western Civilization at Zuni Pueblo for the University of New Mexico—Gallup. I had a class of fifteen students. The general level of writing was better than at our main campus, and three of the students were doing "A" work by any standard. Only one, however, would participate. One week this student was absent, and suddenly the others joined in an animated debate regarding Plato and Aristotle. The next week the absent student returned, and the debate ceased. After the pattern had repeated itself two or three times, I pulled the young woman, who worked for us as a tutor aside and asked her what was going on. "Oh they won't speak in front of me. My uncle is a bow priest and they are afraid."

Gradually I collected a series of stories which utterly shattered my image of Puebloan society as peaceful and egalitarian if also terribly impoverished: houses burned down because newlywed couples refused the "honor" of hosting Shalako and thus feeding nearly 10,000 people, bow priests breaking into houses during ceremonies and destroying electric lights...

The situation with the Diné is rather different. Here there is no official religious hierarchy, but rather informal networks of medicine men who perform ceremonies for individuals on request. But their wisdom is closely guarded, and many, at least, believe that no part of it should be shared in the larger public arena. When I began organizing inter-religious dialogues, for example, the officials in charge of the Navajo Nation Office of Cultural Preservation, both medicine men and the senior cultural officials for the Nation, told me that they did not want such dialogue to take place. Sharing wisdom, they said, cheapens it. And this applied not just to the details of ceremonies regarded as possessing power, but to larger discussion of worldview.

This is not to suggest that there is not real wisdom and value in Zuni and Diné culture. There certainly is. But outsiders who romanticize these cultures and attribute to them a democratic and egalitarian character which they lack do a disservice to those who must live in them and find a way to make their traditions work in a new and more complex world.

The absence of pluralism and democratic participation in horticultural/communitarian and pastoral-raiding/tribal societies is, finally, bound up with the fact that the claims regarding wisdom embodied in myth, however real, cannot be debated and demonstrated. There is, therefore, no real room for difference. New stories, and new interpretations of old stories, are always and only acts of power, whether be it political-military or, more often, cultic.

MYTH IN EMERGING URBAN CIVILIZATIONS

We must, finally, consider the role of myth in the earliest urban civilizations. Indeed, it is from these civilizations—Mesopotamia, Egypt, and the Indus and Yellow River Valleys in Eurasia and the Valley of Mexico and the Andean Highlands in the Americas—that most of our surviving mythic cycles come.

As in the case of hunter-gatherer, horticultural, and pastoral-raiding societies, there is much controversy regarding the nature of the first urban civilizations. Those for which we have really good archeological and literary evidence were all what we call tributary social formations in which warlords had conquered a given territory and extracted tribute (rents, taxes, and forced labor) from villagers, who had been reduced to the status of dependent peasant communities. This does not mean, however, that cities were the product of conquest. There are a few societies such as the Anasazi in Southwestern North America (e.g., Chaco and Mesa Verde) and the Megalithic Cultures of Old Europe (e.g., Stonehenge, and Avebury), which suggest a transitional phase in which villages voluntarily supported cultic centers which in turn served as a focus of meaning and value and carried out astronomical observations and other protoscientific activities which supported agrarian production. There is also some evidence that the earliest cities in Mesopotamia, Egypt, and the Indus and Yellow River Valleys in Eurasia and the Valley of Mexico and the Andean Highlands in the Americas may have had a similar character. Such a hypothetical social formation we call "archaic" because of its ordering of villages to a common ritual center. Unfortunately, we know very little about the mythic cycles of these societies. We have some limited archeological evidence, which is similar to that for horticultural/communitarian societies, and we can try to read backward from the mythic cycles or tributary social formations, "reading out" those elements associated with warfare and exploitation. The result suggests a further development of the largely wisdom and fertility focused and often gynocentric myths of horticultural/communitarian societies, with perhaps some movement in the direction of the development of a better defined high god.

For tributary social formations, on the other hand, the evidence is clear and well defined. The emergence of the warlord state was reflected in the growing influence of patriarchal, sacrificial, and sacral monarchic cults. There are two dimensions to this process. First of all, as warlords extended their control over the villages and displaced the progressive organizing activity of the village chiefs and priests, organizing activity generally came to seem more and more the province of one person alone. Thus the gradual tendency for communitarian polytheism to be replaced by a cult of divine monarchs presiding over a pantheon of heavenly retainers. Increasingly the productivity of the land, on which the community depended for its survival, was attributed to the activity of the monarch and his divine counterpart. We call this the land/lord/god complex. On the one hand the leading members of the emerging ruling class—the local warlords or monarchs—are either deified or regarded as having a special relationship with the deity. On the other hand the already divinized forces of nature (sun, rain, soil, or cultivated plant) are identified with these new warrior gods, creating a complex nexus linking the fertility of the soil with service to, or payment of, rents and taxes to the ruling class. Thus the Canaanite god *ba'al*, whose name means lord, master, owner of land, and husband. The term was used not only for the deity, but for the local warlords who were identified with him. The result was an extraordinarily effective system of social control. Rebellion threatened to bring down not only the sword of the local ruling elite, but also the wrath of the gods. Fail to pay your taxes or perform forced labor and the sun itself will cease to shine, the rains will not come, the soil will lose its fertility. This pattern is nearly universal in the religion of tributary social formations. In some cases, as in Egypt, the ruler was regarded as divine in his own right, the son of the Sun God. Mesopotamian rulers, on the other hand, were regarded as mere tenants of the gods, to whom they conveyed the tribute extracted from the peasant communities.

The second dimension of this process was the emergence in most tributary societies of a more or less developed sacrificial cult. Sacrifice was, to be sure, a well-established practice in tribal hunter-gatherer and pastoral nomadic societies. In hunter-gatherer societies, however, the central element of the sacrifice was the shared meal during which the totemic animal, taboo throughout most of the year, was shared among members of the otherwise scattered clan, reconstituting their social bonds. And in pastoral-nomadic societies the centrality of sacrifice, as well as the specific rituals associated with it, derive from the need to slaughter for food domestic animals with which one had developed a close relationship. Thus the existence of practices intended to reduce the trauma for the animal—e.g., the Greek practice of leading the animal in with scattered grain, of keeping the knife blade hidden until the last moment, etc.

The focus on sacrifice as, precisely, *killing*, and on killing as *the* creative act on the other hand, derives from the fact that violence was, after all, the foundational act of the warlord state. Thus in ancient Mesopotamia, the gods were believed to have created human beings in order to serve them by providing food and drink (Kramer 1963). We have already mentioned the primal sacrifice of *Purusha*, the cosmic first human. According to the *Rig Veda* (X.90) humanity was created when he was sacrificed by the gods.

> When they divided *Purusha* how many portions did they make?
>
> The *Brahman* was his mouth, of both his arms was the *Rajanya* made.
>
> His thighs became the *Vaisya*, from his feet the *Sudra* was produced.
>
> The moon was generated from his mind, and from his eye the sun had birth ...
>
> Fourth from his navel came mid-air; the sky was fashioned from his head;
>
> Earth from his feet ...

It was the pained cry of the horse during the Vedic sacrifices which gave the ritual its power. Similarly the *Satapatha-Brahmana*, says that

> ... the dawn is the head of the sacrificial horse, the sun its eye, the wind its breath, the fire its open mouth. The year is the body of the sacrificial horse, the sky its back, the air its belly, the earth the under part of its belly.

A similar motif is probably reflected in the myth of Isis and Osiris, though here, as is typical of Egypt, where the gynocentric religious dynamic was particularly resilient, it is the wisdom of Isis in piecing Osiris back together, rather than the dismemberment itself, which is regarded as creative and salvific.

The sacrificial cult reached its highest level of development in the religion of the Aztecs. The Aztec empire was a tributary social formation characterized by an advanced hydraulic horticulture. Land was held collectively by the *calpulli*, or village communities, or else by the temples and various state institutions. The *macehualtin* or peasants were required to perform forced labor for the *teuctli* and *pilli*—the ruling classes (van Zantwijk 1985).

But the unique characteristics of Aztec society can be understood only by analyzing Aztec cosmology. According to Aztec tradition, there are to be five epochs in the history of the cosmos, each illuminated by a different sun. Each of these epochs begins when one of the gods sacrifices himself by means of self-immolation and is reborn as the sun of that epoch. Each epoch ends in a cosmic catastrophe.

These suns or epochs are not part of a continuous cycle. Each, rather, is a stage in an ultimately doomed cosmic experiment in creation through self-sacrifice which will come to an end when the present sun, the fifth and last, is extinguished, annihilating not only humanity, but the entire cosmos, and with it the gods as well (Brundage 1985: 27).

In the context of the cosmic economy, the motive force of which is self-sacrifice, human beings are, in effect, food for the gods (Brundage 1985: 36). Just as the cosmos is sustained by the sacrifice of the gods, so the gods themselves are sustained by the sacrifice of human beings. This sacrifice might take the form of bleeding or self-mutilation, but heart sacrifice, in which captured warriors were relieved of their still beating hearts, was by far the most important aspect of the cosmic economy.

Presiding over this process was the god Tezcatlipoca, the "smoking mirror." The name suggests that originally Tezcatlipoca was the god of the night sky, and more specifically of the Milky Way. But as the Aztecs transformed themselves into a militaristic empire this cosmological deity was himself transformed into the most warlike of all gods. Tezcatlipoca was the first god to sacrifice himself and became the first sun. He is known by the names "we are his slaves," and "master of the lords of the earth." He ruled all the cities of the Aztecs through his *ixtpla*, a captured warrior who was offered symbolic obedience by the high priest and ruler throughout the year and was then sacrificed and devoured. As One Death (Aztec Gods were often known by their date-names) he was called Yaotl, "the enemy of both sides," who fomented war in order to insure a steady supply of captives for human sacrifice, and thus an adequate supply of food for the gods. So central was the practice of human sacrifice to the Aztec cosmic economy that when there was no *ratio ad bellum* cities closely allied with each other would engage in flower wars: mock battles which had no other purpose than the exchange of captives who were then held for sacrifice. And as the god One Jaguar, Tezcatlipoca was a warrior painted in black, ensconced in the interior of the earth, wielding sacrificial knives, lying in wait to steal the fifth sun and thus to destroy the cosmos once and for all (Brundage 1985: 84–99).

Tezcatlipoca was worshiped universally throughout all of the Aztec cities. Huizilopochtli, on the other hand, was the tribal god of the Mexica, the dominant Aztec grouping. According to Aztec tradition, Huizilopochtli, whose name means "hummingbird on the left," was the son of the earth goddess, Coatlicue. He slaughtered the stars, or the southern warriors, the Huizilin, and murdered his sister, Coyolxuaqui, and then led the Mexica from their homeland in the north, Azatlan, to the valley of Mexico, where he founded the city of Tenochtitlan. Each night Huizilopochtli re-enacts this drama, doing battle with the Huizlin (the stars). Each day he drives the sun across the sky. And to sustain him in this work he requires, like all of the other Aztec deities, a steady diet of beating human hearts (Brundage 1985: 128ff.).

The Aztecs, of course, were not strictly speaking a Bronze Age society. Their civilization, however, followed a similar course of development using different technology—and along a different timeline. And we do find evidence for human sacrifice in Eurasia. There are numerous references to the practice in the Hebrew scriptures, and some scholars read the story of Abraham and Isaac as, among other things, a decision to break with this practice among the ancient Israelites. We know that the practice was quite common in Shang China and was one of the factors that led to the eventual overthrow of the Shang dynasty by the Zhou at the end of the Bronze Age.

What is the end to which this whole system was ordered? It is in the mythological discourse of the great tributary empires that we find for the first time the emergence of *deification* as a civilizational ideal. At least in

Mesopotamia and Egypt and India (evidence for China and the Americas is less clear), the *purpose* of the whole system we have been describing is to make possible the passage of the King from the human to the divine. Divinity here is, to be sure, still understood as *immortality*, accompanied, perhaps, by certain superhuman powers, and not as *Esse*, the power of Being as such. But it represents the first step in a long process of development, which eventually culminates in the great Christian doctrine of deification as it was formulated by the church fathers and ultimately by Saint Thomas.

Once again, even here, in the sacrificial cults of these oppressive empires, we find a real way of wisdom. This said, the mythic discourse of the great tributary empires still has all of the difficulties associated with myth in earlier societies. Indeed, it is here that they all come to a head. Far from being open to plural interpretation the mythic discourse of tributary social formations was clearly an instrument of social control. And while the peasants and dominated peoples may well have retained their own traditions in the creation and transformation of which they played a significant role, we have no evidence of a public arena in which the meaning of the dominant *mythos* was contested. There is no evidence here to support the contention of Hatab and others that myth is more pluralistic and democratic than philosophy.

THE CRISIS OF THE LATE BRONZE AGE

Gradually the great empires of Bronze Age Eurasia and comparable civilizations elsewhere became impossibly exploitative, and they began to put a real brake on technological development. The ruling class was able to extract almost the entire surplus product from the direct producers. This had the effect of removing any incentive for innovation on the part of the peasantry, which knew that it would not benefit from its own increased productivity. In many cases of course, the peasants were ground down below the subsistence level and had neither the time nor the energy to innovate. The ruling class, on the other hand, invested its energies in extensive accumulation through conquest—extending the area subject to its taxing power—rather than intensive accumulation based on improved agricultural techniques. Warriors and priests increasingly held all forms of manual labor in contempt. The two thousand years after the advent of the warlord state say from 2600 to 600 BC produced few contributions of ... importance to human progress ... They are the "decimal notation" of Babylonia (about 2000 BC); an economic method for the smelting of iron on an industrial scale (1400 BC); a truly alphabetic script (1300 BC) and aqueducts for supplying water to cities (700 BC). (Childe 1951)

The structural impediments to human progress created by the tributary social formations were not confined to the technological and economic realms. An authority structure centered on coercion and mystification, in which the people as a whole had very little interest in building the power of the monarchy, was ultimately very fragile. Tributary states were subject to constant revolt and to invasions assisted by oppressed peasants hoping that their new overlords would be better than the last. Perhaps most destructive, however, was the impact of tributary religious structures on human spirituality. Under the hegemony of sacrificial sacral monarchic cults, human beings came increasingly to regard service to the common good, surplus labor which promoted the development of human society, as a sacrifice, something which negated their own particular interests. To participate in the life of God meant first and foremost to give up one's own life, whether through the payment of rents, taxes and forced labor, martial heroics, or participation in ritual self-sacrifice.

It is at this moment that we witness the first of the "breakthroughs" associated with the Axial Age—those in ancient Israel and Zhou China—and the only ones which don't fall comfortably within Jasper's timeframe (800–200 BCE).

The prevailing religious form of the Canaanite social formation, was, as we have noted, the cult of *ba'al*, which had by this point hegemonized the older, gynocentric cult of the *ashtoreth*. This *ba'al* is generally referred to in the textbooks as a "fertility god," as indeed he was. But the root from which the term *ba'al* is derived means "to own" and the word was used in ways which signify "lord," "master," "owner of land," and ... "husband." It was used for the local warlord as well as for the deity. Identification of agrarian and human fertility with domination and lordship, and of both with the divine, provided the ruling classes with an especially effective system of legitimation. The Canaanite peasantry, to put the matter starkly, worshiped their landlords.

According to Norman Gottwald, the later Bronze Age witnessed a decline in great-power hegemony in the Syro-Palestinian corridor and corresponding internal strife among the warlords who dominated the Canaanite lowlands. The resulting instability in turn led to an increase in rural unrest, which took the form of social banditry (Hobsbawm 1959). These social bandits—referred to as "*'apiru*" in contemporary sources—were essentially marginalized peasants who had been run off their land, or who had gotten into trouble with their lords, and had (quite literally) taken to the hills, from whence they preyed off caravans, or raided the city-states, occasionally entering the service of one or another *ba'al*.

At roughly the same time, the collapse of the Hittite Empire to the north broke the monopoly on iron technology, allowing the techniques for production of primitive bloomery iron to penetrate Canaan. Up until this time metal tools had been a ruling class monopoly, protected by royal control of the tin trade—tin being an essential component of bronze, the only metal thus far widely used in the area. This ruling class monopoly on metal tools had in turn held back the development of the hill country, which required metal tools for clearing and terracing. Bloomery iron, while inferior to the bronze used by the Canaanite aristocracy, was superior to the stone tools used by the Palestinian peasants and could be produced with materials available in the region. The collapse of the Hittite iron monopoly thus put metal tools into the hands of the peasants, removing the obstacle to settlement in the hill country.

The hills were out of the reach of the chariots of the Canaanite warlords and thus beyond the sphere of Canaanite military hegemony. The *'apiru* groups thus began to terrace and cultivate the hillsides, and their banditry gradually transformed itself into a kind of *guerilla*, or prolonged, popular war—the record of which is preserved in the Book of Judges. They organized themselves into *mishpahoth*, or protective associations of extended families. These *mishpahoth* practiced a form of communal land tenure, holding land collectively and redistributing it periodically to individual families, according to need, for purposes of cultivation (Lev 25:8ff.), and also constituted a kind of "popular militia" which helped to defend and extend the "liberated territories" without recourse to a standing army. Israel seems to have provided for a tax of roughly 10 percent of the agricultural produce to support the Levitical priests. At the same time, Israelite law insured that the priests could own no land of their own and thus could not degenerate into an exploitative landowning class.

Norman Gottwald has suggested, based in part on the frequency of Egyptian names among the Levites, and their subsequent role as a religious elite, that the Exodus story is in fact the story of the Levites, and perhaps other elements serving in Egypt as forced laborers, who became the carriers of the cult of *yhwh*, and whose flight from Egypt and penetration of Palestine played a critical role in catalyzing the formation of Yahwistic Israel out of the numerous *'apiru* bands. The Exodus is, according to this hypothesis, the story of the vanguard of the Yahwistic revolution.

The emergence of the cult of *yhwh* was at once a product of, and a catalyst for, this process. The name itself probably derives from an epithet attached to the name of the god El, who was *ba'al*'s father and the actual high god of the Canaanites, but not, for the most part, the object of an actual cult. Revolutionary Israel appealed above the head of *ba'al*, as it were, to his father, who they worshiped as *'el yahwi sabaoth yisrael*: God who brings into being the armies of Israel. This was a mark of the fact that Israel first met her god on the battlefield of the revolution and found in the struggle for social justice the basis of all her religious knowledge. But it is not yet metaphysics. We will see later how this insight was rationalized and formed the basis for the development of a distinct metaphysical tradition.

The case of the Zhou is less clear. We do know that the Shang or Yin dynasty, which ruled China from about 1600–1100 was known as exploitative and that it practiced human sacrifice. The Zhou were originally a subject people and threw off the Shang yoke to become the new masters of China. Perhaps as a result of their experience as an oppressed people, they developed the view that effective and enduring rule depends on what they called the *tian-ming* or the Mandate of Heaven. Those who rule in a way that serves the common good obtain and keep this mandate; tyrants and oppressors do not. These views, which are embodied in the Confucian classics, many of which date back to the early Zhou period, form the basis for the later development of Confucian doctrine (Yao 2000: 1–63).

It is also from this period that the earliest layer of the *I Ching* dates. First and always a tool for divination, the *I Ching* also embodies the rudiments of a distinct metaphysics which was interpreted variously by the Confucian and Taoist traditions: the idea that the universe is driven by a first principle which, whether we regard it as intelligible (as most of the Confucian thinkers would) or ineffable (the Taoist position), manifests itself through an interplay of the active (Yang) and passive (Yin). An excess of the Yang leads to violence and over-reaching; an excessive Yin to passivity and stagnation. Does this idea reflect at the symbolic level an insight into the proper relations between the nomadic tribes which periodically conquered and renewed Chinese society over the ages and the indigenous agrarian populations they sometimes led and sometimes exploited? The Zhou themselves were originally such a nomadic people, as were, in all probability, the Shang before them. It would not have been out of the question for a nomadic people, themselves once exploited and now in a position to exploit, to remind themselves of the dangers of that path.

The discourse created by these two great breakthroughs itself remains mythic. As such it shares the limitations we have already noted. In the absence of formalization, real inference, argument, and thus public debate is not really possible. And while the breakthroughs served the interest of the peasantry, this does not mean ordinary peasants participated in the leadership. The Zhou revolution was the product of an alliance between Zhou warriors and a part of the Shang religious elite—the *ru* or scholars. The Israelite breakthrough was the result of an alliance between bandit leaders and the Levites, many of whom had Egyptian names and who constituted a new kind of religious elite. This said, both pointed beyond myth and at least thematized the idea of the first principle, even if they were not able to actually mount an argument for it. Thus the Zhou revolution replaced the Shang *shang di*, or "lord on high," an anthropomorphic high god, with *tian* or heaven. And the Israelite high god was called *yhwh*, a word which serves as the causative form of the verb "to be."

It should be apparent at this point that myth, while an authentic form of wisdom, is inadequate. It is inadequate first of all because, although it can certainly present answers to fundamental questions of meaning and value, it cannot argue for these answers and thus can do little when meaning itself has been called into question. Second, it is by no means as pluralistic and democratic as its advocates claim. On the contrary, in the absence of formalization and thus of argument, it is quite impossible to have meaningful pluralism. The stories of the dominant group become the dominant stories. Subaltern stories may be allowed, but there is no conceptual metalanguage in which the notion of differing interpretations could be meaningful. And even when myth has not been in the service of an exploitative ruling class, it *has* been the province of a narrow, often hereditary elite.

This all changes, we will see, with the Axial Age, and the advent of dialectics and of a rational metaphysics.

2

The Axial Age

THE AXIAL AGE THESIS has, from the standpoint of the philosophical perspective represented in this book, a questionable pedigree. It derives ultimately from Max Weber's *Protestant Ethic and the Spirit of Capitalism* (Weber 1920/1958), his *Economy and Society* (Weber 1921/1968), and his comparative historical studies of religion. According to this view modernity, and more specifically the economic rationality which makes capitalism possible, is the product of a long process of religious rationalization. This process took place only in certain parts of the world, and then only in varying degrees. *Some* rationalization took place in all of the major civilizational centers of the planet. Magical manipulation of the sacred gave way to worship; priests unified mythic cycles and codified legal and ethical codes. A further wave of rationalization took place in selected parts of Eurasia: Greece, the Middle East, India, and China. Mythic discourse gave way, at least in part, to an abstract philosophical language. Innerworldly aims such as victory in warfare or a good harvest gave way to a search for salvation. There was more focus on ethical conduct and less on sacrifice. Europe, the Mediterranean Basin, and Southwestern Asia went further, eventually opting for an ethical monotheism focused, at least in some degree, on rational innerworldly activity. But even Judaism, Islam, and Catholicism represent incomplete processes of rationalization. This is because they make it possible for the believer to know whether or not he or she has done the will of God, and thus fail to create the psychic tension necessary to drive economic modernization, and, in the case of Catholicism, because the ultimate aim of rational activity is at least in part otherworldly. The process of religious rationalization is completed only in those regions that underwent a Calvinist Reformation. Calvinism alone integrates religious legitimation of inner-worldly activity—including ordinary productive activity—with a doctrine of predestination which leaves the believer constantly uncertain regarding his status and thus constantly engaged in activity aimed not so much at *winning* salvation as at *convincing* himself that he is among the elect. Gradually the religious framework drops away leaving a culture focused exclusively on instrumental rationality.

This theory is problematic for two reasons. First, it is unrepentantly idealist, in the sense that it treats ideas as if they quite literally dropped out of the sky. *Why* does religious rationalization take place? And more to the point, *why does it take place in some regions and not in others?* The result is to treat human history as if it were a kind of gradual evolution towards the one system of beliefs and values which really works, or else simply a battle of ideas—an interminable clash of civilizations driven by radically incompatible views regarding the most fundamental questions of meaning and value. In this sense the thesis defines the contemporary debate between the "end of history" and the "clash of civilizations" camps (Fukuyama 1989, Huntington 1983). Second, such an understanding of history amounts to a straightforward legitimation for imperialism, whether of the more genteel sort which believes that at the end of history—which has either already arrived or is fast approaching—everyone will finally realize that we have been right all along and adopt our modern, capitalist, democratic, and secular way of life, or the more bellicose sort which argues that we must either fight to spread and defend our civilization or watch it die.[1]

Jasper's formulation of the thesis (Jaspers 1953), coming as it did in the period following the collapse of the fascist project, is more cautious. Aware of the close affinity between German irrationalism and the Nazi party, and anxious to avoid the errors of his friend Heidegger, Jaspers carefully avoids the Eurocentric and even Germanocentric formulations of Weber, and focuses instead on the common elements of the "Axial Age" breakthrough which occurred between 800 and 200 BCE in Greece, Israel, India, and China, and which included, among other things, a turn towards more abstract religious language—in effect the birth of metaphysics—and an associated concern for questions of ethics generally and social justice in particular. Even so the theory has problems. It leaves the breakthroughs, and their specific distribution, unexplained, and leaves open the possibil-

---

1. On the relationship between Weberian sociology and imperialism, see Lukacs 1953/1980.

ity of an only slightly more cosmopolitan imperialism, which pits post-axial against pre-axial cultures.

Most dialectical and historical materialists have, furthermore, to the extent that they have addressed the question at all, tended to regard the developments that Jaspers described as part of the Axial Age as essentially reactionary in character. Ellen Meiskins Wood's *Class Struggle and Ancient Political Theory* (Wood 1979) argues, in effect, that rational metaphysics generally, and the Socratic tradition in particular, developed as a defense of the slave mode of production against the democratic peasantry of Athens. Samir Amin's *Eurocentrism* (Amin 1988/1989) argues more broadly that rational metaphysics developed as the superstructure of the great tributary empires. There is, of course, a long tradition in revolutionary China of campaigns against Confucianism which was regarded as a way of legitimating "feudal" exploitation. And who could possibly argue that Buddhism, with its otherworldly pessimism, and Hinduism, with its caste system, represented anything remotely resembling a breakthrough for reason and social justice? One has to look in odd places indeed to find thinkers outside the German irrationalist tradition who have anything positive to say about the Axial Age: the French "left-traditionalist" Pierre Simon Ballenche, for example, who argued that the Axial Age represented a radical democratization of the religious arena as the popular classes struggled to gain full access to the cult and thus claim their full humanity (Milbank 1990: 69).

Why, then, revive the theory, even in modified form? The answer is simple: there *was* a fundamental shift in the way at least several civilizations thought about fundamental questions of meaning and value during the period between 800 and 200 BCE, and this shift needs to be explained. Clearly, furthermore, this shift is intimately bound up with the "birth of metaphysics" and thus bears profoundly on the question at issue in this book: the social basis and political valence of metaphysics. More specifically, it offers us an opportunity to answer the criticisms of metaphysics raised by theorists such as Heidegger and Hatab on the one hand, and Wood and Amin on the other. We will see that far from representing the point of emergence of a distinctively Western nihilism and totalitarianism, the Axial Age was a widespread phenomenon, which actually introduced pluralism and democracy into the debate around fundamental questions of meaning and value. And far from representing a defense of the slave or tributary modes of production, the metaphysical systems which emerged during this period reflected an attempt to reground a discourse regarding social justice which would ultimately allow post-Axial Age intellectuals to restrict the coercive extraction of surplus and redirect investment towards activities which authentically promoted the development of human capacities.

This chapter will offer a radically new version of the Axial Age thesis. Specifically, I will argue that the transformation which took place in China, India, and the Mediterranean Basin between 800 and 200 BCE was first and foremost a response to the possibilities and dislocations created by the development of specialized agriculture and crafts production and the emergence of a petty commodity system. On the one hand, the emergence of specialized agriculture and crafts production opened up the possibility of prosperity based on something other than violence and exploitation. It was suddenly possible to trade commodities, which one's own community could produce cheaply for others that were of great value. This, in turn, gave far broader sectors of the population the possibility of earning enough to participate significantly in the public arena. The emergence of petty commodity production also gave people the basis in experience for understanding the universe as a quantitative system and thus set in motion the transition from mythic to abstract, rational modes of thought—including, especially, the development of the abstract mathematics which made it possible to think God as the One or the Infinite.

At the same time, petty commodity production also led to economic differentiation, as those with better land, better access to markets, or simply better luck prospered, and those who lacked these advantages fell further and further behind. Ideologues for the new, commercial ruling classes legitimated their wealth by developing radically relativistic ideologies such as Sophism, Caravaka Materialism, and Legalism, which argued that there *are* no transcendental principles of meaning and value and thus no such thing as justice. Essentially *all* these phenomena can be documented in the regions that underwent an Axial Age transformation.

From here patterns diverge a bit. Israel, which as we have seen came into being as a result of a peasant revolt in the Late Bronze Age, gave birth to a series of prophets who at once called the people back to their revolutionary heritage, but did so using an increasingly abstract language, eventually giving birth to the divine name—YHWH. This is the causative form of the verb "to be" and marks the dawning of an understanding of God as Being as such. Some of these movements advocated a return to the structures of the premonarchic period (Hosea); others argued for a monarchy (Psalm 72, Isaiah, Micah) which would be faithful to the revolutionary values of earliest Israel but which could protect the people effectively against foreign oppressors as well. The priestly and wisdom literatures, meanwhile, developed a more rationalized cosmology and legal system and mounted a response to the growing skepticism which accompanied the penetration of market relations and latifundialization—to the fools who said in their hearts that there is no God (Gottwald 1979). In China, similarly, a movement arises to return to the values of the Zhou revolution—the movement which eventually became known as Confucianism—but it is accompanied by movements such as Taoism and Mohism which are skeptical about the possibilities of a "just" monarchy which rules in accord with the *tian ming*, the mandate of heaven, and which put forward alternative approaches to fundamental questions of meaning and value (Yao 2000). In India, during the early part of the Axial Age, we witness a gradual rationalization of the Vedic tradition as the Vedic gods gradually give way to a more the abstract concept of Brahman and as the focus on animal sacrifice yields to a doctrine of ascetic, internal sacrifice. The Brahmin monopoly on religious leadership is challenged by these ascetics, something which leads first to the development of the Jaina and Buddhist traditions and eventually to a popular Puranic Hinduism which allows the Brahmins to find a new place for themselves in a complex, pluralistic tradition which speaks more adequately than the Vedas had to the interests of warriors, merchants, peasants, and even outcastes (Thapar 2002). In Greece, finally, we see, in addition to a more generalized process of religious rationalization which issues in the development of pre-Socratic philosophy and of religious democratization, which issues both in the development of new public cults, such as the cult of Dionysus with its associated drama festival and in the emergence of the mystery religions, the emergence of a tradition specifically focused on arguing for the existence of transcendental principles of meaning and value: dialectics. All of these (in many ways very different) developments integrated religious rationalization, religious democratization, a direct or indirect response to the growing injustice engendered by the emergence of petty commodity production—and an attempt to reground a doctrine of transcendental first principles as the condition for resolving the social and spiritual crisis of the era.

The Axial Age

This formulation of the Axial Age thesis helps to explain why some peoples had "breakthroughs" and others did not. Those societies whose cultural forms remained mythical rather than scientific or metaphysical were precisely those into which market relations did not penetrate and in which meaning did not, therefore, become a problem. It also begins to make a case for the principal thesis of this book: that metaphysics, far from being the source of modern nihilism and state terror, in fact emerged as an attempt to reground meaning and value during a period of nihilism, despair, and injustice and as such retains enduring value for the modern world, which suffers from an even more radical version of the same malaise.

We will begin by demonstrating that the Axial Age was defined, at the technological and economic level, by the development of specialized agriculture and crafts production and by the emergence of petty commodity production. We will also show that this was, for the most part, a period of political fragmentation. We will then go on to analyze the principal aspects of the Axial Age breakthrough—religious rationalization and democratization—and show how they represent a response to this political economic situation. We will specifically address both the claims of Heidegger and Hatab regarding the superiority of myth to philosophy and the claims of Wood and Amin regarding the affinity between metaphysics, slavery, and the tributary mode of production. We will conclude by looking at how the principal Axial Age traditions differ from each other and offer some suggestions as to why.

POLITICAL ECONOMY

As we noted in the last chapter, Afro-Eurasia as a whole seems to have undergone a rather protracted period of civilizational decline between 1200 and 800 BCE as tributary structures went into crisis and gradually retrenched. By around 800 BCE, however, there were real signs of a revival. It is, specifically, just precisely around this period that the use of iron technologies becomes really widespread and that we see the beginnings of specialized agriculture and crafts production. In the Mediterranean Basin, this meant above all oil, wine, and the pottery in which to store and transport these agrarian products (Anderson 1974a, Ste. Croix 1982), though there is some evidence that the Greeks also exported the occasional sophist for the amusement of Indian rulers (Thapar 2002: 178).

The West generally suffered a significant balance of trade deficit with both India and China, something which is reflected in the accumulation of vast hordes of Greek and Roman coins in both regions (Frank 1998, Thapar 2002: 242). China exported silk (Frank 1998), India pepper and other spices, teak and ebony, and cotton textiles (Thapar 2002). Southeast Asia entered the system somewhat later, largely as an exporter of spices and specialty woods (Hall 1995, Frank 1998). Peripheries such as the Horn of Africa and Southern Arabia exported frankincense. Gold and textiles came from West Africa. Porcelain and tea entered the system later from India and China.

Initially the development of specialized agriculture seems to have taken place under the sponsorship of archaic or tributary structures. In Greece, for example, civilization seems to have revived around tribal and inter-tribal sanctuaries, which, because they drew pilgrims for seasonal festivals, also became important market centers (Snodgrass 1980). Elsewhere, where civilization had not collapsed altogether, tributary states sponsored investment in these new products (Thapar 2002: 137–279). But in the long run specialized agriculture meant the emergence of markets—first local, then regional, and eventually "global" (i.e., Pan Afro-Eurasian) in scope. Increasingly investment decisions were dictated by the complex interplay of supply and demand. Thales of Miletus, for example, who is generally credited with taking the first steps towards the development of an abstract mathematics, also discovered the law of supply and demand. Foreseeing an unusually good crop of olives one year, he secured control of every olive press in his region and then demanded monopoly prices for the their use—though at least one story suggests that having made his theoretical point he relented and let the presses at their "fair" or "natural" price (Turnbull 1956: 79–82). Archaic and tributary structures became subordinated to what eventually, with the completion of the Silk Road around 200 BCE, became a global petty commodity system in which resources were allocated, at least in large measure, by a global market in luxury goods.[2]

---

2. There is a vigorous debate regarding the point at which an integrated "world economy" or "world system" first emerged (Frank and Gills 1993). In its original form "world systems theory" attributed the formation of a world economy to the European conquest of Africa, the Americas, and Asia (Wallerstein 1974, 1980, 1989), a conquest which was regarded as the origin of the current poverty and underdevelopment of the "Third World." Gradually, however, as scholars began to overcome their Eurocentrism, it became apparent that a world system incorporating all of Eurasia and much of Africa

It is important to be clear what is meant by a petty commodity system. On the one hand, this system must be distinguished from one in which there is trade—even a substantial quantity of trade—but in which resource allocation is still primarily driven by the decisions of some centralizing authority, such as a temple complex or a sacral monarchy. We now know that there were significant trade relations between many of the great civilizations of the Bronze Age—Mesopotamia and the Indus Valley, for example. It is not, however, correct to speak as Andre Gunder Frank now does (Frank and Gills 1992, 1993) of a 5,000 year-old world system, in the sense of a market structure that regulated resource allocation. For the most part, resource allocation in these societies took place through the extraction of surplus, through religious or coercive means, from dependent peasant communities—not through the mediation of a market in which a large number of producers responded to market forces. It is the emergence of authentic market forces, documented, for example, by Thales' decision to buy up all the oil presses and extract monopoly rents, which marks the emergence of a petty commodity *system*.

Petty commodity production differs from capitalism, on the other hand, in that there is a market in goods and services but not in labor-power or capital. Once again, this does not mean that there is no wage labor or usury. Certainly there were. But these forms are marginal and

already existed long before the European conquests (Abu-Lughod 1989). Andre Gunder Frank, originally a proponent of the view that the creation of a unified world system was a result of the European conquests in the sixteenth century, now argues that the existence of global (i.e., Eurasian) trade networks can be traced back some 5,000 years (Frank and Gills 1992) and has argued that the Chinese in fact retained a dominant role in the system until roughly the time of the Industrial Revolution (Frank 1998). He also rejects the notion of "capitalism" as a useful way of distinguishing the modern world system from its predecessors. While I think Frank does a good job of show the long history of global trade, I also believe that he misses three important transitions. First, beginning around 800 BCE we see the development of local and regional trade networks which actually begin to shape what is produced. This is apparent by the recognition of the laws of supply and demand by thinkers such as Thales of Miletus. By around 200 BCE these networks have effectively linked together all of Afro-Eurasia, from Mali, Iberia, and Britain all the way to China (Bentley 1993). These two transitions represent the advent of local and regional petty commodity production: i.e., a system in which resource allocation is shaped by the existence of a global market in luxury goods. Finally, between 1500 and 1800 we witness the gradual emergence of a new system, capitalism, in which not only goods and services but also labor power itself has become a commodity. The construction of capitalism cannot be said to be complete, however, until the full development of capital markets in the twentieth century, which makes capital a commodity as well—a point on which even Marx was not yet in a position to be completely clear.

secondary. The organization of labor remains either coercive—tributary forms persist, for example, and are supplemented by chattel slavery—or else peasant and artisanal, and most borrowing is for the purpose of covering expenses either on the part of the peasantry or on the part of the ruling classes and is not a source of capital. This means that while individual producers, large and small, are beginning to engage in an economically rational calculus, they are not dependent on a pool of investors who require that they guarantee the highest possible rate of return on investments.

Politically, this was a period of fragmentation. The Hellenic *poleis* were, first and foremost, sanctuaries become market towns that extracted surplus from their hinterlands by religious means or later by means of exchange rather than by coercion. Debt servitude and chattel slavery were later developments, which depended in part, at least, on the absence of a state structure that could provide effective economic regulation (Snodgrass 1980, Anderson 1974, Ste. Croix 1982). Small states prevailed in areas which, like China and the fertile crescent, had previously been dominated by large empires. Northern India was just undergoing what seems to have been a primary process of state formation, largely independent of the earlier Indus Valley Civilization, which in any case did not extend east into the Gangetic Plain, north in to the Himalayan foothills, or south into the Deccan or the peninsula. Some of these states were *gana-sanghas*, a sort of republic in which power was held by the senior lineages of what was still in part a tribally organized pastoral-raiding society which had only partly adopted agriculture. Others were small kingdoms (Thapar 2002: 98–173). Where larger tributary structures persisted, they gradually altered their economic strategies, seeking to tax trade rather than direct production and thus to capture for themselves a portion of what was becoming a very healthy commerce.

The emergence of specialized agriculture and crafts production, and of petty commodity production, offered to humanity an extraordinary new opportunity. By using the principle of comparative advantage it was possible for distant regions to profit from trade with each other and thus grow rich without the systematic exploitation of either their own populations or their trade partners. Such an outcome, however, required conscious leadership and intervention into the marketplace. The spontaneous tendency was towards rapid economic differentiation, as those with better land and better access to markets grew rich and those less well endowed grew poor. Peasants, who in many places had just been emancipated from tributary exploitation, found themselves falling into debt peonage and losing access to their land altogether. *Nouveau riche* elements who cared nothing for the traditional obligations between classes challenged sacral monarchs and priestly elites for power, so that political structures lost their integrity altogether (Anderson 1974, Ste. Croix 1982, Chaney 1986, 1993).

Life in a market society, furthermore, is intrinsically alienating. People experience the society—and thus the universe as a whole—as a system of only externally related atoms (individuals) without any obvious ordering to a common end. The result was the emergence of radically skeptical and materialistic ideologies such as Hellenic atomism and sophism (Collins 1998: 86–89, 145–48), the Indian Caravaka school (Chaterjee 1954: 56–64), and Chinese Legalism (Collins 1998: 148–55), all of which restricted the scope of human knowledge to objects of sense perception, denied the ultimate meaningfulness of the universe and the existence (or at least the actual supremacy) of the gods, and regarded morality as at best a set of conventions necessary for humans to live together and at worst as simply a way of legitimating particular social interests (Mansueto 1998b, 1999, 2000, 2002b). These ideologies effectively disarmed the people, giving them no moral leverage against their oppressors.

This was the common social context of all the "Axial Age breakthroughs." Where the great tributary empires of the Bronze Age had used religious meaning to legitimate exploitation, allowing the people to appeal above the heads of their rulers to the gods those rulers claimed as their patrons, petty commodity production called meaning itself into question, and made it a problem—*the* problem which *constituted* metaphysics. Humanity's principal wisdom traditions, which all flow out of this period, are simply different ways of approaching this problem: different ways of answering the question of meaning.

THE PRINCIPAL BREAKTHROUGHS

Those who gave the first answers to these questions were not systematic metaphysicians, but rather sages and prophets. By this I mean that rather than writing philosophical treatises that advanced and demonstrated a whole complex of metaphysical propositions, they gave brief, contextual answers to the questions posed by their social situations. Even when they mounted polemics against myth, poetry, or other forms of imaginative discourse (e.g., Plato) they often used discourse which was in fact more poetic than philosophical. In many cases they appear not to have written at all, but rather to have had their teachings recorded by their disciples. This appears to have been the case, for example, with Socrates and Lao Tzu. Those we call sages taught on the basis of their own acquired wisdom; those we call prophets claimed to be speaking the very word of God.

In all of the principal civilizational centers the basic process leading up to these breakthroughs was, furthermore, the same. On the one hand, there was a gradual process of religious rationalization, as deities understood originally as superhuman persons—as, in effect, characters in a story—gave way to more abstract ways of understanding first principles. On the other hand, there was a process of religious democratization, as the debate about fundamental questions was extended beyond the sphere of the traditional priestly lineages and opened up to anyone and everyone who had something to say, creating a public arena *constituted* by debate around fundamental questions. In essentially all cases, these breakthroughs were catalyzed by and helped reinforce movements to come to terms with the injustices created by the emergence of global petty commodity production.

Greece

This process is most apparent in Greece, where we can trace a step-by-step movement. For Homer, who edited the Iliad at the beginning of the Axial Age—around 750 BCE according to most scholars—the gods are essentially characters in a story, superhuman perhaps, but no less individuals with distinct personalities. Thus, in the opening passages of the Iliad, the human anger of "Peleus' son Achilles" is set side by side with that of "Zeus' son and Leto's, Apollo, who in anger at the king drove a foul pestilence along the host..." (Homer *Iliad* 1:1–10). The only real difference between the gods and the humans seems to be the greater power and immortality of the gods. Indeed, my beginning students, who are often unfamiliar with the names of the Greek gods, often have difficulty telling who is divine and who is human in these stories.

Only a little later, by the time we get to Hesiod, the gods have become personified natural forces.

> First came the Chasm; and then broad-breasted Earth, secure seat forever of the all the immortals who occupy the peak of snowy Olympus...
>
> Earth bore first of all one equal to herself, starry Heaven, so that he should cover her all about, to be a secure seat for ever for the blessed gods...
>
> ...then bedded with Heaven she bore...crooked-schemer Kronos.
> (Hesiod *Theogony* 96–161)

These gods are still individual persons, and we do get stories about them, but they are organized into a genealogy based on the inter-relationships between the natural forces they represent.

The next step in this process was the emergence of a natural philosophy that explains the universe in terms of the transformation of one or more natural forces, without personifying them. Thus Thales taught that the universe was born of water and Anaximenes that it was born of air. Here we have left behind the realm of myth rather definitively, but are still dealing with concrete, sensible entities.

The third and most critical step in the process of rationalization is the emergence of an abstract mathematics. By an abstract mathematics we mean one that operates not on concrete objects but rather on propositions themselves. The mathematics of the great tributary civilizations of the Bronze Age, however complex it may have been, remained irreducibly concrete. Measuring the motions of the heavenly bodies or calculating the number of bricks needed to build a pyramid of a given height may be difficult, but both operations can ultimately be reduced to counting. An abstract mathematics, on the other hand, asks such questions as "What makes a mathematical proposition valid?" or "What is a number?" It is just such reasoning that we see beginning to emerge with Thales of Miletus and later with his student Pythagoras.

The impact of this development on the way in which human beings conceived the first principle was enormous. The Pythagoreans themselves were not simply a mathematical and scientific school, but a religio-political sect—and one that actually seized power in a number of cities in Southern Italy.

The political valence of this tendency is complex and contradictory. On the one hand, the Pythagorean Brotherhood represents a reassertion on a new, more rational foundation of communitarian and archaic forms of leadership—i.e., leadership based on knowledge which contributes in some way to the development of human social capacities, rather than on military prowess or religious mystification. In this sense it represents a refraction of the Greek proximity to the matriarchal and communitarian *arche* through the lens of market-driven rationalization. At the same time, it does appear that the Pythagoreans drew much of their membership from the upper strata of Greek society and that they constitute what amounts to a *rentier* movement. Indeed, the whole outlook of the movement reflects the experience of surveying society as a whole and seeing it as a system of quantitative relationships, an experience which belongs specifically to the *rentier* elite and not to any other social stratum.

The longer-term impact of the development of an abstract mathematics on thinking about first principles was, however, the introduction of what amount to mathematical terms such as the infinite and eternal on the one hand, and the One on the other hand, to describe God. Consider the following selections:

> The first principle of all other things is infinite ... From this the heavens and the worlds in them arise.
>
> The first principle is eternal and does not grow old, and it surrounds all the worlds. (Anaximander *On Nature* 1, 2)
>
> God is one, supreme among gods and men, and not like mortals in body or in mind.
> The whole of god sees, the whole perceives, the whole hears.
> But without effort he sets in motion all things by mind and thought.
>
> It always abides in the same place, not moved at all, nor is it fitting that it should move from one place to another. (Xenophanes *On Nature* 1–4)

Here we have a fully rationalized concept of God, stripped of anthropomorphism, and conceived in wholly mathematical terms.

Alongside this process of religious rationalization was a process of religious democratization. We have already noted that the emergence of petty commodity production, while it opened up the possibility of the accumulation of wealth without exploitation, tended in fact to lead to economic differentiation and eventually to indebtedness, loss of land, and servitude for those peasants who had poorer quality land, were further from markets, or had opted to grow barley and wheat rather than grapes or olives. The result was a series of peasant revolts in the late seventh and early sixth century. These struggles were resolved in different ways throughout Greece. In Sparta, for example, the landed elites co-opted the masses by enserfing the surrounding Messenians and transforming the whole population of the *polis* into a "mass" warrior aristocracy, which played no role in production or commerce whatsoever. In other places the uprisings were suppressed with only a few concessions, and an oligarchic constitution predominated. What interests us here is the Athenian settlement, since it is this settlement that provides the immediate background to the ideological developments we are trying to understand. Here there were fundamental structural reforms, which improved the situation of both the peasantry and the emerging bourgeoisie[3] at the expense of the *eupatridae*. The first of these reforms was carried out by Solon in 594–593 BCE. All debts secured by land or personal liberty were cancelled in what was known as the *Seisachtheia* or "shaking off of burdens." This was accompanied by limited land reform and by the establishment of a mixed constitution that replaced birth with wealth as the criterion of eligibility for higher office and gave even the poorest citizens some voice in shaping public policies. Later reforms further extended the sphere of democratic participation, so that at times essentially all laws were made by a democratic assembly in which all male citizens had voice and vote and many key offices were chosen by lot, though there were also periods of oligarchic reaction.

As we will see, these reforms did not actually bring the Athenian peasantry and artisanate to power. The *nouveau riche* elements which were gradually displacing the *eupatrid* families had the time and resources to participate in public life in ways than the peasants and artisans could not and found ways to manipulate the passions of those who could participate. The effects of the revolutions should not, however, be underestimated. On the one hand, the economic reforms of Solon and his successors guaranteed the continued existence at Athens of a small peasantry, something that cannot be said of Rome and other cities in the ancient Mediterranean. Second, and more importantly, the revolutions brought into being a democratic public arena in which matters that had

---

3. The term "bourgeoisie" is taken here to apply to any social class which drives its revenue from the exploitation of the labor of others and the sale of the resulting goods and services in the marketplace, even if the exploitation in question is not strictly capitalist in character (i.e., based on wage labor), but depends rather on coercion of some kind, in this case on chattel slavery.

formerly been divined or simply decreed by the *basileus* were now matters of public deliberation.[4]

This trend is advanced by the class struggles of the later Archaic, which enlarge significantly the circle of people involved in deliberative discourse, and thus reduce the political weight of the inspired seer or poet. In order to understand the full significance of this change, it is essential to remember that the *basileus*, while not regarded as divine, was a sacred king, and essentially all matters concerning the *polis* were religious matters. As a result of the reforms the hereditary *basileus* was replaced with an elected *basileus archon*, opening up the exercise of a sacred office to public deliberation. The sacred court of the Areopagus was, furthermore, now expanded to include those who had held senior offices, such as that of *basileus archon*.

The reforms also added a second official, the eponymous *archon*, who was responsible for organizing a new religious festival—that of Dionysus. This festival included contests in the various dramatic disciplines: tragedy, comedy, and satyr plays. The development of Greek drama was itself an integral part of the process of religious democratization. The old myths and legends that formed the imaginative content of Greek re-

---

4. Already in the aristocratic councils of the earlier Archaic such as the Athenian *Areopagus*, the practice of deliberation had come to dominate decision making. Jean-Pierre Vernant (Vernant 1962/1982) and Marcel Detienne (1967/1996) suggest that the collapse of the palace system and the development of the hoplite infantry played a critical role in this regard. The collapse of the palace system left much of the older religious structure intact, with the leading families retaining their religious and often their judicial privileges. Wisdom continued, therefore, to appear as the *logos* of the *basileus*, the poet or the diviner. At the same time, the displacement of the *anax* by the collective body of the warrior elite and the expansion of this body into an assembly of citizen-soldiers gave ever increasing weight to the role of deliberation. This is already apparent in Homer. While the *Iliad* and the *Odyssey* present themselves as the products of divine inspiration—i.e., as divine words spoken by the poet on behalf of the Muse, within the context of the epic narrative itself decisions are made as a result of deliberations within either the assembly of warriors (as in the *Iliad*) or an assembly of leading landowners (as in the *Odyssey*). And in the *Odyssey* in particular epic narrative itself is presented as the hero's contribution to a public feast held in his honor. In return for his story, provided it meets with the approval of his hosts, he receives food and gifts. Vernant and Detienne understand this shift from inspired towards deliberative discourse as a sort of secularization—a first step towards the idea, which becomes widespread and even dominant in the classical era, that the Good and the True are merely products of collective human activity, and not objective principles to be discovered and known. It might be more appropriate to see them as reflecting a process of religious democratization. It is not so much that the sacred is purged from public life, as that it becomes a matter of public deliberation.

ligion concerned, for the most part, a vision of human excellence which would have made sense only to the old *eupatrid* families, and then only during the period in which warfare was still their principal occupation. They had little to say to a commercial wine or oil producer, much less to a peasant or artisan. The various forms of drama, but especially the tragedies, took these stories and retold them in a way that made them relevant to contemporary concerns. Thus, rather, than focusing on the divine challenge to excellence—most especially on the field of battle—and on the inevitable limits imposed on human achievement, Greek drama addresses themes such as the contradiction between kinship and political relationships (*Antigone*), between mother-right (still very important among the peasantry) and the patriarchal order of the *polis* (the *Orestaia*), and eventually the conflict between myth and philosophy (*The Clouds*). And each dramatist offered differing answers to these questions, so that drama itself became the locus of an authentic public debate regarding fundamental questions of meaning and value.

The other great locus of religious democratization was, of course, the mystery cult. Traditional Greek religion seems to have afforded hope of immortality only to the semidivine members of the *eupatrid* lineages who were descended from the gods. The new mystery cults extended this promise to literally anyone who underwent an initiation into the cults. The basic structure was always the same: catechesis or instruction regarding the mysteries, initiation, usually through a symbolic experience of death and rebirth by passage through water or a cave, participation in a communion meal, and, later, the possibility of still higher degrees of initiation. The most important of the mysteries in the early period were the cult of Demeter at Eleusis and the Orphic mysteries. By participating in a secret initiation process, members of the mystery cults gained access to knowledge that afforded them the prospect of immortality or at least of a more favorable reincarnation. Eventually, these cults emerged as the principal forms of religious life throughout the ancient world. The form of the mystery cult, which originated in Greece, was joined to content from Egypt (the cult of Isis and Osiris), Persia (the cult of Mithra), and eventually Israel (Christianity).

These mystery cults, with their esoteric beliefs and practices, may seem to have been the very antithesis of a public arena constituted by deliberation around fundamental questions of meaning and value. And it is true that they constituted a new, esoteric realm that played a major role in the cultural life of late antiquity and the Middle Ages. But while there is not very much in the way of deliberation *within* the secret society or mystery cult, the proliferation of such cults creates a public arena in which the various sects compete for adherents and must, therefore, make their cases in a way that is accessible to outsiders. Esoteric discourse presupposes exoteric discourse—an apologetic—and thus something that at least borrows from philosophy.[5] And philosophy, as we will see (Kingsley 1995), conserves its esoteric practical (technical, practical, and soteriological) dimension.

Religious rationalization and religious democratization flowed together into the process that lead, finally, to the emergence of an authentic rational metaphysics in ancient Greece. The work of Heraclitus and Parmenides represent, in many ways, a transitional phase in this regard. On the one hand, they speak about first principles in a way that is characteristic of the final phase of the process of rationalization described above. They understand God in a way that presupposes mathematical formalization. On the other hand, they are also reflecting—albeit still unconsciously—the impact of the revolutionary process that democratized discourse regarding first principles. This is apparent in their concern about the problem of change. Heraclitus (Ephesus fl. 504–501 BCE) was, interestingly enough, one of the last representatives of the old priestly intelligentsia, which had been dominant during Archaic era, and the only one, as far as we know, to become a major philosopher (Collins 1988: 83). At first Heraclitus seems merely to be counterpoising an argument for the primacy of fire (the element of ritual sacrifice *par excellence*) to Thales's argument for the primacy of water (the natural element of the merchant in a sea-going society). But when Heraclitus says that the universe is an "ever-living" fire, he is really saying that it is a constant process of change or flux, which at once consumes and produces, as fire consumes fuel and produces smoke and embers. This flux is, furthermore, rational, Fire being identified with the One, or God, and with the Soul. It at once unites and orders all things. The constant struggle and strife, which we see in the world, is in fact just a complex interplay of opposites, a finely

---

5. Perhaps it would not be too much to see in the exoteric discourse of the mystery cults the beginnings of what in the Christian context is later called "theology." This may also be why theology is, to a certain extent, a distinctively Christian sort of discourse. Christianity was, after all, the last of the great mystery cults to emerge and the one that eventually won out over the others.

tuned tension through which a higher order is produced. Here Heraclitus comes close to Hegel, and to Engels's doctrine of the unity and struggle of opposites. The universe itself is depicted as a kind of ongoing revolutionary process in which meaning is forged through struggle. In the political realm the *class* struggle replaces ritual sacrifice as the central priestly act.

The difficulty, of course, is that Heraclitus does not really explain change; instead he merely posits a process of rational change in order to explain the contradictory phenomena of order and chaos in the universe. The existence of the flux itself remains unexplained. It was this limitation in the Heraclitean doctrine that led Parmenides (Elea, fl. 480 BCE) to carry out a more exhaustive analysis of what it means for something to exist in the first place. What Parmenides realized is that unlike other attributes, Being is absolute—either something exists or it doesn't. Change, fundamentally, involves a coming into being or a passing out of being. But in order for something to come into being it must come either from something or from nothing. But "nothing can come from nothing." Forms or qualities that do not exist at one point in time cannot, therefore, simply appear at a later point in time. If, however, they come from something, then it is difficult to understand in what sense they are actually coming into being. Being *is*, simply and absolutely; all else is mere appearance. Parmenides concluded that the universe is a material, spherical, motionless plenum, eternal and uncreated, beyond which there is nothing (Garrigou-Lagrange 1932).

From a certain point of view, the analysis is brilliant. If Heraclitus was the first to penetrate the nature of change, and to reconcile the existence of order and chaos in the universe, Parmenides is the first philosopher to penetrate the still more profound mystery of Being—indeed to show any real awareness of the idea of Being as such. And Parmenides has also harvested the most important fruit of formal abstraction: the capacity for rational inference. Even when our description of the universe has not yet been completely mathematized, we are still able, by using the same methods of inference used by the mathematicians, to operate on our admittedly rather clumsier concepts to generate new conclusions and thus new knowledge about the world. This move, in turn, opens up the road for the development both of nonmathematical sciences (e.g., history) and of metaphysics.

At the same time, Parmenides' reasoning betrays the limits of formal abstraction. He seems entirely unaware of ideas—such as the idea of the

Good—which can reconcile being and becoming and ends up carrying an important insight—that there is a reality behind what we perceive with our senses, a reality that is fundamental—to the point of absurdity. This tendency is even more apparent in the work of Parmenides' student Zeno, who used similar reasoning to prove that, for example, it is impossible for a runner to complete a race because he would have to traverse an infinite number of points (Garrigou-Lagrange 1932).

This limiting formalism was, in all probability, a reflection of Paremenides' social location as a member of a landed elite now producing for the market. This group, while it embraced the formalization made possible by the emergence of petty commodity production, had every reason to resist the possibility of further "change" by making it appear to be impossible or illusory.

Later pre-Socratic philosophy—especially the work of Empedocles (Agrigentum, 490–430 BCE) and Anaxagoras (500–428 BCE)—can be read as an attempt to effect a synthesis of the Parmenidean and Heraclitean doctrines. Empedocles, for example, argues for the existence of four fundamental material elements: earth, water, air, and fire, but argues that their motion can be explained only by the forces of Love and Hate or Harmony and Discord, which, respectively, cause the aggregation and disintegration of the various elements in different proportions, resulting in the multitude of different phenomena that we experience (Garrigou-Lagrange 1932, Kingsley 1995). Here we lose something, I think, by comparison with both Heraclitus and Parmenides. Empedocles' doctrine of matter falls short of the Parmenidean realization of the absolute and transcendent character of Being, while his claim that there is a perpetual struggle between Love and Discord lacks Heraclitus's insight into the ultimately rational character of all change. Anaxagoras attempts to remedy this latter failure by suggesting that it is *nous* or intellect that orders and directs the unending combination of elements. In both cases, however, the system as a whole, the motion of matter in accord with some ordering principle or principles, remains unexplained. Formalization is incapable of advancing beyond description to explanation. For this it would be necessary to advance to transcendental abstraction—something which, we will see, is intimately bound up with practice, and specifically with political practice. The advent of science is thus always also a turn to the public arena, to the contest over social structure, and the struggle for a just social order.

A real metaphysics could thus only come as the result of a *conscious* reflection on the class struggle. In order to understand how this happened, we need to consider the limitations of the Athenian democracy. Because the public arena was formally democratic, the rich were now forced to obtain the consent of the poor in the midst of the assembly, and for this they required *rhetors* capable of making particular interests appear universal. Schools grew up to teach this art, and those who ran them—the so-called "sophists"—began to produce a relativistic doctrine that legitimated their activity. The spectrum of sophistic opinion was diverse. Some, like Protagoras, were quite moderate, arguing that "man is the measure of all things," that morals were a product of convention and thus subject to revision by law or custom. Others, like Callicles, were more radical, eventually calling into question the very existence of objective reality (Plato *Protagoras, Gorgias*).

There has been a tendency, especially on the left, to regard the Sophists as the spearhead of a fundamentally progressive, if historically premature, attempt by protobourgeois elements to lead a democratic revolution, and that the Socratic philosophers both emerged out of and supported the interests of the old landed elite (Wood 1978). This claim is deceptive. That the sophists represented a broadly "bourgeois" trend, in the sense that they represented commercial elements rooted in and profiting from the petty commodity system, cannot be doubted. But their function was not progressive. On the contrary, their effect was to undermine further the already fragile foundations of public morality and to legitimate policies which made the *polis* an instrument of private interests—those of the agrarian bourgeoisie and the emerging class of merchant capitalists. This is because, in the absence of anything that is Beautiful, True, or Good in itself, moral judgment and thus any judgment regarding the justice of social structures or public policies, becomes impossible. The market system has no better defender than the relativist or nihilist who denies the existence of any criterion that might be used to find the market allocation of resources wanting or to ground some alternative allocation or method of allocation.

Wood (Wood 1979) makes her case for the reactionary character of the Socratic project on the basis of the class position of the individuals involved, the more or less explicitly antidemocratic character of their doctrines, and their involvement with antidemocratic political movements. Let us take each of these points in turn. Socrates, for example, came from a family of at least middling means, having served as a hoplite in the Peloponnesian War and having worked, according to tradition, as a sculptor who received commissions from the *polis* for important projects, including statues that stood on the Acropolis. Plato clearly came from a wealthy land-owning family, and Aristotle from the family of a court physician in the service of the Macedonian royal family. All of the Socratic thinkers, furthermore, were advocates of a monarchic or aristocratic polity, and all were involved with, or at least close, to people who were involved with antidemocratic movements. Socrates was a teacher of many of the men involved in the brutal tyranny of the thirty. Plato came from this same circle and was an advisor to the tyrant Dionysus. Aristotle was an advisor to Philip of Macedon and tutor to Alexander the Great.

No part of this thesis is valid. The historical materialist tradition has never regarded the class origin of a thinker as relevant in assessing the political valence of his or her ideas. By the same standard Wood is using, the entire communist movement would have to be regarded as an idiosyncratic form of bourgeois/aristocratic reaction. Marx, after all, came from a prominent bourgeois family, as did Engels. Marx married the daughter of a baron. Lenin himself inherited noble status from this father.[6]

The same is true of the aristocratic doctrine advanced by Socrates and his followers, but this matter requires more careful consideration. Socrates, and Plato and Aristotle after him, were concerned first and foremost to reground ethics and thus rescue the public arena from the Sophists and the bourgeois interests they represented. This project was carried out in three distinct stages. Socrates himself[7] developed what was primarily a

---

6. 5 Lenin's father, though the son of a serf, attended the University of Kazan and became an educational administrator responsible for primary education in the province of Simbirsk. He increased the number of primary schools in the province from 20 to 434 in just fourteen years, and was promoted to the rank of Actual State Counselor—the equivalent of a Major General in the military. Under the Table of Ranks established by Peter the Great, all officers and civil servants were ennobled, and all who achieved the rank of Lieutenant Colonel in the military, or Court Counselor in the civil service (roughly the equivalent of GS-13/14 in the United States and P-3/4 in the United Nations System), were allowed to pass their titles on to their oldest sons. When Lenin's older brother was executed in 1887 for attempting to assassinate the Tsar, Lenin automatically inherited the title. On at least one occasion, in applying to take his examination in law in 1892, Lenin actually used the title, signing himself "Nobleman Vladimir Ulyanov" (Konrad and Szelenyi 1967).

7. We accept here the scholarly consensus that Plato's earlier dialogues give us a more or less accurate picture of Socrates's own views, while the middle and later dialogues reflect Plato's own developing doctrine.

logical, immanent critique of Sophism, drawing out the implications and internal contradictions of sophistic ideas and demonstrating the need for an ascent to first principles. Thus, in the *Euthyphro* Socrates demonstrates the difficulty of deference to traditional religious norms and the authorities who uphold them. If piety is simply what the gods will, then they are merely arbitrary tyrants. If on the other hand they love what is pious because of its intrinsic goodness, then they are subject to some higher standard in terms of which they must make their judgments—a standard which, at least in principle, might be accessible to reason. Similarly, in the *Gorgias*, Socrates shows that it is logically incoherent to claim that nothing exists, that we cannot know anything, or that there are no general principles that ought to govern public life. The result was the dialectical method, the most important instrument of the philosophical tradition. This method consists in posing agitational questions, which draw out the interlocutor's existing ideas, their implications, limitations, and internal contradictions, and then drive towards a higher synthesis. But it is difficult to find anything like a consistent epistemology, cosmology, or metaphysics in those of Plato's dialogues that represent more nearly Socrates's own position. Indeed, even his ethics is rather sparse.

It is only with Plato that the Socratic project progresses beyond purely methodological issues to begin to trace the outlines of a systematic answer to the sophists. The two most important texts in this regard are, without question, the *Republic* and the *Timaeus*. Let us examine them in detail. Plato opens the *Republic* with a scene that situates the dialogue in its concrete political context. Socrates is returning from the feast of the Goddess Bendis, a Thracian huntress deity associated with a women's revolt at Lemnos that left all of the men on the island dead. This is a suggestive reference to the cult of the *Magna Mater* with which Socratic philosophy has a profound affinity. He is detained by a group of rich young men who insist that he accompany them home (a reference to the arbitrary power of the rich in Athenian society and to the precarious position of the philosopher in the bourgeois city). Once there he engages his host, a rich man of the older generation, and several of the young men who had detained him in a debate regarding the nature of justice. He disposes handily of the traditional view, represented by his host Cephalus, that justice is merely a matter of paying one's debts, a view that reflects the *mores* of a society in which market relations have begun to emerge but have not yet eroded traditional norms of reciprocity. Socrates rejects this position, showing that it fails to address the vitally important question of what people actually *ought* to have. Thus, it is hardly just to give a mad man a weapon, even if it was borrowed from him before he went mad and would ordinarily have been returned as a matter of course (Plato *Republic* 327a–331d).

This insistence on a substantive ethics already challenges market norms. Socrates then goes on to answer three positions that were quite common in Athens at the time. First, he addresses the predominant view among the wealthy Athenians of his day: the idea that justice means helping your friends and hurting your enemies. The difficulty with this is that the worst thing you can do to someone is to make them a worse human being, in which case they would undoubtedly do even more harm to you than they had done before. He then turns to the radical sophistic position—that justice is just the will of the stronger, or that conversely, injustice is more profitable than justice. This view he undermines by showing that the stronger do not always do what is in their best interest, and by showing that justice is an art, and that like all the other arts it is devoted not to its own good but to promoting some end outside itself. Finally, Plato addresses the moderate sophistic view that justice is merely a (necessary) social convention (Plato *Republic* 331e–354c). This position he addresses at much greater length by engaging his interlocutors in an analysis of just what sort of conventions or laws they would establish for a city were they to found one. In the process they discover that they cannot frame laws without reference to some higher principle, some substantive doctrine of the Good in terms of which they evaluate proposed legislation. It also becomes clear that if they are to prevent their city from being exploited by its strongest members—the Guardians who protect it from foreign attack—these Guardians will have to be extraordinary individuals indeed, who not only have a temperament that balances desire and aggression (necessary if they are to defend the city) with reason, but an authentic knowledge and love of the Good itself. This they acquire through a long process of education in which the role of traditional poetry is strictly limited and regulated and largely displaced by mathematics and dialectics. Such individuals are, in fact, philosophers (Plato *Republic* 471c–541b).

This bears directly on the meaning of "aristocracy" in the Socratic tradition. What Plato is advocating here is hardly rule by a hereditary landed elite. On the contrary, the Guardians are to be chosen for their intellectual and moral excellence and to live disciplined lives devoted to the Common Good. Once again he is closer to the communist movement and the larger dialectical tradition out of which it emerged than to anything that would ordinarily be called reactionary. What, after all, is Hegel's "universal class" if not a class of philosopher-kings? What are Marx's communists, who understand the "line of march, conditions, and ultimate general result" of the historical process—Marx who called the philosophers the head, and the proletariat the heart, of the revolution? What is Lenin's vanguard if not an organization of armed philosophers—Lenin who said that to understand Marx's *Capital*, it is first necessary to master the whole of Hegel's *Logic*?

Throughout this discussion, Plato does not so much make his argument as outline it, setting forth a philosophical program that would still need to be fleshed out in other works, or perhaps by other thinkers. Indeed, rather ironically, given the critique of poetry that he has just mounted, he attempts to render his vision compelling by the use of a variety of poetic images.

Having set forth this program, Plato then does something odd. He engages in an extended argument aimed at showing that were a just city to exist, it would inevitably degenerate. Aristocracies, societies governed by the intellectually and morally most advanced elements, degenerate into timocracies, societies governed by the courageous and proud (i.e., warriors). Timocracies degenerate into oligarchies, governed by the rich, oligarchies into democracies, governed by the people as a whole, who do not know the Good, and democracies into tyrannies, which transform the state into an instrument for satisfying the rapacious desires of a single individual. Errors in the training and selection of the Guardians would bring to power leaders more interested in wealth and honor than in truth and justice. Eventually these decadent elements would force a restoration of private property not unlike the *nomenklatura* privatization we have witnessed in the former Soviet bloc. Even if at first the property holders were persons formed under the old system and concerned at least for their own honor, if not for the highest values of truth and justice, gradually, from one generation to the next, the growing opportunities for making money would encourage its pursuit, and the "timocracy," rule by lovers of honor, would degenerate into an oligarchy or a plutocracy—rule by the wealthy. But the degeneration does not stop there. The people see that the rich are able to indulge in the most various pleasures without negative consequences, and they too become infected with greed, rising up at the first possible moment to seize the wealth of the few and share it out among themselves. The rich respond with force, and the result is inevitably tyranny, as the most unscrupulous, playing one class off against the other, make the state their private plaything (*Republic* 543a–576b).

Plato takes up this same theme in the *Timaeus*, but goes further, arguing that social disintegration is part of a larger and inevitable cosmic dynamic. This dialogue, like the *Republic*, takes place at a feast of the goddess—this time the festival of Athena, two months after that of Bendis. The topic, however, is still the just social order. The question arises as to whether or not such an order is possible. A story is told, which Solon learned while traveling in Egypt, of an "earlier Athens," founded by the goddess herself, the laws of which were not unlike those of the just society described by Socrates. This society was, however, destroyed in a conflict with Atlantis, which is now submerged in the oceans.

The cosmology of the *Timaeus* is then presented as if to explain this tendency towards disintegration that appears to be written into the very fabric of the universe. It is interesting to note that Plato has Timaeus (a Pythagorean), and not Socrates, present the theory, suggesting that he regards it as a "best effort," regarding which he has, however, serious reservations. This is not surprising, since the theory has little that is specifically Platonic, but represents, rather, an unstable synthesis of Pythagorean and atomist elements (Cleary 1995: 25).

The principal thesis advanced by Timaeus is that the universe was forged by the Demiurge, a kind of cosmic craftsman, on the basis of an eternal model that Timaeus calls a "living being," indicating a sense of organic unity and completeness. The forms of things are impressed on a "receptacle," which is identified as space and called the "matrix," the "nurse of all becoming." The resonance between the concept of matter and the doctrine of the *Magna Mater* should be apparent.

The principles by which the matrix is ordered are rigorously mathematical, and reflect the influence of the Pythagorean doctrine. Thus the universe as a whole, intended as a copy of the perfect model, is spherical because this is the most perfectly symmetrical shape. The World Soul, which moves all things, is self-moved: it rotates in a manner dictated by the interaction of the Same and the Different: the Celestial Equator and the Zodiac or Ecliptic. Even the properties of the various physical forms of matter are explained in mathematical terms. Timaeus accepts the notion of four elements, as well as the atomist gloss that they are in fact composed of distinct particles. For Timaeus, however, these particles are the result of the impression of mathematical forms on the matrix of space itself—forms that are ultimately reducible to the simplest: that of the triangle. As triangles combine to form solids, one gets the cube, the icosahedron, the octahedron, and the tetrahedron, the particles of earth, water, air, and fire respectively. The dodecahedron, the regular solid that most nearly approximates the sphere, is the sign of the cosmos itself.

The creative activity of the Demiurge extends only to those aspects of the universe that are eternal: the heavens and the world soul, and the stars and planets, which are identified with the gods of mythology. To these in turn is allotted the work of creating the plants, animals, and human beings, whose soul is mixed from the same ingredients as the world soul, but is not so pure.

This ordering work is not, however, all there is to the nature of the universe. The receptacle, Timaeus suggests, is resistant to the work of the Demiurge. Matter, far from being potential organization, in fact resists form, and even when formed begins to disintegrate. Necessity, in this sense, constrains the work of Reason. Here we encounter the atomist element in Plato's cosmology, the sense that the random and probabilistic motion of matter continually reasserts itself, leading even the best works of the Demiurge to disintegrate. This is the basis, for Plato, of the irreversible time that we experience—as distinct from the cyclical time defined by the self-motion of the world soul and marked by the movements of the heavenly bodies. Because of this, while we are able to provide a rational account of the work of the Demiurge, we can offer only a "likely story" to describe the phenomenal universe, which is governed as much by randomness as by reason.

What is going on here? What are we to make of this rupture in the middle of the *Republic* and the turn towards radical cosmological pessimism in the *Timaeus*? The answer is to be found not in the text or even the philosophical context, but in the larger social reality to which Plato was responding. If Plato is pessimistic about politics, then it is because he has reason to be. The history of Greece in his time was one of rapid social disintegration. His own life was marked by the execution of his mentor, Socrates, and by the failure of his own political projects both at home in Athens and in Syracuse, where he attempted to persuade the tyrant Dionysus to implement his political program (Wood 1979). And pessimism in politics tends, as we will see, to produce pessimism in cosmology (Lerner 1990).

There is, however, a more subtle process at work here as well. While Socrates and Plato clearly advance, by means of the dialectic, beyond the merely formal abstraction of the Pythagoreans to a higher, transcendental abstraction capable of grasping the first principle and its transcendental properties, the dialectic itself still depends on formalization and in particular on the distinction between the form or underlying structure and the appearance. And in a period of social disintegration, "form" or "structure" are generally regarded as something static—there is no progress towards more complex forms of organization—while the appearance is identified with the matter or the "receptacle" to use Plato's term, which is constantly changing, which resists form, and which leads to cosmohistorical disintegration. Plato's failure to distinguish clearly between formal and transcendental abstraction leads him to revert to the spontaneous ideology of his time and to regard the first principle in increasingly formal rather than transcendental or teleological terms.

The resulting doctrine is problematic on scientific, metaphysical, and political grounds. Plato is unable to explain growth and development—something that ought to have been apparent to him in the plant and animal world if not in human society. Indeed, more broadly he is unable to achieve a unified theory, which comprehends both celestial and terrestrial motion, and both reversible and irreversible phenomena. Indeed, our analysis of the *Timaeus* suggests that the obstacles to unification along these two dimensions may be more closely connected than historians and philosophers of science have thus far realized. We will see that when Newton unified celestial and terrestrial mechanics he did so only at the expense of any theorization of irreversible processes, which became an object of scientific investigation only with the advent of thermodynamics in the nineteenth century—a science which, at least in its first formulation, reproduced and even radicalized Plato's—or Timaeus's—doctrine.

Even more serious is the fact that Plato's cosmology fails to support the metaphysics he sets forth in the *Republic*. There is no sense in the *Timaeus* that the Good draws all things towards itself, awakening in matter a latent potential for organization. On the contrary, matter is not only inert but chaotic, not only threatening, but actually working disintegration. Order comes from on high, from a sort of celestial monarch—or rather from his vice-regents, who impose it ever some imperfectly on a universe that tends towards chaos and destruction. It is hardly surprising that in his later years Plato should have drifted even further into political pessimism, arguing that philosophers could rule only secretly and from behind the scenes, through a Nocturnal Council that intervenes into what is otherwise an essentially oligarchic regime (*Statesman*), and eventually conceding the inevitability of rule by a (nonphilosophical) landed elite (*Laws*).

It is in this context that we must understand Wood's third charge against the Socratic tradition: that whatever their views the Socratic philosophers conspired with antidemocratic elements. Here, once again, we run up against the difficulty that much the same charge might be made of the communist movement in the twentieth century. Faced with limited alternatives, the left has often chosen to support tyrants willing to take a stand against imperialism and the market order, especially when the tyrants in question have shown some depth and complexity as individuals and some openness to guidance from the Communist Party. How else can one describe a Nasser, a Qaddafi, or a Sadaam Hussein? Indeed, many of the political leaders of the left are better described as tyrants with "philosophical" elements in their temperament than as philosophers endowed with political prudence and the power it yields. Such a tendency to collaborate with tyrants would only be accentuated by well-founded pessimism regarding the prospects for more fundamental change. It is certainly possible, from the vantage point of the present, to question the prudence of such alliances, but one cannot conclude that those who made them did so with reactionary intent.

It is these difficulties in Plato's philosophy that Aristotle's physics and metaphysics attempted to resolve. Aristotle, we should note, began his investigation with physics—with an attempt to explain the universe—rather than turning to that task only *after* having arrived at a first principle. Aristotle also rejects explicitly both materialistic approaches to physics, which reduce change to local motion and to neglect the problem of form entirely (*Physics* 194a), and Pythagorean approaches that understand form in a static way.

> The form is indeed *physis* (nature) rather than the matter; for a thing is more properly said to be what it is when it has attained to fulfillment than when it exists potentially . . . We also speak of a thing's nature as being exhibited in the process of growth by which its nature is attained. (*Physics* 193b)

> Again, "that for the sake of which" or the end, belongs to the same department of knowledge as the means. But the nature is the end or "that for the sake of which." For if a thing undergoes a continuous change and there is a stage which is last, this stage is the end or "that for the sake of which." (*Physics* 194a)

What this suggests is that "motion" or "change" for Aristotle is *first and foremost* growth and development, and that this is conceived of as at once the perfection of a form that is latent in something and the realization of the end for which the thing exists.

From here, Aristotle goes on to treat causation, or that in terms of which motion can be explained. Aristotle distinguishes between material cause, or that out of which something comes to be, formal cause, which Aristotle identifies with the essence, or what a thing is, efficient cause, that by which it comes to be, and the final cause, or "that for the sake of which" a thing exists (Aristotle *Physics* 194b, *Metaphysics* 988a–b). Ultimately, however, change is driven by the attractive power of the final cause. Immediately this is the perfection of form that each thing seeks. Ultimately, however, it is the first Unmoved Mover, the beauty of which moves the heavens and through them the entire universe.

> It is clear, not only in argument but also in fact, that there is something (i.e., the heavens) which is moved with unceasing and cyclical motion. Consequently, the first heaven must be eternal. There is therefore also something which moves it. And since a moved mover is intermediate, there is, therefore, also an unmoved mover being eternal, primary, and in act. (*Metaphysics* 1072a)

This approach allows Aristotle to overcome the pessimism of Plato's cosmology and sociology. While he does from time to time speak of matter as resisting form, the underlying logic of Aristotle's universe is one of growth and development, driven by the attractive power of God. Aristotle is therefore able to develop a much more complex and nuanced ethics than Plato's. He begins with a scientific analysis of human nature, noting that we possess distinctive capacities that transcend those of the other animals. We have an intellect and a will. The Good draws us in to motion, growth, and development just as it does everything else in the universe, but it does so in a different way, by acting on the intellect and thus informing the will. The good for human beings consists in virtue—in habitual excellence in the exercise of our distinctively human capacities. This means, on the one hand, the cultivation of the intellect, through *techne* or excellence in making, *phronesis* or excellence in understanding the means to the ends of human life, *nous* or excellence in understanding first principles, *episteme* or excellence in explaining things, and *sophia* or excellence in rising to first principles, and, on the other hand in the moral virtues of temperance, courage, and justice. The intellectual virtues we develop through study, the moral virtues through habituation, something that requires, in turn, a just social order. While his (like Plato's) preference is for a monarchy in which the king is authentically wise and just, or an authentic aristocracy, Aristotle already begins to recognized the merits of a mixed constitution that includes democratic elements (Aristotle *Ethics*, *Politics*). That democratic potential in Aristotelian thinking is further developed by Thomas and his interpreters.

We are now in a position to evaluate comprehensively the political valence of the Socratic project. It should be clear, on the one hand, that Socratic philosophy is first and foremost a response to and an attempt to tap the potentials and resolve the social contradictions of the petty commodity system and to do so under the constraints imposed by the level of development of the productive forces. In order to understand why this is the case, it is necessary to be quite specific about the potentials and contradictions of the petty commodity system, which overlap with and in some ways foreshadow, but which are by no means identical with, those of capitalism. Like capitalism, petty commodity production offers individuals and small communities the opportunity to exploit their comparative advantages and create and accumulate wealth without coercively appropriating the fruits of the labor of others. And unlike capitalism, it does not *necessarily* involve noncoercive extraction of surplus either. At the same time, some individuals and communities have more comparative advantages than others, and thus prosper, while others may sink into poverty and even lose their productive assets entirely, sinking into debt bondage. And where the people are able to effectively resist this fate, there is a drive on the part of the ruling classes to secure a captive labor force by means of conquest in order to work the large estates they have accumulated. The market, furthermore, which has no access to knowledge of the impact of various activities on the integrity of the ecosystem or the development of human capacities, does not always allocate resources in a way that promotes growth and development. There is, finally, a growing tendency to see human social relationships as merely a means to private ends, with an attendant corruption of whatever sort of regime prevails. And, as we have noted, in a market society of any kind people have no basis in experience for understanding the ordering of systems to a common good, and tend increasingly to see the universe as a system of only externally related atoms, or else as a system of quantities (prices) governed by formal rules but without any global end or purpose. Petty commodity societies are not, on the other hand, affected by the principal contradiction of the capitalist system: i.e., the tendency for the rate of return on capital to be lower on precisely those activities which, because they require high levels of investment in technology or skilled labor, are most likely to promote the development of human capacities, with the result that capital is continually reallocated to low-wage, low-technology activities, which in turn generates a crisis of underconsumption. Shifts in resource allocation in petty commodity societies are, on the contrary, likely to be relatively minor, relatively slow, and to be in response to noneconomic (ecological, technological, political, or ideological) factors.

Resolution of the contradictions of the petty commodity system, unlike those of capitalism, does not require that the system itself be radically transcended. It is merely necessary that economic differentiation be contained, that a mechanism be developed for centralizing and allocating the resources necessary for human development, and that debt servitude, chattel slavery, and other degrading ways of organizing labor be abolished.

It is just precisely these reforms that Plato and Aristotle proposed to carry out—Plato rather more thoroughly, at least in his middle dialogues, than Aristotle. Extremes of wealth and poverty are to be avoided. A considerable part of the social surplus is to be centralized (presumably by means of taxation) in order to support the education and training of the Guardians and Auxiliaries. Further movement in a "socialist" direction, e.g., the expropriation of private property, was simply not called for as a condition for renewed human development, and to regard Plato and Aristotle as reactionary because they did not propose it is antimaterialist and anachronistic.

There remain, of course, the difficult questions of the attitude of the early dialecticians towards chattel slavery, their preference for aristocracy, and the openness of the social order they envisioned. Let us address each of these questions in turn.

Plato, in the *Republic* at least, is clear that there is no room whatsoever for slavery in a just social order. Slavery is seen to emerge only as a result of the disintegration of the ideal state (Plato *Republic* 546). Aristotle, on the other hand, seems to argue that slavery of some sort is a result of natural differences among human beings—that some human beings are merely means to the development of the more advanced, and of human civilization generally, as a result of fundamental differences in their natural endowment.

> For he who can be, and therefore is, another's and he who participates in rational principle enough to apprehend, but not to have, such a principle, is a slave by nature. Whereas the lower animals cannot even apprehend a principle; they obey their instincts. And indeed the use made of slaves and of tame animals is not very different; for both with their bodies minister to the needs of life. Nature would like to distinguish between the bodies of freemen and slaves, making the one strong for servile labor, the other upright, and although useless for such services, useful for political life in the arts both of war and peace. But the opposite often happens—that some have the souls and others have the bodies of free men. And doubtless if men differed from one another in the mere forms of their bodies as much as the statues of the gods do from men, all would acknowledge that the inferior class should be slaves of the superior. It is clear, then, that some men are by nature free, and others slaves, and that for these latter slavery is both expedient and right. (Aristotle *Politics* 1254b)

Two points are in order here. First, we should note that Aristotle acknowledges the difficulty in ascertaining who is fit for freedom and who is fit for slavery, even if he does not draw the obvious conclusion: that slavery will inevitably result in injustice to those who are mistakenly enslaved. Second, we should note that Aristotle's position does not follow organically from his larger system, but rather depends on an unsubstantiated empirical claim: i.e., that some human beings actually lack the ability to make use of their rational faculties. He does not consider the possibility that those who lack the full use of reason need education, not exploitation.

A more fruitful approach to the problem might be to suggest that slavery was not actually an integral part of the petty commodity system, but rather a distinct economic structure that emerged out of it, as a result of the failure to address its internal contradictions, and that the thinking of the dialecticians was not really adapted to addressing this problem.

Indeed, with the collapse of the old archaic order centered on sanctuaries that provided the intelligentsia with a ready source of income, slavery increasingly seemed like the only means by which resources could be centralized to support human development. That it actually held back human development by undermining technological innovation, and thus reducing the total surplus available for investment in activities that promote human development, was not yet clear at this point.

The Socratic critique of democracy is an integral part of the Socratic attempt to resolve the contradictions of petty commodity production. If human society is to be ordered to the Good, then it must be governed by those who know the Good, and this requires a prolonged period of training and education. Due to the low level of development of the productive forces, it is impossible to provide everyone with such an education: thus Plato's option for a philosophical aristocracy, and his failure to even consider the option of a philosophical democracy; thus Aristotle's desire to at least temper democratic participation by including a monarchic and aristocratic element in his constitution. It is only as technological and economic development allow a broader section of humanity the opportunity to cultivate their rational capacities that authentic democracy can really be on the agenda.

And this, of course, is the real point. The political truth that dialectics reveals is a difficult one indeed. Human beings are not, Rousseau to the contrary, born free and only enchained by oppressive social institutions. Rather, we are born slaves and become free only through a long labor of self-cultivation, one that depends on a framework of social institutions capable of nurturing and disciplining that self-cultivation. Democracy, we will argue in later chapters, is more nearly possible than either Plato or Aristotle allowed, but more difficult than most moderns and postmoderns have wanted to claim.

It is in this context that the question of the open society must be understood. Dialectics, unlike myth, *presupposes* pluralism. But it also seeks to discipline it, challenging diverse claims regarding meaning and values to justify themselves by means of rigorous argument. The social order envisioned by Plato and Aristotle is, in this sense, open not in the manner of a free marketplace of ideas in which cultural forms succeed or fail based on their ability to mobilize desires and resources, but rather in the manner of the university, in which liberty of thought and conscience are not only respected but cultivated, but where both are held accountable before the court of reason.

This said, there are real limits even to Aristotle's philosophy. From a *philosophical* standpoint, this limitation has to do with his characterization of the first principle. While Aristotle is quite clear that the first principle can bring things into Being only by means of teleological attraction, it is less clear just why this principle is so attractive. And he does not tell us what it *is*. This will be remedied only by the synthesis of dialectics and prophetic religion worked out by Jewish, Christian, and Islamic philosophers beginning with Philo of Alexandria and continuing up through Thomas Aquinas and his interpreters, who will identify the dialectical principle with the God whose name is revealed in Exodus, and which means *Being*. We will turn to the first stages in this development shortly.

This philosophical limitation also has political implications. To the extent that he discusses it at all, Aristotle characterizes the unmoved mover as a kind of supreme contemplative. At the ethical and political level, this favors the contemplative over the active life and leaves little scope for ordinary workers and peasants to participate in the life of the first principle. Re-theorizing that principle as *Being* as such, on the other hand, stresses the creative act and, without diminishing the role of intellect (creation is, first and foremost, an act of the intellect), validates the role of ordinary labor as a real participation in the life of God.

Israel

We have already seen that there was, in Israel, a breakthrough prior to the timeframe generally associated with the Axial Age, a breakthrough that we associated with the of the crisis of the great tributary civilizations of the late Bronze Age. This breakthrough involved a rejection of sacral monarchy and the war/lord/god complex in favor of a new cult centered on a specific name of the old Canaanite high god 'El: *'el yahwi sabaoth yisrael*. This new cult continued to represent and speak about God anthropomorphically, even if it already rejected graphic representations, and continued, indeed, to think of God as a warrior, but now as a warrior on the side of the poor, a warrior who acted on behalf of justice. Israel met—and served—its God on the battlefield of the revolution.

This should not, however, be taken to imply that Israel traveled on utterly different path than Greece or the other principal civilizational centers of Afro-Eurasia. We noticed, for example, a similar breakthrough in China, the Zhou Revolution, and we have some evidence of comparable developments even in Greece, developments of which a text such as Hesiod's *Works and Days* may represent one of the final products. There remained, in any case, substantial room for further religious rationalization, and for a continued deepening of the spirituality of justice that formed the foundation of Israel's religion.

In order to understand this, we need to sketch out briefly the history of Israel in the period from roughly 1000 BCE on. Earliest Israel, we have argued, was essentially a neocommunitarian or neoarchaic social formation. Villages concentrated in the hill country of Judah, Samaria, and the Galil practiced dry-soil subsistence agriculture on terraced hillsides using slaked lime cisterns in order to catch and hold limited rainfall. Land was held by the village community and periodically re-distributed. Village elders settled disputes within their communities. Ten percent of the product was set aside for the Levites, who formed a kind of priestly stratum that passed on the traditions of Israel's origins and conducted rituals, especially at the major feasts of Pesach, Shavuoth, and Succoth, which corresponded to the barley, wheat, and fruit harvests respectively. There was little in the way of a formal political structure. Above the village level the most important institutions were sanctuaries at places like Bethel, Beersheba, Schechem, etc. These were places to which the peasants repaired at the principal feasts. They also seem to have been the places at which *shophetim* passed judgment on those disputes that could not be resolved at the village level. There was no king, no standing army, and no central temple complex. When external threats arose, Israel responded by producing charismatic military leaders such as Barak and Samson who rallied troops, repelled the invaders, and then returned to their villages.

This pattern persisted from roughly 1200–1000 BCE. At that point a new threat appeared on the scene: the Philistines, probably one of the so-called sea peoples, related to the Achaeans of Homeric fame. The Philistines possessed iron technology and used infantry rather than chariot warfare and were thus able to penetrate and subdue the hill country, which had been Israel's stronghold. This required Israel to develop a more centralized form of organization, which would enable it to raise and maintain a standing army. This took a couple of generations. We see first what amounts simply to a unified military command under Saul, and only later, under David and Solomon, do we see anything like a real monarchy.

Establishment of the monarchy was an ambiguous event from the standpoint of the traditions of earliest Israel. On the one hand, David was able to liberate the lowlands and coastal regions from the Canaanite warlords as well as the Philistines, thus completing the long revolution begun more than 200 years earlier. At the same time, the emergence of monarchy meant, almost inevitably, the reassertion of tributary structures. We know that as early as the third generation—the reign of Rehoboam—the North was chafing under rising taxes and soon withdrew to form its own—but hardly more benevolent—monarchy. Stories such as 1 Samuel 8, which retrospectively imagine the origins of the monarchy, warn that the king will

> ... take your sons and make them serve in his chariots and with his cavalry and they will run before his chariot. Some he will appoint officers over units of a thousand and units of fifty. Others will plough his fields and reap his harvest; others again will make weapons of war and equipment for the chariots. He will take your daughters for perfumers, cooks and bakers. He will seize the best of your fields, vineyards and olive groves, and give them to his courtiers. He will take a tenth of your grain and your vintage to give to his eunuchs and courtiers ... He will take a tenth of your flocks and you yourselves will become his slaves. (1 Sam 8:11–17)

The centralization of surplus and the concentration of land holdings facilitated, in the years after about 800, the development of specialized agriculture. This was more common in the North than in the South, both because the North was better suited ecologically and because it was closer to key trade routes, but the pattern ultimately affected both regions. This led to a gradual erosion of the historic protections that redistributional land tenure—the so-called law of the Jubilee laid out in Leviticus 25—had afforded the peasantry. The story of Naboth's vineyard in 1 Kings 21 probably reflects a memory of this sort of latifundialization. We see, in other words, the same combination of overall increased prosperity and growing inequality that characterized Greece during the same period. We also see the reassertion of strong sacral monarchic tendencies, especially the idea of an *unconditional* covenant between *yhwh* and the House of David in Judah and the reassertion of full-blown *baalism* in the North.

It is against this background that the Axial Age breakthrough in Israel must be understood. The process of religious rationalization was directly bound up with the struggle for a just social order. The site of both this struggle and the new and deeper knowledge of God was the prophetic movement. The earliest attested prophets or *nabi'im* appear to have been court seers, such as Nathan, and to have served largely at the pleasure of the king. Even Nathan, however, did not hesitate to warn the king against wrongdoing. Gradually, we see the prophets emerging as sharp critics of both social injustice (Naboth's vineyard) and of the religious alienation (the re-emergence of *baalism*) that was accompanying it. At first the prophets are merely legendary figures who were remembered for their actions; later, beginning in the eighth century BCE, we begin to have recorded sayings or oracles.

The outstanding feature of these oracles is that they consistently identify social justice (*mishpat wesedek*) with knowledge of God (*da'ath 'elohim*). Thus Isaiah targets directly the latifundialization that developed as a result of the emergence of Israel into regional trade networks.

> *yhwh* opens the indictment against the elders and officers of his people:
>
>> It is you that have ravaged the vineyard;
>> In your houses are the spoils taken from the poor.
>> Is it nothing to you that you crush my people and grind the faces
>>   of the poor? (Isa 3:14–15)
>
>> Woe to you who add house to house
>> and join field to field,
>> until everyone else is displaced,
>> and you are left as the sole inhabitants of the land. (Isa 5:8)
>
>> Woe to you who make unjust laws
>> and draft burdensome decrees
>> depriving the poor of justice,
>> robbing the weakest of my people of their rights,
>> plundering the widow and despoiling the orphan. (Isa 10:1–2)

He then goes on to paint a picture of restored justice, placing fulfillment of the demands of social justice in poetic parallelism with *da'ath 'elohim* or *da'ath yhwh*, thereby equating the two.

> They shall not hurt or destroy in all my holy mountain,
> For as waters of the earth fill the sea

So shall the land be filled with knowledge of *yhwh*. (Isa 11:1–12)

Injustice, on the other hand, is essentially equated with a lack of knowledge of God. Thus Hosea:

> Call your mother to account …
> She does not know that it was I who gave her the grain, the new wine and the fresh oil,
> I who lavished on her silver and gold which they used for the *ba'alim*. (Hos 2:8)
>
> There is no good faith or loyalty, no knowledge of God in the land
> …
> The more priests there are, the more they sin against me …
> As you have rejected knowledge,
> so I will reject you as a priest to me. (Hos 4:1, 7, 6)

And what, precisely, does Israel *know* when she knows God? In acting to create justice—to bring into being the conditions for human development and creativity itself—Israel acts as *yhwh* acts, thus becoming, as Thomas Aquinas would later put it, actually *connatural* with God (Thomas *Summa Theologiae* II-II 89, Maritain 1937, Garrigou-Lagrange 1938). And being connatural with God, Israel knows God directly, experientially, and preconceptually as the power of Being as such. In Exodus 3:13ff., part of the Elohistic narrative of Israel's history from the Northern Kingdom, God tells Moses that His name is *eyeh asher eyeh*. *Eyeh* is the imperfect indicative form of the verb "to be," indicating that this God is Being itself, acting still. In the same passage we also find the revelation of the name *yhwh*, which is the causative form of the verb "to be," and points even more clearly to the recognition of God as the power of Being as such.

In knowing God in this way, Israel lays the groundwork for the development—much later, in the medieval synthesis of Jewish, Christian, and Islamic Aristotelianism—of what we call an *analogical* metaphysics, a metaphysics that understands that God exists in a way fundamentally different from the way in which we or anything else exists, but that we, nonetheless, at the same time, participate in that Being that is the ground of our existence and criterion of all our action. This then provides the basis for the development of a natural law ethics, which recognizes right action as action that promotes the full development of human capacities, and of a just society as one that creates the conditions for such development.

This process of religious rationalization is also, at the same time, a process of religious democratization. If God is known pre-eminently in the just act, then knowledge of God is possible for anyone, and does not depend on priestly mediation. Israel did not yet—and in a sense never did—reject in principle the value of such mediation as part of a larger spirituality. But it was already quite clear that what God demands is not burnt offerings and whole offerings, but rather just conduct and a just social order.

> Thou hast no delight in sacrifice; if I brought thee an offering, thou wouldst not accept it.
> My sacrifice O God is a broken spirit;
> A wounded heart, O God, though wilt not despise. (Ps 51:16–17)

> God has told you what is good;
> And what is it that *yhwh* asks of you?
> Only to act justly, to love loyalty,
> To walk wisely before your God. (Mic 6:8)

Indeed, the prophets themselves represent an opening up of religious leadership. While Isaiah appears to have been a priest, for example, most of the other writing prophets were not. One, at least (Amos), claimed to be a tender of sycamores. As we will see, this democratization of *extraordinary* religious leadership opened up the way for the development of an entirely new form of *ordinary* religious leadership based not on birth within a priestly lineage, but rather on scholarship and the capacity to exercise intellectual and moral leadership. These developments, however, were more characteristic of the Silk Road Era, and will be addressed in the following chapter.

India

In order to understand the Axial Age experience in India, it is necessary first to understand something about the background of Indian Civilization. As we noted in the previous chapter, the principal Bronze Age civilization in the region—the so-called Indus Valley or Sarasvati Civilization—does not fit into the general pattern of Bronze Age river basin civilizations, in that it appears to have developed neither the monumental religious architecture of the sort we ordinary associate with archaic structures nor the sort of palaces and fortifications we generally associate with tributary structures. Instead, we see large cities of shops and private dwellings.

The closest thing to a central structure is what appears to be a large tank of some kind. Some scholars suggest that this was, in fact, a ritual center of some sort, others that it was merely a swimming pool. Statues of dancing women, presumed to be goddesses, are widely dispersed throughout the city, as are smaller shrines.

This evidence is extraordinarily difficult to read. There are, however, two—not incompatible—possibilities. If the tanks did serve ritual purposes, it is possible that the Indus Valley cities were, in fact, at least in part, ritual centers following the model of the earlier Mesopotamian settlements, centers which simply didn't experience conquests by pastoral-raiding peoples and thus never developed tributary structures for centralizing surplus and thus never centralized enough to build temples on the scale of those we find in Egypt or Mesopotamia. On the other hand, we know that Harrapa and Mohenjodaro were both involved in long-distance regional trade serving, among other things, as links between Central Asia (the principal source of antiquity's most precious stone, lapis lazuli) and Mesopotamia. It is possible that this region made an early breakthrough towards a petty commodity system, something that prevented dominance by a single monarch and thus the development of monumental architecture (Thapar 2002: 69–97).

This civilization seems, in any case, to have declined during the middle of the second millennium BCE. Scholars long assumed that this was the result of attacks by the invading Indo-Aryans, but current thinking suggests a combination of factors: changing climate, disease, and internal contradictions, with pressure from the Aryans constituting, at most, a secondary factor. The Indo-Aryans appear to have entered the region gradually, searching for pastures and farmland. Most of their interactions with indigenous peoples, at least as described in their own sources, appear to have been with forest dwellers and villagers, not with a major urban civilization.

When the Aryans came, they brought what was, essentially, a pastoral and raiding economy and a tribal structure centered on patriarchal clans. Clans or groups of clans gradually came to control particular territories governed by a *raja* or chief, assisted by the *purohita* or chief priest and the *senani* or military commander. These *rajas* were far from exercising absolute authority. They were, rather, constrained by various assemblies and councils: the *sabha*, a council of elders, the *vidatha*, an assembly, probably of warriors, which distributed the booty taken in raids, and the *samiti*, the assembly of the whole clan. Initially the *vish* or clan chose the *raja*, who was essentially a war leader whose economic privileges were based on voluntary gifts—*bali*—and a special share of the booty, the *bhaga*.

Gradually, however, the role of agriculture increased and larger settlements were established. This led to a number of changes. The warrior elite seems gradually to have evolved from a stratum privileged but still essentially acting on behalf of the *vish* into a group of exploiters. A popular saying developed that the *raja* eats the *vish* like a deer eats grain. Most likely, at this point, this reflected a tendency for the "gifts" required of the *vish* to become mandatory and onerous. A fourth group of dependent producers, the *sudra*, appeared, probably from among indigenous peoples on whom forced labor obligations were increasingly imposed. (Thapar 2002: 117ff.).

These political-economic changes were reinforced by a perverse synergism between the *Brahmins* and the *rajas*. Increased levels of exploitation required a more sophisticated strategy of legitimation. The *Brahmins* obliged by developing increasingly elaborate rituals that, over a period of many years and at the cost of vast quantities of wealth, promised the *raja* divinization. Thus, after assuming office, the *raja* would perform the year long *rajasuya*, which involved rituals of purification and rebirth. At the end of this, he was expected to make offerings to the "twelve jewels," various members of his family as well as craft and other specialists. The *raja's* rule could be further extended ritually by the *asvamedha*, or horse sacrifice. A horse would be set free to wander for a year, the territory it covered becoming part of the *raja's* domain. At the end of the year it would be sacrificed as part of a fertility ritual that also involved the *raja's* chief wife.

The effect of this dynamic was to set in motion a kind of synergism between the *raja* and the *brahmana*. The largely functional differences between *raja*, *brahmana*, *ksatrya*, and *vaisya* were given ritual significance. The *raja* stood out from the other warriors because, unlike them, he had been divinized—something that one would think would have given him an edge over the *brahmanas* even on ritual grounds. But the *brahmanas* argued that as the *makers* of divinity it was they, in fact, who represented the highest status group. Thus we see the emergence of what was to become a millennia-long status struggle between priest and warrior, which, though certainly not unknown in other cultures, came to play a dominating role in India.

The Axial Age

The religious ideas of this period reflect the dominance of warfare on the one hand and sacrifice on the other. Consider, for example, the following hymn to Indra:

> Let me now sign the heroic deeds of Indra, the first that the thunderbolt-wielder performed. He killed the dragon and pierced an opening for the waters; he split open the bellies of mountains. (*Rig Veda* 1.3)

Or this hymn to Agni, the fire god and the representative among the gods of the priestly function:

> I pray to Agni, the household priest who is the god of the sacrifice, the one who chants and invokes and brings most treasures.
> Agni earned the prayers of the ancient sages, and those of the present too; he will bring the gods here.
> Through Agni one may win wealth, and grow from day to day, glorious and most abounding in heroic sons.
> Agni, the sacrificial ritual that you encompass on all sides, only that one goes to the gods. (*Rig Veda* 1.1)

These same motifs are also apparent in reflections on the sacrificial act itself. Sacrificial violence is at the very origin of the universe and of the social order.

> When they divided *Purusha* how many portions did they make?
> The *Brahman* was his mouth, of both his arms was the *Rajanya* made.
> His thighs became the *Vaisya*, from his feet the *Sudra* was produced.
> The moon was generated from his mind, and from his eye the sun had birth ...
> Fourth from his navel came mid-air; the sky was fashioned from his head;
> Earth from his feet ... (*Rig Veda* 10.90)

It is sacrifice as well that sustains order and creates sovereignty among men.

> Let this racehorse bring us good cattle and good horses, male children and all nourishing wealth. Let Aditi make us free from sin. Let the horse with our offerings achieve sovereign power for us. (*Rig Veda* 1.162)

From here Indian civilization seems to have developed along two distinct lines. In some regions—especially the cities of the Indo-Gangetic plain—the *raja-brahmana* alliance seems to have effectively gained hegemony. In these regions we see the development of what amount to sacral monarchic city-states, some of which controlled significant territories. In other regions—especially in the foothills of the Himalayas—the *ksatrya* effectively resisted the *raja-brahmana* alliance and instead formed *gana-sanghas*, assemblies of "equals" in which the chiefs of warrior clans sat together to frame laws, presiding over not only the members of their own clans, but also dependent *dasa-karmakara* laborers. In both cases, however, there seems to have been a very significant development of specialized agriculture and especially crafts production, including woolen cloth for export, terracotta figurines, etc. Eventually this blossomed into an export trade in ebony, spices, and cotton cloth, and even iron work (Thapar 2002: 141, 160–64, 178).

It was in the context of these city states—just beginning to enter into petty commodity production and still emerging from essential tribal social relations—that the Axial Age breakthroughs took place in India. Broadly speaking, it is possible to identify five broad trends: a skeptical trend that eventually gave birth to the Caravaka School; the Ajivikas, who taught a radical determinism but nonetheless allowed the possibility of release through asceticism; the Jainas, who developed a dualistic metaphysics and also taught release through radical asceticism; the Buddhists, who rejected the idea of the inherent existence of anything whatsoever and sought release through detachment; and the rationalized Brahminism of the *Upanishads*, which taught that the material world was, in some sense, simply an illusion and that everything was ultimately identical with the first principle or Brahman.

We know about Caravaka teachings primarily from later writers who sought to refute them. A possibility of distortion thus always remains. The principal tenets of the school are, however, fairly certain. First, knowledge comes only from perception; even inference from sensation to another sensible object is excluded (Madhva Acarya *Sarvadarsanasamgraha*; Sankara *Sarvasiddhantasamgraha*).

> From this it follows also that there is no possibility of understanding the relation of cause and effect. (Jayarasi *Tattvopaplavasimha*)

> According to the Lokayatika doctrine the four elements alone are the ultimate principles: earth, water, fire, and air; there is no other.
>
> The soul is but the body characterized by the attributes signified in the expressions, "I am stout," ... It is not something other than the body.
>
> The consciousness that is found in the modifications of non-intelligent elements is produced in the manner of the red color out of the combination of betel, areca-nut, and lime.
>
> There is no world other than this; there is no heaven and no hell; the realm of Siva and the like regions are invented by stupid imposters of other schools of thought.
>
> Chastity and other such ordinances are laid down by clever weaklings.
>
> The wise should enjoy the pleasures of this world through the proper visible means of agriculture, keeping cattle, trade, political administration, etc. (Sankara *Sarvasiddhantasamgraha*)

This skepticism was, as in Greece, ultimately a reflex of the petty commodity order, in which wealth, rather than being a means to higher-order activities, had become the principal aim of social life. In India, however, this fundamental basis was overlaid by a more conscious resistance to *brahmana* hegemony, which was seen as an effort on the part of an essentially unproductive stratum to drain away resources that might otherwise have been enjoyed by the *ksatrya* or the more prosperous *vaisya* themselves.

The other schools all represented reactions against the skeptical materialism of the Caravakas and the hedonistic way of life they represented. These trends all shared certain common themes: a focus either on the relationship between self or consciousness on the one hand and the material universe on the other, or on the relationship between the self and the creative power or ground of the universe, the idea that our actions (*karma*) have accumulated results that reach not only through this life but also beyond into later reincarnations or rebirths (*samsara*), and a desire for release from the cycle of death and rebirth (*moksa*).

The Ajivikas, as we have noted, seem to have upheld a kind of determinism, but nonetheless organized orders of monks and nuns to seek release from rebirth. Beyond this we know little.

The Jainas represent the first expression of what would become a long-standing dualistic trend in Indian thought, also later represented by the Samkya and Yoga schools. The Jaina tradition traces its own origins to a long series of *tirthankaras* (literally "ford-makers") reaching back for millennia. Historical Jainism, however, was a response to the teachings of a wandering ascetic of *ksatrya* origin, Mahavira, who was active mostly in the Gangetic plain. Unlike the Caravakas, he recognized not only sensation but also inference as a basis for knowledge and on this basis arrived at the idea that the universe is driven by two fundamental principles, *jiva* or consciousness and *ajiva* or the unconscious. This association is beginingless. Indeed, he recognized no God or first principle even as logically prior. The Jaina upheld an essentially materialistic doctrine of *karma*, which was regarded as a kind of fine substance that accumulated on the *jiva* and bound it to ignorance and rebirth. All action produced such accumulated *karma*. *Moksa* or liberation required radical asceticism—in fact a cessation of all action. All Jainas refrain from occupations that involve killing, which leads to the accumulation of the worst sort of *karma*; some even wear masks so they do not accidentally inhale insects and brooms to sweep the path before them so they will not step on any. One sect—the *Digambara*—actually refuse to wear clothing. The most radical expression of this asceticism was the *itvara* or *sallekhana*, in which the practitioner practices self-starvation over a period of twelve years, burning away accumulated *karma* and ultimately attaining release through death.

It might seem odd to find that the Jaina tradition met with its most favorable reception among merchants in the West of India, especially in Karnataka and Gujarat. It is important to remember, however, that only a small group of religious virtuosos actually attempted to attain liberation; the remainder supported them through almsgiving and tried to avoid occupations and activities that might lead to the accumulation of especially bad *karma*. This had a definite political valence. On the one hand, the religious virtuosos undercut the authority of the *brahmana* priests, arguing, in effect, that spiritual authority was based not on birth or even on learning, but rather on the conquest of matter—something that the privileged *brahmanas* did not even attempt. At the same time, by arguing that killing led to the accumulation of especially bad *karma*, the Jaina tradition also undercut the claims of the *ksatrya*. The result was the religious legitimation of what had historically been *vaisya* occupations. It is little wonder that Jainism eventually became hegemonic in Western India during the height of the Silk Road era, between the eleventh and fourteenth centuries (Thapar 2002: 166).

Buddhism appears, at least in part, as a reaction against the extremism of Jaina teachings. Founded by Siddhartha Gautama, a prince of the Sakya clan in what is now southern Nepal, Buddhism rejected all of the existing metaphysical doctrines—materialist, absolutist, and dualist, in favor of the doctrine of *pratita samutpada* or dependent origination. The principal insight is simple: everything that we encounter in the universe is the result of the a complex of causal interconnections. This is the same insight that was behind Aristotle's doctrine of the unmoved mover. But rather than concluding that there cannot be an infinite regress of causes and that there must therefore be a first cause that is itself uncaused, the Buddhists concluded that *nothing*, in fact, has inherent existence, that everything is ultimately empty.

> Inasmuch as it is dependently on each other and in unison and simultaneously that the factors which constitute dependence originate the elements of being, therefore did the Sage call these factors dependent origination. (*Visuddhi-magga*)

This in turn implied that there was in fact no self (*anatman*), either as an entity autonomous from matter or as an expression of it. Suffering results not from the involvement of some conscious or spiritual principle, such as the Jaina *jiva* with the material world, but rather from ignorance. We spontaneously attribute inherent existence to things and to ourselves and thus become attached to both; liberation is possible only by recognizing that things (including ourselves) lack such inherent existence and that there is, therefore, quite literally nothing to desire and nothing to regret.

Buddhism, like the Jaina tradition, undercut the claims of the *brahmana* priests. Its initial base of support, however, seems to have been not so much among the merchants as among the *ksatrya* elites of the Himalayan highlands. Initially, at least, it seems to have done little to foster a concern for social justice. Indeed, early Buddhist texts indicated a fascination with the institution of slavery as it was practiced by the Greeks, as opposed to the more complex system of *varna* and *jati* stratification that was gradually developing in India, especially in the Gangetic plain. Ultimately, however, the Buddhist critique of *brahmana* privilege allowed the creation of the first large-scale state in India: the Mauryan Empire. Burdened by guilt over those he had killed in completing the conquest of most of Northern India, but also undoubtedly one of the greatest political theologians of history, King Ashoka converted to Buddhism and soon made the Mauryan Empire, once known for its brutality, a model of just social relationships. At the center of Ashoka's strategy was centralization of surplus for a large system of public works—including public granaries, which provided for the poor in times of famine. The property of the rich (the local dynasties and coteries of nobles he had conquered) was seized, but to the poor Ashoka would lend without interest and after three years forgive all debts (Sarkisyanz 1965: 54–56). The surplus extracted from the peasants was relatively modest—between one sixth and one quarter of the total produce. *Sudras* clearing new land were exempt from taxation. Trade was carefully regulated to ensure that the merchant did not make too great a profit and that a share of the surplus was centralized by the state (Thapar 2002: 186–88). This surplus Ashoka used to subsidize temples and monasteries, primarily Buddhist but also Jaina and Brahmin (Sarkisyanz 1965: 28–30, Thapar 2002: 200–204). The result was that he was considered to be a *chakavatti* or universal monarch who restored the rule of *dhamma* or law.

The final trend in Axial Age India was the tradition of the Upanishads. These texts, which date from the very beginning of the Axial Age—the seventh and eighth centuries—understand themselves as a commentary on or an attempt to get at the inner meaning of, the Vedas. They focus above all on the emerging concept of Brahman—the creative first principle, which they understand as the ground of the phenomenal world. Some of the texts refer to *Brahman* in personal terms, as a kind of High God.

> Immortal, existing as the Lord,
> Intelligent, omnipresent, the guardian of this world,
> It is He who constantly rules this world. (*Upanishads*, Svet. 6.17)

Others speak of *Brahman* as an impersonal force.

> Verily this whole world is *Brahman*. Tranquil let one worship It as that from which he came forth, as that in which he will be dissolved, as that in which he breaths. (Chand. 3.14.1)

The later texts speak of both a formed and formless *Brahman*.

> There are, assuredly, two forms of *Brahman*: the formed and the formless. Now that which is formed is unreal; that which is formless is real. (Mait. 6.17, 7)

Coupled with this movement towards a more abstract concept of God was a concern for the relationship between *Brahman* and the self or *atman*. Thus the text that eventually became the *locus classicus* for debate within the Vedanta tradition between nondualistic, modified nondualist, and dualist positions:

> He who is awake in those that sleep,
> The Person who fashions desire after desire—
> That indeed is the Pure. That is Brahman.
> That indeed is called the Immortal.
> On it all the worlds do rest.
> And no one so ever goes beyond it.
> This, verily, is That. (*Katha Upanishad* 8)

The Upanishads were not, for the most part, as overtly hostile to Vedic orthodoxy as the other trends. They did, however, depart from the teachings of the Vedas both regarding the *aims* and the *means* of religious practice. On the one hand, the inner-worldly aims characteristic of Vedic religion give way to a search for *moksa* or liberation.

> I will briefly explain all that is taught in the Vedas, all that asceticism declares, and that which sages seek through religious practice. It is Om.
> This syllable truly is Brahman, it is the supreme syllable. Whoever knows it obtains all wishes.
> This is the best support. Knowing this support a person attains happiness in the world of Brahma.
> The wise one is not born, does not die; it does not come from anywhere, does not become anything. It is unborn, enduring, permanent; this one is not destroyed when the body is destroyed....
> (*Katha Upanishad* 2.1.15–18)

The Upanishads, similarly, make a strong case for the inadequacy of sacrifice as a means achieving religious aims.

> The sacrificial rituals, eighteen in number, are, however, unsteady boats, in which only the lesser work is expressed. The fools who delight in this as supreme go again and again to old age and death. (*Mundaka Upanishad* 1.2.7)

Finally, while the Upanishads did not represent as radical an assault on Brahmin hegemony as did the other trends, it did tend to open up new possibilities for religious leadership. Thus, for example, by reducing the

Vedas to the syllable "om," the Katha Upanishad reduces substantially the quantity of text that must be memorized and recited in order to achieve wisdom.

All of these trends, then, despite their fundamental differences, reflect the principal tendencies of the Axial Age: religious rationalization and democratization. It might be argued that the drive towards social justice was, at the very least, less apparent in India than in Israel or Greece, but we must remember that by disrupting the *raja-brahmana* alliance, all of these movements contributed to undermining the principal form of legitimation for the neotributary structures that were emerging in India at the time, and forced the ruling classes to adopt more progressive policies and to opt for legitimation strategies that placed much higher moral demands on the state.

As in the case of the Mediterranean Basin (henceforth the Greek and Jewish breakthroughs will need to be considered in relation to each other), the Axial Age breakthroughs in India posed questions and suggested particular directions; the elaboration of metaphysical systems that attempted comprehensive answers and justifications was a characteristic of the later Silk Road period.

China

Chinese thought, especially during the early period, is often regarded as non-metaphysical, avoiding fundamental questions of meaning in favor of a concrete approach to addressing social problems. This is not really accurate. We have already seen in the previous chapter that the Zhou revolution was accompanied by a movement away from the anthropomorphic *Shang Ti*, or "lord on high," the high god of the Shang or Yin dynasty, towards the more abstract *T'ai Chi* (Great Ultimate) and *tian* or "heaven" (Fang 1981: 101–16) favored by the Zhou. The term *T'ai* means great or supreme. The term *chi* was originally quite concrete, and taken literally means "pole," in the sense both of "tent-pole" and "pole star" (Ching 2002: 33). During the Zhou dynasty, in other words, we see a process similar to that which took place in early Archaic Greece, as anthropomorphic gods give way to natural forces.

The Axial Era in China was, as elsewhere, characterized by the development of specialized agriculture and crafts production and the emergence of petty commodity production. This in turn resulted in the erosion of the Zhou land tenure system, under which land was divided into nine equal plots, eight private and one public, so that the peasants in effect contributed only one ninth of their total product to support the ruling classes (*Zhou-li*). In 722 BCE Zhou authority effectively collapsed, setting in motion a period of political fragmentation and warfare known as the Spring and Autumn and Warring States periods.

As elsewhere, one response to these developments was the emergence of a skeptical and pragmatic trend—Legalism—which argued that order and progress depended on the development of a strong state. Some Legalists stressed the role of coercion in building a strong state, others the role of law, but all denied the existence of transcendental first principles and all upheld an essentially relativistic ethics (Collins 1998:148–53).

The other principal trends represent a reaction against this sort of skeptical relativism. Mo Tzi reintroduced the idea of a personal creator God who demanded of humanity an ethic of *bo ai*—universal love. Later Mohists moved in a more naturalistic direction, developing empirical and mathematical methods in the sciences (Collins 1998: 138–43). These developments were not unlike the simultaneous movement in Hesiod to emphasize the cult of Zeus as a god of justice, while naturalizing the other gods.

We also see a growing tendency towards the use of mathematical language to speak about first principles in what eventually emerged as the Taoist and Confucian trends. This is particularly apparent in the *I Ching* or Book of Changes, which proposes to derive quite literally everything from a series of trigrams consisting of broken and unbroken lines.

> In the changes is the Great Ultimate.
> This produces the Two Forces.
> The Two Forces produce the Four Images.
> The Four Images produce the Eight Trigrams.
> The Eight Trigrams determine fortune and misfortune.
> Fortune and misfortune give rise to the great activities.
> (Wilhelm and Baynes 1967: 318–19)

It is only one small step from here to Taoism, which identifies the *Tao* or Way with the *Wu-Chi* or the "limitless."

> The Way begets the One; One begets Two; Two begets Three; Three Begets the Myriad Creatures ... (*Lao Tzu* 42)

> Know the male
> But Keep to the role of the female
> And be a ravine to the empire...
> Then constant virtue will not be wanting
> And you will return to the Infinite. (*Wu Chi*) (*Lao Tzu* 28)

This in turn paves the way for the fully metaphysical, rather than merely naturalistic, use of the terms *tian* and *T'ai Chi* that we find in Confucius and in the later Confucian tradition.

> The gentleman stands in awe of three things. He is in awe of the Decree of Heaven. He is in awe of great men. He is in awe of the words of the sages. (*Lun-yu* XVI.8)

> What Heaven imparts to man is called human nature. To follow our nature is called the Way. Cultivating the Way is called education. The Way cannot be separated from us for a moment. (*Chung Yung*)

This said, there can be little doubt that the dominant concern of Axial Age Chinese thought was with questions of social justice. We have already seen the focus on universal love characteristic of the Mohists. The Mohists rejected the emphasis on rites and ceremonies associated with the Zhou tradition, and instead looked back to the legendary pre-Shang Hsia dynasty, and in general seem to have argued for a return to something like a communitarian or archaic structure. This appears to have led them to develop a disciplined political organization that actually contested for power (Collins 1998: 138–43).

The concern for social justice is, however, most apparent in the emerging Confucian trend. This trend reflected the influence of scholars or *ru* displaced by collapse of Zhou authority and forced to sell their services to the princes of the now autonomous states. Their aim was, in effect, to restore the Zhou system. They were forced, however, to actually argue their case for this system, and ended up not only developing a metaphysical rationale for it, but also rationalizing and democratizing it and radicalizing its emphasis on rule in service to the common good.

The *T'ai Chi* or Great Ultimate gives birth to *tian* or Heaven. It is the *tian-ming* or the Mandate of Heaven that in turn gives order to human societies and legitimacy to their rulers. Concern for the well-being of the people is fundamental to any society governed in accord with the Mandate of Heaven.

> The Master said, "Give them enough food, given them enough arms, and the common people will trust you." (Confucius *Analects* XII.7)

Confucius rejected the Legalist emphasis on force in favor of a strategy centered on rule by virtue.

> The Master said, "Guide them by edicts, keep them in line with punishments, and the common people will keep out of trouble but will have no sense of shame. Guide them by virtue, keep them in line with the rites and they will, besides having a sense of shame, reform themselves." (Confucius *Analects* II.3)

Confucius identified five virtues: *zhi* (wisdom), *li* (propriety or religion) *ren* (benevolence), *xin* (fidelity), and *yi* (justice). The main burden of cultivating wisdom is on the ruler, who must authentically be superior to those he would claim to rule. The *zhi, jen,* and *yi* of the ruler together lead to the *xin* of the subjects and thus ensure social harmony. *Li,* or religion, plays a critical mediating role. By participating in the ancient rituals, the principal relationships that defined the social order were rectified and maintained, and thus brought into harmony with the larger order of the cosmos.

> This *li* is the principle by which the ancient kings embodied the laws of heaven and regulated the expressions of human nature. Therefore he who has attained *li* lives, and he who has lost it dies. ... *Li* is based on heaven, patterned on earth, deals with the worship of the spirits, and is extended to ... rites and ceremonies ... Therefore the Sage shows the people this principle of a rationalized social order, and through it everything becomes right in the family, the state, and the world. (*Li Ki* XXVII, in Lin Yu-tang 1938)

Confucius, like the Israelite prophets and the Hellenic dialecticians, wants, in effect, to restore the archaic order undermined by the rise of the warlord state and of petty commodity production, but to do so on the basis of a rationalized understanding of the meanings behind, and the social functions carried out, by myth and ritual. The result will be

> Kindness in the father, filial piety in the son
> Gentility in the eldest brother, humility and respect in the younger.
> Righteous behavior in the husband, obedience in the wife.
> Human consideration in elders, deference in juniors
> Benevolence in rulers, loyalty in ministers and subjects.

The Confucian system was hierarchical, making distinctions between the sage, the superior man, and the ordinary man, but its nobility was one of merit, not of birth (Confucius *Lun-yu* IV: 15; VIII: 2, 7; XIII:20; XVI: 8).

Taoism, finally, despite its reputation in the West for quietism, also had definite political implications.

> Why are the people starving?
> Because the rulers eat up the money in taxes.
> Therefore the people are starving.
> Why are the people rebellious?
> Because the rulers interfere too much.
> Therefore they are rebellious. (*Tao Te Ching* 75)

The emergence of a warrior aristocracy, which invested the surplus product in military conquests rather than in raising agricultural productivity, and of petty commodity production, which makes the generation of surplus a means of private profit, mark the departure of Chinese society from its natural course of development, its deviation from the *Tao*.

> When the Tao is present in the universe
> The horses haul manure.
> When the Tao is absent from the universe
> Warhorses are bred outside the city. (*Tao Te Ching* 46)

Taoist monasteries cultivated the martial arts as well as scholarship and meditation, and at certain points in Chinese history became centers of political military resistance to the Empire (Deng Ming-Dao 1990: 13). The Taoist masters of Huainan were actively engaged in the process of reconstruction that followed the end of the period of Warring States (Cleary 1990: vii). The Taoist tradition in effect counsels a return to the communitarian norms of pre-tributary China, which, they believed, represented a natural and healthy pattern of social development.

As in the Mediterranean Basin and India, in other words, the Axial Age in China—the birth of metaphysics—was intimately bound up with the struggle to address underlying injustices created by the emergence of petty commodity production. While hierarchy remained central for some trends—especially Confucianism—the hierarchy in question was one of real excellence rather than birth, and the period as a whole represented a period of real opening up both in the sense of access to participation in debates around fundamental questions of meaning and value and in the sense of the range of perspectives reflected. We will see these trends continued and extended during the Silk Road Era.

It is to that period—which was arguably the Great Age of Metaphysics—that we now turn.

3

The Great Age of Metaphysics

INTRODUCTION

OUR READERS WILL, at this point, no doubt be posing the following objection: "We grant that you have demonstrated that there was, in fact, an 'axial era' and that it was a period of religious rationalization and democratization, of a deepening recognition of injustice and of the disharmonies of existence generally, and of a deepening commitment to address those injustices. But this doesn't prove your point. After all, you have acknowledged that the innovators of the axial era were not systematic metaphysicians but rather prophets and sages. Isn't the systematic metaphysics that developed in the epoch that followed—more often than not in conjunction with remythologizing salvation religions—fundamentally an attempt to co-opt Axial Age traditions and use them to legitimate oppressive world empires?" This was, in effect, the position of the Enlightenment, which traced its own "light" back to the Greeks but which rejected the religious metaphysics of Neoplatonism and of Neo-Platonizing and Aristotelianizing Judaism, Christianity, and Islam. This was also the position of the later Heidegger. Heidegger's early critique of metaphysics, we will remember (Heidegger 1927, 1928), focused on the failure of thinkers, beginning with Plato, to grasp the distinction between Being and beings. Instead, he argues, they theorize Being as the beingness of beings—they think Being in entitative terms. Later (Heidegger 1941) Heidegger modified both his historical analysis and his philosophical position. Increasingly identifying ancient Greek and German romantic thought, he claimed to hear in Plato and Aristotle echoes of the earlier Greek *aletheia* or unconcealment of Being and located the crystallization of metaphysics in the "translation" of Greek thought into Latin, "the language of road builders and empire makers," a crystallization that is completed in the Middle Ages when Being is identified with the supreme maker, the Christian Creator God. This process culminates, of course, in Thomas, who is *the* philosopher of the "ontotheologic," the universal causal-explanatory system in which Being is simply an instrument for explaining and ultimately manipulating entities (Caputo 1982).

This chapter will argue that the Enlightenment and late-Heideggerian theses are no more defensible that Heidegger's earlier claims regarding Plato and Aristotle. On the contrary, we will show that while metaphysical systems with their roots in the axial era certainly *were* joined with (partially) remythologized salvation religions and that together these ideological systems certainly *were* used to legitimate world empires, that they also had the effect of restricting exploitation and redirecting surplus towards activities that promoted human development and civilizational progress. The resulting synthesis was also *more* rather than less open and democratic than the original dialectics of the Axial Age. And the elaboration of the insights of the prophets and sages of the axial era into metaphysical systems and the fusion of these systems with partially remythologized salvation religions to generate what the Christian tradition called "theology" represented real intellectual progress—specifically the completion of the journey of the dialectic begun during the axial era in credible doctrines of the first principle understood variously as *Esse* (Being) as such, the *tathagatagarbha* (Buddha nature) or *Brahman,* or the *T'ai Ch'i* or Great Ultimate. These doctrines all, on the one hand, reflected the tremendous civilizational progress of the period, which made humanity more and more connatural with the creative principle that lies behind the universe, but also depended in significant measure on the contributions of prophetic religion (the idea of God as *Esse,* for example, derives ultimately from the revelation of the divine name in Exod 3:13) or the spiritual practices of the Buddhists, Taoists, and Hindus.

Our argument will proceed as follows. We will consider each of the principal post-axial civilizations—the Hellenistic-Roman Civilization, Byzantium, *Dar-al-Islam,* Western Christendom, India, and China. We will begin in each case by demonstrating the presence of certain underlying political-economic patterns: integration into the developing Silk Road trade networks on the basis of specialized agricultural and craft technologies pioneered during the earlier axial era and the emergence of large imperial structures that, while they continued the earlier tributary pattern of taxing the peasantry, were in fact ordered to profit from taxation of this Silk Road trade. We will then show how axial and post-axial movements interacted with these structures at once lending their legitimacy and at least partially hegemonizing them, profoundly altering both the ways in which they extracted surplus and what they did with the surplus they extracted. We will show that the result was an internally differentiated but interrelated complex of civilizations sharing similar civilizational ideals: i.e., a common focus on participation in Being through the search for meaning and the cultivation of human creativity.

HELLENISTIC-ROMAN CIVILIZATION

It is, of course, with respect to the "West" that Heidegger elaborated his thesis, and it is with respect to the West that we must first show it to be wrong. We begin by analyzing the basic character of Hellenistic-Roman civilization and showing why neither dialectics nor the prophetic religions—Judaism and Christianity—were able to redeem it. We will then analyze the internal dynamics and interactions of Rome's successor civilizations—*Dar-al-Islam* and Christendom—and show how each developed a specific synthesis between prophetic religion and dialectics, and how each variant shaped, and was shaped by, the civilization in question.

Civilizational Patterns

Political Economy

The roots of Hellenistic-Roman civilization lie in an attempt to save the ideal of Hellenic civilization from a profound structural crisis that afflicted the Mediterranean world from about the fourth century on. This ideal was, we will remember, centered on a radical democratization of the life of the city—which was, first and foremost, a *religious* life. The real *work* of Hellenic civilization, in other words, took place not in its olive groves and vineyards, its workshops or markets, but rather in the cultic centers of its mystery religions, in its drama festivals, and above all in the public forum in which, in principle at least, any male citizen could earn sufficient respect from his peers to rise to the office of *basileus archon* and sit for life on the Areopagus.

This ideal was, to be sure, never fully realized. Athens went much further than most cities in extending participation in the public arena to the full body of citizens, and even there this participation was, for the vast majority, a mere formal possibility. The peasants and artisans of the Athenian *demos* remained bound by *ananke* to the toil of vineyard and olive grove, workshop and market, held back by material constraints from ever *really* becoming citizens.

By the fourth century, however, even this modest realization of the Hellenic ideal was endangered. The economic strategy of the Hellenic *poleis*—the exploitation of new technologies (specialized agriculture, especially wine and oil, and specialized crafts, especially pottery) to develop a vigorous export trade—had been dramatically successful. The very success of this model lead, however, to imitation, much of it encouraged by the Greek cities themselves, which spawned numerous colonies throughout the Mediterranean Basin and north into the Black Sea. The result of this was growing competition and a gradual decline in revenues in Old Greece as the comparative advantage that made the *polis* possible in the first place was lost to new entrants (Ste. Croix 1982).

"Democratic" adaptations that combine low rates of exploitation and broad political participation with an open economy permitting at least some to accumulate significant quantities of wealth are almost always associated with a high-end export economy. As revenues declined over the course of the fourth century, the result was an intensification in the class struggle as the ruling classes attempted to maintain their position and/or recover lost ground, something that required 1) intensified exploitation, either of their own working classes or a much expanded base of chattel slaves, or both; 2) successful development of imperial taxing structures that transformed colonies from competitors into a new source of revenue; and 3) insertion into—and a measure of control over—the developing Silk Road trade networks, so that products that were now being produced for export throughout the Mediterranean could be traded globally and thus retain their comparative advantage.

Alexander's conquests opened the door for all of these adaptations. On the one hand, wars of conquest increased the supply of chattel slaves and opened up new lands to exploitation, either by slaves or by dependent tenants for whom Macedonian rule meant simply a change in masters. At the same time, Macedonian hegemony lead to a gradual erosion of democratic institutions so that the working classes lost much of the political protection they had won during the struggles of the Archaic and Classical epochs, and the ruling classes were able to once again begin accumulating land and pushing an ever larger fraction of the population towards servitude. Control over the entire Eastern Mediterranean and Western Asia meant that cities which for Athens had been competitors now became a source of revenue for the Macedonians, while at the same time securing access to trade routes with India and China. The Carthaginians, themselves an old colony of the Phoenicians, did much the same for the Western Mediterranean. Indeed, by 200 BCE, most of civilized Eurasia, from China in the East and India in the South, to Britain, Iberia, and West Africa in the West, had been linked together in one single "global" market in luxury goods.

It was, however, the Romans who completed this process and unified the entire Mediterranean Basin, together with most of Europe and parts of Western Asia, into a single imperial structure. In order to understand the precise character of this structure it is necessary to say a few words about the history of Rome itself. Like most of the *poleis* of the Mediterranean basin, it grew up on the basis of specialized agriculture and crafts production. Like them, it experienced sharp economic differentiation during the first two centuries after its founding, a period corresponding roughly to the Greek Archaic era. And, as in Greek cities during this period, economic differentiation led to sharp internal struggles. Most Greek *poleis*, however, resolved these contradictions by carrying out authentic land reform and establishing more or less democratic polities (the Athenian model), or else opted for outright oligarchies, which reduced either their own citizens or those of the surrounding countryside to servitude (the Spartan model). Rome did neither. The Roman constitution was, to be sure, thoroughly oligarchical, paying only lip service to democracy. While laws could officially be made only by the Assembly, this Assembly was by tribes and under the effective control of the patrician families that made up the most prestigious lineages in the various tribes, or later by *nouveau riches* plebeians. Real authority remained with the Senate, which was gradually opened up to plebeians who had held senior magistracies, but this simply transformed it from a hereditary oligarchy into an economic oligarchy—what amounted to a council of the city's largest landowners. The consuls or senior magistrates held far more authority than their counterparts in even oligarchic cities in Greece, especially with respect to military matters.

Where Rome differed most from the Greek oligarchies was in the fact that it cushioned its own population from the most brutal forms of exploitation and opted instead for empire. The Roman ruling classes effectively bought off their own people with the promise of "bread and circuses," and above all with the opportunity to secure a plot of land through service in the imperial army. This created extraordinary economic pressures for imperial expansion. Both the modest "welfare state" enjoyed by the Roman people and the continued wealth and power of the ruling classes depended on empire.

In this sense the transition from the Republic to the Principate was inevitable. The drive for empire increased the political weight of the military to the point that it outweighed the historic institutions of the Republic, which were not so much abolished as they were simply overshadowed. As in the case of the Hellenistic Empires, the Roman state was never the principal means by which the ruling classes extracted surplus from the population. Rather, it created opportunities for private individuals to engage in exploitation. The (very substantial) surplus extracted from the conquered peoples was used first and foremost to buy into the Silk Road trade. Wine, oil, and gold flowed East; silk and spices flowed West.

The resulting structure amounted to this: a military dictatorship that extended throughout the Mediterranean *oikumene* and made it possible for the Roman and provincial ruling classes to establish vast latifundia worked by slaves (in the West) and dependent peasants (in the East). The extent of latifundialization, as well as of effective taxation, varied considerably from one region to the other. In the West, for example, Sicily, Libya, Mauritania, and Numidia in North Africa, and much of Gaul and Iberia were all transformed into "bread baskets" with vast estates worked primarily by slave labor. Towards the periphery of Europe, on the other hand, in Britain for example, there is some evidence that pre-Roman patterns persisted. The same is true in the East, where latifundia were more often worked by tenants or wage laborers than by slaves. Galilee was latifundialized long before the Roman conquest; Judea on the other hand remained home to large numbers of independent peasants well into the Roman period (Freyne 1980: 156–70).

Rates and forms of taxation also varied, and recent research has made the picture even more complex, as scholars debate just how early the *capitum* or head tax was imposed. Generally speaking, however, all areas under Roman rule were subject to the *tributum* in the amount of one forth of the harvest (Freyne 1980: 174). Those regions directly under Roman administration were subject as well to the *annona* or yearly produce to support the Roman population, and the *annona militaris*, paid in kind or forced labor to support the Roman garrisons (Belo 1981: 63) and to various tolls, excises, and duties, known collectively as the *publicum*, whence the name "publican." The tax burden would have been further compounded by the exactions of the indigenous ruling classes, at least some of which had historically derived their revenues from taxes and tithes rather than from the exploitation of latifundia.

The multiple forms of exploitation to which the people were subject meant that the class structure of, and the pattern of social contradictions in, the Roman Empire was complex indeed.

1. Within the ruling bloc we must distinguish:
    1.1. the Roman metropolitan ruling classes, which included:
        1.1.1. The Senatorial Order—eventually defined as those who had a *census* of HS 1,000,000, and who controlled all of the most senior posts in the imperial administration, of whom there were never more than 600 in the Empire as a whole;
        1.1.2. The Equestrian Order, whose members had a *census* of HS 400,000 or more, and who provided the cadre core of the Roman imperial administration, and depended on imperial exactions for its revenues and advancement.
    1.2. the provincial ruling class, which included:
        1.2.1. The curiales, or members of the city councils, who were generally required to have a census of over HS 100,000.[1]
2. Outside the ruling bloc we should identify:
    2.1. Two types of middle strata:
        2.1.1. Privileged freedmen and slaves who were entrusted with important administrative responsibilities, who were often able to accumulate significant wealth, but

---

1. Ste. Croix suggests that the curial census marked the lower limits of ruling class status—i.e., the amount of wealth necessary to free the individuals in question and their families from laboring to earn a living and leaving them free to participate in the governance of their cities.

who lacked the personal liberty characteristic of ruling class status; and

2.1.2. A relatively large middle stratum of merchants, artisans, intellectuals and others who had effective control over their time and labor, but who did have to sell the goods and services they produced in order to survive.

2.2. The vast majority of the population consisted of various types of agricultural produces, subject to systematic exploitation of various kinds:

2.2.1. Independent and community peasants subject only to taxes, tithes, and occasional forced labor;

2.2.2. Tenants, subject to rents and to varying degrees of constraint on their liberty of movement, which generally increased during the later years of the Empire; and

2.2.3. Chattel slaves, who were generally men taken as prisoners of war and often worked to death in the fields or in the mines.

Hellenistic-Roman civilization was, in other words, from the very beginning, characterized by the most profound contradictions. It emerged as an attempt to salvage the Axial Age ideal of spiritual self-cultivation and democratic citizenship, but it did so by means of an exploitative and oppressive structure that soon began to undermine that ideal.

Metaphysics and Politics

This is nowhere more apparent than in the transformation of the dialectical tradition during this period. The Academy first moved back, under Speusippus, towards a Neo-Pythagorean position syncretized with an astrological cult, which was probably of Babylonian origin, and then to an idealist skepticism along the lines of Berkeley and Hume. The first position—the vision of a universe dominated by numbers or by stellar deities accessible only by means of a mathematized astronomy, and then only very partially and imperfectly—is a reflex of the market system seen from the standpoint of the *rentier* elite which alone can penetrate the mysteries of the market order, and then only in a partial and incomplete manner. Like the earlier Pythagorean movement, it represents an effort on the part of an advanced section of the *rentier* elite to establish itself as an intellectual and moral leadership core, a project that was doomed from the beginning.[2]

If the doctrine of Speusippus and his followers developed the mystical and religious potential of the Socratic dialectics, Skepticism developed its critical side, eventually arriving at the conviction that authentic knowledge was effectively impossible. This conclusion was the product of a careful analysis of the internal logic of sensation. By establishing sensation as inherently subjective and unreliable (a position to which Plato himself had been sympathetic) the Skeptics were able to undercut the objective basis of all human knowledge, turning the Platonic dialectic into its own opposite. The turn to Skepticism reflects the retreat of the rentier elites from active participation in the marketplace and public life into private consumption, with an attendant focus on the subjectivity of sensation and perception and a growing recognition of its inability to transcend this position.

The Aristotelians, meanwhile, under Aristotle's successor Theophrastus, rejected his teleological cosmology and turned towards a radical materialism. Randall Collins explains this development in microsociological terms. Platonists and Aristotelians defined themselves in relationship to each other, he argues, a dynamic that pushed each to adopt more radical positions than their founders had held. Another school, meanwhile (the Stoics), took up the philosophical middle ground between idealism and materialism that Aristotle had formerly occupied (Collins 1998: 107–8). While this thesis undoubtedly has some merit, it does not explain the larger context in which this jostling for position took place, and more specifically it does not explain why the Stoics were able to seize the mid-

---

2. It is not unheard of for intellectually and morally advanced segments of the ruling classes to establish an effective position of leadership vis-à-vis the larger population, but this takes place only when there is some sort of reciprocal exchange between the people and the intellectuals in question, as was, for example, the case during the middle ages, when monasteries played a central role in opening up new lands for cultivation and provided avenues for upward mobility for members of the peasantry. Ironically the fact that monasteries often engaged in direct extraction of surplus from the peasants made it easier for them to exercise leadership because the peasants felt that they were contributing, through the monastery, to something of immeasurable value. Rentier elites, precisely because they have withdrawn from direct involvement in economic activity, find it difficult to develop such reciprocal relationships and thus to exercise effective leadership.

dle ground from the Aristotelians, and why the Aristotelians so willingly yielded it. A more likely explanation is to be sought in the original social base of the Aristotelian school in the privileged stratum of the artisanate. Its political ambitions defeated, this stratum now settled down to focus on the scientific research that can support its principal activity, which is *techne*. Rejection of the doctrine of the unmoved mover reflects this political acquiescence. Without a metaphysical principle to ground it, the dialectical critique of the market order, as well as any potential critique of the Macedonian Empire, cannot stand. At the same time, the Aristotelians resist any impulse to directly or indirectly legitimate the imperial order by adopting something like the Stoic position. In this sense, Aristotelianism ceases to be a global ideology and becomes a partial stance proper to a social stratum with no prospects for hegemony.[3]

The rise to prominence of Stoicism itself requires some comment. The Stoics saw the universe as a material system infused by a rational World Soul or Logos that organized and directed its activity in a more or less deterministic fashion. What this doctrine did was to conserve the Aristotelian distinction between matter and form, and thus Aristotle's "centrism" in the struggle between idealism and materialism, while at the same time eliminating the teleological element that was fundamental to Aristotelian science and metaphysics. This was a reflex of a social order in which people, at least in the larger cities, no longer had a day-to-day experience of participation in a whole ordered to a common end, and thus were no longer able to think of the universe on this model. Order, rather, came from the outside, from the state, which brought some measure of form to an increasingly chaotic social system governed by the operation of market forces. The sharp distinction between matter and the rational soul is, furthermore, a reflex of the distinction between slave and free. Unlike the Aristotelian understanding of matter as the potential form, the Stoic doctrine effectively foreclosed any possibility of an internal dynamism within matter leading to growth and development, and thus reflects quite well the situation of the slave under the Hellenistic and Roman Empires.

---

3. The distinction between global and partial stances is due to Antonio Gramsci, who distinguished between fundamental classes that are able to offer a global vision for the reorganization of human society, and are thus able to mount a credible contest for hegemony, and nonfundamental classes, which develop political and ideological forms that simply advance their interests within the context of existing social structures and existing class alliances (Gramsci 1949b).

Crisis and Reform

Internal Initiatives: Pagan Neo-Platonism

Soon, of course, the fabric of Hellenistic-Roman civilization began to unravel. There have been no end of theories advanced to explain the "decline and fall of the Roman Empire," which is, perhaps, the original *locus classicus* of Western historiography, dating back to Gibbon and perhaps, in a certain sense, even to Augustine himself. Some theorists have focused on ideological factors, such as the moral decline that accompanied the rise of prosperity (Rostovzeff 1960) or the growing influence of otherworldly salvation religions such as Christianity (Gibbon 1909). But prosperity had no such impact on *Dar-al-Islam* or Han, Tang, or Song China. And it was Christianity that built the civilization of the European Middle Ages.

Within the historical materialist tradition three different theories are current. Perry Anderson focuses on the underlying economic crisis created by the closing of the *limes*. The Sahara Desert to the South and the Russian forests to the North and East meant that there was in fact a limit to the lands that Roman armies could conquer. But the closing of the *limes* meant a shortage of slave labor, which had been drawn primarily from among prisoners of war (Anderson 1974a: 76, 80). In order to remedy this situation, *servi* were settled on the land, with families (Ibid., 94). This naturally began breaking down the distinction between free and servile labor. At the same time, beginning with Diocletian, increasing restrictions were placed on the freedom of movement of the *coloni* (Jones 1974: 302). What had, in the West at least, been a slave society was slowly transforming itself into something more like feudalism.

Geoffrey de Ste. Croix (Ste. Croix 1982), on the other hand, sees the crisis of the empire as first and foremost a legitimation crisis. From the very beginning the Empire had put unlimited power in hands of a ruling class that gradually concentrated more and more wealth into its own hands. When slave supplies dwindled, they resorted to transformation of free peasants into *coloni* in order to make up lost revenues. For a while this stabilized the economic situation, but it also led to more frequent rebellions. Gradually the burden of maintaining the empire was extended to the lower strata of the ruling classes, the *curiales*, who in turn also withdrew their allegiance, especially as the empire proved itself unable to protect them against peasant revolts and barbarian invasions. Christianity, in this analysis, simply added to the economic burden born by the working classes as ever-larger segments of the population sought clerical status in order to escape tax burdens, and as the Church itself was gradually transformed into a large landowner. Eventually there just isn't anyone left with the willingness and wherewithal to resist the "barbarian" invasions.

Both of these explanations have merit, but neither really comprehends either the underlying economic weakness of the Empire or the significance of the structural changes that took place beginning in the fourth century. Andre Gunder Frank (Frank 1998) has shown that the Mediterranean Basin generally and the Roman Empire in particular had a long standing balance of trade deficit with its trading partners further east. This is because, while Roman agriculture stagnated under the impact of chattel slavery, India and China were busy implementing progressive new agricultural technologies that made it easier and cheaper to produce grain and thus to free up more of the population to produce the luxury goods the Romans craved. Thus India during this period was already implementing wet rice agriculture, one of the most productive agricultural technologies known to preindustrial humanity (Thapar 2002), while Han China was introducing crop rotation, the use of soybeans to restore the fertility of the soil, and increased use of animal power (Gernet 1985). The Mediterranean Basin was, in other words, paying for its response to the class struggles of the late Archaic period, which emancipated native debt slaves only to replace them with imported chattel slaves, while India and especially China were moving towards more progressive forms of labor organization.

Probably all three factors had an impact. The underlying economic weakness of Roman civilization explains the eclipse of the West by India and China during the millennium between 500 and 1500 CE. The closing of the *limes* and the conversion of slaves (in the West) and free peasants (in the East) into *coloni* defines at a structural level the transition from Hellenistic Roman to Christian civilization. This, and the fact that the West was more exposed to Barbarian invasions than the East, and thus more prone to question the value of the Empire, all help explain why the crisis was so much more severe in the West than in the East. And clearly the late Empire suffered a profound crisis of legitimation, apart from which the various attempts at reform—and their ultimate failure—cannot properly be understood.

Ultimately, however, the crisis of the Roman Empire and the larger Hellenistic Roman civilization of which it was part was not merely structural. It was civilizational: i.e., it was a crisis of the Axial Age ideal of spiritual self-cultivation and democratic citizenship, which simply could not be realized in the context of a "global" empire founded on slave labor.

It is in this context that the emergence of Neo-Platonism and of the various strategies for imperial reform associated with it must be understood. By Neo-Platonism we mean that cluster of doctrines which, while tracing its origins to Plato, goes well beyond him in the elaboration of an idealist epistemology and metaphysics. Plato put forward a number of different theories of knowledge, including at least one that suggests that knowledge begins with the senses and that we rise to knowledge of intelligibles only by means of the dialectic. Similarly, he put forward at least two cosmologies—that of the *Republic*, according to which the universe is drawn into being by the attractive power of the Good, and that of the *Timaeus*, according to which the physical universe is a result of the action of a Demiurge on a prime matter already subject to certain mathematical laws. Whether Plato advances his theory of reincarnation as a doctrine or merely as a way of making a point about moral accountability is unclear. The precise status of the Ideas and their relationship to the material world is unresolved in Plato, as is the relationship of the Good to the other ideas. And while there is a broadly consistent ethic of subordinating the spirited and desiring faculties to reason, Plato gives us three distinct political theories, each one increasingly pessimistic. None of this is the result of indecisiveness or inconsistency. Rather, it is because Plato was attempting to address a very specific problem in a very specific social context. He wanted to reground ethical discourse in a *polis* that was lurching towards crisis.

In the works of the leading Neo-Platonists—Plotinus, Proclus, and Iamblichus—all of these ambiguities are resolved in an emanationist metaphysics in which everything in the universe is a manifestation of the first principle, understood first and foremost as the One. The One is not Being or Intellect, but is beyond both, infinite and ineffable. The One, however, is also the Good and thus tends to overflow, sharing itself, as it were, and thus brining the universe into being. The first product of this overflowing or emanation is Intellect (*nous*). This is the realm of Ideas, the archetypes, as it were, of everything that might come into being. The second emanation is that of the World Soul, which contains within itself all of the various forces that govern the physical universe.

On the one hand Neo-Platonism (Collins 1998), with its emphasis on the One, clearly represents an accommodation to the monotheism promoted by Judaism and, in a more moderate form, Christianity. Gone is the idea that the various gods of Greek mythology are actually separate and discrete beings utterly independent of each other or of any higher principle. At the same time, the Neo-Platonists were concerned to defend the polytheistic tradition of the Greeks. The Gods were thus identified with the various emanations of the One, resulting in a complex celestial hierarchy. Thus there are, according to Iamblichus, both intellectual gods, who are the principles of the active and passive intellects, and terrestrial gods, among whom he distinguishes three hundred celestial beings, seventy-two orders of subcelestial beings, and forty-two orders of deities responsible for various natural forces. Below all these come those human beings who have achieved sainthood, such as the heroes of old and great philosophers such as Pythagoras and Plotinus.

Human beings are, in this system, part matter and part intellect or spirit. We have within ourselves an emanation of the divine spirit, the One, to which we struggle, however clumsily, to return. This we do by first purifying ourselves of material concerns and then by cultivation of the intellect, which is able to penetrate the secrets of the World Soul and to understand the operations of the Intellect. The final stage of development, however, involves a sort of revelation or divine illumination in which the One bestows on the philosopher a direct and immediate vision of its own nature. This intuition of the One reduces the intellect to passivity and results in a state of ecstasy, which excludes consciousness of all else. This in turn confers on the philosopher prophetic power as well as knowledge of the operation of all of the forces of the universe.

This latter conclusion led to the synthesis of the dialectical tradition with theurgic practices derived from Greek and Asian religions. By becoming one with God, the philosopher attains what amounts to divine powers, which are exercised through oracles, divination, and sacrifice.

Neo-Platonism in this form provided the ideological framework for the policies of the pagan reforming emperors, Diocletian and Julian, who tried to rationalize and systematize both the extraordinary plethora of pagan cults that were operating in the Empire and to regularize and reform the pagan clergy. Both projects were characterized by attempts at authentic economic reform. This is reflected, among other things, in the shift from slavery to the colonate as the principal way of organizing labor

(Anderson 1974), in at least some limited attempts at land reform, and in a growing willingness on the part of the Empire to intervene on the side of the peasantry to prevent the worst abuses (Ste. Croix 1982).

From here on out, however, the two strategies differed radically. Diocletian's reforms, which were eventually adopted and modified by Constantine, included an attempt to bind all of the various orders of society in service to the empire. Thus the imposition, perhaps for the first time, of significant taxes on the senatorial elite; thus the imposition of taxes on merchants who were seen as profiting from the *Pax Romana* without contributing anything to its maintenance. Julian's strategy, on the other hand, centered on a global reduction in taxes, cutting back on the size of the imperial bureaucracy, and on an attempt to restore the institutions of the *polis*. Indeed, from Julian's point of view the empire was first and foremost a federation of *poleis* governed by independent city councils.

Both strategies shared, at the ideological level, a commitment to sacral monarchy. For Diocletian, however, this meant a coercive requirement that everyone in the empire sacrifice to him as a god. For Julian it involved holding himself to such high standards that the claim of divinity became credible. Julian was known, in fact, for his informal and democratic manner and for his respect for the equal dignity of all human beings.

Ultimately both pagan Neo-Platonist strategies for reform failed. Julian's strategy failed largely because the Hellenic ideal it served had already died. The ruling classes had long ago retreated into lives of private luxury and were not receptive to calls that they restrict consumption in order to save a system that, as far as they were concerned, existed to make them rich. Diocletian's strategy, on the other hand, failed largely for ideological reasons. It was, quite simply, no longer possible in a post-axial society to organize a civilization around the divinization of a single ruler. Only a religion of *universal* deification could save the empire, and only at the cost of reordering it to a very different civilizational ideal.

Resistance from the Periphery: Judaism, Christianity, and Islam

It is in this context that we must understand the contributions of prophetic religion. Israel and its religion emerged, as we have seen, out of an effort to build a just social order and more specifically out of an effort to restore communitarian and archaic structures during the crisis of the late Bronze Age. In the process of actually building that society, it achieved a new insight into the first principle. Israel realized that her God, who she first understood as just another warlord god—but on the side of the poor rather than their oppressors—was not just *El yahwi sabaoth yisrael*—God who brings into being the armies of Israel—but *yhwh*, the power of Being as such, creator of heaven and earth and the ground of humanity's own creative activity.

Israel's existence as a liberated zone in a world of great empires was temporary. She soon found herself forced to accommodate herself to the realities of subjugation by new empires with more powerful military technologies. There were, broadly speaking, three possible responses to this situation. One could develop an effective strategy for resistance and build the power necessary to actually create a just social order. Failing this, one could either hold on to the underlying commitment to social justice, living as creative minority within a larger oppressive civilization in the hope that one's way of life would eventually prove attractive to the majority and result in gradual transformation, or one could conclude that justice is actually impossible for ontological or anthropological reasons and seek something else—something that turned out to be eternal life or deification.

Early on, Judaism clearly gravitated towards an effort to liberate itself from imperial rule and use a restored monarchy to rebuild the just social order that it remembered from the "days of its youth." While the prophets sometimes counseled submission to the great powers in the short run, they nearly all looked forward to a future of liberation and restoration. The relatively benign rule of the Persians and the Ptolemies temporarily eased the revolutionary impulse, but when the Seleucids attempted to erect a statue of Zeus in the holy of holies as part of their Hellenization project, the Jews responded with a successful revolt, that of the Maccabees, which won them a brief period of independence. And while Rome's relative tolerance and sensitivity to Jewish religious sensibilities led many in Israel to counsel accommodation during the early years of the Principate, by 66 CE a broad spectrum of Jewish parties had been won over to the revolutionary project. Ultimately it was only the overwhelming force of the Roman legions, which crushed the Jewish uprising of 66–70 CE and the Bar Kochba revolt of the next century, which convinced Israel that national liberation and restoration were not on the agenda (Horsely 1985, Eisenman 1997, Tabor 2006).

The result of this process was the emergence of the Pharisees, who had been merely one of many political-theological tendencies in Second Temple Judaism, as the branch out of which most later Judaism—what we now call rabbinic Judaism—emerged. The Pharisees, while not rejecting the Temple and while certainly sharing a long-term hope in liberation and restoration, had focused the bulk of their attention on adapting the legal traditions of Israel to the new realities of petty commodity production and insertion into the Silk Road trade. For example, rather than waiting for a time when the Jubilee Law could once again be strictly observed to act justly, they focused on the central moral norm embodied in Leviticus 25—"When you buy or sell ... amongst yourselves, you shall not drive a hard bargain ... You must not victimize one another" (Lev 25:14–17a)—and asked what it meant for merchants in the new global economy. As events turned against the people of Israel during the Jewish War, a group of rabbis gathered at Jabneh (the Roman Jamnia) to begin to codify the oral traditions they had been developing. These they organized under six headings. The resulting collection is known as the Mishnah, which was completed by 220 CE at the latest. Further commentary on the Mishnah continued both in the land of Israel and in Babylon, where there was an important Jewish community. These further commentaries, which consist fundamentally in debates between rabbis regarding the proper interpretation and application of the Law, eventually became the Palestinian and Babylonian Talmuds, which were completed sometime in the sixth century, shortly before the Arab invasions. In the absence of a Temple and with the prospects for political independence shattered, the Pharisaic trend gained effective hegemony within the Jewish community.

The Talmud is, in the first instance, simply an adaptation of a legal tradition that grew up in an agrarian, communitarian social order to the realities of petty commodity production and imperial domination. This is especially apparent in the tractates dealing with economic issues. Moral principles that were enshrined in the agrarian law of Leviticus 25 rejecting absolute private property, requiring periodic redistribution of the land, prohibiting the taking of interest on loans, and in general directing Jews not to "drive a hard bargain" become the basis for a detailed analysis of the ethics of buying and selling. But there are also adaptations in the ritual law, as the focus of ritual life shifts from the Temple to the family, and the household itself becomes the locus of the only possible cult.

It is undoubtedly this focus on providing ethical and ritual direction under the difficult circumstances after the Jewish War that gave the rabbis their credibility. As Jacob Neusner (Neusner 1975) has pointed out, however, there is more to the Talmud than simply adapting Jewish law, with its historic focus on social justice, to new social circumstances. The Talmud also suggests a new model of leadership. While the Jewish communities in Palestine and Babylon, and indeed in other cities as well, often had an official leadership recognized by the political authorities, and while in some cases, as in Babylon, there was even an Exilarch claiming descent from David, real authority belonged to the rabbis. But it did not belong to the rabbis as an officially sanctioned body, the judgments of which were taken as legitimate. Rather, authority belonged to whichever rabbi was able to make the most logically convincing argument regarding the particular point of law in question. While earlier opinions might, furthermore, serve as a point of reference or departure, there was, in principle, no point that was not subject to criticism and re-evaluation. The people of Israel became, in effect, a logocracy, where neither law nor persons but rather logic alone ruled. This model of authority exercised powerful influence both under Islam and in Catholic Europe as the universities gradually assert themselves as a real center of authority.

Second, this pattern of political authority helped redefine the way in which Israel thought about her God. Originally a warrior on behalf of the poor and later a creator, the power of Being as such, Israel's God became in the context of rabbinic Judaism himself a scholar, whose principal activity was Talmudic debate.

The resulting spirituality added a new dimension to the historic Jewish focus on knowing God in the just act. Earliest Israel was a revolutionary peasant society focused on restoring the historic rights of peasant communities against the predatory claims of the warlords. The Jewish Diaspora was a complex multiclass civilizational force that, while retaining its historic commitments to economic justice, now also insisted that claims regarding justice—and therefore God—be subject to critical scrutiny and mediated through rational deliberation.

The result of this was to transform the Jewish people, deprived though they might be of land and king and Temple, into one of the leading forces—indeed perhaps *the* leading force—in the development of Western society and the reason we call it Western rather than Christian or European. They became practitioners of "a ruthless criticism of everything existing" (Marx 1843/1978), a criticism grounded in a primordial experience of divine justice. It was, above all, the deliberative practice of the rabbis that shaped that of the Islamic *ulema* and through them that of the Christian scholastics (Makdisi 1989). And everything authentically critical in the modern Western tradition (as opposed to what is merely messianic) bears this same rabbinic seal.

Talmudic Judaism was not, however, the only tendency within the Jewish communities of the Hellenistic and Roman Empires. Especially in the Diaspora, there was a powerful syncretism between Judaism and the dialectical tradition. We see the first evidence of this in the Wisdom literature. As Israel reflected on its religious traditions in the light of Hellenic philosophy, it gradually discovered in its God an intelligible principle, which orders all things.

> In wisdom there is a spirit intelligent and holy, unique in its kind yet made of many parts, subtle, free-moving, lucid, spotless, clear, neither harmed nor harming, loving what is good, eager, unhampered, beneficent, kindly towards mortals, steadfast, unerring, untouched by care, all-powerful, all-surveying, and permeating every intelligent, pure and most subtle spirit. For wisdom moves more easily than motion itself; she is so pure she pervades and permeates all things. Like a fine mist she rises from the power of God, a clear effluence from the glory of the Almighty; so nothing defined can enter into her by stealth. She is the radiance that streams from everlasting light, the flawless mirror of the active power of God, and the image of his goodness. She is but one, yet can do all things; herself unchanging, she makes all things new; age after age she enters into holy souls and makes them friends of God and prophets, for nothing is acceptable to God but the person who makes his home with wisdom. She is more beautiful than the sun, and surpasses every constellation. Compared with the light of day she is found to excel, for day gives place to night, but against wisdom no evil can prevail. She spans the world in power from end to end, and gently orders all things. (Wis 7:22—8:1)

At the same time, unlike those strains of Hellenic philosophy that developed in isolation from Judaism, and retreated further and further into otherworldly, gnostic withdrawal, the wisdom tradition regarded philosophy as a means for arriving at knowledge not only of God, but also of nature—and history.

> God ... gave me true understanding of things as they are: a knowledge of the structure of the world and the operation of the elements; the beginning and end of epochs and their middle course; the altering solstices and changing seasons; the cycles of the years and the constellations; the nature of living creatures and behavior of wild beasts; the violent force of winds and human thought; the varieties of plants and the virtues of roots. I learnt it all, hidden or manifest, for I was taught by wisdom, by her whose skill made all things. (Wis 7:17–22)

It was this wisdom that made possible Israel's historic victories over her oppressors.

> It was wisdom who rescued a god-fearing people, a blameless race, from a nation of oppressors. (Wis 10:15)

And it was wisdom that would lead to their ultimate vindication.

It was, above all, Philo of Alexandria who transformed these poetic reflections into a real philosophical synthesis. Drawing on a mixture of Jewish, Stoic, and Middle Platonic ideas, Philo argued that the ideas, or the forms of things, exist in the mind of God as a kind of intelligible world. In their latent form, Philo called these ideas *sofia* or the divine wisdom. In their active, creative form, they became the *logos*, the word through which all things came into being. Unlike the Hellenic tradition, however, Philo rejects the eternity of matter and teaches that matter itself was the product of divine creative activity. Thus, while he retains the form/matter dualism that is characteristic of philosophy in all pre-industrial societies, he takes an important step towards the recognition of the material world as a realization of, rather than a falling away from, the divine will.

According to Philo, the Law of Moses is nothing other than the law of the cosmos itself, fully accessible to reason and binding on all humanity. On this basis, Philo develops a harmonizing ethics that integrates Jewish and Greek elements, arguing that authentic freedom consists not in citizenship in Rome or some reconstituted Greek city-state, but rather in service to the one true God who alone is authentically self-existent. It is the Jews, who know and follow this law—and not the Greeks and Romans, with their devotion to wealth and earthly political power—who are the true cosmopolitans. Knowledge of the law flows out from the Jews to the other peoples of the earth who will eventually be united as in a single city, under the one law of the living God.

This metaphysics had definite political implications. Specifically, it represented the very first claim from within the dialectical tradition, that the creation of a just society was actually possible, something that Platonic and Aristotelian metaphysics, with their claim that matter inevitably resists form, rendered ultimately impossible. It also put philosophers in a leading role in creating such a society. In this sense, Philo wrote the charter for later Jewish, Christian, and Islamic philosophy, and framed the problems they would have to address in greater depth: the relationship between religion and revelation, the question of creation *ex nihilo*, the nature of the human intellect, its relationship to the intelligences emanating from God, and the extent and method by which it might rise towards the divine, and the relationship between the philosopher and philosophy on the one hand and the prophet and revealed religion on the other.

The Hellenistic Judaism of Philo of Alexandria was not the only appropriation of the dialectical tradition, and of Platonism in particular, by the Jewish community. While it was the rabbis who became the real leaders of the people of Israel in the period after the destruction of the Temple, the priestly tradition did not entirely die out. It was, rather, elaborated into an esoteric Wisdom. It is difficult to tell just how much of the Kaballah actually dates from late Antiquity, but there is good evidence that the *Sefer Yetzirah*, for example, dates back as early as the second century. At issue here is a fusion of Judaism with Neo-Platonist or proto-Neo-Platonist metaphysics of emanation and return. We will consider the Kaballah more fully later in this chapter. Here it will suffice to point out certain characteristics that are already apparent at this early date:

1. The process of emanation is understood in a distinctly Jewish way as being embodied in language and especially in the divine name—the pronunciation of which, in the Temple cult, was thus a real participation in the creative life of God.

2. The whole fabric of creation has somehow been ruptured, something that is reflected on earth in wrong action and social injustice.

3. The process of return is also understood in a distinctively Jewish fashion as rooted in ethical conduct. By means of the just act we "raise sparks" towards God. Kabalistic ritual affects "things above," in the higher worlds, creating more favorable conditions

for the redemption of Israel and the establishment of a just social order here below, but right conduct and the struggle for social justice also helps to mend the torn fabric of the universe in a process known as the *Tikkun Olam*.

This fusion of Neo-Platonic theurgy with Jewish ethical commitment would ultimately lead to the creation of a distinct form of Jewish resistance within *Dar-al-Islam* and Christendom, an issue to which we will return later.

Christianity represents a very different accommodation of prophetic religion to the realities of life under the Roman Empire. There continues to be considerable debate regarding the position of Jesus within the political-theological spectrum of first-century Palestinian Judaism. One school understands him as, essentially, a radicalized Hillel-school Pharisee. The Jesus we encounter in the synoptic Gospels was, clearly, a teacher of the oral Torah "reinterpreting the Hebrew Scriptures in a manner more in line with the social setting in which he found himself." Furthermore, the general pattern of his ministry "with its emphasis on teaching and healing" is characteristic of the rabbinic pattern for the period. "He likewise seems to have participated in Pharisaic-type fellowship meals, instituting the Christian Eucharist at the final one he attended" (Pawlikowski 1982: 92–93).

The *content* of Jesus's teaching also shows significant Pharisaic influence. This is evident in any number of places. Jesus's answers to the questions posed to him while teaching in the temple (Mark 12:13–34), and particularly the question concerning the great commandment, put him more or less squarely in the Pharisaic camp, marked as it was by a focus on love of God and neighbor (Mark 12:28–34) as the central aspect of Jewish life, a belief in the Resurrection (Mark 12:18–27), and internal division regarding such questions as the lawfulness of paying tribute to Caesar (Mark 12:13–18). The prayer that Jesus taught to his disciples—elements of which are preserved in the so-called "Lord's Prayer" (Matt 6:9–13, Luke 11:1–4)—also contains several characteristic Pharisaic elements—a sense of intimacy with God, who is addressed as "Father," a desire for the coming of the Kingdom, for the accomplishment of God's will on earth, a sense of the importance of forgiveness, etc.

Recent scholarship has, however, increasingly questioned this consensus, arguing that Jesus was the leader of one of the last revolutionary messianic uprisings (Eisenman 1997, Tabor 2006) and perhaps even the catalyst for the Jewish War. This thesis depends on a more skeptical reading of the Synoptics, regarding them as not merely attempting to differentiate emerging Christianity from the Pharisaic Judaism of which it was originally a branch, but as actually falsifying events to hide the dangerous memory of one who understood himself, and who was initially accepted by many Jews, as the authentic Davidic messiah. We cannot engage here all of the evidence brought to bear by scholars like Eisenman and Tabor. Suffice it to say that even in the Synoptics we find significant support for this image of Jesus: the high note of eschatological expectation that characterizes what even the most critical scholars acknowledge as authentic sayings (e.g., Mark 4), the march on and messianic entry into Jerusalem, and the fact that he was executed by the Romans as a Jewish royal pretender.

Ultimately, however, this debate is theological and has little bearing on our argument. This is because the Christianity that eventually gained hegemony over the Roman Empire grew up outside of Israel, in the cosmopolitan cities of the eastern Mediterranean, in places like Antioch and Alexandria, Ephesus, Corinth, and Philippi, and eventually in the center of the empire, in Rome itself, and was characterized by a theology that was neither Pharisaic nor Messianic, nor indeed Jewish in any sense.

There has been a good deal of ink spilled in debate around the social composition of these Christian communities. Some, such as Kautsky and Weber, claimed that Christianity found its constituency among the exploited and lower-middle strata. Others, such as Dimitris Kyrtatas (1987), have suggested that Christianity, at least outside of Israel, was primarily a movement of the wealthy. Recent scholarship (Theissen 1982) has begun to bring some closure to this debate by pointing out the internal diversity of the Christian communities, and focusing attention instead on the political valence of Christianity within the complex social world of the Hellenistic city.

A few general comments are in order. First of all, a social location within the Hellenistic cities of the eastern Mediterranean *excludes* the possibility that Christianity was a religion of the Roman ruling class—i.e., the imperial family, or the Senatorial aristocracy, who owned the vast slave-driven estates of the Western Mediterranean. It *also* excludes the possibility that Christianity was a religion of the principal exploited classes—i.e., the agricultural slaves of the Western part of the empire, or the rural wage laborers or dependent peasants of the East. The entire population of the Hellenistic city, diverse as it was, occupied a range of intermediate and ambiguous class positions. It is possible to identify within these cities:

1. the aristocracy including

    1.1. a very small number of Equestrians occupying senior military and civilian positions in the colonial administration, and

    1.2. the decurionate or city council, which had the unenviable responsibility of collecting the taxes owed to Rome, or making up the difference out of their own resources;

2. a middle stratum of merchants, artisans etc. some of whom were very wealthy and others of whom were poor indeed;

3. an urban plebianate of wage laborers and the marginally employed; and

4. slaves, some of whom would have been rather well off and secure, others of whom would have been severely exploited.

Theissen (1982: 69–119) has demonstrated the presence of most of these elements in the Pauline community in Corinth, and we have no reason to believe that the situation would have been any different elsewhere. We should also note that the Pauline communities appear to have been ethnically diverse—containing both Jew and gentile, and probably gentiles of very diverse origin.

The story of Jesus was, however, read by Hellenistic Christians in many different ways. The larger framework for this reinterpretation was given by the principal form of popular religion in the Mediterranean Basin—i.e., the mystery cult, which we discussed in the last chapter. These cults promised eternal life to anyone who went through a process of catechesis and initiation, leading up to revelation of the central mystery and a communion meal. The story of Jesus, as it was handed down by his followers, fit well in this framework. He looked like yet another dying and rising god, and there was no reason why a format that had adopted Egyptian and Persian stories as well as Greek could not accommodate one from Israel, whose religion had acquired a certain mystique because of its rationality and focus on ethical conduct.

Within this context, however, the story of Jesus could be read in very different ways. There were, broadly speaking, three possibilities. The first possibility is *liturgical*. Here, the death and resurrection of Jesus are read as a final and supreme sacrifice that completes and supersedes the temple cult and various practices that already existed within Judaism—the Pesach meal—or that derived from the Hellenistic mystery cults—baptism—become part of a series of mysteries participation in which takes on a salvific character. Initially this salvation is understood in traditional Hellenistic terms as immortality. But gradually, as Jesus himself is recast as an incarnate God, the mysteries are reinterpreted as leading to *theosis* or deification, a view that reaches its fullest development within the Orthodox tradition. We cannot trace out fully here the lineage of this theology. Suffice it to say that we find elements of it already present in the "background" Christian mysteries that Paul engaged: the idea of baptism into Christ and resurrection with him, for example (Romans 5). We also find elements of it in the Johannine tradition, with its emphasis on the mutual indwelling of the Father in Christ and of Christ in the members of the Christian community. From here, the lineage winds through the Christian fathers to Athanasius, who makes explicit the claim that "God became Man that Man might become God" (Athanasius 325 CE/1989: 93).

This is the most conservative interpretation of the Christian mysteries, in the sense that it conserves the most of the Hellenistic-Roman tradition, and it is the one that ultimately defined Byzantine Christendom. Because the problem it addresses is *ontological* (finitude and contingency) rather than ethical, and because its solution to this problem is liturgical, it requires no transformation of the social structure. We will see that it made it possible to legitimate the imperial reform program, which Diocletian initiated but could not sustain on the basis of the imperial cult alone.

Second, the Christian mysteries could be understood as expiatory and atoning. This is the interpretation Paul himself put on the Christianity he encountered on his missions. Let us listen to Paul's account of the very core of the Christian proclamation.

> But now the righteousness of God has been manifested apart from the law, although the law and the prophets bear witness to it, the righteousness of God through faith in Jesus Christ for all who believe. For there is no distinction; since all have sinned and fall short of the glory of God, they are justified by his grace as a gift

through the redemption which is in Christ Jesus, whom God put forward as an expiation by his blood, to be received by faith. (Rom 3:21–25)

Two points are in order here. First, the *problem* that Pauline Christianity addresses is not ontological (finitude and contingency) but rather ethical (sin). Second, the solution that Paul proposes is not fulfillment of the Law, either in the Pharisaic sense of ethical conduct within the context of and as a leaven within an unjust society, or in the Messianic sense of a revolutionary-apocalyptic break with injustice, but rather what Protestantism eventually named substitutionry atonement. God's justice requires that sin be punished. The crucifixion of the innocent victim (Jesus) accomplishes this, leaving humanity free from guilt and extending to them, as a free gift, eternal life.

This reading of the Christian mysteries also has definite political consequences. First of all, Paul liquidates completely, in a way Jesus never did, the Jewish aspiration for national liberation. For Paul "there is no distinction" between oppressed Jew and Roman oppressor. Salvation is defined not in national terms but in terms of faith in the crucified and risen Christ. The fact that Paul looks forward to the eventual salvation of the Jews (Rom 9–11) does not change this. Their salvation is no longer a *Jewish* salvation—no longer a restoration of the people of Israel to the land of Israel to live under Jewish law, but rather just another specific application of the generalized Christian salvation and thus a negation of Jewish national identity.

Second, because justice is done by the merits of another—i.e., Jesus—this reading as well requires no fundamental social transformation.[4] Paul is quite clear that,

4. This reading of Paul has, to be sure, been called into question by advocates of the "new perspective" and the "fresh perspective," of whom we will take James D. G. Dunn (Dunn 2005) and N. T. Wright (Wright 2004) respectively as typical. This new perspective in turn builds on E. P. Sanders's (Sanders 1977) earlier work on Palestinian Judaism. While there are significant internal differences in this trend, its claims may be summed up broadly as follows.

First, Palestinian Judaism was not a legalistic religion that sought salvation by means of "works of the law," but rather a "covenantal nomism" in which salvation was grounded in God's free election of the people of Israel and works of the law were a mark of fidelity to the covenant (Sanders 1977).

Second, because of this, Paul's adversaries could not have been Palestinian Jews but were, rather, other Jewish Christians, the "men from James," who contended that membership in the Church required circumcision and/or other Jewish cultural practices.

These, and not ethical conduct broadly understood, are the "works of the law," which are in question, and "justification by faith" is not to be pitted against a demand for ethical conduct, but is rather a claim on behalf of Gentile Christians who believe in Israel's God (Dunn 2005).

Third, this argument must be set in the context of a broader polemic against what advocates of the "fresh perspective" argue was the principal and most important religion of the Roman Empire: the cult of Caesar. In this context, Paul's gospel must be understood to be first and foremost a proclamation *against* Caesar and *against* Rome, that it is Jesus, the crucified and now risen and vindicated Jewish Messiah, who is really and truly Lord. In this sense Paul's mission is fully in continuity with that of Jesus understood as a Jewish revolutionary and deeply anti-imperial, even if it is acknowledged that he urged prudential obedience to the Roman authorities and seemed not to have intended a political revolt (Wright 2004).

The new perspective and fresh perspective are based on complex and diverse arguments not all of which can be addressed here. And we have no intention of denying that the trend has produced some fruitful insights. From the standpoint of our argument, however, neither the new nor the fresh perspective succeeds in answering either our earlier critique of Paul's antisemitism (Mansueto 2002a) nor our argument here that his position did not point towards authentic social justice.

First, the idea of a legalistic religion in which salvation is earned by works of the law has always been a straw man. I know of no tradition that has ever argued for such a thing.

Second, whoever Paul's adversaries may have been (and I am not at all certain it is "new" to say that they were Jewish Christians associated with the figure of James, rather than non-Christian Jews of any of the other Jewish parties), in the course of his polemic with them, Paul develops a soteriology which, I would argue, is not merely different from but actively hostile to classical humanistic ("pagan") and Jewish and Catholic spiritualities of meaning and self-cultivation in which human beings, drawn by the incredible beauty of God as reflected in the universe and/or by the struggle for the conditions for their own development, gradually becomes capable of knowing and loving God, first as a means of self-development and eventually—because the struggle for beauty and truth and justice turns out to be about much more than that self-development—in essence, for Her own sake. In this sense Paul is anti-pagan and anti-humanistic (which advocates of the fresh perspective especially will acknowledge enthusiastically), anti-Jewish (in the sense that he argues that, as N. T. Wright puts it, Jews miss out on the eschatological fulfillment of their own tradition and in the sense that the argues that what became the core of later rabbinic Judaism, fulfillment of the law, is in fact impossible) and anti-Catholic, in the sense that, as Luther quite correctly saw, Paul provides little support for the Catholic vision of salvation as the cultivation of infused capacities that allow us to grow, in significant measure at least through our own efforts, towards being *capax dei*, capable of and connatural with God, something that is the historic position of the Thomistic if not the Augustinian tradition within Catholicism.

Third, I very much doubt that the cult of Caesar, however widely diffused it may have been, was in any meaningful sense the most important religion in the Roman Empire, a claim that, in any case, requires further specification of what is meant by religion. Do Paul's letters reflect at least an implicit rejection of the claims of that cult? Sure. No one would ever have claimed that even a Gentile Christian of the first century, much less a Jewish Christian, supported the imperial cult. But that does not make Paul anti-imperial

> there is no authority except from God. Therefore he who resists the authorities resists what God has appointed, and those who resist incur judgment. (Rom 13:1-2)

Paul does not command the wealthy members of his Corinthian congregation to share their wealth with the poor, as was the custom in the Jerusalem community, but only to refrain from turning the Eucharist into an occasion for conspicuous consumption (1 Cor 11:17-22; Theissen 1982: 145-74). He does not command Philemon to manumit the Christian slave Onesimus, but only to treat him as a brother in Christ. How one does this to a person one is keeping as a slave may be a bit obscure, but Paul's interest is clearly more in the subjective motive than in the objective relationship. "I preferred to do nothing without your consent so that your goodness might not be by compulsion but of your own free will" (Kyrtatas 1987: 63-71; Philemon 1:14).

Gerd Theissen has characterized Paul's social ethics quite appropriately as a kind of "love patriarchalism."

> Paul knows only a few of the sayings of the Lord. And even if he had known more, the ethical radicalism of the Jesus tradition ... would have found little room to survive in the congregations founded by him.
>
> In these congregations there developed an ethos obviously different from that of the synoptic tradition, the ethos of primitive Christian love-patriarchalism ... This love-patriarchalism takes social differences for granted, but ameliorates them through an

---

in any meaningful sense. Augustine was a far more explicit critic than Paul of both paganism and the imperial cult and he clearly mourned the waning of imperial power in the West. It is quite possible to oppose the imperial cult without being be anti-imperial and to be anti-imperial without arguing for a profound, liberating structural transformation of Roman society. As we will see, the empire eventually *does* recognize Jesus as Lord—and Caesar as his vice-regent. And the change does catalyze *some* structural transformation, but only from chattel slavery to feudalism—precisely the sort of system we would expect to find legitimated by what Theissen aptly calls Paul's love-patriarchalism. And it does so by making the change, which was initiated by the imperial authorities themselves, easier for the ruling classes to accept, not by organizing the exploited. Indeed, Paul does not even address the most oppressed classes under the Roman system: the agricultural slaves of the West and the exploited peasants of the East.

Ultimately, a theology such as Paul's, which understands God as an infinitely powerful divine sovereign who demands from his creatures radical obedience, can only reproduce a social structure based on domination and submission, even if it also counsels rulers to be gentle and loving towards their charges who—like humanity generally in relation to God—are never anything more than treasured pets or loyal servants.

obligation of respect and love, an obligation imposed upon those who are socially stronger. From the weaker are required subordination, fidelity and esteem. (Theissen 1982: 107)

Especially as interpreted by Augustine, the Pauline reading of the Christian mysteries would have a profound impact on Western Christendom, though it would be embraced for very different reasons by the Germanic warlords who eventually displaced the Romans there and Romans and Romanized elites hoping to salvage something of their past.

A third reading of the Christian mysteries is both ontological and ethical. It understands the mysteries as divinizing, but not by means of a purely liturgical process. Rather, the mysteries provide a framework for intellectual and moral self-cultivation, mediating to the intellect truths that transcend—but never contradict—human reason and moral demands that transcend natural justice. The cross, understood in this context, is the sign of a justice pursued to the very end, beyond what natural law requires, and the resurrection a sign of God's vindication of that justice. When we take up the cross we live out God's justice and thus share in God's nature, undergoing a real, if accidental rather than essential, divinization.

This reading of the mysteries resonated especially powerfully among the Celts, who had their own very powerful tradition of intellectual and moral self-cultivation. It was they who saved what little remained of Jewish Christianity and then carried it into the complex synthesis of trends that defined Catholic Christendom. But more on that later.

We will see shortly just how Judaism and these different Christianities interacted with each other and with the post-Hellenistic Roman world. But before we can do this we must look at what was, at least initially, the most powerful expression of prophetic religion in the post-Hellenistic-Roman Mediterranean World: Islam.

Henri Pirenne (Pirenne 1937/1939) has written that we cannot really speak of the end of the Roman Empire until the emergence of Islam. It was Islam that took from emerging Christendom the entire Southern and most of the Eastern Mediterranean, a region that included many, if not most, of its richest lands, keeping the Byzantine Empire tied up in a defensive struggle on its southern flank and preventing the incorporation of the new Germanic kingdoms in the West into the imperial structure. But it was also the emergence of Islam that catalyzed the extraordinary civilizational progress that made the European Middle Ages possible.

The Great Age of Metaphysics

Islam prides itself on the idea that, unlike the other great monotheisms, it emerged in the "clear light of history." A middling Meccan merchant of the Quraysh tribe began to have visions. He consulted his wife, for fear he was losing his mind, but she reassured him that the visions were authentic. These visions, which he was commanded to write down, were eventually compiled as the Qu'ran. He then began public preaching, calling on the people of Mecca to reject their polytheistic religion and to return to what he claimed was their original monotheism. The Meccans rejected him, so he fled north to Yathrib, and established himself there as a prophet and *de facto* ruler. Within his lifetime the Arab tribes he converted united much of the Arabian peninsula; within a generation Islam had liberated most of the Eastern Mediterranean and Western Asia; and within another century it had built one of the largest empires known to humanity.

Unfortunately, like the stories that Jews and Christians tell about their origins, this story is simply untenable. The archeological record contains powerful evidence that the Arab expansion preceded the formation of anything like an established Islam: Arab coins issued in conquered lands, for example, show no evidence of the Islamic inscriptions that later became normative until the eighth century (Cook and Crone 1977). Nor does the text of the Qu'ran become anything like definitive before the ninth century (Wansbrogh 1977, 1978), which it surely would have if the document had already been completed in the Prophet's lifetime and—composition or revelation—functioned as the "little green book" of the Islamic revolution. Unfortunately, the historical-critical study of the Qu'ran and the historical sociological study of the origins of Islam are terribly underdeveloped by comparison with the historical-critical study of the Jewish and Christian Scriptures and the historical-sociological study of Jewish and Christian origins, and the best that we can offer is a rather schematic and probabilistic account.

We begin with an overview of the conditions in pre-Islamic Arabia. Much of the Arabian peninsula, the so-called *Rub al Khali* or Empty Quarter, is impassible desert, with sands so deep even camels cannot cross it. There is a line of oases across the northern part of the peninsula, and another down the western coast—the *Hijaz*—on a high plateau with harder soil that permits travel. The far south of the peninsula, which the Romans called *Arabia Felix* and the Arabs themselves Yemen, is a bit wetter and more fertile and the home of frankincense and coffee trees. The eastern coast offers access to the Indian Ocean and to ports in southern Mesopotamia and India.

In such an ecosystem, the only adaptation that permitted anything above village-level organization was trade, and it was above all the incense trade that allowed the Arabs to become more than tribal sheep herders moving from oasis to oasis and subsisting on mutton and dates. By Roman times the Nabatean Arabs had established an important city at Petra, which was, in effect, the first truck stop heading east out of the Roman Empire. The Romans, however, grew tired of paying the tributes and tolls the Nabateans imposed and re-routed trade through Alexandria and the Red Sea, effectively cutting the Arabs out of the Silk Road trade.

Social organization remained essentially tribal, with cities controlled by the senior lineages of the senior clans of the most powerful tribes—such as the Quraysh from which the Prophet was born. The heads of these lineages formed an urban patriciate that governed through what the Romans imagined to be city councils like those throughout the rest of the empire, but which were, in reality, more nearly just inter-tribal negotiating sessions.

The peninsula was religiously quite diverse. There is some evidence for an indigenous monotheism, but most Arabs seem to have practiced a South Semitic polytheism in which Allah, the high god, was worshiped along with his daughters—al Uzzah, al Lat, and al Manat, the sun, the moon, and the planet Venus. There were significant Jewish and Christian communities, and substantial evidence, especially in Yemen and the East, of influence from Babylonian and perhaps Persian religion.

The decline of Roman power presented the Arabs with both an opportunity and a problem. On the one hand, they had a chance to break out of the peninsula and gain sufficient territory to secure a more favorable position in the global trade networks. On the other hand, they could not do this without finding a way to overcome tribal divisions and unite. It is in this context that the emergence of Islam must be understood.

Cook and Crone (Cook and Crone 1977) put a very specific interpretation on just how emerging Islam met the needs of the Arab tribes. Working largely off of Greek sources, they argue that the initial preaching of Mohammed, whose historicity they do not question, was essentially a Jewish-influenced messianism aimed at uniting all of the Semitic peoples to throw off Roman (Byzantine) hegemony and to liberate Jerusalem. Because of the centrality of the idea of a common Abrahamic heritage, they call this early movement Hagarism, after Sarah's handmaid who was the mother of Ishmael, legendary father of the Arabs. Some historical sources suggest that Mohammed lived much longer than Islamic tradition acknowledges and actually participated in the liberation of Jerusalem. That done, however, the Arabs soon fell out with the Jews and began trying to carve out for themselves an independent religious identity, drawing on elements of Jacobite and Nestorian Christianity, Samaritanism, and Persian and Greek philosophical traditions as well as the Rabbinic Judaism that formed their point of departure. "Islam" emerged only gradually as various groups vied for leadership. These included varying types of religious scholars on the one hand (*'ulemma* or jurists, *mutakallim* or theologians, and practitioners of *falasafa* or philosophy) and generals on the other, as well as groups claiming descent from or designation by the Prophet or his kin and/or companions according to varying tribal traditions.

Whether or not we accept the details of this account, the broad outlines make sense. For one thing, had the movement not had a strong apocalyptic tone, it is difficult to imagine that the problem of succession, which drove later Islamic politics, would not have been better resolved, given the otherwise highly effective and pragmatic character of Islamic political strategy. More broadly, as one moves through the plethora of socioreligious movements and political-theological tendencies we meet during the first centuries of Islam, all of the various influences identified by Cook and Crone can indeed be identified, as Crone points out in her later book on Islamic politics, *God's Rule* (Crone 2004).

This said, it seems to me that Cook and Crone miss, or perhaps merely understate, the distinctive feature of Islam by comparison to the other Semitic monotheisms. Where Judaism grew up in an environment of political disenfranchisement and thus had to find a way to realize the law without political power, and where most variants of Christianity gave up early on the idea of actually building the Kingdom of God on earth, and redefined messianism in an otherworldly direction, thus laying the groundwork for an alliance with the Roman Empire and its successor states, Islam actually joined, from the very beginning, a religious orientation centered on realizing the law with the political power necessary to actually do so, or at least to attempt to do so. In this sense, the defining feature of Islam is no so much its radical monotheism (this is actually compromised significantly in certain forms of popular Shi'ism) but rather *al-amr bi'l-ma'ruf wa 'nahy 'an al-munkar*: commanding right and forbidding wrong.

This said, Islam develops this orientation in the context of an emerging Silk Road empire which, like all other such empires, aims first and foremost at profiting from insertion into the Silk Road trade, and is able to secure the support of Arab and later Persian, Berber, and Turkic elites because it provided the ideological basis for the wars of liberation and conquest that were necessary in order to build the empire. And just what constitutes right and wrong, as well as how one discerns them and who has the authority to command and forbid them, remain open to diverse, competing, and ultimately incompatible interpretations throughout the early centuries of Islamic civilization. We will consider the way in which these struggles played themselves out shortly.

BYZANTIUM

We are now in a position to analyze the civilizations that emerged out of the crisis of Hellenistic Roman Civilization—and to measure the impact of the dialectical tradition on them. We will look first at then at Byzantium, then at *Dar-al-Islam*, and finally at Western Christendom.

Byzantine Civilization represents, far and away, the most conservative accommodation to the crisis of the Hellenic ideal. If *Dar-al-Islam* and Western Christendom developed new structures in order to realize new ideals, then Byzantium embraced new ideals in order to save as much as possible of the old imperial structure.

This said, there were real differences between Byzantium and the Later Roman Empire at the level of social structure as well as of civilizational ideal. It is, perhaps, easiest to sum up these differences by saying that Orthodox Christianity provided a means for not only legitimating but also retheorizing and radicalizing the transformation of the Empire originally envisioned by Diocletian.

Like pagan Neo-Platonism, Orthodox Christianity was focused on liberating humanity from finitude and contingency and had, at best, a weak sense of sin. Where it differed was in offering an actual strategy for deification or *theosis*. This might seem, at first, simply to be a change at the level of anthropology and soteriology rather than at the ontological core of the system. The anthropological and soteriological changes required by the doctrine of *theosis*, however, required ontological changes as well.

These changes are, above all, concentrated on the doctrines of the Trinity and the incarnation. Christianity needed a language in which it could speak of God as one in essence, but of three persons and of Jesus as at once truly God and truly human. The Platonic language of *ousia* (essence or nature) and *hypostasis* (person) provided a way to do this. Christian Neo-Platonism was, first and foremost, a theorization of the Holy Trinity and of the person of Jesus in terms of the successions of hypostases that emanate from the Neo-Platonist One.

By thinking God as Trinity rather than as the One, while maintaining the underlying unity of the divine essence, Christianity began to think this essence in a new way: as something in which persons could participate in varying degrees. The divine persons of the Holy Trinity participate in it by nature: they *are* it; others share in it as a superadded quality, as a food becomes hot when cooked, without itself becoming heat. By thinking of Jesus as one unified person who is both human and divine, Christianity opened the road for human beings to take on the divine nature. Working out the details of all this was beyond the Neo-Platonists, and would have to wait the subtlety of the medieval Aristotelians, and of Thomas in particular, who applied to the problem the categories of substance and accident, potency and act. But the beginning of the process was here. And it was enough to provide an ontological foundation for the perfect mystery cult—one that conferred not just immortality (which is how the early Greeks had understood divinity) but divinity proper, as it was understood by the peculiar synthesis of dialectics and prophetic religion that was gradually replacing the Hellenic ideal. Only such a mystery cult could provide the ideal for an entire civilization.

This metaphysics of participation was systematized and passed on to the West in the work of Dionysus the Areopagite. In Dionysus the Christian Trinity and the various orders of angels replace the Greek and Asian gods and the hierarchy of the Church replaces that of the Empire, but the underlying logic of his system is little changed from that of his pagan teachers, except that here, in the Christian context, full divinization has become possible. The universe as a whole is sacred, an overflowing of God's creative power; we return to God by means of participation in the mysteries, ascetic purification, meditation on the divine nature, and infused contemplation of a Divine Nature that radically transcends any possible discursive knowledge. As in the case of the pagan Neo-Platonists, the function of human society is to facilitate humanity's return to God.

It is just that the society in question is that of the Church. Gradually Orthodox Christianity developed a complex theology that rationalized this process, theorizing the liturgy as a kind of "heaven on earth," participation in which, especially because of its beauty, elevates human beings above the earthly realm, lifting them towards heaven (Ware 1993).

This theology had, in turn, definite political implications. It led to a theorization of the whole society as a kind of liturgical system, in both the older sense of a system of public works undertaken for the common good and in the sense of the organized system of the mysteries themselves. Liturgy, in other words, which had always been a part of the civic life of the Hellenic and Hellenistic-Roman civilizations, effectively displaced public deliberation as the principal form of civic engagement. The empire existed in order to support the mysteries; the people existed in order to support the empire.

This political theology supported the transformation of the organization of labor in the Empire. While antiquity had been characterized by a sharp distinction between slave and free, the Byzantine ideal made everyone into a servant of the sacral state. Slaves were transformed into *coloni*, settled on the land and bound to it but no longer subject to sale, but the same fate beset free peasants as well, who found themselves subject to increasing burdens. Indeed, artisans and merchants were increasingly bound to their hereditary trades and required to meet the needs of the state, and the traditional senatorial order, which had been distinguished by its autonomy from the Empire, was merged with the equestrian order to form a unified service nobility (Jones 1974: 302, Anderson 1974: 100).

It is in this context that we must understand the patristic denunciations of private property and of the rich, of which some liberation theologians have made so much (Miranda 1981). The Church Fathers were not, strictly speaking, advocates for the peasants or artisans, but rather for the public, liturgical economy as against the private economy of luxury consumption, which certainly persisted even among the somewhat chastened aristocracy.

At the pinnacle of this system was a sacral monarchic ideology that legitimated what was left of the Roman Empire for nearly another millennium.

> As the knowledge of one God and the one way of religion and salvation, even the Doctrine of Christianity, was made known to all man-

kind, so at the self-same period, the entire dominion of the Roman empire was being vested in a single sovereign. Profound peace reigned throughout the world. And thus by the express appointment of the same God, two roots of blessing, the Roman Empire and the doctrine of Christian piety, sprang up together for the benefit of men ... (Eusebius *Or. Con* 16: 4–7 in Ruether 1974: 142)

The emperor himself comes to be regarded in much the manner of a God-King,

> The emperor, like the rays of the sun whose light illuminates those who live in the most distant regions, enlightens the entire empire with the radiance of the Caesars as with the far reaching beams reflected from his own brilliance ... Thus he is present everywhere, traversing the entire earth, being in all places and surveying all events.
>
> Having been entrusted with an empire, the image of the heavenly kingdom, he looks to the ideal form, and directs his earthly rule to the divine model and thus provides an example of divine monarchic sovereignty. (Eusebius in Cunningham 1982: 51)

This strategy was, we should note, less demanding in what it required of the ruling classes than that of Julian, whose claims to divinity were based on his actual virtue, and required that the emperor be at the very least a Platonic philosopher king. Here, it is the emperor's office, magnified by the sheer extent of his realm—the reach of his laws and his intelligence service, in effect—which guarantees his sacral character. It also, furthermore, guaranteed the primacy of the royal (or rather imperial) office over the priestly office. The emperor is himself a kind of sacrament, a living image of what others might achieve; the priest is merely the maker of that sacrament. There is little or no integration of the Jewish understanding of the first principle as Being itself—and the prophetic office appears not at all.

This pattern persisted for some time in the Eastern Mediterranean. But Byzantium represented, in the end, a kind of rear-guard action. The reasons for this are not hard to find. Orthodox Christianity rationalized the way in which surplus was extracted and the way in which it was used, but did not address the underlying structural problem of the Western economy: its backward position in the larger system of the Silk Road. The colonate replaced slave labor and more of the surplus really was used for public purposes than had been the case in the Hellenistic and Roman empires, but there was, in effect, no investment in developing new technologies and new products that might improve the balance of trade deficit with India and China. The result was an underlying economic weakness and a tendency for the revenue needs of the sacral state to be met by increased rates of exploitation. In the end, most of the people of Byzantium found the Islamic ideal more attractive.

The Byzantine pattern is important, however, because it provided a model for the development of urban civilization in a region that had not previously seen organization above the village level: the vast domain of the Slavs to the North and East. Because this region eventually gave birth to the Russian Empire and the Soviet Union, which represents one of the principal attempts to realize in practice the ideals of the dialectical tradition, its history is important to our argument.

The persistence of the village community throughout the Slavic domain created a constituency for rationalizing the liturgical economy in a way that was not possible in Byzantium. Land was owned in common by the village and redistributed periodically among its member families. It was the village that was responsible for paying rents and taxes—in effect for carrying out public liturgies. But the village was not only an economic institution. It created the basis in experience for understanding the universe as an organized totality. Indeed, the Slavic word for village, *mir*, also means universe and peace.

As in Byzantium, but much more quickly, the emerging states of the Slavic north reduced the smaller warlords to a state of dependency, a process that gave rise to the Grand Duchy of Moscow, and eventually to the Great Russian Empire. Every member of this noble class (like the *decuriones* of old Rome) was required to perform service, initially military, and later bureaucratic, at the course of the *Tsar*. Later on, in the seventeenth and eighteenth centuries, provision was made for non-nobles who served dutifully in the lower ranks of the military and bureaucracy to themselves obtain noble status. The result was the formation of an intelligentsia with real confidence in its potential as a ruling class.

This intelligentsia, in turn, found in the organized peasant communities of Russia and the other Slavic states a ready constituency for their revolutionary aims. The Russian Revolution and the formation of the Soviet Union can be seen, in the end, as an attempt to (further) rationalize the liturgical economy by making it actually serve the common good. This led to a very different reading of the dialectical tradition generally and of Marxism in particular than we find in the West—or in India, China, or the rest of the Third World, for that matter. The focus on deification would remain, even if this was not admitted. It was simply the means that would change.

DAR-AL-ISLAM

Civilizational Patterns

It was in large measure in response to the conservatism of the Byzantine response to the crisis of Hellenistic-Roman civilization that Islam, with its focus on actually *realizing* the historic ideals of Judaism, had emerged in the first place. But defining a civilizational ideal and realizing are two different matters. It is not possible in this context to discuss all of the various tendencies that emerged in this struggle. Patricia Crone's *God's Rule* (Crone 2004) already does an excellent job of this. Instead, I will outline the principal social forces that shaped *Dar-al-Islam* by way of setting the stage for understanding Islam's unique contribution to the history of metaphysics. There was, first of all, the empire-building dynamic noted above. It was this dynamic that led to the selection of Abu Bakr, who was known more for his political military skill than his learning or piety, as the first *kalifah* or successor to the Prophet and that, in general, favored election of the *kalifah* rather than his designation of descent from a narrow line of relatives. It was also this dynamic that provided the social basis for the eventual formation of the *ahl al sunna wa'l-jama'a*, the Sunni "party of tradition and community," which rejected the persistent messianic tendencies in early Islam and compromised commitment to ideological purity and social justice in the name of the unity and peace necessary for civilizational progress. At times this dynamic could breed ruthlessness and oppression, and did so early on. Almost no one, even later Sunnis, regarded the Umayyads, who can nonetheless be credited as the real founders of *Dar-al-Islam*, as model Islamic rulers. And by the time of al-Ghazali (d. 1111), it was widely accepted that those who wielded political power (*dhu shawka*) were little more than rough soldiers with a fondness for luxury and a tendency towards cruelty. Often this oppression was rationalized as divine punishment. Thus the *hadith* that attributes to the Prophet the saying that when God is angry with a people, he sends the Turks to rule over them, and al-Ghazali's claim that however badly behaved the Turks may be, they are doing the will of God (al-Ghazali *Fada'ih* 113 in Crone 2004: 237).

This dynamic of pragmatic empire building was, however, balanced by a recognition that unity and thus peace could be achieved only on the basis of a common religious identity and a higher degree of social justice than was common in the surrounding empires. It was this that served as the basis for divisions: how and by whom religious unity and social justice were to be defined. One very important force in this regard was the still essentially tribal tradition of the Arabs themselves, which pulled in two conflicting directions. On the one hand, the prestige of the Quraysh was already very strong, and the idea that authority descended within a closely defined lineage widespread. On the other hand, the tribes also had a tradition of selecting leaders by *shura* or election, though just who constituted the electorate varied and provided a basis for ongoing dispute.

Cutting across this division deriving from tribal practices was the conviction, characteristic of the early stages in the institutionalization of most charismatic religious movements, that the leader must be the most qualified person religiously. In emerging Islam, this requirement was often stated in maximalist terms: if the *kalifah* finds that he is no longer the most qualified he must step down. Early on the idea of religious pre-eminence as a qualification for the caliphate became associated with support for maintaining the succession within the Prophet's family, variously defined, but usually understood as involving descent from Ali, his son-in-law, giving rise to the "Shi'ite" *shi'a al-Ali* or "party of Ali." There were, however, groups that upheld the requirement of religious pre-eminence, while allowing that it might appear or be verified by some means other than descent and designation.

The requirement of religious pre-eminence, in turn, raised the question of just what constituted the basis for religious unity. Here there were a number of competing and inter-penetrating tendencies. There was, first of all, a veneration of the text of the *Qu'ran* and the *Hadith* (sayings) and *Sunna* (practices) of the Prophet, and there developed very early on a tradition of scholarship devoted to preserving, validating, and interpreting these texts. As Cook and Crone suggest, emerging Islam probably drew on the model of the Jewish rabbinate as it developed this model of religious scholarship, which like the rabbinate was centered on textual and especially legal interpretation. But while there was significant room, at least according to some of the legal schools, for *ijtihad* (independent judgment) regarding the interpretation and application of the law, the Islamic *'ulemma* never developed the idea, which, we have seen, became central to rabbinic Judaism, that debate itself is a participation in the life of God.

Second, we see very early on the emergence of *kalam* or theology, which attempts to support revealed doctrine with rational arguments and ends up, as theology always does, entering as well into its interpretation. The relationship between this sort of theology and the tradition of Greek philosophy is not entirely clear. Perhaps *kalam* represents an appropriation of the tradition of Christian apologetics, which used rational arguments derived ultimately from the Greek tradition but which could, at the same time, often be quite hostile to philosophy as such. The first school of *kalam*, the Mutazilites, stressed the unity of God, the basic goodness and freedom of humanity, and the power of human reason to discern what is right. Very quickly, however, an opposing school appeared, the Asharites, which stressed the sovereignty of God to the point of arguing that God creates each instant of the universe separately, so that there are no real causal relations between things that might for the basis for a physics, metaphysics, or natural law ethics. Moral judgment is radically dependent on divine command.

Third, we see early on the development of *falasafa*, which consisted mostly of a fusion of Neo-Platonic and Aristotelian philosophy and which was patronized by rulers primarily because its practitioners were also skilled physicians, astrologers, and alchemists, and could thus contribute to the welfare of the court and community in practical ways. The philosophers, for their part, following Platonic and Aristotelian tradition, regarded themselves as most qualified to rule, and in many cases even identified the *kalifah* with the Platonic philosopher king. We will, of course, have more to say about *falasafa* later on.

Fourth, there was a very strong tradition of esotericism, which seems to have had multiple sources: the Gnosticism that was pandemic in the Eastern Mediterranean, emerging Kabbalism, and possibly some Persian traditions. This esoteric tradition was picked up especially by the partisans of Ali, who declared that their *imam* had, in addition to the highest possible mastery of the exoteric tradition, i.e., the *Qu'ran*, *Hadith*, and *Sunna*, a knowledge of the esoteric meaning of the tradition. This esoteric meaning was identified, in varying degrees, with *falasafa* by the party of Ali in general and especially by the Ismailis, who eventually established a dynasty in Egypt, the Fatimid Caliphate (909–1171). But it also provided a framework for the emergence of Sufi mysticism, which initially eschewed politics, but eventually gave birth to powerful orders that founded dynasties throughout *Dar-al-Islam*. Philosophical and Sufi esotericism, meanwhile, later flowed together to give birth to the highly imaginative *ishraqi* tradition, which blended philosophical speculation with Gnostic illumination.

The tension between the dynamic of empire building and the dynamic of religious and philosophical reformism made the early history of *Dar-al-Islam* unstable to say the least. Many of the partisans of Ali were too extremist and purist to effectively exercise political power. The vast majority of Shia—the Twelver or Imami communities—believe that there was an unbroken line of twelve Imams, the last of whom became hidden rather than dying, and who will eventually return to usher in a reign of justice. While they remain far more insistent than most Sunnis that the only legitimate ruler is one who is just and who has a profound grasp of the law or *sharia*, they tended, until the development of the ideology of Islamic Republicanism by Grand Ayatollah Ruollah Khomeini in the 1970s, towards political quiescence.

The Ismailis, on the other hand, who trace their own leadership from the seventh Imam, Isma'il bin Jafar, eventually built a state—the Fatimid Caliphate—based in Egypt, where they were responsible for making Cairo a major civilizational center and for founding the Al-Azhar University. They believe that there is a continuing and unbroken line of living Imams represented in the present period by His Highness Prince Karim Aga Khan. The Ismailis also believe that behind the external forms of the law there is a deeper mystical content that is passed on from one Imam to the next. This led the Ismailis to play an extraordinarily important role in the intellectual history not only of Islam, but also, indirectly, of Europe. This is because the hidden or *batin* content of the religion became identified with Hellenic philosophy. Ismailis played a critical role in translating the Greek texts of Plato and Aristotle into Arabic. It was in this form alone that most survived to be passed on, via Jewish translators in *Al-Andalus* (Muslim Spain), to Christian Europe. Ibn Sina, whose text on medicine was used not only in the Islamic world but also in the West up until the seventeenth century, and whose philosophy profoundly influenced that of Thomas Aquinas and thus the whole Catholic tradition, came from an Ismaili family. Other important beneficiaries of Ismaili patronage include the mathematicians al-Haytham and Nasir al-Din Tusi and the poet and philosopher Nasir e-Khusraw. It was the Ismailis who established the great university of al-Azhar and effectively built the city of Cairo.

On all sides, relatively few of those who actually exercised power had sufficient learning or virtue to qualify as fully legitimate caliphs even by the more relaxed standards of the emerging Sunni tradition. Almost none, for example, were really *mujtahids*, scholars sufficiently learned to exercise independent judgment in matters of law, a task that fell increasingly to the scholars. This created enough discomfort that even Sunni scholars asked whether or not it was permissible to use public works built by oppressive kings (Crone 2004: 306)—a question that seems never to have occurred to even the most sectarian Christians.

Pressure from the legal scholars, theologians, philosophers, and esotericists, however, tended to hold the caliphs accountable to a higher standard than that of other earlier empires in the West. Of critical importance here was the *zakat*, or wealth tax, which took between 2.5% and 5% of the net wealth of those living in *Dar-al-Islam* each year. This tax—unlike the Roman impositions which it replaced—fell most heavily on the wealthy while providing an ample source of revenue which could be used to support the poor, subsidize debtors and slaves seeking to buy their freedom, and support institutions such as mosques, *madrasas*, and hospitals. The latter institutions were also supported amply by *waqfs* or charitable trusts. There were additional taxes: the *jizyah* or poll tax imposed on *dhmmis* or protected religious minorities and the *kharaj* or land tax, imposed on lands seized during the conquest, but both were to be used for the benefit of the whole community. While many rulers attempted to impose other taxes, they faced constant opposition on this front from legal scholars who warned that such taxes were uncanonical (Crone 2004: 304–7).

It was, no doubt, due to these low levels of exploitation and the productive use to which the surplus extracted was put that the Arab armies were most often greeted as liberators rather than conquerors and that once established, Islamic rule proved quite civilizationally progressive. Revenues were invested in the arts, sciences, and philosophy as well as religion. The Abbasid Caliph al-Mamoun, for example, established the *bayt-hikhmah* to translate scientific and philosophical manuscripts from every language, but especially Greek and the languages of India. This, in turn, set in motion extraordinary progress in mathematics, science, and philosophy. It was the Muslim al-Khwarizmi who developed algebra. And investment in the alchemy led to the flourishing of laboratory techniques, including distillation, which proved essential for later scientific and technical progress. The Arabs also invested heavily in bringing water to their cities, which were like vast gardens, and in horticulture, developing many of the most important vegetables in the modern Mediterranean kitchen, importing others from India and China, and refining the techniques which, applied later on by the Portuguese and Spanish to plants from Africa and the Americas, reshaped diet world-wide.

The Social Basis and Political Valence of Islamic Metaphysics

It is in the context of this dynamic but internally contradictory civilizational pattern that we must understand the development of metaphysics in *Dar-al-Islam*. On the one hand, there can be little doubt that rational metaphysics generally, and Aristotelian metaphysics in particular, reached one of its high-water marks under the Abbasid caliphate, and another just a little bit later in *al-Andalus*. More specifically, it was during this period that the identification of Plato's Good and Aristotle's Unmoved Mover with the God of Exod 3:13 was finally completed and that we see the emergence of a fully developed analogical metaphysics of Being as Such. At the same time, the situation of those who practiced *falasafa* was always tenuous. One caliph would patronize *falasafa* and the next would repress or at least ignore it, and the turn against philosophy came much earlier in *Dar-al-Islam* and was of broader effect than that in Christendom.

It, would, perhaps, be most accurate to say that *falasafa*, like so much else in *Dar-al-Islam* was caught in the crossfire between the two motors of Islamic civilization: the drive to build a military empire which would allow marginal, nomadic peoples—first the Arabs and then the Turks—to control a large section of the Silk Road trade and the insistence, originating the earliest preaching of Mohammed, that that military empire also be an effective instrument for commanding right and forbidding wrong—that it be God's Rule on earth. It was only because of the intersection of these two dynamics that philosophy found a home at all in Islam; either dynamic by itself would have excluded dialectics. But the requirement that the fantastically wealthy empire the Arabs were building also be a *just* empire posed problems, which neither messianic preaching nor legal scholarship could resolve, and thus created a niche which the practitioners of *falasafa* tried, as best as possible to fulfill. In the end, however, with the ascendancy of the Turks, the twin dynamics of military expansionism and prophetic austerity took over and philosophy found itself marginalized.

More specifically, philosophy entered the Islamic world as one of the amenities which the early caliphs accorded themselves. Philosophers were also astrologers, alchemists, and physicians—functionaries that every Silk Road court required. And so beginning with the establishment of the *Bayt-Hikhmah* by the Caliph al-Mamoun, the Abbasids in particular subsidized the collection and translation of wisdom from every civilization with which the Arabs had come into contact, but most especially the Greeks, the Persians, and the Indians. Translation eventually gave way to elaboration, and soon the caliphs and the various other rulers who gradually took their place, were subsidizing extensive research in what might be called the Aristotelian physical and biological sciences, and in their practical application in alchemy, horticulture, and medicine. Metaphysics, and its extension into psychology, ethics, political theory, and spirituality, were something that the philosophers did, so to speak, on their own time. Even so, it was not at all unusual for a philosopher to be called to serve as *wazir* or to be appointed *qadi* or judge, and in this sense they had significant influence over public policy and the larger direction of development of Islamic civilization

The philosophy which entered *Dar-al-Islam* was an eclectic mixture of Aristotelianism, as interpreted by Alexander of Aphrodisias and Neo-Platonism, as represented in the misnamed *Theology of Aristotle*, which was really a paraphrase of sections of Plotinus' *Enneads* and the *Liber de Causis*, also incorrectly attributed to Aristotle but actually a summary of Proclus' *Elements of Theology* (Nasr 1964:9). The principal transmitters seem to have been dissident Christians—Nestorians and Monophysites who had fled East into Mesopotamia and Persia in the wake of the Christological controversies, as well as the few remaining pagan philosophers who fled after Justinian closed the last of the philosophical schools, Plato's Academy, in 529 (Rubenstein 2003: 75–77).

When philosophy began to be produced in Arabic by thinkers like al Kindi (801–866) and al-Farabi (870–950), it could hardly be called Islamic in any meaningful sense. It was, rather, simply a restatement, with perhaps some light rationalization and systematization, of the Platonized Aristotelianism of late antiquity. It was put forward as the rational or, in the case of those philosophers influenced by Shi'ism generally and the Ismailis in particular, the esoteric or *batin* content of the revelation made to Mohammed. It was, to be sure, necessary to credential it in the Islamic world, and this meant showing how it related to revealed or prophetic religion. Al-Kindi, took the first steps in this direction, making a distinction between *al-ilm al-ilahi*, which is given directly by God to the prophets, and *al-ilm al-insani* or rational knowledge, and argued that certain truths, such as creation *ex-nihilo* had to be accepted on faith, but there was no attempt to develop a philosophical doctrine of prophecy (Nasr 1964: 12). Al Farabi went further, and raised the status of philosophy, by arguing that religion (*milla*) and *falasafa* put forward the same truths, just in different forms: philosophy by means of demonstrative proofs (*burhan*), for those who could comprehend them, and religion by means of images and persuasion (*iqna'*), for the masses (al-Farabi. *Tahsil* 56, Crone 2004: 173). Philosophy comes first, grasps the truth in pure form, and is unchanging. Religions come about when lawgivers mediate philosophical truth the masses in an attempt to found a just polity (Crone 2004: 173).

Al-Farabi was the first to define philosophically what is meant by prophecy—at least prophecy of the first rank. The prophet must *first* be a philosopher, and must be intellectually and morally perfect to such an extent that his intellect comes into contact with the Agent Intellect (*al'aql al-fa''al*) or intelligence of the sublunary realm, which is the agent of divine "revelation." Whether this is the result of a purely rational dialectic, as Crone claims (Crone 2004: 172), dismissing the claims that al-Farabi was a Sufi, or the result of a sort of mystical illumination which builds on philosophical speculation, as Nasr claims (Nasr 1964: 16) remains unclear. In any case this contact with the Agent Intellect not only perfects the potential intellect of the prophet but also forms his imaginative faculties, so that he becomes a great popular preacher, able to move the masses (Crone 2004: 178), thus establishing himself as paramount leader (*al-ra'is al-awwal*).

Al-Farabi further extends Plato's vision of the philosopher king by arguing that such a lawgiver could found not only a single city (*madinat*) but also a whole community (*umma*), that several such cities or communities could coexist, even if their religions were different, because the philosophers who governed them would constitute a kind of cosmopolitan elite who knew the real truth behind the differing imaginative forms embraced by the masses, and by specifying what happened after the lawgiver died—an issue, as we have seen, which was of fundamental importance for Islam. Ideally the lawgiver would be succeeded by one like himself. In practice, however, lawgivers seemed to appear only to found new communities: thus the long years between Moses, Jesus, and Mohammed. Generally speaking, the community would be governed instead by a *ra'is* or *malik al-sunna*, and new laws elaborated from those given by the prophet on the basis of *fiqh* or juristic science or by a group of philosophically trained individuals who did not rise to the level of prophecy: *riyasat al-afadil*. But where an outstanding philosopher did exist, he ought to rule directly if he could. If not, he remained *al-malik fi 'l-haqiqa*, the real, uncrowned king, and governed indirectly by advising the rulers as did the *'ulamma* and *mutakallim* who mediated philosophical truth to the masses (Crone 2004: 179–80).

It is only with ibn Sina (980–1037) that we really get what might be called an authentic synthesis between philosophy and Islam. Here the critical achievement was ibn Sina's analysis of being. He distinguishes between the essence of a thing (*mahiyah*) and its existence (*wujud*) and between its necessity, possibility, or impossibility. With respect to the first distinction, and contrary to the impression one gets from reading Gilson (Gilson 1952), it is existence that is principal (*asil*). Essence is a limitation on being. Beings are, further, divided into impossible (*mumtani'*), possible (*mumkin*), and necessary (*wajib*). Essences that, on analysis, are incompatible with existence are impossible. Those that are compatible with but do not require existence are possible. If, finally, the essence of a thing includes existence, then it is necessary. For such a thing, essence and existence are the same: it *is* Being. And this, for ibn Sina, is true only of God (ibn Sina *Shifa', Najat, Danishnamah*, Nasr 1964: 27).

This understanding of God as Being as such sets ibn Sina apart from all earlier attempts at synthesis between philosophy and prophetic religion, which had either primarily used philosophy as an apologetic tool, as was the case with most of the early Christian Neo-Platonists, or else treated philosophy itself as the real truth, and regarded prophetic religion as a means of popularizing it. Even the great Philo of Alexandria, who clearly appreciates both traditions, manages at best an eclectic synthesis, using the Jewish idea of God to find a "place" for Plato's ideas and using philosophical methods to interpret and argue for the superiority of Jewish law. Here, on the other hand, we have an integrated synthesis. On the one hand, an idea clearly drawn form the Jewish tradition is used to solve a core problem in the philosophical tradition: what is so attractive about the Unmoved Mover? Ibn Sina answers that the unmoved mover is attractive because it *is* Being, which is what all things seek in proportion to their nature. At the same time, philosophy militates against the concept of divine sovereignty that was emerging within Islam. God is, to be sure, radically transcendent. There can be no greater gulf than between possible and necessary being. But God is not arbitrary. He acts, rather, in accord with his nature, and his commandments are those that are written into the very nature of things, all of which, in the end, amount to one: Seek Being.

This said, it is also true that ibn Sina does not realize the full potential of his insight. He envisions the universe as a process of essentially intellectual emanation from God rather than as a real process of creative activity, and human beings as returning to God, again primarily by means of an intellectual ascent—completed by mystical union, if Nasr is correct, rather than sharing in God's creative activity by means of their own labor, with the intellect playing a leading and regulating role. Nasr describes ibn Sina's cosmology lucidly.

> From the One Necessary Being . . . is brought forth a being whom Avicenna calls the First Intellect and who is made to correspond to the first archangel. This Intellect contemplates the Necessary Being as necessary, its own essence as necessary by virtue of the Necessary Being, and its own essence as a possible being. It thus has three dimensions of knowledge which give rise to the Second Intellect, the Soul of the first heaven, and the body of the first heaven, respectively. The Second Intellect generated in this manner contemplates in a similar way the First Intellect, generating thereby the Third Intellect, the soul of the second heaven, and its body. This process then continues until the Tenth Intellect and the ninth heaven, which is that of the moon, are generated. From here one the substance of the Universe has no longer sufficient purity to generate another heaven. Therefore, from the remaining "cosmic possibilities" the world of generation and corruption comes into being.
>
> In the sublunary world, the Tenth Intellect performs several basic functions. Not only does it give existence to this world, but it issues forth all the forms which in combining with matter bring into being the creatures of this region . . . The Tenth Intellect also serves as the illuminator of the mind of man. (Nasr 1964: 29–30)

This, in turn, shapes ibn Sina's psychology. Ibn Sina expands Aristotle's analysis of the intellect, defining four rather than merely two degrees of actuality. The material or potential intellect is the pure possibility of acquiring intellectual knowledge. When we exercise this capacity we develop the habitual intellect, which can receive knowledge, and the actual intellect, which can create it. When our intellect becomes, in effect, a copy of the universe, we have developed the adept intellect (Nasr 1964: 38–40).

As for al-Farabi, the prophet goes one step beyond this, his intellect actually becoming united to the Agent Intellect or Tenth Intelligence. But for ibn Sina, in addition to thus perfecting his intellect and forming his imaginative faculty so that he becomes a great poet and preacher as well as philosopher, the Tenth Intelligence also gives the prophet the power of making external matter obey his commands (Nasr 1964: 43). This union with the Tenth Intelligence represents the highest degree of development possible for human beings and the aim of all authentic spirituality. This is true even if one accepts as authentic his *Mantiq al-mashriqiyin* or Logic of the Orientals and the last chapters of the *Ishararat wa'l-tanbihat* (Nasr 1964: 43–44). Here he identifies his Aristotelian philosophy as exoteric and turns to an imaginative exposition of the soul's journey towards God. Even so, the journey in question is fundamentally an escape from the material universe, and terminates in liberation from physicality, not in connaturality with God. In this sense, ibn Sina leaves the dialectical project incomplete.

Ibn Sina's political philosophy is similar to al-Farabi's except that he goes further in identifying Mohammed as, at the very least, the final and definitive lawgiver, and Islam as the final and definitive imaginative presentation of philosophical truth. He develops what amounts to an incipient sociology of religion, explaining how various Islamic laws draw attention to God and help to maintain social order (Crone 2004: 187–88).

It is important to point out here that Islamic *falasafa* advanced for the first time an ideal that would be further elaborated—and developed in two different directions—in dialectical materialism. On the one hand, full deification is ruled out—in the case of *falasafa* by the fact that it is logically impossible to cross the line between contingent and necessary Being, in the case of modern dialectics by the conviction that matter itself is the first principle and there is, therefore, no "god" one might become. The pinnacle of human development is understood to be perfect knowledge of material world *and the ability to use this knowledge practically to control matter, physical, biological, and social.* In *falasafa* this is the role of the prophet. For dialectical materialism it is the role of the Communist Party, which becomes the "unique subject object of human history" (Lukacs 1921/1971). The scientific strain of dialectical materialism focused on transforming social structure in order to unleash development of the productive forces (making external matter obey its commands); the humanistic strain focused on the transformation of social relations themselves.

It was not long after ibn Sina produced his synthesis that the tide turned against metaphysics in the Islamic world. Here the underlying factor was the failure of the Islamic project itself: the effort to build a just social order presided over by a ruler who was not only just but himself actually the best and wisest man alive, and in some meaningful sense the heir of the Prophet. It was this common idea that united even the most literalist Muslims with the most rationalist practitioners of *falasafa*. And the ideal was resilient. It could survive caliphates and even whole dynasties that lacked even the most minimal qualifications for rule, whether by the standards of the jurists or those of the philosophers. It could even survive delegation of *de facto* political-military authority to a group of foreign invaders, so long as it was possible to argue credibly that real guidance was being exercised by the "best"—in reality the practitioners of *falasafa*, the *mutakallim*, and the *'ulamma*, and symbolically the *kalifah*. But when the Seljuks began blinding and dismissing caliphs at will, when it became apparent that *they* were the real power, the basis in experience for *falasafa* as a credible social force disappeared and Islamic Aristotelianism began to crumble.

This problem was exacerbated by the fact that *falasafa* and its close cousin, Mutazilite *kalam*, were, to a very significant degree, tied specifically to the Islamic political authorities. The Abbasid Caliph al-Mamoun, who founded the *Bayth Hikmah* and set in motion the development of Islamic *falasafa*, had attempted to impose the tenets of the rationalizing Mutazilite school on the caliphate as a whole. Traditionalist textual scholars reacted by forming legal guilds, which defended competing approaches to the interpretation of the Quran and the *hadiths*, or sayings and practices of the Prophet. These guilds trained legal scholars and granted them recognition as *faqih*, *mufti*, and *mudarris*, master, professor, and teacher of the law after they had passed an oral examination demonstrating their capacity for independent and original legal reasoning (*ijtihad*). It was these guilds of legal scholars—and not the philosophers—who led the struggle for scholarly autonomy in *Dar-al-Islam* (Makdisi 1989). When the intellectual tide turned against them, the philosophers were left without much protection.

Leading the charge against philosophy was the theologian al Ghazali (d. 1111). Al-Ghazali had fully mastered the tradition of *falasafa* at Nishapur, where he studied, but turned against it, rooting himself instead in an emerging and unstable synthesis of Asharite *kalam* and Sufi mysticism. His most important work was his *Tahafut al-Falasafa*, the Incoherence of Philosophy. In this text, he undertakes a critique of ibn Sina's synthesis, arguing that on closer logical examination the philosophers core arguments fall apart. It is not possible to consider the work in detail in this context, but the key link in his argument is a critique of the idea of necessity, which he insists is a purely logical concept, that cannot be applied to physical and metaphysical relations—a position that many Western philosophers have themselves taken, following Hume. The realization of a possibility requires power and will—in effect it requires God. This was, in effect, a reflex of the political situation under the Seljuks and their great Persian *wazir* Nizam-al-Mulk, who was al-Ghazali's patron and who appointed him to the most eminent chair in *Dar-al-Islam*. It also represented the victory of Asharite *kalam*, the principal claims of which became established points of Islamic orthodoxy:

- an epistemology in which human knowledge is restricted to what we know by means of the senses, by discourse with other human beings, and by divine revelation;
- a cosmology purged of any realms of emanation from God, and in fact any intermediate causes, so that God creates each and every instant separately, making him the sole real agent in the universe;
- a strategy for proving the existence of God that stresses the act of creation, so that it does not undermine divine sovereignty;
- a rejection of the earlier Mutazilite claim that the unity of God implies that God lacks attributes, undermining the use of Islam's central theological claim as a battering ram against literalism; and
- a claim that God's decrees are, in fact, prior to and the sole basis of any moral law.

Such a God can, of course, be approached only by means of a personal relationship, and so after performing his great ideological service to the Seljuks, al-Ghazali renounced his chair and began a long search for mystical experience, which ultimately eluded him. Eventually he formed a small Sufi community (Collins 1998: 412–14, 421–23).

From here, Islamic metaphysics develops in two very different directions. We have, on the one hand, the so called *ishraqi* or illuminist school associated with Suhrawardi (1153–1191) and ibn Arabi (1165–1240), and the resurgent Aristotelianism of ibn Rusd (d. 1198) on the other. This first school builds on the mystical dimension of ibn Sina's work, taking al-Ghazali's criticisms as a corrective to excessive rationalism and extending the philosopher's tentative overtures towards Sufism. But it also draws on and synthesizes two long esoteric traditions: that of Egypt and that of Persia. Indeed, Suhrawardi believed that all wisdom had originally been revealed by Hermes or Idris, who he regarded as prophet rather than a god, and had then been transmitted through Egyptian lines that included Pythagoras and Plato, and Persian lines that included the ancient Zoroastrian priest kings, eventually coming to rest in *Dar-al-Islam*.

Suhrawardi defines a complex hierarchy of degrees of knowledge. The lowest level is represented by those whose thirst for knowledge has just been awakened. Then come the philosophers, who seek wisdom by means of discursive knowledge. Pure mystics stand above the philosophers, but above both stand those who join discursive reason and intellectual intuition and who he calls *hakim mutaallih*, a term perhaps best translated as theosophers. These *hakim mutaallih* are in turn joined through a hierarchy of celestial beings to the *Qutb* or *imam* who stands as the pole joining God and the created world (Nasr 1964: 64).

The universe for Suhrawardi is essentially a descending hierarchy of degrees of light. Materiality is darkness and the form of each thing is nothing other than the angel who guards it and makes its existence possible. Because of this he rejects ibn Sina's claim that being is prior to essence and asserts instead the view that essence is prior to being and is in fact what gives things their actuality. He draws significantly on Persian traditions in developing a complex angelology, with considerable attention devoted to describing the various orders of angels, their functions, etc. There is, first of all, a longitudinal series of archangels with the highest giving rise to that below it. Each archangel has a masculine dimension of domination (*qahr*) and a feminine dimension of love (*mahabbah*). The masculine dimension of this hierarchy gives rise to a latitudinal or horizontal complex of angelic archetypes. The feminine dimension of the hierarchy of archangels gives birth to the fixed stars, and through them to the other heavenly bodies, which are, in effect, a materialization of the angelic beings. The horizontal order of angels, on the other hand, generates an intermediate order of angels that rules the various material species directly. These *al-anwar-almudabbarah* or *al-anwar al-isfahbdiyah* (regent or lordly lights) move the heavens and guard all creatures on earth. Every human being has one planted in his soul and humanity as a whole is governed by one: the Angel Gabriel, or the Holy Spirit who, among other things, inspired the prophet Mohammed. When humans are born, part of our soul becomes trapped in the body; the other part remains in heaven. Our aim is to be reunited with our heavenly counterpart, which is our real self (Nasr 1964: 70–74).

By comparison with ibn Sina, the last of the great Islamic commentators on Aristotle, ibn Rusd (d. 1198), represents a step forward with respect to cosmology, but a step backward in the fields of psychology and metaphysics. As Leaman points out, his revolutionary impact on the West notwithstanding, ibn Rusd was first and foremost a jurist, and a jurist of the conservative Maliki school, which wanted to restrict the role of the Hadith, of consensus, and of independent reasoning in the application of the law and return to a more Quranically based Islam. He seems to have brought this same spirit to his reading of Aristotle. Specifically, he tries as much as possible to purge Aristotelianism from the Neo-Platonic accretions that had accumulated over the years. In the field of cosmology, this leads him to reject ibn Sina's emanationism in favor of an emergentist paradigm that, at least implicitly, radically revalues the material world. Ibn Rusd seems to have rejected the idea that form came to matter from the outside, and argued instead that

> the primary, unformed matter contains potential forms as "seeds." Forms are therefore not extrinsic to but immanent in matter. If the forms were to come to matter from the outside, this would be a sort of *creatio ex nihilo*. The forms are as eternal and uncreated as is matter. God creates neither matter nor form. The task of the "prime mover" is to convert possible forms into actual forms, i.e., to develop the seeds contained in matter . . . Prime matter is uni-

versal potency that hides the seeds of the forms; the prime mover does nothing but turn potency into act. (Trachtenberg 1957: 66)

At the same time, ibn Rusd seems to have lost the realization that we see in ibn Sina of God as Necessary Existent. Whether in the name of the same faithful, if somewhat literalistic, exegesis he applied in the interpretation of *sharia'*, or in the name of more purely inner-worldly evolutionism, ibn Rusd reinstates the contradiction we saw in Aristotle's original formulation: we know that there must *be* an unmoved mover that draws things into being by attraction, but we do not know what is so attractive about it.

Ibn Rusd's position would seem at least to have laid the groundwork for a more positive view of human nature, and it did in the sense of putting greater emphasis on the human civilizational project by comparison with otherworldly salvation. At the same time, ibn Rusd seems to have radically devalued the individual human person and its prospects for anything like a full realization of our immanent drive towards divinity. This is because he reads Aristotle as upholding unicity not only of the agent, but also the potential intellect, with the result that human beings are reduced to the status of mere data collectors, with a single collective intellect doing our thinking for us.

This, in turn, has two consequences. First, it means that we have different ideas only because and to the extent that we have different experiences. This undercuts the role of difference and deliberation in political life and tends to accentuate the authoritarian dimension in dialectical political theory. Second, it means that there is no meaningful possibility of personal immortality, since there is no part of *us* that is immortal. We are, in effect, material instruments of the Agent Intellect for the collection of data and the transformation of matter—and no more.

This is reflected in ibn Rusd's political theory. On the one hand, ibn Rusd stresses the historic commitment of the dialectical tradition to the struggle for social justice. This is why he abhors democracy (*siyasat al-jama'iyya* or *al-hurriyya*), which he associates not with popular participation in decision making (something which, for reasons we will come to understand shortly, he seems not even to have considered) but rather a society in which everyone pursues their own aims. Patricia Crone explains:

> What he actually meant by a democracy was a society in which the public sphere had turned into a private playground for big men, whose competition for power tended sooner or later to result in the establishment of tyranny: the privatization of public power and revenues was common to both regimes. Magnate families who plundered the masses had been characteristic of Iran and were found "in many of these cities of ours;" most of the cities "today" were democratic, he said. It was against this dissolution of the sphere of collective interest by private households that he endorsed Plato's abolition of the household for the guardians of the city (i.e., rulers and soldiers). People with access to public power should not have private property or wives and children of their own. (Crone 2004: 190)

This concern for the welfare of the people does not, however, extend to a confidence in their capacities. On the contrary, ibn Rusd's response to al-Ghazali's critique of philosophy, as well as his "definitive treatise," make it quite clear that philosophy—which is the condition for authentic participation in governance—is only for the few. For the vast majority, myth, which presents the truths of philosophy in imaginative form, and a rigorous application of the *sharia'* are in order. Indeed, while ibn Rusd rejects literalistic interpretations of the scriptures as a matter of principle, he is also critical of rationalizing *kalam* as merely a half measure and confusing to the people.

The difficulty with this position is that, while there are many doctrines in Islam (as in Judaism and Christianity) that can be interpreted as imaginative representations of Aristotelian truth, there are many others, including some core doctrines such as the creation of the universe and the immortality of the soul, which cannot. It is easy to see how positions such as that taken by ibn Rusd and later by his Latin followers could have given rise to the claim that they taught a doctrine of "dual truth" in which philosophy and revelation point to radically different truths. But it seems unlikely that this was the interpretation that ibn Rusd intended. Rather, it is likely that he upheld the priority of philosophical truth, and simply regarded Islam as the best imaginative approximation possible, and a useful tool for social control—a control exercised on behalf of, though not by, the people.

This said, it should be clear that whatever reservations we may have regarding ibn Rusd's position, there can be little doubt that his work sustains our basic thesis: that metaphysics, far from serving to simply legitimate oppressive social structures, represented an attempt to at the very least reign in exploitation, and more especially the focus on private wealth that was associated with the emergence of petty commodity production.

We should also note, as in the case of ibn Sina, that ibn Rusd in many ways anticipates the approach of dialectical materialism. In this case the similarity is intensified by an explicitly emergentist (as opposed to emmanationist) cosmology. He also anticipates the position of the Leninist tradition specifically with regard to the people: solicitous for their welfare and pessimistic about their potential for full, conscious political participation. We will return to this question later.

Medieval Jewish Metaphysics

Our account of the development of metaphysics in *Dar-al-Islam* would be incomplete with an account of developments among the Jewish minority. We have already noted that Islam represented, from the very beginning, at once an expression of the Jewish tradition and a sharp break from the political-theological strategy of rabbinic Judaism. On the one hand, Islam took from Judaism the synthesis between radical monotheism and a spirituality centered on ethical conduct generally and the struggle for social justice in particular. On the other hand, where the Jews had largely accepted the limits placed on proselytization by the now Christian Roman empire, and had given up aspirations to both universalism and political power (even in the sense of self-determination for the people of Israel), Islam understood itself as having a universal vocation and was, in a certain sense, constituted by the commitment to effectively "command right and forbid wrong."

Not surprisingly, the overall effect of this dynamic was to neutralize any really effective Jewish resistance to or ferment within *Dar-al-Islam*. Judaism had, after all, opted for particularism and political passivity by necessity rather than choice, and the distinctive ethos that it was developing—the idea that there is no authority but a good argument—would turn out to have more critical force in Christendom and later on in modern Europe than in the Islamic world. It is hard, after all, to say why it is better to debate what is just rather than to actually *achieve* justice, even if the justice achieved is imperfect. Because of this, as Collins points out (Collins 1998: 434), Jewish thought in *al-Masreq*, the eastern part of the Islamic world, was not especially original. Jews produced variants of ka-

lam and Neo-Platonism, and provided the model for the development of Islamic scriptural and legal scholarship. It was only in the far West, in *al-Andalus*, and only very late, as the Islamic *al-Andalus* was succumbing to internal and external pressures—those of the invading Berber tribes—the *Almohads* and *Almoravids*—on the one hand, and of the *Reconquista* on the other—that Judaism generally, and Jewish philosophy in particular, really found a voice. Both Berber groups began at least as reform movements, the *Almohads* actually giving those they conquered the alternative of conversion or death, and many Jews fled, either for friendlier regimes in *al-Masreq* or for Christian lands where the spurts of crusading alternated with refined cosmopolitanism.

There were, broadly speaking, three responses to this situation. On the one hand, many Jews opted to re-affirm their particularism. The most important such thinker was Judah Halevi, whose *Kuzari* goes much further than al-Ghazali in rejecting philosophy: humanity's only real knowledge of God comes from his special revelation to the Jews. This network was dominated by rabbinic scholars. Second, there was a powerful cosmopolitan philosophical trend, which in turn included Neo-Platonist and Aristotelian wings. Of particular interest among the first tendency was ibn Gabriol, who argued that the emanations from God are themselves material in character, and that matter is in no sense negative or evil. As Collins points out, "ibn Gabriol's *Fountain of Life* contains no scriptural references and Latins were unable to tell whether" he "was Muslim, Christian, or Jew" (Collins 1998: 436). It was the Aristotelian tendency, however, which proved more influential. Ibn Daud, for example, who took refuge with the Christians at Toledo after the *Almohad* invasion, and who wrote a history of Latin Christianity in Hebrew in the hopes of sparking a dialogue, actually began the work of purifying Aristotle of Neo-Platonist influences that ibn Rusd continued. Unlike ibn Rusd, however, ibn Daud and his successor Moses ben Maimon made an effort to actually reconcile Aristotelian philosophy with Jewish doctrine, an approach that points ultimately to the strategy adopted in Christendom by Thomas Aquinas. This work was aided considerably by the systematization of Jewish doctrine by Maimonides, whose "creed" and list of the commandments or *mitzvoth* was considered authoritative even by Jews who found his philosophical work suspect.

The third trend is represented by Kabbalism. We have already mapped out the early stages in the development of Kabbalism above. It appears that early Kabbalism was, however, simply a Jewish variant of Neo-Platonist theurgy. It was in the period of the retreat of *Dar-al-Islam* in the face of an advancing Christendom, that the truly distinctive characteristics of the Kabalistic tradition emerged—characteristics that point forwards towards modernity.

Neil Asher Silberman (Silberman 1998) traces out this development quite neatly. Analyzing the Kabbalism of the prosperous and relatively protected Jewish communities of Provence during the time of the *Cathari* controversy, he writes:

> ... the *Sefer Bahir*, the Book of Brilliance, provides a key to understanding the intimate and complex *connection* between an Unknowable God and His creation ... It combines many earlier, distinct systems of symbols to show that varieties of trees, the organs of the human body, the heavenly constellations, colors, sounds, and biblical heroes are all variations of a *single* pattern from which the world and everything in it is made. Like the sublime symmetry of the vortexes and whorls of modern fractal geometry, the creators of the Sefer Bahir saw a single master pattern endlessly reproduced. (Silberman 1998: 60)

> ... through its unique biblical interpretations, mystical parables, and vivid juxtaposition of images, the Sefer Bahir offers a powerful Jewish alternative to the mystical speculations of the Cathari. Its image of the Tree of Life extending between earth and the heavens showed that the material and spiritual worlds—the realm of the here and the realm of the hereafter—were not opposites or opponents but were both part of the unity of God. (Silberman 1998: 64)

This essentially positive outlook on the world is reflected in an embrace of the doctrine of reincarnation, not as something to which sentient beings are chained and must seek liberation, but as a kind of circulation of divine energy through an essentially good world, and as a school in which souls gradually grow towards God.

The situation in *al-Andalus* was very different. During the period between 1085, when Christians took Toledo, and the completion of the *Reconquista* in 1492, and especially up through the middle of the thirteenth century,

> ...a small number of Jewish aristocrats noted for their skill as diplomats, translators, and court officials ... were granted new urban properties, dues and agricultural estates in return for their service as loyal administrators ...

> Yet while a few Muslim and Jewish nabobs enjoyed the fruits of Christian conquest, the simpler craftsmen, farmers and workers who remained in the conquered territories found that the world they had known for generations was no more. Ancient mosques, synagogues, and cultural monuments were destroyed or reused ... And more important than the individual acts of desecration and appropriation was the rise of aggressive frontier chaos of conquistadors, cowboys, and land barons that would create an entirely new world. For the vast expanses of central Iberia, formerly cultivated only in the river valleys and around the towns and cities—were gradually transformed into range land, with enormous herds of cattle and sheep providing great wealth for the few ... (Silberman 1998: 80–81)

It was in this context that Kabbalism assumed its fully developed form. Central to this tradition was the idea that something had gone deeply and profoundly wrong during the creation of the universe—something that had resulted in the emergence of the aggressive civilization of Christian Spain. Thus:

> ... Rabbi Isaac [ben Jacob ha-Cohen of Soria] recognized that the main characteristic of the forces of evil was their ambition to conquer the world. "These are the worst of all," he explained in the Treatise on the Emanations of the Left. "It is their wish and ambition to be on top of the divine, to distort and cut the divine tree with all its branches ..."
> ... It is said that from Asmodeus and his wife Lilith, that a great prince was born in heaven, the ruler of eighty thousand destructive demons, and he is called *Harba de-Ashmedai Malka,* the Sword of King Asmodeus, and his name is *Alpafonsias,* and his face burns like fire. He is also called *Gorigor* ... (Silberman 1998: 85–86)

These are, of course, transparent references to King Alphonso and Pope Gregory X.

These themes are extended in the *Zohar*. King Alphonso had made devotion to the Blessed Virgin central to the ideology of the emerging Spanish state. The *Zohar* countered this with a claim that the *Shekhinah* or divine presence, conceived of as feminine, had been captured by the forces of darkness, and would have to be rescued (Silberman 1998: 91). This dark vision seemed to be confirmed by the repression and double taxation, which followed on the failure of Alphonso's bid for the crown of the Holy Roman Empire.

The question of course, given our aims in this work, is whether or not the Kabbalistic tradition developed a unique metaphysics. This is a complex question, given the diversity of perspectives reflected in the tradition. It seems, however, that unlike the Jewish Aristotelians around Moses ben Maimon, Kabbalism tended, at least, towards a univocal metaphysics. This is apparent from the beginning in the idea that the universe could not bear the creative overflowing of divine power, and that the vessels into which the divine nature poured were somehow ruptured. This is possible only if we conceive of the divine power as somehow in contradiction with the existence of created things. It is further reflected in the representation of the highest of the *sephiroth*, Keter, as Divine Will, which is characteristic of some, and especially later, Kabbalistic texts, such as the *Pardes Rimmonim* (The Grove of Pomegranates) attributed to Moses Cordovero (Silberman 1998: 154–55). It is even more apparent in the work of Isaac Luria, who argued that evil was present in the divine nature itself, which is conceived of as a simple infinity or unlimited (the *Ein Sof*), and that creation took the form of a withdrawal of God from the universe, something that alone made possible the existence of finite creatures, which were gradually purified as evil demonstrated its long-term unworkability (Silberman 1998: 172–74).

This univocal metaphysics in turn led to two very different types of political and spiritual practice. On the one hand, if the divine power was a simple infinity, it was in principle *divisible* and thus subject to (partial) human control. Thus the idea that the *sephiroth* (though not, of course, the *Ein Sof*) could, in fact, actually be manipulated by ritual means. Rabbi Joseph della Reina, for example, used special incantations to try to capture the demons of which they believed the Castilian monarchy to be the earthly reflection (Silberman 1998: 114). Ultimately this emphasis on taking charge of the portion of the divine power that had been transmitted to humanity, or at least to the people of Israel, lead to Judaism's last major flirtation with messianism, in the movement around Sabbatai Svi, which culminated in his conversion to Islam in 1666 (Silberman 1998: 198–216). We will see this tendency further developed by the great secular Jewish thinkers of modernity, who, of course, substitute rational technical or political for ritual action or messianism. Indeed, Yiramayhu Yovel (Yovel 1991) attributes the origins of modernity itself to the transmission of certain tendencies from Judaism by way of the *converso* community.

For the most part, however, the idea of creation by *withdrawal* tended to serve as a counterpoint to the modern Christian obsession with sovereignty and is, perhaps, best seen as a precursor to certain strains of postmodernism, which identify spirituality with respect for the Other who, like God, remains always and only incomprehensible. One thinks especially of Levinas and Buber, but also of late Derrida. But this is a much later part of our story. For now we must turn to an examination of developments in Christian Europe.

WESTERN CHRISTENDOM

Civilizational Patterns

It might have been possible for Islam to continue its expansion beyond the Iberian peninsula and up through Western Europe. Certainly there was no question, in this region, of a "Byzantine" solution: the crisis was too deep, and it was impossible to sacralize an empire that was already visibly collapsing. Perhaps for purely contingent reasons—the course of this battle and that—or perhaps because a deeper synthesis between Roman, Germanic, and Celtic traditions was already underway that made Islam less compellingly attractive than in the Magreb and al-Andalus, this did not happen. Instead, a new civilization grew up defined by the interaction of three very different variants of Christianity, reflecting the diverse cultures of the peoples who inhabited the region.

The first of these was the Celtic tradition. Celtic tribes had moved into Europe over a long period beginning around 1000 BCE and had some presence throughout the region, but were concentrated in the far West: in Iberia, Gaul, and the British Isles. Like most Indo-Europeans, the Celts were originally stockbreeders and raiders, and preserved a strong warrior tradition. But, perhaps because of the way in which they interacted with the indigenous communities they encountered or perhaps because of internal dynamics within Celtic society itself, they gradually settled down and embraced a way of life that integrated stockbreeding with agriculture. They also developed a culture that, without ever losing its irascible edge, was characterized by profound respect for learning. This was reflected in the preservation of a "tripartite structure" that George Dumenzil claims was once universal among Indo-Europeans: a division of the society into producers, warriors, and scholar-priests, with the latter clearly dominant.

In the case of the Irish, who preserved the Celtic pattern in purer form than other groups, the structure worked something like this. Land was owned collectively and parceled out to individual families. The lands of warriors and priests were worked partly by free producers and partly by dependent peasants, though the relative proportion between the two is not entirely clear. Kings were elected from among the warriors by a complex process that involved the kin network of the deceased king, which meant that the electoral college changed with each generation. The electoral process, however, was controlled by the druidic priests, who also had to "make" the king by means of a series of rituals that left them with substantial control over him. These druidic priests were not so much ritualists but scholars, were at the top of a complex priestly hierarchy that included bards of various kinds as well as ritualists and others. They mastered a complex lore that included, during the later period, material from the Hellenistic and Roman as well as their own traditions.

The Germanic cultural pattern was very different. While many Germanic groups settled down to engage in agricultural pursuits, stockbreeding and raiding continued to play a much larger role in their economy. There appears, furthermore, to have been little or no independent, full-time, priesthood. Warriors legitimated themselves by winning and distributing the spoils of war among their followers, a process that led to the development of a loose and informal hierarchy of warrior nobles ruling over a peasant population that they at once exploited and protected. The central relationship within this system was the pledge of fealty, which bound a man to his lord and a lord to his overlord. In return for this fidelity in service, the lord was bound to share freely what he won for his men. Germanic war leaders performed sacrifices on behalf of the communities they led, and if there were priests involved they were very much in the background.

On the fringes of the Mediterranean Basin, finally, in Italy, and in and around major Roman colonial cities, elements of the old Roman latifundial pattern remained side by side with new forms created by the Germanic invasions. Germanic invaders generally took one third of the estates of the old Roman aristocracy, and established themselves as a military aristocracy, while the Roman and Romanized populations gravitated towards positions of leadership in the Church, which was the institution that now represented continuity with the old order.

Christianity was appropriated differently by each of these populations. In the Celtic regions, for example, the Christianity that emerged reflected the historic Celtic emphasis on learning and on intellectual and moral virtue as the condition for leadership. Institutionally, it meant a Christianity centered on monasteries, which people went to pursue wisdom and to live in a just community. Ideologically, it meant a Christianity that, in addition to various traditional Celtic elements, fused Jewish Christianity with Neo-Platonism. Indeed, in the Celtic regions we find more emphasis on Jewish Christian traditions than in any other part of Christendom. It is reflected in the teachings of thinkers like Pelagius, who taught that human beings are essentially good, that we have free will, and that salvation is the result of a long process of intellectual and moral development in which the savior, Jesus, plays the role first and foremost of guide.

The Germans and Romans, on the other hand, assimilated Christianity, in a way that emphasized the theology of Saint Paul, especially as mediated by Augustine of Hippo. We will consider Augustine's theology at great length later. Here it is sufficient to point out the two very different aspects of Paul's theology that appealed to the Germans and Romans respectively.

The attraction for the Germanic warlords was relatively straightforward. Pauline theology legitimated their authority as agents of order without imposing severe religious obligations on them in order to maintain that legitimacy. But it also provided the matrix for the eventual development of a distinctively Germanic Christianity centered on an idea shared between German culture and Pauline Christianity: the idea of the free gift of a lord to his loyal retainers. According to this theology, Jesus is first and foremost a warrior who does battle with Satan much as Beowulf does battle with Grendel, and binds him deep in hell. He then bestows his booty, which is salvation, as a free gift to those who have been faithful too him. This theology reaches its full development, of course, only much later, in Martin Luther and the other reformers, something illustrated amply by Luther's hymn *Ein Feste Burg*.

Pauline theology was attractive to the emerging hierarchy of the Roman Church for entirely different reasons. They read Paul—perhaps more accurately than his Germanic interpreters—as the theologian of what amounted to a mystery cult and stressed the role of baptism and the larger sacramental system. This reading made them, in effect, the unique channel of the divine grace, which alone made salvation possible. At first they pressed this claim only with respect to the religious realm. Gradually, however, they began to claim more—that the authority of the warlords was little better than that of thugs, and that only ecclesiastical sanction could render it legitimate. The warlords rejected this claim, but valued the prestige that ecclesiastical sanction could offer, and thus entered what eventually became a complex game in which the Church (particularly the papacy) and the warlords (particularly the Holy Roman Empire and the French monarchy) played off each other, building power through a complex dance of collaboration and competition.

One might, on the basis of this sketch of the situation during the years after the collapse of Roman authority in the West, predict that the future for Europe was dark indeed, dominated as it was by marauding warlords seeking booty and displaced Roman aristocrats trying to eek out an existence for themselves mediating otherworldly salvation. And that, indeed, is the standard Protestant and Modern picture of the earlier Middle Ages. Nothing, however, could have been further from the truth. The years after the collapse of Roman authority were, in fact, a period of unprecedented growth and development for Europe, as the region developed agricultural technologies suitable to its specific climate, and as it was, for the first time, fully integrated into the Silk Road trade networks.

We must begin with the ecosystem. From a modern standpoint it hardly looks difficult: a West Marine climate with mild winters and cool summers shading almost imperceptibly into the Mediterranean climate that had sheltered the Greek and Roman civilizations for centuries. And it had not proven an impossible ecosystem even for the Celts and Germans with their relatively simple iron age technologies. But Europe is far to the North and while temperatures are rarely frigid due to the warming effects of the Atlantic Ocean and the Gulf Stream, light is at a premium and growing seasons short. And soils were dense and rocky, and needed more working than those of the Mediterranean rim. This made it difficult to produce an agricultural surplus of the sort necessary to support a complex urban civilization.

Two key technological developments changed this: the three-field system and the alpine plow. Both were associated with a quantum leap in the use of animal power and other non-human power sources. The three-field system involved leaving fallow roughly one third of the land each year. The land was used as pasture and the manuring that resulted from this practice left it fertile and ready to plant the next year. The alpine plow, unlike the Mediterranean *ard*, turned over soils deeply and made possible the cultivation of rocky uplands that were previously useful only for hunting or pasturelands. Being heavier than the *ard*, it required more use of animal power and was thus symbiotic with the three-field system.

The greater use of animal power was, in turn, at least partly a result of the complex migrations and cultural interactions of the period. While the Italic peoples of the south had always had animals, they had developed a cultural pattern that emphasized the cultivation of grain, oil, and wine. The Germanic peoples, having historically been stockbreeders, introduced into the region a new focus on pastoralism, especially transhumant pastoralism, which brought large herds of sheep and cattle into the agricultural lowlands during the winter where they provided a very important service to the soil.

In addition to animal power, emerging Christendom made increased use of wind and water power. Both technologies had been used by the Romans, but only in a limited way. Now they were used to grind grain and, eventually, in the later Middle Ages, to run textile mills.

The reason for this shift is not hard to find. A ready supply of slave labor had made it cheaper for the Romans to force humans to do what might have been done by animals or even by geological energy sources—something that was reinforced by the disdain for labor that they inherited with the Hellenic ideal. Now, with the slave regime broken, the Hellenic ideal abandoned, and labor in short supply, humanity needed to make more efficient and effective use of human creative capacity—and did. The result was a rapid increase in agrarian productivity. The period between collapse of the Roman Empire and the middle of the twelfth century saw agricultural yields increase from 4:1 to 9:1, the first real increase since the agricultural revolution (Anderson 1974a). And of course higher agricultural yields made it possible to withdraw more labor from agriculture and redirect it to other activities. This meant that gradually, over a period of several centuries, Europe evolved from a real technological backwater, to a center of significant innovation in the crafts sector. Economically, the most important expression of this was probably in the production of dyed wool cloth for export, which became Europe's principal contribution to the Silk Road trade networks. But Europeans also made advances in navigation, the three-masted ship; in the chronometry, the mechanical clock;

and in printing, movable type. These later inventions were ultimately to play a significant role in the destruction of the medieval synthesis.

Closely connected with these technological developments were changes in the economic structure that at once reflected and reinforced the new value placed on human labor power. In order to understand this we must re-evaluate the historic characterization of medieval economic structure as "feudal." According to historical materialist formulations, "feudalism" is a mode of production that integrates agrarian forces of production with the extraction of labor from dependent peasants, either in the form of rents, taxes, or forced labor. "Dependent" in this context means that the peasants were less than fully free, but not chattel slaves. The most common designation for such peasants has been "serfs," a word derivative from the Latin *servi*, used for slaves, but now designating peasants who cannot leave the land to which they are born but who also cannot be bought or sold. Definitions of feudalism preferred by bourgeois historians have associated with the exchange of land for service—which in the case of the peasantry meant manual labor—or with a more specifically Norman pattern in which the land is divided into three parts—the *demesne* or lord's land, the *virgate* or peasant lands, and the commons, which is used by both. Peasants work three days of each week on the demesne and three days on the *virgate*.

By none of these definitions can the economic structure of medieval Europe be described as globally feudal. On the one hand, we find a bewildering array of different land tenure patterns. Allodial tenure was common in many Germanic areas and in the more remote parts of Scotland. In some cases these allods were noble—many of the German principalities were held in this way—but some were owned by peasant families. In the Slavic east, communitarian tenure patterns were dominant. And even where "feudal" patterns, in the broad sense of land held in return for service, were dominant, the nature and quantity of the service required and the degrees of freedom enjoyed by the peasants varied enormously. One student of the Diocese of Bayeux in Normandy found essentially no evidence of anything that might be called "serfdom" at all (Gleason 1936)! We know, furthermore, that after the Black Death undercut the labor supply in Europe, that peasants rapidly began renegotiating their contracts with their lords. Were most European peasants "serfs" in the classical sense, this would not have been possible and would have required a global revolutionary transformation more fundamental than that worked by the peasant revolts of the fourteenth century.

We should also note that the surplus extracted by "feudal" means was not all used on warfare and luxury consumption. There was a distinction, in Norman areas, for example, between land held in *homage*, which required military service, and land held in alms, which supported the activities of monasteries and other ecclesiastical institutions—activities that included almsgiving, teaching and scholarship, and the provision of healthcare.

It was in the cities, however, that the progressive character of the medieval social structure was most apparent. Here the institution of the guilds played the leading role. The guilds were at once economic regulators, modes of political representation, educational institutions, and cultic communities. If someone wanted to practice a trade he enrolled as an apprentice for a period that generally lasted for between four and seven years. After he demonstrated his proficiency, he became a "journeyman," and could ply his trade freely in return for wages. If and when he developed a reputation that attracted students, he became a master and could set up his own workshop, training apprentices and employing journeymen. The guilds formed the model for the organization of scholars that developed in the twelfth century. Indeed, the term *universitas* originally referred to any association of guilds, something that is reflected in the Latin *universitas studiorum* and the modern Italian *università degli studii* to designate associations of the guilds of scholars.

This system set strict standards for entry into the trade, and since craftsmen were reluctant to admit competition, required workers to demonstrate the very highest degrees of ability before they entered the field. Prices and wages were, meanwhile, strictly regulated, making competition on the basis of price essentially impossible. Craftsmen competed on the basis of quality alone, something that helped Europe gradually overcome its technical backwardness and become a global quality leader in the sectors it entered.

It was the guilds that took the lead during the communal revolutions of the Middle Ages, in some cases actually controlling the government of important cities. The guilds also each had their own patron saints, and were responsible for the feast of that saint and sometimes for aspects of larger religious festivals. In this sense they constituted lay religious confraternities, and formed the basis for the development of the mendicant orders in the twelfth century.

At the political level, medieval Christendom was characterized by a profound dispersion of political authority. Once again, understanding this requires reconsideration of the concept of the "feudal," this time as a political concept. It is, on the one hand, true that at least limited political jurisdiction came with the right to land, so that in some places even ordinary knights exercised at least a modicum of political authority, adjudicating cases involving those subject to them that did not involve the use of the death penalty. Most jurists agreed, however, that in order to convene a court, a lord had to have at least three vassals, so that his judgment was checked by that of his peers. But even the authority of great lords with far more than three vassals was checked by the existence of overlapping jurisdictions and by the numerous privileges and exemptions enjoyed by the Church and by the clergy. Thus a knight or even a great lord might hold land from more than one *suzerain*, requiring him to do military service to lords who might even go to war against each other. In such cases, one was always his *liege* beside whom he was required to fight, but he had, nonetheless, to supply knights to the other side. Within the territory of any great lord there would be clergy exempt from his control and subject instead to the bishop, monasteries that enjoyed varying degrees of immunity, and any number of churches and other holy places where those seeking to escape the lord's justice could seek sanctuary. The result was the effective absence of anything resembling sovereignty in the modern sense—complete and effective authority and control over a territory and its people—at least until the Norman conquests, the Crusades, and the *Reconquista* began to bring real monarchies into existence.

The Great Age of Metaphysics in the West

We are now, at long last, in position to analyze the social basis and political valence of dialectical metaphysics in the post-axial West. Here there were, basically, two competing traditions: one that used Platonic metaphysics to support a Pauline and Augustinian interpretation of Christianity, and another that also made use of Platonic thought, but emphasized Aristotelian metaphysics to work a synthesis between Latin and Celtic Christianities.

Augustinianism

As we have explained above, the sort of conservative transformation of the Hellenic ideal carried out by the Byzantine Empire made sense only in regions in which imperial reform was working (after a fashion) and the imperial structure remained largely intact. In the West things looked very different, as Germanic warlords vied with Roman hierarchs and Celtic abbots for leadership of a new civilization. It was in this context that a second and very different Christian Neo-Platonism, that of Augustine, took root.

Augustine was born in North Africa, and it is impossible to understand his thought apart from that context. North Africa was one of the breadbaskets of the Empire. Large latifundia produced grain using first slave and later *coloni* and wage labor. The rate of exploitation was unusually high, and anti-imperial sentiment especially strong. Christianity here was assimilated first and foremost as an ideology of resistance to the Empire. It was above all in North Africa that Christians, especially young women of the decurion class, whose families' civic responsibilities often left them without a dowry, actively sought martyrdom. And when, during the persecution of Diocletian, many bishops and other clergy cooperated with the imperial authorities, making the required sacrifices and handing over copies of the holy scriptures, many of the people refused to recognize their continuing authority, giving rise to the Donatist controversy.

As Bishop of Hippo in North Africa during the late fourth and early fifth centuries of the common era, and a son of the provincial aristocracy, Augustine was a friend of neither the empire, which had ruthlessly exploited his homeland for centuries, nor of the Donatist peasants who raided the estates of the wealthy, wielding large clubs and crushing the skulls of the landowners while shouting *Deo laudes!* (Praise God!). As a member of the exploiting classes, he looked to the public authorities to maintain order. As a member of an oppressed people, he rejected the empire's claim to sanctity.

All this required some ground or basis for moral judgment. In this respect his starting point is not unlike Plato's. Augustine thus begins with a critique of the Skepticism that he believed was undermining morality in the empire. His argument is simple.

> ... I know for certain that I exist and know and love. About such truths I fear no arguments from the Academy's skeptics. "What if

you are deceived?" they protest. If I am deceived I exist! For one who does not exist cannot be deceived. (Augustine *City of God* XI, 26)

This is, of course, nothing other than the *cogito* that Descartes did not so much discover as restate in a slightly more rigorous way. Our own existence is analytically self-evident, because in order to deny it we must first exist.

Clearly the point is well taken. And it is understandable why this would be such a tempting point of departure for philosophy. If one can begin with an analytically self-evident starting point and derive all knowledge from that starting point, one need not deal with the messy business of the senses or show how, if at all, it is possible to derive knowledge of the universal from the sensible particular. But matters are not so simple. The *cogito* may be a secure starting point, but its security is that of a prison. It provides no obvious exit to knowledge of things outside ourselves.

There are, broadly speaking, two ways out of this prison. The first is through analytic reason itself—a path that the rationalists of the seventeenth century would attempt with limited success. The second route out of the prison house of the *cogito* is to claim that the intellect is illuminated from the outside by an intellectual light in which it can directly perceive the essence of things in themselves. In order to ground the objectivity of this knowledge, it is generally claimed that the illuminating light is divine. This is the approach taken by Augustine (Augustine *Contra Academicos* II:5; *De libero arbitrio* II: 3–5). The basic thrust of this argument is that we have in our minds the idea of God—that is, of Being—which is infinite, perfect, necessary and so on. Clearly this idea does not arise directly from the rational self-knowledge we have in the *cogito* or from whatever vague knowledge we may derive from the senses, since in both cases the knowledge in question is of a finite system. But the idea must come from somewhere, indeed it must come from something capable of producing the idea of infinite, perfect, necessary Being. But only such Being itself could explain the presence of this idea. Thus we have an immediate rational intuition of God. This knowledge of God then guarantees the objectivity of our knowledge of finite systems, which are seen in a divine light that bathes the intellect, revealing the intelligible properties of things just as natural light reveals their sensible properties. Indeed, the fact that we know anything changeless and eternal, such as the Pythagorean theorem or other mathematical formalizations, was for Augustine evidence of an eternal light, which made such knowledge possible, and thus evidence for the existence of God.

Once the existence of God has been established, Augustine has the principle of order that he requires. Human beings participate in this order to the extent that their love was directed towards God. Humanity is divided into two cities, the City of God, composed of those who love God, and the City of Man, composed of those whose love was disordered, and directed towards the creature rather than the creator. Augustine was, however, able to identify a certain limited order within the City of Man. Those who love honor, he argued, are generally more disciplined, and are able to prevail over, those who love pleasure. This, he argued is the foundation both of slavery and of the state, which derive their legitimacy from the capacity of lovers of honor to raise lovers of pleasure to a higher degree of order. Neither institution, however, really participates fully in the life of God.

Nor can human beings depart of their own free will from the City of Man and return to God. This is because once we have sinned we are bound in sin until freed by divine grace. Let us examine this problem in more detail. Augustine's initial analysis of evil, as simply the privation of the Good, is fully in accord with a Platonic metaphysics of participation. "There is no such entity in nature as 'evil;' 'evil' is merely a name for the privation of good" (Augustine *City of God* XI, 22).

Sin, furthermore, is simply a turning from the greater, immutable to the lesser, mutable good. "This failure does not consist in defection to things which are evil in themselves; it is the defection in itself which is evil" (Augustine *City of God* XII, 8).

Thus far there is nothing in Augustine's analysis that would suggest that human failure either merits eternal damnation or results in a fundamental inability to do good. The turn comes when Augustine asks about the *cause* of sin. The straightforward answer, and the one which would be coherent with the larger Platonic background of his analysis thus far, would be that we sin because of the relative weakness of our knowledge of higher goods, and especially of God, by comparison with our knowledge of lesser goods, which seem more vivid. But Augustine rejects this option, on the basis of a very thin argument, in favor of the view that our "defection" from God to ourselves and other creatures is "without cause." When we sin our activity is "futile" and has "defective causes." ". . . when an evil choice happens in any being, then what happens is dependent on the will of that being; the failure is voluntary, not necessary and the punishment is just" (Augustine *City of God* XII, 8).

The defect, furthermore, consists in disobedience of and rebellion against God. Thus According to Augustine, God

> ... created man's nature as a kind of mean between angels and beasts, so that if he submitted to his Creator, as to his true sovereign Lord, and observed his instructions with dutiful obedience, he should pass over into the fellowship of the angels, attain an immortality of endless felicity, without an intervening death; but if he used his free will in arrogance and disobedience, and thus offended God, his Lord, he should live like the beasts, under sentence of death, should be the slave of his desires, and destined after death for eternal punishment. (Augustine *City of God* XII, 22)

The weakness of human nature, which prevents us from doing what is right, is not so much a direct and natural consequence of original sin, as it is a punishment for our disobedience.

Full participation in the life of God is possible only by divine grace, which orders the love of the believer and incorporates him into the City of God. This City of God is not the Church, but rather the invisible body of the saved. The Church includes both the saved and a far greater number of the damned.

The political valence of Augustine's theology in its original context is clear. On the one hand, he strips the Empire of any pretense to holiness. Its function is simple: to maintain order. Real authority belongs to the Church. At the same time, he saves the Church from the requirement that its clergy actually be virtuous. That is quite impossible, for they are drawn like everyone else from an impossibly sinful humanity. But their authority and their sacraments are, nonetheless valid; they are a means of grace even if they are not themselves personally just. The result was a spirituality of authority and submission that could legitimate both warlord and Church without demanding too much of either.

Christianity, to be sure, did not last long in Augustine's North African home—in no small part because of his efforts. Shorn of its anti-imperial valence, Christianity could no longer hold the interest of the North African people, who welcomed the invading Arab tribes of the seventh century as liberators. Augustinian theology did prove attractive to two other groups: the Germanic warlords who were gradually establishing their sway over Europe and the emerging hierarchy of what eventually became the Roman Church.

For the warlords it provided first a kind of limited legitimation of their authority as agents of order—if only that of the City of Man—and second a metaphor of salvation as a free gift bestowed by a victorious Christ on his loyal followers—a metaphor that resonated deeply with the warrior ethos of Germanic culture. Gradually these warlords began to revive the idea of the Roman Empire as a unifying framework for European society and to create "imperialist" theories that argued that while the spiritual power descended from God to the pope and the other bishops, the temporal power descended from God to the Emperor. Emerging monarchs outside the framework of the Holy Roman Empire—such as the Norman Kings of England—did the same. Thus Anonymous of York argued that the king was superior in every way to the priest because the latter represented Jesus's human nature, while the king represented his divine nature.

The Church countered these arguments with complex reasoning of its own. The early Augustinian acknowledgement of a limited but autonomous legitimacy of secular authority gradually gave way to the view that the warlords were no better than bandits unless their authority was confirmed by the Church, something that in turn required submission to the Church. Pope Gelasius put forward the view that all authority came from God—and through the pope—who handed the sword of secular power to the various kings of Europe, but always maintained his right to withdraw it.

This struggle between the temporal and spiritual authorities culminated in the investiture controversy of the twelfth century. Reforming popes such as Gregory VII and Innocent III fought vigorously but not always successfully to wrest from the warlords and especially from the emerging monarchs the right to name bishops and thus to have in place local religious leaders who could challenge the warlords when their rapacity exceeded customary bounds. These reform bishops were, furthermore, encouraged to build and defend an independent economic and political base so as to be less dependent on the economic favor of the ruling classes. The difficulty of course is that while this gave bishops and abbots a measure of *relational* autonomy, it did not really give them *structural* autonomy. They became, in effect, great feudal landowners themselves. There is good reason to believe that their estates were administered less brutally and that the revenues generated were used in ways that better served the community than those of most feudal lords, but the fact remains that they were *structurally* quite similar, if not identical, to secular estates.[5]

From Celtic Neo-Platonism to Catholic Aristotelianism

In the Celtic regions we find a very different appropriation of the Neo-Platonist tradition. Here the Byzantine Neo-Platonism of Dionysus the Areopagite was transformed at the hand of his translator, John Scotus Eriugena, an Irish theologian of the ninth century, into a powerful metaphysics of participation in which Creation replaces Unity as the defining characteristic of the divine. John divides Nature into four parts: that which creates and is uncreated, that which is both created and creative, that which is created and does not create, and that which is neither created nor creates. By the first division he understands God, from whom all things flow. The divine nature is so profoundly ineffable that not even God can understand himself. Were he to do so, he would place himself in a limiting category, something that would contradict the definition of God as infinite or unlimited. Creation is first and foremost a theophany, God's self-revelation to the intellect and the senses. The second division in John's system corresponds to the Neoplatonic intellect. It is the realm of ideas that exist, in this case, first and foremost in the Word, or the second person of the Trinity, without in any sense being identical with it. From here God's creative power overflows in the realm of number, space, and time—the physical world in which the divine essence becomes visible, however, imperfectly, to the senses. The dimness of our vision of God leads, however, to becoming mired in sensation, something from which we are saved only by divine grace, expressed in the institution of the Church, which, by means of the sacraments, transforms the things of the senses into means of salvation. We thus rise from sensation through the various degrees of intellectual perfection—John distinguishes three (*dianoia* or internal sensation, *logos* or ratiocination, and *nous* or intellection), to the unity with God for which we were predestined. It is not just humanity, though, but the whole of creation, which is ultimately restored to God.

---

5. Sarell Everett Gleason, however, found no evidence of serfdom on the estates of the Bishop of Bayeux between 1066 and 1204, even though his diocese was located in Normandy, in the "heartland" of classical feudalism (Gleason 1936). Conditions in the Diocese of Lucca in the twelfth and thirteenth centuries were, if anything, even more favorable for the peasantry (Osheim 1977).

When God became incarnate he took on not only humanity's intellectual soul but also its animal and vegetable souls and indeed the very elements themselves, which are thus joined forever to the divine nature of which they were always, in any case, a partial expression.

Here we see joined together the optimism of the Celtic tradition with the larger framework of Neoplatonic metaphysics. Christian elements—specifically the doctrine of the Trinity and the Incarnation—are mobilized to help flesh out the system and to articulate symbolically the return of all things to God. And for the first time we see God characterized as, first and foremost, *creative activity*. The existence of the material world is not the result of some error or accident but an expression of what God *is*—of God's *is-ness*—at the very deepest level. And we have a share in that creative capacity.

The full implications of this new ontology are not, to be sure, fully elaborated. The return to God is not through the cultivation of human creativity but through a more traditional Neoplatonic variant of the dialectical ascent. This no doubt reflects the only incipient development of the productive forces characteristic of ninth-century Ireland. Full development of the new metaphysics would have to wait for the creative cross-fertilization between the dynamic civilizations of *Dar-al-Islam* and the new urban centers of high-medieval Europe.

It is just precisely this cross-fertilization that is reflected in the Catholic Aristotelianism that reaches its high point in Thomas Aquinas. The process by which Aristotle was transmitted has already been traced out in detail by scholars and popularized admirably by Richard Rubenstein in his masterful *Aristotle's Children* (Rubenstein 2003). Here we will focus on clarifying just precisely what was added to medieval Aristotelianism by Christian philosophers—with what social and political consequences—and on some of the internal struggles within the Aristotelian party.

It has become a commonplace among Catholic Neo-Thomists, due largely to the influence of Etienne Gilson's influential study *Being and Some Philosophers* (Gilson 1952), that essentially all earlier Aristotelians followed Aristotle himself in believing that it is *morphe* or form that gives things being, and that it was not until Thomas's *De ente et essentia* that philosophy arrived at an understanding of Being as such. This he further associates with the doctrine of creation *ex nihilo*, which, he argues, Thomas defended against the Radical Aristotelians and the Islamic commentators. Gilson makes a special point of stressing the association of being and form in ibn Sina who, he argues, passed it on to the Augustinian trend. It was Thomas's preference for ibn Rusd's more literal commentary that created room in his system for a doctrine of Being that derived ultimately from the Jewish scriptures.

There are a number of problems with Gilson's claim. First, he misreads Aristotle himself. While it is certainly true that Aristotle lacked a fully coherent doctrine of Being, and while form certainly plays a role in giving individual things their being, Aristotle's larger system is ultimately dominated not by morphology but rather by teleology—by the immanent drive of all things towards the unmoved mover. He leaves this drive—and the attractiveness of the unmoved mover—unexplained, but it is precisely this *aporia* that made possible the synthesis with the concept of God as Being as such, which emerged in Judaism and was carried into Christianity and Islam. Things seek the unmoved mover because they seek Being. More to the point in the present context, we have already shown in our analysis of ibn Sina's *Danish* that Gilson's reading of the great Persian commentator is simply impossible. While Thomas's doctrine of Being is more refined and developed, the *idea* is clearly present in ibn Sina in the idea of the Necessary Existent and Thomas's third argument for the existence of God. This argument, which Gilsonian or "Historical" Thomists so praise, is essentially just an elaboration of ibn Sina's insight.

What, then, did Thomas contribute to the metaphysics of *Esse*? First, at the philosophical level, he developed a complete or nearly complete doctrine of the transcendentals—the properties of Being in so far as it is Being in which all things share. These include the Good, the True, the One, and—as Umberto Eco argued ably in an early work (Eco 1970/1988: 20-48)—Beauty. Beauty is Being considered as an object of perception, sensual or intellectual. The Good is Being considered as an object of desire or the will. The True is Being considered as an object of judgment. The One is Being considered in itself. This in turn provides for a more complete and integral synthesis between the teleological theology and cosmology of Aristotle and Jewish, Christian, and Islamic monotheism, a synthesis that affirms the essential goodness of the universe and God's immanence in it while safeguarding the divine unity and transcendence more securely than the doctrines of the Asharites or the Augustinians ever could. On the one hand, God is *in* all things as the power of Being that makes their existence possible. It is God that we seek in every motion of the passions even if we do not know it. At the same time, the recognition of God as Being as such guarantees the unity of God—there can be only one such power—and God's radical incomprehensibility, not only by reason, but also by revelation. *Being* is not susceptible of definition.

Second, Thomas's doctrine grounds individuality in a way that the Islamic commentators failed to do. Human beings—and indeed everything in the universe—are a composite not only of form and matter but also of a created share of God's Being. Indeed, form does not so much bring us into being as constitute a limit. *What we are is a particular form of Being.* This way is shared *in part* with others in our species, genus, and whatever higher *taxa* we may identify, but it is ultimately uniquely *ours*. This provides a solution to the problem of personal identity, which has so vexed modern philosophers of both materialist and formalist persuasions.

Third, however, and most importantly, Thomas provides a new and distinctive way of resolving the problem of salvation that is faithful to the Jewish roots of Catholic philosophy, but shows how a fuller and more complete divinization of human beings is possible than either Judaism or Islam allowed. The key here is the concept of connatural knowledge. The basic idea is simple: that like knows like. This is the basis of the whole Aristotelian-Thomistic theory of sensation: that human beings and other animals know material things because being material ourselves we can be affected by material objects. But Thomas develops the idea further, and suggests that it is the key to a sort of intellectual knowledge as well. For example, there is a certain sense in which someone who is just or temperate knows what justice of temperance is, even if he has studied no philosophy at all. And this is true whether the justice in question is natural—acting in accord with the natural law, seeking God and the development of our neighbors because they are the condition of our own existence and development—or supernatural: seeking God and the good of others as ends in themselves. When we act with this latter, supernatural justice, which Thomas calls *caritas,* we act with God's own justice and love and thus have a direct, nonconceptual experiential knowledge of God. It is this "caritative wisdom" that constitutes the basis of Thomistic mystical theology and which is perfected in the beatific vision. But what we are seeking when we seek God is of course Being, and what we promote when we act for the good of others—or for that matter for our own good—is nothing other than Being as such. This is, in effect, a philosophical and theological elaboration of the Jewish concept of *da'ath 'elohim*. Generally translated "knowledge of God," the prophets continually placed *da'ath 'elohim* in poetic parallelism with phrases denoting justice and ethical conduct (see, for example, Hos 4:1–2; 6:3), something that essentially equates them (Thomas *Summa Theologiae* II, Q 45, a2; Maritain 1937).

This, in turn, allows Thomas—without in any way diminishing the glory of the human intellect as our highest natural participation in the life of God—to overcome the hyper-intellectualism of the Islamic *falasafa*, which seemed perpetually on the verge of denying any sort of salvation to those who are not philosophers. As we noted above, the closest we can come to a doctrine of salvation in ibn Rusd is identification of the potential intellect with the Agent Intellect—i.e., knowledge of the lowest of the angels. And this is something that comes about exclusively through philosophical study. Ibn Sina suggests something similar, but late in life elaborated an esoteric "oriental philosophy" that suggested the possibility of more, but again only for a select few who, *after* philosophical preparation, receive divine illumination. Thomas allows acquired philosophical and theological wisdom their rightful place. Only conceptual knowledge can be the basis for public discourse and thus leadership *in foro externo*. But it is quite possible to be illiterate and still be wise, in the sense of knowing God by means of the still higher caritative wisdom, the wisdom that even the philosopher and theologian need for salvation. Mystical theology is saved from esotericism and the elaboration of baroque theosophical landscapes, and made fully accessible to all who act justly.

Thomas's doctrine also allows him to speak meaningfully of the doctrine of the Incarnation without slipping into philosophical nonsense or theological absurdity. On the one hand, Thomas is quite clear that God cannot *become* flesh, for the simple reason that God, Being as such, is absolutely changeless, outside space and time. What Christians call the Incarnation represents a change on the part of *humanity* that becomes joined to God in a qualitatively new way (Aquinas *Summa Theologiae* III:1:1a2). While Thomas does not spell out the details—nor could he, for fear of reprisals from a hierarchy already turning away from his Aristotelian approach—this new way is just precisely that of caritative wisdom. The story of Jesus is an apt imaginative account of this joining precisely because of its ordinariness. Jesus was not a great philosopher or even a great prophet. He was not a priest and he was not a liberating king. All he did was to fulfill the law, consistently, to the very end. He represents Israel's fidelity to the covenants, a fidelity that, as was already painfully clear in Jesus's time, was not ordered to Israel but to the development of humanity as a whole. And his resurrection represents God's vindication of Israel, God's promise that by acting beyond the demands of merely natural justice, by losing ourselves in the pursuit of Being, we do not perish but *become*, in ways we could not imagine, gradually growing towards God.

All this is, to be sure, embedded in texts that can be read in a far more traditional way. They represent not so much Thomas's teaching as the unfulfilled potential of his teaching, the basis for some future Thomism no longer afraid to step outside the bounds of dogma where dogma contradicts reason, but which still sees, however dimly, beyond reason, through the supernaturally just act, into the heart of Being itself.

This distinctively Catholic development of the metaphysics of *Esse* was at once a reflex of and served to reinforce the distinctive civilizational pattern that was emerging in Christendom. The advances in agricultural technology had made *materially* possible a flourishing of human civilization unprecedented in the region. On the other hand, the peculiar tension between the spiritual and temporal lords had created a social space in which that civilization could flourish: the autonomous chartered city. These cities, most often chartered by Bishops, but occasionally chartered by the Emperor or some other temporal lord, became centers in which ordinary human beings cultivated excellence in *techne*, in making—and thus a new sort of connaturality with God. This created a basis in experience for humanity to understand the possibilities of its autonomous participation in Being, quite apart from anything the Church might add and quite apart from the need for any sort of "baptism." At the same time, the presence of the Church—and especially of the monastic communities and later on the mendicant orders as distinctive communities within the larger human city—pointed towards a still higher degree of participation in the life of God, one that was not in contradiction with, but rather completed, that provided by ordinary labor and human civilizational progress. That is why, as the mendicant orders emerged, thousands if not millions of merchants, artisans, and peasants sought to participate in their ministry through third orders that recognized fully the sanctity of the lay state and sought to unlock the hidden potential of an authentically lay spirituality. But this remained an ideal and an attractor, not something that could be imposed or required. Where Islam could only wrestle with the problem of how best to "require good and prohibit evil," creating a just social order dedicated to civilizational progress, promising the masses a kind of earthly paradise and the philosophical elite a sort of mystical union not with God but with the least of his Angels, Christendom imagined a civilizational progress completed in full and complete enjoyment of God: the very divinization of humanity.

Thomistic metaphysics had very definite political-theological implications. On the one hand, it safeguarded the autonomy of civil society. Every creative act was understood as a real participation in the life of God, and humanity was understood as quite capable of governing itself on the basis of natural reason. The civil authorities required no baptism or anointing by the Church in order to be legitimate. At the same time, the Church stood over and against the civil order both as a reminder of humanity's ultimate destiny—deification—which transcended mere civilizational progress, *and* as a guarantor of natural law.

But Thomism went even further than this, envisioning *within the Church* a division of offices, which provided an even higher order accountability. Where Islamic Aristotelianism had allied itself with the *caliphs* and ultimately depended on their support, Thomism argued not only for the autonomy of the Church from the state, but also for the autonomy (and in a certain sense for the superiority) within the Church of philosophers and theologians in relationship to the Bishops. And this was not mere wishful thinking, but a theorization—if also an extension—of established practice.

Catholic universities were ecclesiastical institutions, and their members clerics, and they thus enjoyed the same exemptions and immunities as other clerics. At the same time, they also fell under the authority of Bishops, who, together with the Pope, claimed final authority over matters of faith and morals, matters regarding which they also taught. This led the universities to struggle for, and often to win, special privileges. Thus, according to Roger Gryson:

> The University constituted one of the three ruling powers of the state, along with the Church and the Monarchy. These three powers were compared to the three persons of the Trinity and wee symbolized, according to certain authors, but the three points of the stylized *fleur-de-lys* on the arms of the kings of France ...
>
> ... Since, according to the terms of Frederick Barbarossa's famous constitution, it was their knowledge which enlightened the world, since they were for our intelligences what the sun and stars are for our eyes, as declared Pope Honorius III, they ben-

efited from privileges similar to those of nobles and clerics. They were exempt from taxes and corvées. They could not be arrested or searched, kept under surveillance or tortured. They could only be subpoenaed with special consideration and could not be sentenced to "infamous punishment" (mutilation, forced labor) even less to capital punishment, nor could their goods be seized for debt ... The doctorate was a dignity (*praelatio*) the same as the episcopate; it was equivalent to a title of nobility. (Gryson 1982 citing Grundmann 1951–1952, Barbarossa, Gregory IX, LeBras 1954)

Nicholas of Cusa even accorded the "teachers of the great universities" senatorial rank (Cusa 1440/1960: 509).

Thomas theorized this system by distinguishing between the *magisterium cathedrae magistralis* and the *magisterium cathedrae pontificalis*. The former determined what was true, the latter governed. Again according to Gryson, Thomas compares the work of the Church to a building site.

> [He] likens the parish priests to the workers, the bishops to supervisors, and the teachers to architects. For St. Thomas, the specific character of the Episcopal ministry ... was ... in the concrete organization of pastoral work. (Gryson 1982: 184–83, citing Thomas *Quodlibitales* III a. 9 and I, a 14)[6]

This vision achieved its most complete—if imaginative rather than philosophical—expression in the poetry of Dante Alighieri. Trained in and deeply attracted to Radical Aristotelianism, Dante sought a middle position between the party in whose philosophy he had been nurtured and the teachings of Saint Thomas. Dante (Alighieri *De Monarchia*), who had been influenced by the Latin Averroists but rejected metaphysical monopsychism, stressed that it took humanity as a whole, collectively, to realize the full potential of the human intellect. He thus implicitly recognized knowledge as a social reality that develops over time and that is bound up both with the structures that organize human civilizations and with the larger struggle for a just social order that makes possible the full development of human capacities (Gilson 1968: 167). It was the function of the Empire to guarantee the conditions for human development and civilizational progress. At the same time, he upheld the possibilities of a higher knowledge and a high love—indeed a higher destiny and a higher

---

6. For further support for this understanding of the *magisterium cathedrae Magistralis* see Congar 1978, Lytle 1981, and Taber 1990. For an alternative view see Olsen 1980.

civilization—which humanity was called to by the "love that moved the sun and all the other stars." Setting out on the path of self-cultivation and civilizational progress we found ourselves called to transcend the limits of the natural and challenged to become more than we are. This is symbolized in Dante's ascent into the heavens accompanied by Beatrice, lured by physical beauty to pursue a beauty that transcends even the intellect.

Latin Averroism

By comparison with this, the "Radical" Aristotelians—Almaric of Bena, David of Dinant, and Siger of Brabant—as well as later "Latin Averroists" such as Marsiglio de Padova, are all conservatives. They are not, to be sure, conservative *Christians*. They represent, rather, an importation into Christendom of the cautious spirit of Islamic *falasafa*: cautious in the sense that they limit what reason can achieve—at the outside we can know everything the Agent Intellect knows—and thus what humanity as a whole can achieve.

In order to understand this claim it is necessary first to clarify the principal doctrines of the Radical Aristotelians. First, they upheld, along with Aristotle and most of his non-Christian commentators, the eternity of the world, a conclusion that flowed quite naturally from the Aristotelian doctrine of the unmoved mover. If the unmoved mover was eternal, and drew the world into being by its attractive power, then the world must naturally have been in existence as long as the unmoved mover itself—forever. Even Thomas conceded that this claim could be rejected only on the basis of revelation. Second, however, they upheld the unity of the Agent, and in some cases the Potential Intellect. As we have seen above, in our analysis of the Islamic commentators, this doctrine radically undercuts human individuality and undermines the philosophical basis for belief in anything like personal immortality. Individuation comes exclusively as a result of our materiality, which is precisely what is charged with overcoming. For followers of Ibn Sina, we might obtain a kind of union with the Agent Intellect in—a very imperfect—contemplation of the divine as it is reflected in the material reality of the sublunar realm. For followers of ibn Rusd, even that seems difficult to imagine. Material civilizational progress represents not only our natural *telos* but the outer limit of our potential. Human beings are, in the end, simply information collection devices and manual laborers for the Agent Intellect, sharing in its work of creation, and then dying. As individuals, we mean nothing. We will see this spirit replicated in modern dialectics—both that of Hegel and that of Marx, Engels, and their interpreters.

Finally, the conservatism of the Radical Aristotelians is reflected in their doctrine of God. We see little evidence here of any assimilation of the innovations of ibn Sina and Thomas Aquinas. Indeed, they even seem to retreat from Aristotle's own identification of God as first and foremost the *final* cause of the universe—an identification that ibn Rusd had sustained.

> The primary, unformed matter contains potential forms as "seeds." Forms are therefore not extrinsic to but immanent in matter. If the forms were to come to matter from the outside, this would be a sort of *creatio ex nihilo*. The forms are as eternal and uncrated as is matter. God creates neither matter nor form. The task of the "prime mover" is to convert possible forms into actual forms, i.e., to develop the seeds contained in matter ... Prime matter is universal potency that hides the seeds of the forms; the prime mover does nothing but turn potency into act. (Trachtenberg 1957: 66)

Among the Latin Averroists, this position is documented for Siger of Brabant, and later by Giordano Bruno. Most, however, interpreted Aristotelianism in a much more radically pantheistic way. For some this meant idealism. Almaric of Bena, for example, reasoning that it was form, not matter, which characterized actual being, Almaric argued that in a very real sense everything is form, and thus implicitly, at least, everything is God (Dahm 1988: 94). David of Dinant, on the other hand, argued that since God is the source of all things, God must *be* prime matter.

> The philosophy of David of Dinant is ... a materialist pantheism ... The basic ground of this philosophy is the pantheistic unity of the material, spiritual, and divine principles ... this unity lies not in the empirical world, and not in the reason of the individual, and not in the matter of single things, but in a higher realm, where reason *as such* melds into God and "prime matter." (Trachtenberg 1957: 96–97)

As in the Islamic context, Radical Aristotelianism—here often called Latin Averroism—points forward toward dialectical materialism. Lacking a way to theorize the deification of humanity, it focuses its attention instead on civilizational progress. Lacking a coherent doctrine of connatural knowledge it cannot trust that ordinary people can achieve wisdom, and so casts itself in the role of an esoteric truth reserved for the elite—or revolutionary vanguard—while the people are led to an approximate truth by means of the imaginative language of religion. Ultimately, however, this would prove a dead end. Civilizational progress that does not point beyond itself toward deification is not the work of philosophers, but rather of scientists and technologists on the one hand or organizers on the other. The philosopher is reduced to the role of under laborer.

We will trace out this process in the next chapter. For now, we need to examine the way in which the Augustinian Party reacted to the Radicals.

The Augustinian Reaction and the Averroist Counter-Reaction

It would be easy to blame the Augustinian rejection of Aristotelianism on the excesses of the Radicals, but the record is clear that it was not only Averroist, but also Thomistic propositions that were condemned in 1270 and 1277. We need then to ascertain just what it was that motivated this reaction, and to explore its impact on Christendom's understanding of God, the universe, and humanity's place therein.

John Milbank (Milbank 1991, 1999) provides an important clue, pointing to the Scotist doctrine of the univocity of being as a critical turning point in this regard. Thomas—and most of his Platonist and Aristotelian predecessors according to Milbank—had understood the difference between God and the universe as qualitative. God is *esse*, the power of Being as such; contingent or created beings participate in this act of Being. This at once rendered everything sacred—because everything participates in the divine act of Being—and rendered impossible and even ludicrous the idea of a human assault on the throne of heaven. If, however, the difference between God and the universe is *quantitative*—if both exist in the same way, and differ only in that God is infinite and everything else finite, then it is quite possible for human beings (and especially for humanity collectively) to become divine simply by means of building power. There is thus a contradiction, which is foreign to the Thomistic tradition, between divine transcendence and human self-development. For those who continue to uphold the idea of a transcendent God, human self-development, if not in itself wrong, can easily over-reach itself and become rebellion against divine sovereignty, and thus cannot become the basis for an ethics. Thus the turn, which we see in marked form in Scotus (Boler 1993, Ingham 1993), towards a divine command ethics. For those less concerned with divine sovereignty (even if they remain theistic in some sense) the human drive to *become* God by understanding and gaining control of the universe becomes the basis for a new civilizational ideal. This is, in fact, *the* civilizational ideal of modernity: liberal and socialist. In this sense, the turn towards a univocal metaphysics *defines* the modern alternative between fundamentalism and (liberal or socialist) modernism. From this point of view modernity (and postmodernity) are not so much about a rejection of metaphysics as they are about a shift from an analogical to a univocal metaphysics.

What Milbank fails to do is to explain why the new doctrine of the univocity of being emerged and gained currency in the first place. In order to answer this question it is necessary, first of all, to point out that while Milbank is quite correct to date the emergence of at least a partial consensus in favor or a univocal metaphysics to the fourteenth century or later, the turn in fact begins much earlier. Graham MacAleer (MacAleer 1996), for example, has shown a similar concern with human over-reaching in the ethics of Anselm of Canterbury. This is especially significant in light of the fact that it is Anselm, above all, who puts forwards a "quantitative" concept of God as "that than which nothing greater can be thought." I have shown elsewhere that his ontological argument is convertible with a mathematical proposition known as Zorn's Lemma (Mansueto 2002b), which has never been proven. Similar concern for divine sovereignty can be found in Stephen Tempier's condemnations of Aristotelian science in 1270 and 1277 (Duhem 1911). And it is, of course, easier to arrive at a strong doctrine of original sin on the basis of a univocal metaphysics, which cannot help but pit human beings against God and against each other, than on the basis of an analogical metaphysics that does not. Because of this I am inclined to believe that the doctrine of the univocity of being is rather deeply embedded in the whole Pauline and Augustinian tradition, even if Augustine himself, and some medieval Augustinian thinkers such as Bernard and perhaps Bonaventura, at times transcended it.

The social basis for this trend is not hard to find. We have noted above the extraordinary civilizational progress that characterized Western Christendom after the fifth or sixth century. There were, however, limits to the Christian regime of accumulation. The expansion of the areas under cultivation led, by the middle of the twelfth century if not earlier, led to land shortages. These were not so much *absolute* shortages in the sense that the carrying capacity of the land was being pushed, but rather relative shortages engendered by feudal landholding patterns. The law of primogeniture, followed in varying degrees by most European warlord families, meant that nearly the whole of a lord's land was bequeathed to his eldest son. Dowries were provided for daughters and perhaps for a second son who chose to enter a monastery or who was able to obtain a senior clerical post. The other sons were sent to be trained as knights and to serve as retainers for other lords. They lived in their lord's castle as "knights bachelor" until such time as their lord was able and saw fit to grant them a fief, after which they could settle down, marry, and have children. The difficulty is that as the land under cultivation was extended so too was the land, which was already enfeoffed. This meant more knights bachelor—and what amounted to a sort of aristocratic gang problem, as these armed, unmarried young men did what such men have always done, preying on women and peasants and generally undermining the social order.

Many aspects of medieval culture can be traced to efforts to address this problem. The codes of chivalry were, no doubt in part, at least, an attempt to control armed men by ideological means. But a shortage of land and a surplus of armed men in the long run could only mean one thing: pressure for conquest. This dynamic was overdetermined by the last of the great Germanic migrations: the Norman conquests. While some of the pressure for conquest was played out within Christendom—the Norman conquest of England, for example—for the most part it resulted in pressure for expansion. From the end of the eleventh century on, Christendom adopted a far more aggressive posture towards *Dar-al-Islam* (and the Byzantine Empire), with the "the crusades" in the narrower sense of the effort to conquer the land of Israel and the Reconquista of Sicilia and *al-Andalus* flowing into each other and ultimately into the conquest of Africa, Americas, and Asia.[7]

These conquests had two results. First, they gradually improved the position of Europe in the global trade networks and provided the "first installment" as it were in the primitive accumulation of capital, which led eventually to the emergence of an authentic bourgeoisie and to the industrial revolution. Second, wars of conquest helped bring into being strong monarchies that gradually put forward claims to sovereignty

---

7. The institutional and ideological continuity between the crusades, the *Reconquista*, and the conquest of the Americas is well established. Ramon Gutierrez (Gutierrez 1990) for example points out that the office that financed pacification of the Indians in New Mexico in the seventeenth century was called *la cruzada* and that the Spanish regarded the indigenous peoples of the Americas as "Moors."

which were hitherto unheard of in Europe. Indeed, it is *only* in those regions of Europe that were touched significantly by these conquests that we see early developments in the direction of the sovereign nation states: England, which was formed by the Norman Conquest of Britain, France, where the monarchy played a leading role in organizing the crusades, and Spain, which was the product of the *Reconquista*. Elsewhere state formation lagged, sometimes well into the nineteenth century.

It was the process of state formation that first had an impact on Christian metaphysics. The link is, in fact, startlingly simple. As long as Christendom knew nothing like sovereignty, and the public authorities, temporal and spiritual, functioned more like ideals or attractors than as coercive authorities, people thought of God as an ideal or attractor as well. But the emergence of absolutist monarchies created both a *basis in experience* and a *social interest* in thinking of God as a heavenly sovereign. On the one hand, the experience of emerging political sovereignty provided a model for thinking about God. On the other hand, the emerging monarchies sponsored intellectuals who not only argued for the superiority of the king to the priest and prophet, but also sought to undercut the emergence of a natural law that might constrain royal imperatives.

The result was a series of condemnations of Aristotelian philosophy and theology and a resurgence of Augustinian theology, which ultimately culminated in the Reformation. A whole host of "corrective" strategies, from Anselmian formalism and Bonaventurian exemplarism to Scotist voluntarism and Occamist nominalism, was employed to reign in metaphysics and safeguard revelation and divine liberty.

In Anselm this impulse is still relatively weak and the connection between a univocal metaphysics and royal imperatives is only implicit. Defining God as "that than which nothing greater can be thought" clearly marks the difference between God and the universe in quantitative terms, but it does not directly magnify divine sovereignty. Anselm's account of the fall and the ethics implicit in it stress God's demand for obedience and human over-reaching, but they do not stress God's *arbitrary* power.

Bonaventura goes further. Exemplarism is the notion that everything in creation reflects in some way the divine nature. For Bonaventura this meant specifically the Holy Trinity. This may, at first, seem like a rather positive outlook on the material universe, but for Bonaventura this reflection of the divine nature is wholly and completely the product of God's creative activity. The active potency of matter and secondary causes such as human labor play little or no role. The beauty of the natural world is simply an occasion for praising the greatness of God, the recognition of which seems to be the principal function of the human intellect. Thus the insidious link, in all Franciscan spirituality, between the romantic adulation of nature and the rigid repression of the whole upward drive of complex organization, life, and intelligence (Bonaventura, *Quaestiones disputate de Scientia Christi*).

John Duns Scotus and William of Occam go even further. God is defined, for Scotus, as the infinite, and his proof for the existence of God is essentially an analysis of the concept of infinity. Formalized, it runs like this.

> God is the Infinite or Unlimited.
> Nonexistence is a limit.
> Therefore God must exist. (Scotus *De Primo Principio*)

Augustinian ethics draws out the conclusions from this metaphysics quite neatly. For an analogical metaphysics there is, quite simply, no contradiction between the full development of my capacities *properly understood* and the full development of everything else in the universe. This is because what all things seek is, quite simply, the undivided and inexhaustible power of *esse* as such. Ethics is all about understanding properly what we seek. For a univocal metaphysics, on the other hand, the universe is a zero-sum game. While it is *possible* for me to grow and develop in ways that do not take away from others, it is also quite possible for the development of two systems, even when rightly understood, to come into conflict. Ethics is more about containing human over-reaching than it is about combating ignorance.

For medieval thought this problem was framed in terms of the *casu diaboli*, the "case of the devil" (MacAleer 1996). The question was, quite simply, how Lucifer, who had a clear vision of the divine good unclouded by sensuality, could possibly have chosen a lesser over a higher good. The answer given by Augustinian thinkers, such as Anselm and Duns Scotus (Boler 1993, Ingham 1993), is that he didn't. He chose exactly as a good Aristotelian would have advised: he chose to *be* God, a choice that led him into fatal rebellion against his rightful divine sovereign. This is taken to show that, at least under some circumstances, choosing the full development of one's capacities can, in fact, be sinful.

This reasoning led Scotus—who advanced the most complete and consistent form of this ethics—to make a distinction between the *affectio commodi* and the *affectio justiae*. The first seeks its own development, the second what is right. When my development comes into conflict with that of another, I am obliged to do as God commands, loving my neighbor as myself and God above all. Some contemporary thinkers (MacAleer 1996) see in this line of reasoning the basis for a postmodern ethics of *caritas* understood as respect for the radical otherness of the Other, not unlike that elaborated by Levinas (Levinas 1965). The more straightforward reading, though, is that this is an ethics of obedience: to God and to his earthly representatives.

On the question of just who those earthly representatives are, the thinkers of the Augustinian reaction are nearly unanimous: it is the king or Emperor, depending on the precise geopolitical allegiance of the thinker in question. We have already noted the early apologist for the Normans known only as Anonymous of York who entered the struggle between the spiritual and temporal lords by arguing that the King was superior to the priest because he represented Jesus's divine nature and the priest his human nature. It was Stephen Tempier, the Bishop of Paris, who was essentially a creature of the French monarchy, who undertook the purge of Aristotelianism from the University of Paris in the 1270s. And it was in Oxford, in what was the most advanced absolutist state of the late middle ages, that the Augustinian reaction reached its peak in the works of Scotus and Occam. The Dominican Order, which courageously preserved the thinking of Thomas Aquinas, stood clearly on the side of the Papacy in its struggle with the Empire; the Franciscans, whose intellectuals led the charge against Aristotle and Thomas, sided overwhelmingly with the Empire.

• • •

What does this analysis tell us about the principal question we have been exploring: i.e., the social basis and political valence of metaphysics? First, it should be clear, the analogical metaphysics of *Esse*, far from legitimating totalitarianism of any kind, in fact laid the groundwork for a political theology and ethics that held the political authorities accountable before the court of natural law, restricting exploitation and redirecting surplus in a way that promoted human development and civilizational progress. It did this by constituting the Church and the University as autonomous teaching authorities independent from and superior to the state. It is, rather, the univocal metaphysics of the Infinite, which emerged as a result of the Augustinian Reaction, that points in the direction of a spirituality of authority and submission. We will see, in the next chapter, that it also laid the groundwork for the emergence of the modern ideal of divinization through scientific and technological progress.

This said, Radical Aristotelianism presents problems of its own. The larger dialectical tradition, especially in conjunction with prophetic religion, precisely because it advances a coherent doctrine of God, defines deification as the ultimate aim of human being. This in turn requires a credible strategy for realizing this aim—something that is present only in the Catholic tradition, and then only implicitly, in the works of Thomas Aquinas. Failing this, there is a tendency for dialectics to invest innerworldly civilizational progress—an aim that, however worthy, falls well short of deification—with a metaphysical burden it cannot bear. This is, as we will see, the real tragedy of modern dialectics generally and of dialectical materialism in particular.

We will turn to the story of modernity in the next chapter. For now, however, we must analyze the metaphysical systems of post-axial India and China.

INDIA

In so far as the Heideggerian critique was developed with reference to Europe and the Mediterranean Basin, our analysis of developments in India and China will be more abbreviated. Specifically, we will be attempting to show broadly parallel developments: i.e., 1) that the original insights of the Axial Age sages were gradually developed, in dialogue with partially remythologizing salvation religions, into metaphysical systems; 2) that the resulting synthesis was not only more complete and intellectually coherent than the fragmentary insights of the sages, but also tended in a common direction—towards a metaphysics that understood the first principle as, in some sense, radically creative; and 3) that these metaphysical systems—or more specifically their advocates—partially hegemonized the great Silk Road empires of these regions, redirecting surplus towards civilizationally progressive uses and, in one way or another, democratizing them, thus extending and partially fulfilling the promise of the Axial Age. We will also be at pains to show, against the popular variants of the postmodern critique of Western metaphysics, that "Eastern" traditions, even when they differ significantly in the way they approach certain key questions, are every bit as "intellectual" and "hierarchical" as those of the West.

Political Economy

The Ashokan System

In India as in western Asia and the Mediterranean Basin, the formation of the Silk Road trade network was accompanied by the formation of a new type of empire centered on taxing trade. The first such formation in India was the empire of the Mauryas. And, as in the West, the construction of empire was a brutal and bloody affair. Consider this account of Ashoka's campaign against Kalinga:

> When he had been consecrated eight years the Beloved of the Gods, the King Pyadassi conquered Kalinga. A hundred fifty thousand people were deported, a hundred thousand killed, and many times that number perished. (Major Rock Edict XIII, tr. R. Thapar, in Thapar 2002: 181)

Here, however, the similarity ended.

> On conquering Kalinga the Beloved of the Gods felt remorse, for when an independent country is conquered the slaughter, death and deportation of the people is extremely grievous to the Beloved of the Gods and weighs heavily on his mind. What is even more deplorable to the Beloved of the Gods is that those who dwell there, whether *brahmanas*, *shramanas*, or those of other sects, or householders who show obedience to their superiors, obedience to mother and father, obedience to their teachers and behave well and devotedly towards their friends, acquaintances, colleagues, relatives, slaves and servants—all suffer violence, murder, and separation from loved ones . . . This participation of all men in suffering weighs heavily on the mind of the Beloved of the Gods. *Major Rock Edict* XIII, tr. R. Thapar, in Thapar 2002: 181)

Because of this, Ashoka, "the Beloved of the Gods very earnestly practiced *Dhamma*, desired *Dhamma* and taught *Dhamma*" (Major Rock Edict XIII, tr. R. Thapar, in Thapar 2002: 181).

Whether as a result of a sincere personal conversion or part of an unusually mature and sophisticated legitimation strategy—or both—

Ashoka undertook the first effort to organize and administer a Silk Road empire in accord with the principles of the new salvation religions.

In many ways, the Ashokan system looks very much like an enlarged tributary state. By this time, the Indo-Gangetic plain had become a major agricultural center, though villages continued to engage in stockbreeding. While the state attempted to assert control over the land, private property rights were gradually established. Two crops annually were common. State and private lands were cultivated by tenants of various kinds, as well as *dasa-karmakara* laborers, who appear to have been wage laborers and slaves of various types. Taxes were assessed on the area of land cultivated (*bali*) and on the produce (*bhaga*), with the surplus extracted someplace between one sixth and one fourth of the total agrarian product. Nonagrarian activities were subject to a tax known as the *kara*, while craftsmen in particular were obliged to perform free labor for the state (*vishti*). Water was also taxed. Craftsmen were organized into associations known as *shreni* and *puga*, which gradually became large and complex, which at once organized large scale production, protected their rights, and facilitated the collection of taxes. Trade was strictly regulated, with superintendents of commerce inquiring into supply, demand, and costs of production, before approving pricing. A toll of 20% and a trade tax of 4% were levied on all transactions. Interest rates were fixed at 15% (Thapar 2002: 184–90).

Within the context of this basically tributary structure, however, Ashoka pursued policies that gave him a well-deserved reputation for justice. First, much of the revenue he collected was directed towards uses that served the common good. Thus, the imperial capital at Pataliputra is the only city at which we find monumental palace architecture (Thapar 2002: 189). Instead, the surplus he centralized was used for a large system of public works—including large scale irrigation systems, public granaries that provided for the poor in times of famine, and endowments for Buddhist and Jaina monasteries. The property of the rich (the local dynasties and coteries of nobles he had conquered) was seized, but to the poor Ashoka would lend without interest, and after three years forgive all debts (Sarkisyanz 1965: 28–30, 54–56).

What did Ashoka gain by this generosity? First, the Buddhist doctrine of dependent origination taught Ashoka that ultimately his power rested on the consent and even the support of the people. A king who improved the lot of his people would enjoy their firm support and his kingdom would be secure. In short, Ashoka used a program of public works and public piety to build an alliance with the masses against the local aristocracies who presented the greatest threat to his empire. Second, Buddhism solved one of the principal difficulties facing a prospective emperor in India: the system of *varnas* that made Brahmins superior to warriors or rulers, and that made all rulers members of a relatively egalitarian caste community in which, up until 500 BCE, a kind of rough internal democracy had prevailed. This system had made kings dependent on the *brahmanas* who performed the sacrifices that made them divine. Buddhism and Jainism made spiritual authority dependent on the individual characteristics of the person claiming it, not on their birth or ritual knowledge. A just king could thus claim to be superior to a priest. This did, to be sure, present a new problem. What about the *bikkhus* and other ascetics Ashoka patronized? Where they not superior to him in terms of their personal sanctity, especially from the standpoint of world-renouncing traditions such as Buddhism or Jainism? This question was probably not resolved within Askoka's lifetime, but he became the central figure in later Buddhist solutions to this problem. Ashoka was regarded as *chakavatti*, a monarch whose rule is *constituted* by the turning of the wheel of the *dharma*, and ultimately as a Bodhisattva, a being who has achieved or who is close to enlightenment, but who continues to be reborn in order to help ripen other beings. This made him, of course, superior to the ordinary *bikkhus*, who had only just started out on the road to enlightenment, and who, in the Theravada tradition at least, were only aiming at personal liberation rather than at the liberation of all sentient beings.

The Mauryan empire eventually fell, but Ashokan state Buddhism became the model for smaller kingdoms in Sri Lanka, Burma, Thailand, and Kampuchea. An entire tradition of lay Buddhism grew up, centered in the *Ashoka-sutras*, which spoke of just kings who had fed the poor, pardoned criminals, and invested the surplus they centralized in public works and the support of the Buddhist *Sangha* (Sarkisyanz 1965: 33). This lay Buddhism, like the monastic tradition of the Buddha himself, pursued liberation from the illusion of selfhood. Its principal means, however, was not meditation assisted by monastic withdrawal from worldly attachments, but rather works of *Metta* or charity, through which one gained *karuna*, or a sense of identification with others. Ashokan Buddhism provided fertile soil not only for the emergence of reforming monarchies, but also, when these monarchies ceased to serve the common good, for the emergence of peasant revolts directed at restoring *dharmaraj* or the rule of cosmic law and setting humanity once again on the path to liberation. And we will see that movements rooted in Ashokan Buddhism, and in structurally similar variants of Indian philosophy, continue to this day to play an important role in humanity's struggle to fulfill its destiny in the cosmos, defining a unique "Indian road" of human development and civilizational progress.

The Development of the "Hindu" System

The period following the collapse of the Mauryan Empire was accompanied by a complex of diverse and often conflicting dynamics, so that it took a long time before a new coherent pattern emerged. The years following 185 BCE were characterized by the reassertion of tribal and clan polities, the *gana-sanghas* (Thapar 2002: 210–11) and by a series of invasions from the northwest, including the Kushanas and the Sakyas, each of whom established their own states (Thapar 2002: 213–28). At the same time, there was a massive expansion of trade both through Central Asia and by sea, with textiles, pepper, and ivory being the principal exports, and wine and gold coins being the principal imports (Thapar 2002: 141, 248). We see the emergence of more or less autonomous organizations of artists and merchants—the *shreni* or guilds. We also see the emergence of Buddhist monasteries as major economic actors in their own right, with monks and nuns pooling their capital and investing it in trade, or with rulers and landowners making loans to guilds with all or some of the interest to be paid to the monasteries (Thapar 2002: 268).

This was also the period in which we begin to see the emergence of a real urban civilization in the south. Up until this point the south had been dominated by chiefdoms that showed only a very limited ability to centralize surplus, which they invested in large megalithic burial sites and other ritual structures. Much of the real authority had remained in the hands of the heads of households, and local village headmen (Thapar 2002: 231–32). Now, however, trade with Rome and with the eastern Mediterranean began to spark the emergence of urban centers devoted to this trade, in which black pepper and beryl, textiles and ivory were the most important commodities. Buddhist and Jaina monks made their way south, establishing monasteries and, as kingdoms emerged that could offer them patronage, Brahmins followed (Thapar 2002: 233–34).

The Great Age of Metaphysics

Gradually, however, by the beginning of the Gupta dynasty (319 BCE), a distinctive pattern did emerge. This has often been regarded as a period of economic decline, especially in the cities, due to the crisis of the Roman Empire and the consequent decline in demand from one of India's principal trading partners and to climate change that resulted in an expansion of the arid regions (Thapar 2002: 298). In fact, however, Roman decline was rapidly offset by new development within India and by the development of a new trade network in which the Arabs were the principal intermediaries. Where the Mauryan empire had been focused primarily on taxing the existing economy, the new system focused on systematically expanding the area under cultivation and on catalyzing economic growth in general. Development was fostered largely by offering large grants of land to both Buddhist and Jaina monasteries and to Brahmins, who then undertook responsibility for development. Land granted to monasteries and to Brahmins was held tax free, in return for teaching and ritual services provided. Grants to collectivities of Brahmins were called *agrahara* grants, those to individual Brahmins *brahmadeya* grants (Thapar 2002: 291–92).

This pattern had a number of consequences. At the political level it set in motion a process of centralization, which ultimately left state structures in the Indian peninsula weakened. Provincial, district, and village officials came to hold their posts on a hereditary basis and when the central authority weakened often tried to establish individual kingdoms. This, in turn, meant claiming *ksatriya* status, which required Brahmin sanction and thus opened up new possibilities for patronage for Brahmin intellectuals (Thapar 2002: 290). At the religious level it meant both the emergence of great Buddhist monastery-universities, such as that at Nalanda, which were the recipients of *agrahara* grants, but also the gradual eclipse of these centers as more and more land was granted to individual Brahmins in the context of Gupta and post-Gupta development policies.

A similar pattern developed in the south, except that monastery and Brahmin settlements were, if anything, more prominent. These latter settlements came in two waves: first *agrahara* and *brahmadeya* settlements like those in the north, then *devadana* or *devadeya* settlements in which the land was actually held by the temple (Thapar 2002: 338). Brahmin domination was especially strong in Kerala (Thapar 2002: 380, 387), where temples often had their own militias trained in the martial arts. The South also witnessed the development of bonded *atimai* labor. Private property was stronger than in the North and taxes higher—up to one third of the total product. The south tended to benefit more from the emerging Arab trade and it was better situated to take advantage of the emerging trade with Southeast Asia, which supplied many of the spices which were then transshipped to the Mediterranean (Thapar 2002: 338–42).

The gradual re-assertion of Brahmin hegemony was further facilitated by the development of Puranic Hinduism. This was, in effect, an entirely new religion, with new gods, probably derived from those of the indigenous peoples being absorbed as Sanskrit culture extended into the south, with new rituals and an entirely new kind of spirituality. Where Vedic religion had been focused on the act of sacrifice itself, with the gods understood as being bound by rituals properly performed, and eventually disappearing almost completely, Puranic Hinduism was centered on the worship of Gods, especially Vishnu (the creator) and Shiva (the destroyer). These gods were understood as conferring a variety of benefits, including *kama* (pleasure) and *artha* (wealth and power), as well as encouraging right conduct and social justice (*dharma*) and providing various modalities of *moksa* or liberation, understood in many different ways. Offerings to the gods continued to be an important part of the ritual, and still required ritual specialists, though Brahmins who undertook these roles were generally regarded as of lower status than those who performed the old Vedic rituals. Animal sacrifice was no longer obligatory.

Buddhism had won support away from the old Vedic tradition in part because its practitioners could be regarded as authentically holy and because Buddhist monks were willing to make some accommodation to popular tradition. The *stupa*, for example, probably derives from traditional megalithic burial sites. Puranic Hinduism, however, had *both* authentic holy men (and women) of its own, *and* a more generous outlook on those for whom the idea of *nirvana* seemed unattractive. Gradually, indeed, the idea developed that one could achieve *moksa* simply by devotion to the god (usually one of the avatars of Vishnu) or even by engaging in orgiastic rituals (left-handed *tantra*, usually in the Shaivite tradition).

Buddhism responded to the Hindu challenge with innovations of its own. The original Buddhist ideal of seeking release from suffering through an enlightenment gained by long years of asceticism and meditation, and understood as something that everyone must do for themselves, with the Buddha's teachings as a guide but with his merits good for himself alone, gradually gave way to the ideal of *bodhisattva*, who dedicates himself or herself to continuous rebirth until all sentient beings have been released from suffering and whose merits are good for others as well as for himself. *Nirvana* itself, never clearly defined in the Buddha's teachings but looking suspiciously like total annihilation, was redefined as a kind of omniscience in which the consciousness, recognizing that nothing is permanent, can enjoy the flux of phenomena without becoming attached to them. The result was the *Mahayana*, the great vehicle, which eventually became the dominant form of Buddhism in China and Japan. Meanwhile, practitioners of the Theravada, the tradition of the elders, developed a far more tolerant attitude towards those who were not yet ready to seek enlightenment, but who could accumulate merit by almsgiving and other good works, and absorbed a good bit of the popular religions of the regions into which the tradition migrated.

Ultimately the Hindu strategy proved the more powerful. There are a number of reasons for this. First, Brahmins proved themselves better pioneers than Buddhist monks, who were not supposed to be so involved in worldly affairs. Monasteries seemed to flourish best in established agricultural zones with thriving trade centers (Thapar 2002: 487). Second, state-building strategies in India came to lean heavily on Brahmin legitimation (Thapar 2002: 487). Third, Puranic Hinduism could integrate Buddhism into itself (as the cult of one of the avatars of Vishnu) in a way that Buddhism itself could not reciprocate. By 900 CE Buddhism had all but vanished from India, except in the east, where it continued to enjoy royal patronage (Thapar 2002: 488).

This pattern dominated in India until its incorporation into *Dar-al-Islam*. This was itself a gradual process, with the Arabs taking Sind as early as 712 and then fighting a war of position in the northwest and along the west coast of several centuries. Their progress was no doubt held back by the internal divisions within the *'ummah*. Eventually they were displaced, at least in the political field, by the Turks, who were initially attracted simply the by opportunities for plunder—and most especially by the fantastic riches of many of the temples along the western coast. Hindu state structures were simply too fragmented to resist, and in 1206 Qutb-ud-din-Aibak established a Sultanate at Delhi. Later Turkic rulers eventually asserted authority over the entire subcontinent.

The Development of Indian Metaphysics

It is against this background that we must consider the development of Indian metaphysics. As in the West, the basic dynamic involved the elaboration of the insights of Axial Age sages into complex metaphysical systems sustained by subtle dialectics in the context of dialogue and debate with competing traditions. Broadly speaking, Indian metaphysics began with four fundamental perspectives:

1. the atomistic and determinist materialism of the Caravakas and the Ajivikas;

2. various matter/spirit dualisms, deriving especially from the Jaina, but also represented in the *Gita* and other orthodox Hindu sources;

3. the idea of Brahman as a universal creative principle, which derived from the Upanishads; and

4. the idea of *pattica-samupada*, the principal metaphysical teaching of the Buddha.

Of these, the last two turned out to be the most powerful, and the story of Indian metaphysics is largely the story of the struggle between them.

Hinayana Metaphysics

During the early years of the Silk Road Era, Buddhism was clearly dominant, especially in the historic centers of Indian civilization in the northwest and the Indo-Gangetic plain. From a metaphysical standpoint, the principal challenge facing Buddhism was to explain the status of things, and especially persons, in a system that denied that anything at all has inherent existence. This is a problem because things, their ambiguous metaphysical status notwithstanding, are recognized as the objects of desire and fear and thus as occasions of suffering, and because persons, while lacking a self in any strong sense, are thus regarded as seeking liberation and thus as in some sense meaningful subjects. One person in particular, furthermore—the Buddha—is regarded as in various ways the agent of the liberation that all eventually seek, thus perhaps a subject in some special sense.

The range of responses to this problem is staggering, and detailed consideration of each alternative is well beyond the scope of this work.

Broadly speaking, it is possible to identify two distinct approaches. The Hinayana tradition developed a sort of minimal metaphysics that acknowledged the reality of things as at the very least the intersections of causal networks independent of the mind and focused on the idea of detachment as a practical goal; the aggregates to which we become attached are mental constructions and meditation helps us achieve detachment to the extent that it helps us realize this. The Mahayana tradition, on the other hand, explored in depth the full ramifications of the idea that things are "empty" (*sunya*) of inherent existence and that reality consists of a kind of mental flow, developing a variety of metaphysical positions ranging from seminihilism to absolute idealism. The Hinayana regard the Mahayana as a departure from the original teachings of the Buddha. The Mahayana argue that its insights are based on later esoteric teachings of the Buddha and that the teachings preserved by the Hinayana represent simply an exercise in skillful means designed to lead those seeking enlightenment but still largely undeveloped along the early stages of a long process of development.

It has become fashionable in recent years to stress the anti-metaphysical character of the Buddha's original teachings and to read not only Hinayana but much early Mahayana philosophy in this light. David Kalupahana (Kalupahana 1992) is typical of this trend, arguing that Buddhism is based an on rejection of metaphysics understood as a rational search for meaning, or rather on a rational recognition that there is no such meaning and thus on a radical anti-substantialism. This work rejects his claim, will argue that the Buddhist doctrine of *pattica samupada* in fact represents one of the principal alternative metaphysics available to human reason, and will analyze the history of Buddhist metaphysics as an attempt to explore the possibilities—and limitations—of this central idea. Both Hinayana and Mahayana solutions will be treated as possible readings of *pattica sammupada*, though the full potential of this doctrine was realized only in Chinese Buddhism and will thus be explored in a later section of this work.

The first major solution to the metaphysical problems posed by Buddhism was that of the Pugdalavadins, who argued that "there is a *pudgala,* or person over and above the bundle of aggregates which makes up human experience." Their argument is quite straightforward: "If there is no soul, what is it that is reincarnated from one life to another?" (Collins 1998: 215; see also Kalupahana 1992: 126ff.) This was one of the largest and most enduring Buddhist schools in India until about 600 CE and still had some support as late as 1200 CE. Ultimately, however, it suffered from the fact that it seemed to reject the Buddha's central insight and its terrain was eventually taken over by Hindu sects that were able to put forward similar teachings without the liability of rejecting simultaneously the authority of the Vedas and the manifest teaching of the Buddha.

The second major solution was, as we have suggested, that of the Sthaviras or Theravadins, who saw themselves as adhering most closely to the teachings of the Buddha as preserved by his earliest followers. They were originally strong in western India, which is the home of the Pali language in which the Buddha taught and survive due to their role in the colonization of Sri Lanka about 250 BCE (Collins 1998: 215).

Theravada metaphysics is centered on a series of commentaries on a body of literature known as the Abhidharma, which draws on the results of meditation to analyze experience into elements, leading to recognition that there is no self or indeed anything else to which one can become attached. The Abhidharma is essentially a compendium of these elements—five *skandas*, thirteen sense fields, eighteen elements, and between four and twenty-four types of causal relations (Collins 1998: 215; Kalupahana 1992: 144–48).

There were, to begin with, two principal interpretations of the Abhidharma. According to the Sarvastivadins, "the so called objects of everyday life are not real, for they are mere transitory aggregates, but the elements of which they are composed are real and permanent ... the one item they are at pains to show does not exist is the subjective self" (Collins 1998: 216). The Sautrantikas, on the other hand, "rejected the doctrine of the intentionality of consciousness by which the Sarvastivadins defended their realism. Instead they distinguished between the things of experience, which exist, but only as transitory point-instants of space-time, and non-concrete categories, which do not exist; the latter are permanent and real but only as abstractions. There is a non-referential aspect of mind by which dharmas which are not existing substances can be real objects of valid cognition" (Collins 1998: 217).

The struggle between the Sarvastivadins and the Sautrantikas forms the background not only for Theravadin but also for much Mahayana speculation. The difference is that where the Mahayana tried to expose contradictions and draw logical implications, the Theravadins concentrated on defending what they regarded as core Buddhist dogmas and on harmonizing what remained. Thus Moggaliputa-tissa's *Kathavatthu* (Kalupahana 1992: 132–43) is essentially a refutation of the personalism of the Pugdalavadins, the realism of the Sarvastivadins, and the doctrine of a transcendental, eternal Buddha, which was emerging among the Mahayana. Buddhaghosa's *Visuddhimagga* (ca. 410–431, see Kalupahana 1992: 206–16) on the other hand, focuses on harmonizing and systematizing the texts and teachings that arrived in monasteries in Sri Lanka during reign of King Mahnama. In the process, however, he ends up laying groundwork for what eventually emerges as the distinctive Theravadin metaphysics. "Buddhaghosa's philosophical language eliminated not only metaphysical conceptions, such as permanent and eternal subjects and objects, but also empirical distinctions such as woman (*itthi*) and man (*purisa*), retaining only the aggregates (*khanda*) ... We have here recognition of an "unconscious" consciousness, referred to as the life continuum (*bhavanga*) to account for the continuity in the otherwise dissected and momentary mental events. Philosophically, this is not that different from the metaphysical conception of the *alya*-consciousness presented in the *Lanka*, expect that it is not originally pure (Kalupahana 1992: 21–213).

From this point forward, Theravada philosophy was primarily a matter of working out the details of this metaphysics of "evanescent point instances" and mental constructs. Vasubhandu II (400–480)—so called to distinguish him from the Mahayana philosopher of the same name—synthesized Sarvastivadin and Sautrantika theories, arguing that some elements are evanescent point instants, while others are "nonforceful, escape chain of causation because they are basically concepts." His *Abhidarmakosha* is a classic statement of this tradition (Collins 1998: 237–39).

The result of these refinements was, ultimately, a development in the direction of the emerging Mahayana schools, which stressed the emptiness of everything, even the basic *dharmas* and the role of the mind as the agent of experience. Thus Dharmakirti (ca. 650 CE), who is claimed by many different schools, retheorized Theravada realism, arguing that what is real is what causes. The real, in other words, is "action not entity." This meant that certain things that earlier Theravadin philosophers had regarded as real—space and time for example—are rejected as mere conceptual constructs. At the same time, Dharmakirti insists, against Madhyamika seminihilism and Yogacara idealism, that the world really does exist (Collins 1998: 239–40).

It was in the same context that Dignaga (480–540 CE) developed a Buddhist logic in response to the emerging Hindu Nyaya tradition, reducing the sources of knowledge to two, perception and inference, and simplifying the syllogism. Dignaga also moves in the direction of the Mahayana, and more especially the Madhyamika. Rejecting the emerging Mimamsa doctrine of the eternality and permanence of the sounds of language he held that all names are negative—that words are defined, in a sense, in relation to each other, and that sensation is all that exists. At the same time, because thought is fundamentally negation, thought itself should not be reified as in any sense the source of things. Through meditation we recognize things as they actually are: fleeting particulars (Collins 1998: 231–32; Kalupahana 1992: 197).

Mahayana Metaphysics

Whether we accept the traditional Mahayana claim that their sutras represent later, esoteric, and more advanced teachings of the Buddha (which is doubtful) or not, there is a strong case to be made that they more successfully draw out the metaphysical implications of the central Buddhist idea of dependent origination. This is apparent from the very earliest Mahayana literature, the *Prajnaparamita* (Transcendent Wisdom) sutras, a group of sutras that first began to emerge in the period between 100 BCE–100 CE, and which were then elaborated between the years 100–300 CE, reaching completion sometime between 300–500 CE, though the texts later began to absorb some Tantric influence in the period between 600–1200 CE (Conze 1960: 9ff., 1968: 11ff.). As Paul Williams points out:

> The principal ontological message of the *Prajnaparamita* is an extension of the Buddhist teaching of so-Self to equal no essence, and therefore no inherent existence, as applied to all things without exception. This is not some form of Monistic Absolutism, negating in order to uncover a True Ultimate Reality. The ultimate truth is that there is no such thing. (Williams 1989: 46)

Similarly, Beyer argues that

> the metaphysics of the Prajnaparamita is in fact the metaphysics of the vision and the dream: a universe of glittering and quicksilver change is precisely one that can only be described as empty. The vision and the dream become the tools to dismantle the hard categories we impose on reality, to reveal the eternal flowing possibility in which the Bodhisattva lives. (Beyer 1977: 340)

Practically, this is associated with an emerging emphasis on the Bodhisattva ideal, the aim of persisting in rebirth until all beings have been liberated, and with the idea of skillful means—the notion that the Buddha and his followers must use a variety of different teachings in order to meet the needs of beings at different levels of development (Williams 1989: 46, 50–52).

There were, broadly speaking, two different ways in which this basic insight could be elaborated. Nagarjuna (who lived in the second century CE) and the Madhyamika tradition that followed him focused on the concept of *sunyata* or emptiness, which replaces for them the concept of *svabhava* (self existence or essence) as the basic metaphysical category. For the Abhidharma, *svabhava* was the defining characteristic of a dharma, as hardness is of the earth dharma. Only dharmas have essences. Conventional things do not. For the *Prajnaparamita*, all entities, including dharmas, are conceptual constructs. There are, therefore, no essences at all. In Madhyamika, *svabhava* means inherent existence. And as Nagarjuna argues,

> The origination of inherent existence from causes and conditions is illogical, since inherent existence originated from causes and conditions would thereby become contingent. How could there be contingent inherent existence, for inherent existence is not contingent. Nor is it dependent on another being. (*Madhyamikakarika* 15, 1977 vv. 1–2 in Williams 1989: 60)

What Nagarjuna is doing here is, in effect, to reject the key assumption that governed the Western metaphysics of *Esse*—namely the idea that there can be no infinite regress. For Nagarjuna, the concept of dependent origination is, in effect, a claim that there is no first cause, no cause that is its own cause and thus grounds contingent existence. Everything is contingent.

Practically speaking, the *Madhyamika* pointed to the importance of a rather austere sort of meditative practice—one designed to clarify and simplify, and in this sense it remained in continuity with the Theravada tradition, the analytic emphasis of which it simply carried to its logical conclusion.

The *Yogacara* or *Cittamara* (Mind Only) School traces its origins to the monk Asanga and his half-brother Vasubhandu, who lived between roughly 310 and 390 CE. Central to their teaching was the doctrine of the three aspects (*trisvabhava*) of things: the conceptualized or constructed aspect (*parikalpitasvabhava*) in which we perceive the objects of ordinary everyday life, the dependent aspect (*parantrasvabhava*) in which we recognize that these objects don't really exist in any absolute sense, and the perfected aspect, (*parinispannasvabhava*) (Williams 1989: 82–86).

> According to the *Samdhinirmocana Sutra* it is the "Suchness" or "Thusness" (*tathata*), the true nature of things, which is discovered in meditation (6:6). It is said to be the complete absence, in the dependent aspect, of objects—that is, the objects of the conceptualized aspect (*Mahayanasamgraha* 2:4). This is not as difficult as it seems. What it amounts to is that through meditation we come to know that our flow of perceptions, of experiences, really lacks the fixed enduring subjects and objects which we have constructed out of it. There is only the flow of experiences. The perfect aspect is, therefore, the fact of non-duality, there is neither subject nor object but only a single flow. It is also emptiness, explained for this tradition as meaning that one thing is empty of another. That is, the flow of perceptions—the dependent aspect—is empty of enduring entities—the conceptualized aspect. What remains, the substratum which is empty of those enduring entities, is the flow of perceptions themselves. (Williams 1989: 84–85)

This is not, therefore, a subjective idealism of the Berkeleyan variety in which mind is real and "things" are merely ideas in our minds and that of God, but rather a rejection of the duality of subject and object itself.

> Maitreyanatha begins his *Madhyantavibhaga* with a clear assertion of existence which serves to differentiate the *Cittamara* from the *Madhyamika*: "the imagination of the nonexistent (*abhutaparikalpa*) exists. In it duality does not exist. Emptiness, however, exists in it." ... Thus we have a reinterpretation of the notion of emptiness, which has ceased to mean 'absence of inherent existence', since the imagination of the nonexistent, whatever it is, is empty but never the less has inherent existence... Our new opposition is emptiness versus subject-object dualism. (Williams 1989: 86)

This has definite practical implications, as Collins points out:

> Whereas Madhyamika emphasized salvation through a simplifying skeptical wisdom, Yogacara made salvation dependent on a very complex training process of mastering many refinements of meditation simultaneously with their philosophical basis. (Collins 1998: 223)

The Great Age of Metaphysics

The result was the elaboration of complex hierarchies: numerous degrees of ultimate nothingness, ranks of bodhisattvas and monks, etc. Where the Madhyamika represented a turning of Buddhism to its lay base, Yogacara reflected the reassertion of the monastic impulse within the Mahayana context.

From here it was inevitable that Mahayana philosophy would develop back in a quasi-theistic direction. It is difficult to tell just how far this process actually went in India itself. There are texts that reflect such tendencies in Sanskrit, but we do not know if they were originally composed in that language or translated back into Sanskrit in order to give them an air of authority. The *Avatamska sutra*, which later served as the core text of the Hua-yen school in China, is actually a compilation of various texts. References to two of these, the *Dasabhumika* and the *Gandhavyuha*, appear in Indian literature. The rest of the text probably is probably of Central Asian origin, from the region of Khotan (Kamegawa 1949 in Cook 1977: 21, 124; Williams 1989: 121). The *Saddharmapundarika* (Lotus) Sutra, which serves as the principal text of the T'ien Tai (Japanese Tendai) tradition, was first translated into Chinese as early as 286 CE and scholars believe that it dates to sometime between the first century BCE and the first century of the common era, roughly the same time as the early *Prajnaparamita sutras* (Williams 1989: 142). Most philosophical reflection on the content of the sutras took place, however, in China, Korea, and Japan rather than in India.

This said, it is useful to reflect briefly on the content of these sutras, to suggest the powerful impulse towards something like an analogical metaphysics of *Esse* within a tradition founded on a rejection of the idea of inherent existence. The first step in this process was the emergence of the idea of the *tathagatagarbha* or Buddha-nature, which resides within all beings.

> All the living beings, though they are among the defilements of hatred, anger, and ignorance, have the Buddha's wisdom, the Buddha's Eye, the Buddha's Body sitting firmly in the form of meditation. Thus, in spite of their being covered with defilements, transmigrating from one path ... to another, they are possessed of the Matrix of the Tathagata [*tathagatagarbha*], endowed with virtues, always pure, and hence not different from me ... (*Tathagatabargha Sutra*, trans. in Takasaki 1958: 51, Williams 1989: 97)

One sutra, the *Mahaparanirvana Sutra*, even goes so far as to call this latent capacity for Buddhahood "*atman*" (Williams 1989: 98–99).

> We also find in this context an emerging doctrine of potentiality and actuality. The *Srimaladevisimhanada Sutra*, for example, distinguishes between the *tathagatagarbha* and the *dharma-kaya*. The former is potential and still in defilement; the latter is realized and undefiled. (Williams 1989: 100–101)

> ... beginningless, increate, unborn, undying, free from death; permanent, steadfast, calm, eternal; intrinsically pure, free from all defilement store' and accompanied by Buddha natures more numerous than the sands of the Ganges ... (Williams 1989: 101)

But what does one become when one achieves complete Buddha-hood? This is the question answered by the *Avatamska* sutra, which attempts to show how the world looks from the standpoint of a Buddha or advanced Bodhisattva. This sutra mixes Madhyamika and Yogacara themes, acknowledging that all things lack inherent existence but at the same time arguing for the a pure consciousness as the source of all things. Paul Williams (1989: 121–23) argues that the purpose of this move is to endow the Buddhas and advanced Bodhisattvas with enormous creative power. If nothing exists besides mental constructs, then the images created by the Buddhas and advanced Bodhisattvas in their meditations will be as real as anything else. And their motive in creating these images will be nothing other than their compassion for all beings, who they seek to liberate.

The result is, in effect, to reinstate an analogical metaphysics of creativity in which the ultimate ground of the universe is Mahavairocana, the Great Illumination Buddha, who looks rather more like the God of Western monotheism than most traditional Indian deities.

> The realm of the Buddhas is inconceivable; no sentient being can fathom it ... The Buddha constantly emits great beams of light; the Buddha body is pure and always tranquil. The radiance of its light extends throughout the world ... In all atoms of all lands, Buddha enters, each and every one, producing miracle displays for sentient beings: such is the Way of Vairocana. (*Avatamska Sutra* I.1 and I.4, in Williams 1989: 122; and in Cleary trans. 1984/6)

This universe, which the sutra calls the *dharmadhatu* or realm of *dharma*, is Vairocana Buddha, or in another image, the jewel net of Indra, a system of interdependent causality represented as a unified whole (Cook 1977).

And each and every human being has within them the potential to become a Buddha, seeing the *dharmadhatu* as it really is, bringing forth infinite worlds, ripening an infinite number of beings. In this sense, the doctrine parallels the emerging Western idea that human beings can, through some combination of wisdom and justice action, actually *become* divine.

> Clearly to know that all dharmas
> Are without any self-essence at all; To understand the nature of dharmas in this way
> Is to see Vairocana. (in Williams 1989: 123)

> They perceive that the fields full of assemblies, the beings and aeons which are as may as all the dust particles, are all present in every particle of dust. They perceive that the many fields and assembles and the beings and the aeons are all reflected in each particle of dust. (in Williams 1989: 124; in Gomez 1967: lxxxviii)

The question, of course, is why this doctrine did not take hold in India as it did in China. The answer may well be that it did, but in a form more nearly compatible with the popular religions of the peoples of India who were gradually being integrated into Sanskrit civilization during this period. As we will see, Puranic Hinduism, as it struggled against the hegemonic Buddhism of the post Mauryan period, gradually created a doctrine that looks suspiciously like the Buddhism of the *Avatamska Sutra*. It is to that story that we must now turn.

Hinduism

As we noted above, the emergence of Puranic Hinduism was fundamentally a result of the fusion of Vedic Brahminism with local cults in response to the challenge presented by Buddhism and Jainism. This response drew substantially on the tradition of the Upanishads and the Bhagavad-Gita, but was highly innovative and syncretistic, resulting in the emergence of entirely new—indeed of many entirely new—forms of religious life (Thapar 2002: 275ff.).

At a deeper level, the emergence of Hinduism represents a re-assertion of the ideal of the self and of creation against the Buddhist emphasis on the void, and in this way parallels developments within Buddhism itself. Indeed, the principal aim of Hindu philosophy is to establish just precisely these concepts.

A word is in order regarding the traditional organization of Hindu philosophy into the "six acceptable *darshanas*." This classification was originally developed by Jaina scholars during the eighth century as a way of classifying the Hindu intellectual field from the outside. The scheme was not used within Hinduism until the fourteenth century, by which time it was already long obsolete, since some of the *darshanas*—Yoga for example—had never really been philosophical schools in the first place, while others, such as Vaisheshika, were no longer really complete and autonomous systems. By this point, Hindu philosophy *meant* Vedanta, with borrowings from the other traditions. Indeed, while later Hindu philosophers read the *darshanas* back into the Upanishadic period and beyond, there was almost certainly never really a period during which we could find these six *darshanas*, understood as living philosophical schools, competing against each other (Collins 1998: 227, 269). They are, rather, more like modes of speculation, somewhere in between specialized fields (*Nyaya*, for example, focuses on logic and epistemology, *Vaisheshika* and *Samkya* on cosmology, *Vedanta* on metaphysics) and competing perspectives. What makes them "acceptable" is their deference to the authority of the Vedas, though their actual engagement with the Vedas varies considerably.

Behind the ideology of the "six acceptable *darshanas*" there is, however, an underlying reality. The defense of the world and of worldliness against the Buddhist ideal of *sunyata* united an exceptionally wide range of competing tendencies, including many that in the West would never have been regarded as compatible with "religion" of any sort, such as the Nyaya-Vaisheshika atomism.

The struggle against Buddhism proceeded in two stages. During the first, a variety of realistic perspectives took the field against Buddhist semi-nihilism. In the second, Hinduism, probably building on the emergence within Buddhism of a doctrine of a creative cosmic consciousness, claimed for itself the terrain previously held by the Mahayana and secured more or less complete hegemony over the Indian ideological field. The emergence of Mimamsa represents, as we will see, a kind of transition between these two phases.

Puranic Hinduism's first attack on Buddhism was in the field of logic. Early Buddhism made ontological claims on the basis largely of insights gained in meditation, and paid little attention to dialectics. The Nyaya school, which emerged beginning around 100 CE, sought to exploit this weakness by analyzing the sources of knowledge and the methods of argument in order to define an intellectual field on which Buddhism could be defeated.

The Nyaya identified five sources of knowledge: intuition (*pratyaksa*), inference (*anumana*), comparison (*upamana*), and testimony (*sabda*). Intuition referred originally to sense-perception, though it was later used to describe anything apprehended directly, even if not by the senses. The school upheld a realistic understanding of sensation, in which the senses (*indriyas*) come into contact (*sannikarsa*) with their objects (*arthas*), producing cognition (*jnana*). Inference proceeds using a unique five step syllogism, which includes:

1. the proposition to be established—e.g., "the hill is on fire"
2. the reason for this proposition—e.g., "it smokes"
3. an example—e.g., "whatever has smoke has fire, such as a kitchen"
4. an application of the example to this case—e.g., "so does this hill"
5. the conclusion—e.g., "the hill is on fire"

Upmana or analogy allows us to know things by comparison with other things which we already know.

The inclusion of *sabda* or testimony among the sources of knowledge allows the Nyaya tradition to reconcile a basically empirical approach to knowledge—essential, in the mind of the founders of this school, to the defense of realism—with a recognition of the authority of the Vedas. Nyaya scholars continued the tradition of Brahminical grammar and began a long process of rationalization that led eventually to the Mimamsa doctrine of the creative power of the word and to the Buddhist nominalism we have already analyzed above (Radhakrishnan 1957: 356–57).

Closely allied with the *Nyaya* school was the *Vaisheshika*, which also emerged around 100 CE, becoming a coherent school around 500 CE (Collins 1998: 234ff.). This school joined to an empiricist epistemology probably derived from the *Nyaya* an atomistic, pluralistic cosmology. It classified the objects of experience (*padarthas*) into six categories: substance, quality, activity, generality, particularity, and inherence. Some Vaisheshikas also recognized nonexistence as a separate category. The first three categories we can perceive directly, the others are inferred. Substances, which are the substrate of qualities, include earth, water, light, air, ether, time, space, soul, and mind. Consciousness is not a perceived property of bodies, thus the soul must be a distinct substance. Since different souls have different experiences and states, they must be really distinct. These experiences and states are the consequence of actions.

Early Vaisheshika texts, such as the *Vaisheshika-sutra*, do not mention God. Later Vaisheshika thinkers, like most Nyaya, advanced a version of the eutaxiological argument. While the atoms that make up the universe are eternal, their ordering into an organized cosmos as well as the origins of the Vedas and the meanings of words cannot be explained apart from an intelligent designer. (Radhakrishnan 1957: 386).

Nyaya and Vaisheshika taken together probably represent the reflection back into Hinduism of the materialist tendencies originally represented by the Caravaka. It is a mark of the uniqueness of the intellectual situation created by Buddhism that a materialistic and originally atheistic ideology would be called on to defend religion.

The Samkya school, similarly, represents the reflection within Puranic Hinduism of the dualistic trend represented by the Jaina, substantially moderated in accord with the emerging Puranic spirituality. This trend can trace its roots back to the *Bhagavad Gita,* though that text is not so clearly dualistic as the fully developed Samkya that emerges around 200–400 CE (Collins 1998: 234–236). According to this school, the universe consists of two principles: *prakriti* or matter, which is pure potential, and *purusa* or consciousness. *Prakriti* is, in turn, informed by three qualities or *gunas*: *sattva, rajas, tamas*. The first of these is the potential for consciousness and is the cause of pleasure. The second is the potential for action and struggle and causes pain. The third resists consciousness and action and is a source of indifference and apathy. *Prakriti* evolves under the influence of *purusa*, leading to the development of *mahat*, or the great one, *buddhi*, or intelligence, and *ahamkara* or self-sense, which is the principle of individuation. The *sattva* aspect of *ahamkara* gives rise to *manas* or mind, the five organs of sensation, and the five instruments of action. The *tamas* aspect of *ahamkara* gives rise to the five fine or subtle elements, which in turn give rise to the gross elements. *Rajas* supplies the energy necessary for both of these developments. The individual or *jiva* is *purusa* limited by its involvement with *prakriti*, and includes a subtle body that a distinct mixture of the three *gunas*. Bad deeds lead to the accumulation of *rajas* and *tamas*, good deeds and yogic practice to the accumulation of *sattva* and to more rapid liberation. Indeed, later Hindu schemes attribute to the four *varnas* differing mixtures of these *gunas*. While it is the catalyst for evolution, *purusa* itself remains free. The experience of limitation gradually leads to the recognition of this freedom and its liberation from a *prakriti*, which exists for this purpose alone. The idea of a divine creator is explicitly rejected (Radhakrishnan 1957: 424, 425).

The Mimamsa school, on the other hand, emerged first and foremost out of efforts to defend the Vedic sacrifices against not only Buddhism and Jainism, but also against Upanishadic critiques and Puranic Hinduism. Legends place its origin with Jaimini, who lived some time between 200 BCE and 200 CE, and who continues to be one of the principal authorities for Vedic astrology. The basic strategy of this school is to uphold the Vedas and the Vedic sacrifices as eternal and as themselves the underlying creative force behind the universe and as the source of all rewards. Originally the school rejected fundamentally the ideal of *moksa*, and regarded religion as directed to worldly goods or at most to a better, even heavenly rebirth. Later, however, it adopted the ideal of *moksa* for itself.

The school developed some highly creative ideas. In the field of epistemology, it added to the sources of knowledge already recognized by the Nyaya negation and postulation. This latter is rather like the Kantian idea of a transcendental argument that proves the existence of something because it is the condition for the existence of something we already know exists. They stressed, furthermore, the role of the perceiving subject as the basis of knowledge, something that led eventually to the development of a variant of the *cogito* within the Vedanta tradition.

The school is best known, however, for its logocentric ontology: the idea that the actual *sounds* that compose the Vedas are eternal and that they are the ultimately source of the universe, concretizing, as it were, into material beings. When the Brahmin pronounces the Vedic formulae, he invokes this same process of creation, which commands—indeed brings into being—the gods themselves (Collins 1998: 241–47).

Vedanta, in turn, emerged out of the rationalization of the Mimamsa ontology of language. Sometime around 400 CE the grammarian Bhartrihari revived the old Upanishadic cult that sought union with Brahman through pronunciation of syllable *aum*. He broke, furthermore, with the Mimamsa cult of the sounds of the words. He argued that meaning is different from pronunciation and emerges only in the context of the sentence as a whole. This *sphota* doctrine laid the groundwork for a break with pluralism and the emergence of Vedanta monism (Collins 1998: 230–31). This position, in turn provided leverage for rationalizers within the Mimamsa tradition, such as Mandana (eighth century) who argued that *sphota* or meanings can be realized only in individual phonemes, creating the idea of universals manifested in particulars (Collins 1998: 246–47). From here, it was only a small step to the idea of a single creative principle—Brahman—manifesting itself in the myriad particulars of the universe.

It was Sankara, a South Indian who studied in the North before returning South to establish monasteries to replace the declining Buddhist establishments, who took this step. Sankara identifies three different levels of knowledge: the absolute, appearance, and illusion. The first is knowledge of the first principle, the second the ordinary knowledge we have of things around us, and the third error in the ordinary sense of the word—the classic example is confusing a rope with a snake. Using a variant of the *cogito* he argues that doubt about the inherent existence of phenomena—the foundational experience of the Buddhist—presupposes something doing the doubting. This ground, however, is not the individual subject of Augustine or Descartes—the reality of which might well be doubted—but rather Brahman, which, being eternal and self-existent, is beyond doubt (*Brahma-sutra-bhasya* 3.2.22). The reality of the external world is grounded on the basis of the intentionality of consciousness: knowledge of self is always over and against objects. But the reality of the world does not imply pluralism: the transcendent, as ground, already contains the phenomena (Collins 1998: 248–49).

This *advaita* philosophy was closely connected with Shaivism in Kashmir and in the South. Even at the popular level, the cult of Shiva was associated with the idea of underlying energies manifesting themselves in the phenomenal world, and Sankara provided this cult with a highly developed metaphysics. Emerging Vaishnavism, on the other hand, needed more scope for devotion to particular deities with well-defined characteristics. The first step in this direction was taken by Ramanuja (ca. 1100 CE) whose *vishishta* (modified) *advaita* argued that precisely because consciousness is intentional and always involves an object it is not absolute but plural. There must thus be some distinction between Brahman and the individual *atman*, even if Brahman is in all things as ground and creative principle. While Brahman is ultimately one, it has both material and spiritual modes of existence. The material aspect may be regarded as the body of the universe, so that the world cannot be mere illusion, an interpretation sometimes put forward by followers of Sankara (Collins 1998: 262-65).

The *dvaita* doctrine of Mahdva (1197-1276 CE) goes further, arguing that being is the power of everything to be itself. Salvation is by the grace of the saving deity—Vishnu—and consists not in mystical union but in unending adoration. The result, as with the Asharite and Augustinian reactions in the West, was a tendency towards nominalism (Collins 1998: 264-66).

This, indeed, was the general trend of Hindu metaphysics as the Turks gradually established a more and more effective state structure, a trend that once again parallels developments in the West. Thus in the fourteenth and fifteenth centuries, Gangesh and Raghunatha Shirmani revived the Nyaya tradition and developed it into an authentic formal logic, mounting a powerful attack on the concept of the universal and extending further the trend towards nominalism (Collins 1998: 267-68). This development was cut short only by the emergence, beginning in the sixteenth century, of a movement of cultural resistance that emphasized those aspects of the tradition that were most distinctive—i.e., most anti-Islamic. Thus, we see the emergence of a Hindu Scholasticism that developed in two different directions. The first trend, represented by Vijnanabhikshu, advocated a non-*advaita* syncretism. The second, under the leadership of Appaya Dikshita did the same thing from a monist perspective, so that *advaita* Vedanta gradually emerged as the quasi-official philosophy of India (Collins 1998: 269-71), a tendency which persisted well into the twentieth-century struggle for national liberation.

The Social Basis and Political Valence of Indian Metaphysics

The question from the standpoint of this work is, of course, whether or not the whole enterprise of Indian metaphysics represented a fundamentally totalitarian impulse and whether or not the specific trajectory of Indian metaphysics during the Silk Road Era—its evolution from a tradition of sayings by sages into a cluster of authentic metaphysical systems, and its development from the semi-nihilism of original Buddhism to the absolutism of the *Avatamska-sutra* and the monisms and theisms of the Vedanta—contributed to such an impulse.

This question takes a very specific form in the Indian context, because early Buddhism, at least as it is understood by contemporary scholars like David Kalupahana, seems to supply perfect evidence that it is, in fact, possible to take seriously the problem of meaning and to develop an authentic and even profound spirituality without metaphysics, simply by coming to terms with the hard fact of impermanence and living in a way that is grounded in this realization.

Matters are, however, not quite so simple. In order to assess the real social basis and political valence of the various schools of Indian metaphysics, it is necessary to look at their actual impact on the development of Indian society. This is a difficult task given the problems involved in fixing some of the basic data—e.g., dating texts, etc.—and given the fact that we have yet to arrive at a definitive explanation for the sudden rise and then gradually dying out of Buddhism. What follows is hopefully somewhat better than conjecture, but perhaps something short of a fully demonstrated conclusion.

First, it seems clear that the larger tendency of Theravada Buddhism is towards the formation of fairly strong monarchic states governed by the Buddhist ideals of the *chakavatti*, the monarch who turns the wheel of *dharma*, and the Bodhisattva-king. Like most ideals, we have no reason to believe that it was ever followed rigorously, even by Ashoka, much less by his Sri Lankan, Khmer, Burman, and Thai imitators, but such ideals serve as effective means of legitimation only if they have some effect. And, at least in the case of Ashoka, the evidence is there: large scale investments in infrastructure and in religion and land reform, debt forgiveness, and tax relief for the peasantry.

Does the emergence of the Mahayana and of Hinduism, therefore, represent a falling away from this ideal? Not necessarily. As we have seen, the rise of Puranic Hinduism and the transformation and decline of Buddhism were bound up with the emergence of a fundamentally new political-economic pattern in India: that of relatively weak monarchies that focused their efforts on putting new land under cultivation and on strengthening participation in trade networks. Fully developed Mahayana Buddhism, with its large monastic establishments and its offer of a sort of salvation to the laity through rebirth into a "pure land"—i.e., the kind of Buddhism that would develop in China just as Buddhism was fading in India—was reasonably well adapted to these tasks. Indeed, it is not difficult to see in the radicalization of the focus on the doctrine of dependent

The Great Age of Metaphysics

origination, which itself was originally a reflex of the interdependence characteristic of a petty commodity society, the emergence of still more intense and complex market relations in which the commodities themselves all but disappear, becoming first the fleeting point instants of the Sautrantikas and eventually the void intersections of causal networks of the Madhyamika and empty mental constructs of the Yogacara.

In the long run, however, Buddhism was too otherworldly to remain hegemonic in a prosperous society that valued wealth and worldliness. The same thing would happen in China, albeit less completely and a bit later, as Buddhism gave rise to a Neo-Confucian metaphysics that had absorbed much of its insights. The only difference is that in China the new hegemonic ideology was sufficiently disdainful of mercantile activity that Buddhism was able to conserve a niche for itself as a religion of merchants. In India, on the other hand, emerging Puranic Hinduism made the strategically brilliant move of acknowledging the legitimacy of a wide range of different aims in life—*kama, artha, dharma,* and *moksa*. It also rejected definitions of *moksa* that suggested annihilation. At the same time, it hierarchized these aims in a way that gave priority to spiritual development and social justice.

The result was that as Sanskrit civilization spread through the peninsula, it did so in a way that, while by no means free of oppression and injustice, tended to channel resources into human development and civilizational progress, funding first monasteries and then temples that served as centers not only of spiritual development but also for artistic creativity and scientific research. And, as we have seen, many of Ashoka's original reforms—tax breaks for peasants clearing new land, for example—were retained. Indeed, we are beginning to see a pattern—and one that will be confirmed in China as well. Distaste for oppressive structures leads to the development of otherworldly ideologies—first among the elite in the form of the teachings of sages, then in the form of otherworldly salvation religions such as Buddhism and Christianity. These otherworldly religions build monasteries that contribute to economic revival and create a more just social structure. Gradually, however, the resulting prosperity renders the monastic impulse less attractive, resulting in the re-assertion of inner-worldly tendencies carried by lay intellectuals.

Both the internal transformation of Buddhism and the emergence of distinctively Hindu metaphysical systems reflect precisely these dynamics. What we see in the long period between the Buddha himself and the full flowering of Vedanta is first a reassertion of the reality of the external world, then a growing emphasis on the creative—first just the creative power of the human intellect as the source of the mental constructs of ordinary experience, but eventually as the source of entire worlds—as the Buddhist Vairocana or the Hindu Brahman, both of which bring into being and nurture countless souls, souls that themselves mature to find that they, too, *are* this creative principle.

This is not a totalitarian ideology. It is, rather the product of a long evolution that began with the rejection of a world given over to oppression and injustice and that led, along diverse paths, to recognition of a principle by which the universe could be explained and human action could be judged and ordered. Vedanta and the metaphysics of *Avatamska-sutra* are not "the same" as the Western metaphysics of *Esse*, but they emerge as a result of a similar social process, play a similar role in the development of their respective civilizations, and grope towards a common principle the full comprehension of which eludes all three.

Let us now turn to Chinese metaphysics and see what an analysis of its basic tendencies can add to our argument.

CHINA

China, like India and the West, demonstrates a very specific pattern of civilizational development during the Silk Road Era. There is, first of all, an attempt to establish an empire capable of maximizing and capturing the revenues generated by the newly established Silk Road trade networks. In China, this was the empire of the Qin, who began unifying the Chinese lands in the fourth century and established China's first real empire in 221 BCE. This empire was guided, very specifically, by the doctrines of the relativistic Legalist School and, while it played a critical role in establishing long lasting institutional patterns, was known throughout the rest of the history of China for its brutality and oppression. An unsuccessful attempt was then made to reform the empire under the guidance of axial-age ideologies. It was, above all, during the Han period that the original insights of the Confucian and Taoist sages were developed into a coherent metaphysical system that provided both legitimation and accountability for the imperial system. During this period we also see the emergence of a Taoist opposition among the gentry and peasantry of the Southeast. When the effort to build a reformed empire failed, China fell prey to a long period of minor dynasties of "barbarian"—i.e., Turkic or Mongolian—origin. It is during this period that Buddhism becomes a major force in China, and when the country was finally reunited it was under dynasties—the Sui and the Tang—which show significant influence from the steppes and which build a system that is less centralized than the Han and in which the leading civilizational influence is a network of large landholding monasteries motivated by an ideology (Buddhism) that is at least nominally otherworldly. These monasteries, however, as in the West, proved themselves to be powerful engines of technological and economic progress, and ultimately laid the groundwork for the emergence of the Song system, which represents a pinnacle of political influence for the now "completed" Chinese metaphysical system—Neo Confucianism or *dao xue*. The Song system was characterized by effective hegemony by the Neo-Confucian civil service that maintained close ties to the people by means of a complex system of consultation and by repeated attempts to contain growing tendencies towards latifundialization and economic polarization. The Song experiment was cut short by the Mongol invasion. When China regained its independence, it did so under the far more authoritarian Ming dynasty during which, however, the Neo-Confucian schools continued to exert a powerful force for social reform.

There are, of course, some patterns that are specific to China. First, it is in China that we see the full development and eventually the exhaustion of the metaphysical potential of Buddhism. It was the challenge presented by Buddhism, with its doctrine of *sunyata* or emptiness, which forced the Confucians to develop an adequate metaphysics. In this sense Buddhism played a role in China comparable to that played by Christianity in the West. The difference is that while in Christianity the tendency towards a univocal metaphysics centered on a sovereign god, eventually won out over the analogical metaphysics that developed through the interaction between the prophetic religion and the dialectical tradition, in China it was the analogical metaphysics of the Neo-Confucians that eventually triumphed. The result was a unique situation in which the Chinese could continue to believe in their superiority as a global center of civilization without pursuing world conquest and could continue to develop technologically and economically while trying to make that development serve higher values.

It is impossible to consider the golden age of Chinese civilization without asking what it can tell us about the complex relationship between Chinese culture, and especially Confucian *ru xue* and the problem of modernization and capitalist development on the other hand. Was Confucianism an obstacle to industrialization and capitalist development as Weber and Chinese scholars such as Ho Ping-ti have argued? Or was China the victim of noncultural forces—the devastating effects of the Mongol invasion or a "high-end equilibrium trap" that made it more profitable to use cheap labor than to invest in labor saving machinery? Is the Confucian tradition part of what has facilitated the rapid growth in East Asian economies, both capitalist and socialist, in recent years? Or is something else at issue?

In order to answer these questions, we need to look closely at the complex interaction between metaphysics and political economy during China's long Silk Road era.

The First Empire

The Qin

It must be noted, first of all, that the early years of the Silk Road were a period of rapid technological progress for China, in a way that they were not in the West. This meant, first of all, improvements in agriculture, with the growing practice of crop rotation, and the increased production of soy, which helped restore depleted soils. We also see increased reliance on animal power, with the development of the ox-drawn plow, better methods of harnessing horses, a cart with two shafts, and the cultivation of Lucerne as fodder for horses. This is a sort of agrarian pattern that did not become widespread in Europe until the second half of the first millennium of the common era. But Qin and Han China was by no means exclusively agrarian. This was, among other things, the time when the Chinese made major improvements in the production of cast iron and developed a kind of steel technology. Indeed, there is some evidence that by the Qin or Han periods, iron and steel were, along with salt, China's most important nonagricultural economic activities (Gernet 1985: 139–40)! Trade in silk, lacquer ware, and copper remained important (Gernet 1985: 139–41).

The Qin Empire was founded on an act of conquest by a state—the Qin—that was guided from the beginning by a Legalist ideology (Gernet 1985: 103–8). The first aim of this state was to break the old aristocratic families who had dominated China during the Warring States Period and found itself on the direct support—and control—of small peasant communities. The idea was to take the dependents of the old noble families and to transform them into free soldier peasants directly dependent on the state—a goal that was to be pursued by many Chinese dynasties up through, one might argue, the Maoist era (Gernet 1985: 81). Old states and aristocratic domains were broken up and reorganized into thirty-six commanderies. A universal system of ranks was established, as well as standards for reward and punishment, promotion and demotion, based on service to the state. Everything imaginable was standardized: coins, weights and measures, characters, even the gauge of cart wheels. Old walls defining and defending historic states were torn down and a new wall built to protect a now-unified China from the steppe, while an attempt was made to link China together internally with a system of roads and canals (Gernet 1985: 103–8).

The Legalist empire had no use for knowledge that lacked an obvious practical application—or for wisdom that might challenge the authority or constrain the freedom of the Emperor. All books other than treatises on medicine, agriculture, and divination were burned in 213 BCE, and over four hundred opponents of the dynasty were executed at Xien-yang. There were, no doubt, many Confucians among them (Gernet 1985: 109).

The Legalism that guided the Qin derived from the work of Xunzi (313–238 BCE) and his student Han Fei (280–233). Xunzi had been trained in the *ru xue* but understood the first principle in a radically naturalistic way and argued that, contrary to the teachings of Confucius himself and of Mencius, human beings are fundamentally selfish in character, though they can be restrained and cultivated through education and ritual (Yao 2000: 76–80). Han Fei took these teachings much further; he adopted a nominalist theory of knowledge and an extreme naturalism in cosmology and metaphysics. The world was, for Han Fei as for the Greek atomists and Epicureans and the Indian Caravakas, essentially just the play of material forces. Human beings are motivated by greed, and the aim of politics is to satisfy that desire as much as possible by enriching the state (*fuo-kuo*). The state must be based on military might (*ch'iang-ping*), and must affect human beings by means of a system of rewards and punishments rather than relying on education and ritual to cultivate virtue. This said, the system of laws must be objective and impersonal, and there is a sense in Han Fei, unlike some of the more radical Legalists, that they reflect natural laws understood in a materialistic sense. This doctrine, not surprisingly, found favor among the emerging class of great merchants, many of whom served as key advisors to the emperor under the Qin dynasty (Gernet 1985: 79, 90–93, 204; Collins 1998: 148–55).

The Han

Qin oppression lead to resistance across a broad spectrum of social strata—peasants, scholars, and old nobility. This led ultimately to a rebellion led by Liu Pang, a minor Qin official of peasant origin who succeeded in 206 BCE in establishing the first Han Dynasty. The Early Han maintained much of the Legalist structure, including the ranking of essentially the entire population along a scale of twenty-four degrees of dignity, the system of rewards and punishments based on service, the organization of the country into centrally defined commandries and prefectures, and in general the policy of breaking down human communities into smallest possible units, moving large numbers of people to wherever they could be used most effectively. The Han further undercut the aristocracy by eliminating primogeniture so that aristocratic domains would become subdivided and impoverished, and it limited the rights of princes to the ability to tax grain in a certain territory (Gernet 1985: 110–16).

What changed was the civilizational ideal that these structures were increasingly mobilized to serve. It was under the early Han that we begin to see both the reassertion of the tradition of *ru xue*, now increasingly in synthesis with ideas from the *tao xue*, and the emergence of a more purely Taoist opposition.

The strategy on the Confucian side was simple. Even under the Qin there had been room for engaging the Emperor on the basis of materialistic arguments deriving from the five elements school and the yin-yang school, which argued that political events as well as physical and biological processes were governed by the law-like behavior of material forces. It was also possible to engage him by using ancient divination texts—texts that made reference to such core metaphysical concepts as T'ien (Heaven) and K'un (earth) and the Tao. Resurgent *ru xue* drew on these texts to set cosmology and politics—and thus imperial policy—in a broader metaphysical and thus moral context (Gernet 1985: 158). This was reflected at the religious level by the re-establishment of the core Confucian cult of Heaven (Collins 1998: 154).

An early stage in this process is reflected in the work of Tsou Yen (305–240) (Collins 1998: 153), who rationalizes divination by using the five elements theory as a cosmology and argues that the rise and fall of political power is governed by a natural succession of the five elements, in the order of earth, wood, metal, fire, and water (Gernet 1985: 158). Tung Chung-shu (179–104 BCE) (Collins 1985: 155; Yao 2000: 83, 88) made the link to *ru xue* explicit by treating the five agents as "ministers" or "sons" of Heaven, resulting in a fully moralized cosmology and sociology. Yao explains:

> Heaven is the transcendental reality and the source of human life, and humans must faithfully follow the principles of Heaven and fulfill Heaven's mandate. In this relation, Heaven is the spiritual power and the great grandfather (*zeng zufu*) of humans, and Heaven alone can reward the good and punish the bad. Not only are humans considered to be physically shaped by Heaven but their moral and political ways are similarly determined. Human qualities are endowed and animated by Heaven. Insofar as Heaven loves people they should be human (*ren*); Heaven acts regularly in the progression of the four seasons and day and night, so people should observe the principles of propriety (*li*); Heaven has authority over Earth so the Sovereign has authority over his subjects, a father over his son and a husband over his wife. Human behavior must model the operating forces of Heaven, yang and ying, Yang signifies virtue and is associated with spring, thus symbolizing the giving of life and education; yin completes yang and is thus associated with autumn, the season of destruction, and symbolizes death and punishment. To carry out the will of Heaven, a ruler must rely on education and the propagation of virtue, and not on punishments and killing. (Yao 2000: 84–85, referring to Shyrock 1966: 50–51)

The precise political impact of these ideas is hard to gauge, but we know that they were influential in the later Han period and that this was a period characterized by *both* continued centralization *and* by a growing commitment to social justice and civilizational progress. Thus the great reformer Wang Ming (9–23), founder of the short-lived Xin Dynasty, systematically nationalized estates and slaves and attempted to reorganize agriculture on the basis of the Chou-li (Gernet 1985: 149–51).

Unfortunately, the redistribution of land promised by Wang Ming was not carried out. The result was the emergence of strong anti-centralist tendencies. These were to some extent reflected in the policies of the restored Han Dynasty after 23 CE, which based itself on the large landowning families of Honan and allowed the emergence of an agrarian structure characterized by growing inequality. This substructure integrated various degrees of dependency and tenancy with a tributary overlay in which the state extracted taxes and corvée labor. This agrarian economy in turn supported an increasingly specialized craft and mercantile sector centered on the production of salt, iron, silk, and local specialties such as lacquer ware, controlled by a mixture of private merchants and state monopolies (Gernet 151–57).

The failure of the centralizing reform strategies of the Confucians in turn created room for a more radical opposition inspired by ideas now generally regarded as Taoist, though the term is probably a bit anachronistic. Especially characteristic in this regard are the ideas reflected in the *Huainanzi*, which eventually inspired a rebellion led by the prince of Huainan in 122, which was put down, interestingly enough, by a disciple of Tung Chung-shu. (Collins 1998: 157)

It is in this period when the principal metaphysical difference between *ru xue* and *tao xue* begins to emerge. Confucians generally opt for a positive understanding of the first principle, though they may understand this principle in more idealistic or more materialistic terms. Taoists on the on other hand, focus on the concept of *wu wei* or nonbeing, as a way of capturing the ineffability of the first principle and thus the impossibility of deriving definite moral principles and political norms from it.

> Vacuity gave rise to Tao, which gave rise to space and time, which in turn gave rise to material force, and then to the manifestations of the material universe. There was a time before yin and yang, Heaven and Earth, and even before non-being ... (Collins 1998: 157)

This does not mean that the Huainan group was without a social platform. On the contrary, they reflect a distinct approach to social justice centered on allowing things to follow their natural path of development, as against the centralizing reformism of the Han Confucians.

> The basic task of government is to make the populace secure. The security of the populace is based on meeting needs. The basis of meeting needs is in not depriving people of their time. The basis of not depriving people of their time is in minimizing government exactions and expenditures. The basis of minimizing government exactions and expenditures is moderation of desire. The basis of moderating desire is in returning to essential nature. (Masters of Huainan in Cleary 1990: 3–4)

Taoists did not reject the use of armed struggle to restore human society to harmony with the Tao.

> When greedy and gluttonous people plundered the world, the people were in turmoil and could not be secure in their homes. There were sages who rose up, struck down the forceful and violent, settled the chaos of the age, leveled the unevenness, removed the pollution, clarified the turbulence, and secured the imperiled. Therefore humanity was able to survive. (Masters of Huainan in Cleary 1990: 49)

What the Taoists rejected was warfare for the sake of conquest.

> The martial Lord of Wei asked one of his ministers what made a nation perish. The minister replied, "Numerous victories in numerous wars."
>
> The lord said "A nation is fortunate to win numerous victories in numerous wars—why should it perish thereby?"
>
> The minister said, "When there are repeated wars, the people are weakened, when they score repeated victories, rulers become haughty. Let haughty rulers command weakened people and rare is the nation that will not perish as a result." (Masters of Huainan in Cleary 1990: 12)

Wars of liberation, however, were sometimes necessary.

> The military operations of effective leaders are considered philosophically, planned strategically, and supported justly. They are not intended to destroy what exists but to preserve what is perishing. Therefore when they hear that a neighboring nation oppresses its people, they raise armies and go the border, accusing that nation of injustice and excess.
>
> When the armies reach the suburbs, the commanders say to their troops "do not cut down trees, do not disturb graveyards, do not burn crops or destroy stores, do not take common people captive, and do not steal domestic animals."
>
> Then the announcement is made. "The ruler of such and such a country shows contempt for heaven and the spirits, imprisoning and executing the innocent. This is a criminal before heaven, an enemy to the people."
>
> The coming of the armies is to oust the unjust and restore the virtuous. Those who lead plunderers of the people, in defiance of nature, die themselves . . .
>
> The conquering of the nation does not extend to its people . . .

> The peasants await such armies with open doors, preparing food to supply them, only worried that they won't come. (Masters of Huainan 1990: 50)

The Taoist masters argued for an organization of society based on relational power.

> ...those with common interests will die together; those with common feelings will strive together; those with common aversions will help each other. If you move in accord with the Way, the world will respond to you; think of the interests of the people and the world will fight for you. (Masters of Huainan in Cleary 1990: 52)

The Taoist strategy was defeated, for the time being, by the victorious Han, but in the long run it had two effects. First, it paved the way for the Chinese reception of Buddhism, which radicalized the emphasis on nonbeing or emptiness and, even when it enjoyed imperial sponsorship, tended to favor development of a decentralized, monastery-based social structure. Second, as China's economic center of gravity shifted from the north and west, with its wheat-based agriculture, to the south and east with its wet rice cultivation, which required a higher level of investment in the land and thus tended to foster a stronger sense of ownership, this decentralizing impulse would begin to assert influence even in the Confucian camp, leading to resistance to centralizing reforms under the Song Dynasty. Perhaps a premonition of this is to be seen in the Old Text School of Confucianism, which rejected the metaphysical and cosmological speculations of the Tung Chung-shu group and his New Text school in favor of careful scholarship based on ancient texts—and which, interestingly enough, had affinities with the opposition to the Han (Collins 1998: 157–58; Yao 2000: 88–89).

The Wei, Jin, Southern and Northern Dynasties (220–581 CE)

The collapse of the Han dynasty was followed by a period of disunity. In the north, we witness at one and the same time the emergence of a series of dynasties of nomadic origin and the large-scale settlement and sinicization of the nomadic peoples of the northwest. At a deeper level, however, the political economy established by the Qin and Han continued. A centralized state continued to play a leading role in organizing the economy, redistributing not only resources but population, organizing large-scale public works, etc. Pressure from as yet unassimilated nomadic groups, coupled by the desire to control trade routes, resulted in continued military expansionism. In the south, this was also a period of the assimilation of neighboring peoples, but the Thai, the various Tibeto-Burman groups, the Miao, the Yao, the Mon, and the Khmer were militarily much weaker than the nomads of the northwest and found their lands seized and their populations either decimated or pushed further south. Relatively thin population, primitive agriculture, and the failure to develop anything like a specialized craft economy, led to the development of a closed landed aristocracy of Han settlers that effectively resisted attempts at centralization. Szechwan and the southwest showed elements of both patterns (Gernet 1985: 174–75).

At the philosophical level, this period was characterized by growing influence on the part of the *tao-te jia* and retrenchment and re-examination within the Confucian trend. A note is in order her regarding terminology. Some argue that the philosophical debates of the *ch'ing t'an* (Pure Conversation) and *xuan xue* (Dark or Mysterious Learning) schools have nothing to do with the popular Taoism that spread like wildfire in south China during this period, and which continues to exert influence to this day. Collins (Collins 1998: 166), on the other hand, points out the existence of a broad common ground, or at least common interests and patterns, the most important of which was opposition to the official Confucian cult, associated with northern imperial authorities, and a focus on longevity through gymnastics, medicines, metals, alchemy, etc. Even if "philosophical" and "religious" Taoism had different points of origin—the first in the teachings of axial-age sages and cosmologists, and the second in the indigenous religious traditions of the South—there was an authentic syncretism that resulted in the formation of a coherent cultural tradition.

The Pure Conversation School is of little interest from the standpoint of our argument. It developed out of the Old Text School, but without the foil of the Han cult became essentially a group of aesthetically sophisticated hedonists (Collins 1998: 170–71). The Mysterious Learning, on the other hand, became the focus of metaphysical speculations, which essentially drove the future development of Chinese philosophy. The school was founded by Wei state officials, Ho Yun (d. 249) and Wang Pi (226–49). They took as their starting point the synthesis of yin-yang and five elements cosmology with Taoist ontology that had been formulated, for the Confucian side, by Tung Chung-shu (Collins

1998: 171), but focused attention on the relationship between *wu* and *you*, nonbeing and being, emphasizing, for the most part, the priority of *wu* over *you* and developing much of the philosophical vocabulary in terms of which later debates were conducted, including the distinctions between substance (*ti*) and function (*yong*), one (*yi*) and many (*duo*), nature (*xing*) and emotion (*qing*), principle (*li*) and material force (*qi*) (Gernet 1985: 206; Yao: 2000: 89–90).

The extent of the Taoist hegemony is apparent from the tenor of debates within the Confucian trend. These debates focused first and foremost on the relationship between moral codes (*mingjiao*) and human tendencies (*ziran*). There were, broadly speaking, three positions. The first tendency, which included thinkers such as He Yan, Wang Bi, and Guo Xiang, held that "moral codes come from nature" (*mingjiao chuyu ziran*) and that "any moral codes that do not fit human nature must be abandoned. " (Yao 2000: 94) The second trend, associated with Ruan Ji and Ji Kuang, argued that "since moral codes come from nature, then it is natural for us to go beyond these codes to follow our own nature" (*yue mingjiao er en reran*). The third tendency, associated with Xiang Xiu and Guo Xiang, emerged as a defense of the classic Confucian position and held that it was necessary to counteract the emphasis being placed on *wu* or nonbeing and to recognize that "moral codes and social institutions are themselves natural" (*mingjiao hi ziran*). One member of this group, Pei Wei (267–300) wrote a critically important treatise, the *chong you lun* or *Justification of Being*, which "argues that nature (*ziran*) is what is so (*ran*) by itself (*zi*) and that Nature is in "being" rather than nonbeing because nonbeing cannot create by itself (Yao 2000: 93–95).

This was also the period during which Buddhism penetrated Chinese culture, carried first and foremost by merchants who came first by land and then by sea, and later by pilgrims, who journeyed to India seeking manuscripts and studying at the great Buddhist centers such as Nalanda before returning home to undertake the work of translation and acculturation. In the North Buddhism was largely dependent on state sponsorship. Non-Han kings such as Shi Hu (334–349) invited Buddhist monks to court and eventually began endowing large monasteries. In the South, on the other hand, support came from the landed aristocracy who also began to endow monasteries that modeled themselves on large aristocratic estates (Gernet 1985: 220–21).

Chinese Buddhism built on and radicalized the Taoist emphasis on *wu* or nonbeing, which was seen as a way of translating the Sanskrit *sunyata* and regarded meditation (*dhyana*) as an extension of Taoist techniques for inducing trance. *Karma* was understood in terms of traditional concepts of individual destiny (*ming*) and parallels were even sought between Buddhist and Confucian morality (Gernet 1985: 215).

Sui and Tang Dynasties

It was not, however, until China was reunited under the Sui and Tang Dynasties that Chinese Buddhism really came into its own. These dynasties, like others before them, continued to exert an element of centralized control over the economy. A system of life plots (*kuo fen t'ien*) was established, with land allocated based on the number of adult men in a family. This system was applied to land used for cultivating grain. *Yung-yeh* land used for growing hemp, mulberries, and other fiber crops remained private property. And was subject to three forms of taxation: *tsu* (a tax on cereals), *yung* (corvée), and *tiao* (a tax on cloth), including silk (*chuan*) and hemp (*pu*) (Gernet 1985: 245–47). These taxes were used to support large scale public works, including the construction of a vast system of canals linking the Huang He, Wei, and Yangtze rivers (Gernet 1985: 239–42) and a public administration staffed by learned officials, who were later to become dominant in the Sung. The Tang developed a systematic legal code with penalties depending on one's relation to the victim and the relative position of the criminal and victim in the social hierarchy as well as the seriousness of the offense, (Gernet 1985: 242–45). All this reflects the persistence—indeed the further development under the Sui and Tang—of the state driven model focused on maintaining social justice which had emerged under the Han and which would become dominant under the Song.

There was, however, another aspect to the Tang social structure: an aristocratic military class intensely focused on horsemanship, reflecting the influence of and response to the steppes. Warriors were expected to provide own horses (Gernet 1985: 247–52), which encouraged the development of large landed estates (*chuang-yuan*). Under the Sui and Tang the owners of these estates retained more influence than the scholar elite. It was also these landed estates that shaped the development of Sui and Tang Buddhism. Both the Emperor (and Empress) and the landed elites made substantial donations of land to the monasteries, so that by the time Buddhism was finally repressed in 842–845 the monasteries may well have controlled up to 25 percent of the land in China (Gernet 1985: 263, Collins 1998: 277–79)! In some parts of the country, the local population was even enslaved and bound to provide grain for the monasteries, which were used, as in Europe, to clear frontier lands and place them under cultivation. Monasteries were exempt from taxation. However they obtained it, many monasteries had far more grain than they needed and began to loan it at interest, establishing what they called "Inexhaustible Treasuries"—i.e., banks. They also invested heavily in crafts production and trade, becoming among the most important economic players in the Silk Road system. Ching-tu monastery in Tun-huang got half of its income from loans, another third from temple lands and rents on oil presses, investment in water mills, caravans, etc. The monasteries thus played a central role in promoting the development of petty commodity relations in the countryside and tended to draw the marketized peasants under their sway through the medium of pure land cults which promised rebirth in a "pure land" where enlightenment would be easier to achieve, simply through faith in Amitabha Buddha.

It was in this context that an increasingly sophisticated and distinctively Chinese Buddhism emerged. Paul Williams points out that the foundational development in this regard was the transformation of the concept of the *tathagatagarbha*, which in Indian and Tibetan Buddhism had been a soteriological idea, into the basis of a cosmological and metaphysical theory (Williams 1989: 109). The key text in this regard is the *Ta-cheng ch'I-hsin lun*, the *Awakening of Faith in the Mahayana*.

> "The principle is the mind of the sentient being. This mind includes in itself all states of being of the phenomenal and transcendental world." According to the commentator Fa-tsang (643–712) this One Mind is the *tathagatagarbha* (p.32). The *Awakening of Faith* itself takes the *tathagatagarbha* as the substratum of *samsara* and *nirvana* (pp 77–8). The Mind has two aspects—the Mind as Suchness or Thusness, that is, the Absolute Reality itself, and the Mind as phenomena. . . . Differentiation . . . arises through illusion, fundamental ignorance of one's true nature. (Williams 1989: 109–10)

What this did, of course, was to substantially undercut the centrality of the doctrine of *sunyata* or emptiness, which became an understanding of the *way* in which things exist rather than a claim that all things lack inherent existence and a redefinition of the Chinese ideal of the sage, or rather a new understanding of what it meant to be a sage: i.e., to understand that phenomena are empty and dependent and that it is only on the basis of this knowledge that they can be cultivated or "ripened."

There were many variants of this philosophically sophisticated monastic Buddhism. The two most important, however, were the Tien Tai, which enjoyed the patronage of the Sui and the Hua-yen, which enjoyed the patronage of the Tang (Collins 1998: 285). The two schools are quite close, with the latter simply building on and drawing out more explicitly the metaphysical implications of what is essentially a common position.

The Tien Tai school, so called for its mountain home, argued for the centrality of the *Saddharmapundarkia* (Lotus) Sutra as the most complete revelation of *dharma*. Using the technique of *p'an chiao*, in which the teachings of various Buddhist schools were ranked in terms of their relative completeness, with the lower ranked schools treated as skillful means (*upayakausalya*), teachings directed at the less developed. The Tien Tai school essentially argued away centuries of Buddhist semi-nihilism as a way of helping the less developed get past their attachment to phenomena in order to prepare them for a future as advanced Bodhisattvas or fully developed Buddhas engaged in the work of "ripening being." They taught a complex cosmology of ten worlds, including numerous heavens and hells, as well as the persistence of Buddhas as agents for the cultivation of enlightenment, distinguishing between the eternal, cosmic Buddha and his various manifestations.

The Hua-yen (Collins 1998: 286) carried this process even further. There have, historically, been two different interpretations of Hua-yen metaphysics among Western scholars. Francis Cook (Cook 1977) reads Hua-yen as an elaboration of the Madhyamika doctrine of *sunyata*; Paul Williams (Williams 1989) reads it in the light of the doctrine of the *tathagatagarbha* and the One mind.

Cook's reading focuses on the doctrine of interpenetration, according to which, because of the mutual dependence of everything in the universe on everything else, each phenomenon actually contains all others. The universe is understood as the "jewel net of Indra," Vairocana, the eternal or cosmic Buddha, is just a symbol of this interdependent network.

> If each part does not wholly cause the whole to be made and only exerts partial power, then each condition would only have partial power. They would consist only of many individual partial powers and would not make one whole, which is annihilationism ... Also, if the part does not wholly create the whole, then when one part is removed, the whole should remain. However, since the whole is not formed, then you should understand that the whole is not formed by the partial power of a condition but by its total power. (Fa-tsang, *Hua-yen I ch'eng chiao I fen-ch'I chang* 508c in Cook 1977: 12)

> Everything, from an atom to the universe itself, functions as the cause for everything else. In Buddhist terminology, this is the emptiness of things, and if there were anything which is not empty, which is to say anything that is not causal in this manner, then that is really a nonentity. Emptiness does not at all rob existence of its vitality and color, rather the full, round, solid form of the object and its vigorous life of activity are in reality precisely its emptiness. Its concreteness, discreteness, and true individuality are indeed realities of the most vivid kind, and it is the manner in which the object exists that is an issue, not these qualities. (Cook 1977: 73)

Williams, on the other hand, focuses on the distinction between *li* and *shih*, noumenon and phenomenon in Fa-tsang's *Chin-shih-tzu chang*, (*Treatise on the Golden Lion*). In this treatise, Fa-tsang argues that while a statue of a lion made of gold *appears* to be a lion, it is actually made of gold. He also notes Tsung-mi's rejection, in the *Yuan jen lun*, of Madhyamika teachings that refuted the phenomenal appears of things as representing a lower stage in the hierarchy of Buddhist teachings (Williams 1989: 130–34).

> The Teaching of the One Vehicle that Reveals the Nature holds that all sentient beings without exception have the intrinsically enlightened, true mind. From time without beginning it is permanently abiding and immaculate. It is shining, unobscured, clear and bright ever present awareness. It is called the Buddha nature and the *tathagatagarbha*. (Tsung-mi. *Yuan jen lun* 710a11, in Gregory 1995)

The answer to this dispute is, I would like to suggest, rather more complex than either party recognizes. Tsung-mi's intention, at least, is to reject both Madhyamika and Yogacara formulations in favor of something new and distinct. This is apparent from the way in which he hierarchizes the various revelations of *dharma*. His chapter on "Deluded Attachments" criticizes Taoism and Confucianism. The "Teaching of the humans and the gods" explains a very rudimentary and broadly defined Puranic Hinduism. The "Lesser Vehicle" explains the most basic teachings of the Buddha in order to initiate the process of detachment. The "Teaching of the phenomenal appearances" refers to Yogacara Buddhism and the "Teaching which refutes the phenomenal appearances" to Madhyamika Buddhism, from which his own Hua-yen "Teaching of the One Vehicle that Reveals the Nature" is to be understood as distinct. The question is whether or not he delivers on this promise. His own explanation of the "Teaching of the One Vehicle" sounds suspiciously like Yogacara doctrine developed in the direction of an absolute idealism. My own inclination is to believe that he was looking for something new but found himself constrained by Buddhist doctrine, which allowed nothing besides interdependent phenomena and the mind that either understands their real nature or fails to and thus falls into illusion.

What is most interesting about Hua-yen metaphysics generally and Tung-mi's formulation in particular is that it shows both the power and the limitations of Buddhist metaphysics. It would be a very long time before Western philosophy clearly grasped the radical interdependence of phenomenal being. We see elements of such an insight in Spinoza and it is central to Hegel's *Logic*, but it becomes widespread only in the light of developments in quantum physics that undercut the older forms of atomism. In this sense Hua-yen must be credited with drawing out fully a critical insight into the nature of Being—that all *contingent* being is empty in the sense of being just a complex network of interrelationships. At the same time, a pure metaphysics of interdependence is unable to explain why there is anything at all—i.e., why there is a network of interdependent causes in the first place. It was, undoubtedly, the cosmological focus of their tradition that forced Chinese Buddhists to address this problem and to opt for the idea of One Mind as the necessary source of phenomena. This, however, created yet another problem: why is the pure, unsullied awareness of the One Mind disrupted by illusion, giving rise to phenomena? This question remains unanswered—indeed it remains unasked.

The early part of the Tang period would be the last time Buddhism was hegemonic in China. Gradually the deeper dynamic of Chinese civilization, which was centered on the reforming activity of a centralizing state informed by a largely Confucian scholar-gentry, reasserted itself.

This Confucian resurgence was, no doubt, ultimately related to deeper contradictions in the Tang system. The growth of rice cultivation and the concentration of wealth in great estates lead to a shift from taxation of persons to a taxation of land, further increasing the burden on the poorest classes (Gernet 1985: 262–66). The economy was further undermined by the closure of the roads of Central Asia as a result of Islamic expansion, especially after the defeat by the Arabs at Talas in 751 (Gernet 1985: 261–62). The emergence of a regional command structure undermined the control of the central government over an already decentralized and aristocratic military (Gernet 1985: 262–72).

The result of these setbacks was a radical rejection of all things foreign, and thus an attack on Buddhism as well as other foreign religions, such as Nestorian Christianity and Manichaeism. In 842–845, 260,000 monks and nuns were forcibly returned to lay life. 150,000 of their former dependent peasants and servants were added to the census lists (and thus to the tax rolls). Fully 460 monasteries and 40,000 small places of worship were destroyed or converted to other uses. Nearly all of the vast lands of the monasteries were seized. And Buddhism fared better than other "foreign" religions. Mazdism, Manicheanism, and Nestorianism were completely proscribed (Gernet 1985: 295).

This does not, to be sure, mean that Buddhism disappeared completely from China. Rather, it changed, essentially abandoning sophisticated metaphysical speculation or at least displacing such speculation from the center of the path towards liberation. What was left was, at the elite level, the Ch'an tradition that had emerged out of the Hua-yen and upheld much of its metaphysics, but focused on the pursuit of sudden enlightenment (or rather on uncovering the latent enlightenment already present in all beings, through meditation on subtle paradoxes) and, at the popular level, various Pure Land sects that promised salvation largely on the basis of faith and that appealed primarily to the merchant population and to some marketized peasants. The intellectual center of gravity had shifted back to the Confucian camp (Collins 1998: 290).

The Song Dynasty and Dao Xue (Neoconfucianism)

It is in the following period that we witness the full flowering of Chinese metaphysics. The new empire that grew up as China recovered from the crisis of the Tang system was radically different from its predecessors.

Where the Tang Empire had been a relatively decentralized agrarian and aristocratic structure in which most of the progressive potential was lodged in the great monasteries, the Song Empire was commercial, democratic, and centralized—and effectively controlled by its Confucian intelligentsia.

This new system was made possible by a number of key technological developments. It is during this period that we witness the rapid expansion of wet rice cultivation throughout the south, making what had once been a hinterland the economic center of China, as well as the spread of such commercial crops as silk, hemp, cotton, and tea, (Gernet 1985: 319–20). We also see a massive development of complex handicrafts, including the emergence of large workshops in essentially all of the traditional areas of craft production (Gernet 1985: 320–22).

The underlying tendency towards latifundialization and towards the erosion of patriarchal relationships and their replacement by purely commercial forms of tenancy, which naturally accompanied the development of petty commodity relations, continued. We know that this was the case because only peasants, not large landowners, were taxed and only 30% of a total of 24 hectares of arable land was taxable in 1064–1067 (Gernet 1985: 312–16).

There were a number of attempts to reform this system, the most important of which were the reforms of Wang An-shih (1069–1076), who proposed taxing landlords, imposing price controls, extending low cost credit to small farmers, and reforming the system of exams to include engineering and science instead of just the literary classics (Gernet 1985: 305–9; Collins 1998: 301–2). Somewhat later Chia Ssu-tao (1213–1275) tried to limit land ownership to 500 mu (about 27 hectares) and have the state buy a third of the surplus to support the armies (Gernet 1985: 315).

The Song political structure represented a substantial rationalization and democratization of the imperial system. The Emperor presided over, ratified, and if necessary resolved differences in the Council of State but did not have and did not claim autocratic power. Policy was developed by the *xue-shih-yuan* or Court of Academicians who drew up documents based on consultation with broad ranks of the civil service and, through them, with the people. Appointment to and promotion within the civil service was based, at least nominally, on scholarship, though political considerations certainly also played a significant role (Gernet 1985: 303–5).

It was in this context that the Neo-Confucian synthesis, or what contemporaries called *dao xue* finally emerged (Collins 1998: 299ff., Yao 2000: 98ff.). *Dao xue* was, in effect, an elaboration of the earlier synthesis between Confucian ethics and Taoist metaphysics that had first emerged during the Han era modified by the debates of the Wei, Jin, northern, and southern dynasties and above all by the struggle with Buddhism. The foundational text was, in this regard, Zhou Dunyi's (1017–1073) *T'ai-chi t'u shuo* or *Explanation of the Diagram of the Great Ultimate* (Yao 2000: 98–101). Given the centrality of this text, it is worth quoting from it extensively.

> The ultimate of nonbeing and also the Great ultimate. The Great ultimate through movement generates yang. When its activity reaches its limit, it becomes tranquil. Through tranquility the Great Ultimate generates yin. When tranquility reaches its limit, activity begins again....
>
> By the transformation of yang and its union with yin, the Five Agents of Water, Fire, Wood, Metal, and Earth arise. When these five material forces are distributed in harmonious order, the four seasons run their course.
>
> The five agents constitute one system of yin and yang and yin and yang constitute one Great Ultimate. The Great Ultimate is fundamentally the non-ultimate ...
>
> When the reality of the ultimate of nonbeing and the essence of yin, yang, and the five agents come into mysterious union, integration ensues. *T'ien* (Heaven) constitutes the male element and *K'un* (Earth) constitutes the female element. The interaction of these two material forces engenders and transforms the myriad things. The myriad things produce and reproduce, resulting in an unending transformation.
>
> It is humanity alone which receives the five agents in their highest excellence, and therefore is the most intelligent. The five moral principles of human nature (humanity, righteousness, propriety, wisdom and faithfulness) are aroused by and react to the external world and engage in activity, good and evil and distinguished, and human affairs take place.
>
> The sage settles these affairs by the principles of the mean.... Thus he establishes himself as the ultimate standard for humanity. Hence the character of the sage is identical with that of Heaven and Earth; his brilliance is identical with that of the sun and moon; his order is identical with that of the four seasons, and his good and evil fortunes are identical with those of spiritual beings. The

superior human cultivates these moral qualities and enjoys good fortune, whereas the inferior man violates them and suffers evil fortune.

Therefore it is said that the yin and the yang are established as the way of Heaven, the weak and the strong as the way of Earth and humanity and righteousness as the way of man. It is also said that if we investigate the cycle of things we shall understand the concepts of life and death. (Zhou Dunyi *T'ai-chi t'u shuo* 1, in Fieser and Powers 1998: 170ff.)

This text is, clearly, extraordinarily condensed and obscure. There are, furthermore, debates over the original form of the text. The version quoted above begins, in the Chinese, "*Wuji ehr taiji,*" but another version of the text beings "*Tzu wuji ehr taiji.*" The difference is significant. The longer version, which Julia Ching, among others, argues (Ching 2000: 22, 235–41) is original, gives more play to *wuji* as the source of *taiji* and thus emphasizes nonbeing over being.

It was, however, the ambiguity of this text that made it so fruitful as a *locus* for metaphysical speculation. On the one hand, it outlines a metaphysics, cosmology, and ethics in which a transcendent first principle gives rise to a hierarchy of cosmic forces, which in turn give rise to the physical, biological, and social universe. Human beings represent the pinnacle of what amounts to a cosmohistorical evolutionary process, and the sage, who understands and follows the laws that govern this process represents the most evolved form of humanity, and is thus the standard by which all others should be judged.

This said, fundamental ambiguities remain. Of these, two were most important. The first was epistemological and concerned the relative role of investigation and meditation in the search for wisdom. Do we know the *taiji* by means of a kind of rational dialectic that begins with the "investigation of things" and concludes to a transcendental first principle? Or do we know that first principle through a kind of intellectual intuition achieved through meditation? While most of the practitioners of *dao xue* engaged in both scientific investigation and meditation in a broadly Ch'an tradition, the tradition diverged sharply around this question.

Second, what is the relationship between *wuji* and *taiji* and what is the nature of the *taiji* itself. The first question defines one's position in the broad Chinese intellectual spectrum that extends from Buddhism on the one side through Taoism to the more rationalistic and materialist variants of Confucianism. The second divided Confucians between those who emphasized *li* or principle, those who emphasized *xin* or mind/heart, and those who emphasized *qi* or material force.

Within this context a wide range of different positions emerged. Shao Yong (1011–1077), for example, identified the *taiji* with *xin* and thus emphasized meditation or intellectual intuition in the understanding, but opted in *Huangju Jing shi* or *Cosmic Chronology of the Great Ultimate* for an essentially mathematical or numerological understanding of the Great Ultimate. By reflecting on ourselves we can discern the basic structure of the universe, through a kind of mathematical intuition. The Great Ultimate gives birth to yin and yang, which in turn give birth to the four emblems (the heavenly bodies, the earthly substances, the sense organs, and the periods of human history—the ages respectively of the Three Sovereigns, the Five Emperors, the Three Dynasties, and the Five Despots). He argued that if the mathematical structure of the Great Ultimate can be decoded, it is possible to predict the course of events (Yao 2000: 100–101).

At the other end of the spectrum we find thinkers such as Zhang Zai (1020–1077), who advanced a materialistic version of *dao xue*. For Zhang, the supreme ultimate is *qi* or material force. The universe came into being when the Great Void contracted. The light part became yang, and the heavy yin. All things are the result of the interaction between these two types of material force and all things ultimately dissolve into them. Human beings are a combination of the two forces. The more yang one has, the better one is. Zhang cautioned against seeking physical immortality, which is quite impossible in this cosmology and argues that it is better simply to cede to the will of heaven (Yao 2000: 101–3).

Ultimately, however, speculation became focused on an intense two-line struggle, the terms of which were defined, ironically, by two brothers whose work was initially regarded as constituting a single school, the *luo xue*. What the Cheng brothers shared in common was a focus on the complex interaction between *tian li* or heavenly principle and *ren yu* or human desires. The task of human beings was to reduce or extinguish their human desires in order to preserve and realize heavenly principle, a position that reflects enduring Buddhist influence. Cheng Yi (1033–1107) emphasized the importance of principle and logic and laid the groundwork for the development of Zhu Xi's *li xue*; Cheng Hao (1032–1085) emphasized humaneness, and extended *xin* to include heaven, laying the groundwork for the *xin xue* of Lu Jiuyuan and Wang Shouren (Yao 2000: 103–4).

Zhu Xi's (1130–1200) synthesis was simple but profound. Human beings acquire knowledge of first principles by investigation of the world around them. What this realizes is a complex interaction of *li* or principle and *qi* or material force. *Li* orders things to their proper ends; *qi* makes the manifestation of things possible and confers form, but also distorts or limits the way in which *li* is expressed.

Many thinkers have seen the relationship between *li* and *qi* in the thought of Zhu Xi as rather like that of *morphe* and *hyle* in the Aristotelian tradition, and the comparison is not without merit. *Qi*, however, carries rather more internal dynamism that the Aristotelian *hyle*, which is a pure potential for receiving form. *Qi* may even be regarded as containing the seeds of form. In this sense it is closer to the way matter was understood by ibn Rusd and the Latin Averroists; *Li*, on the other hand, is above form. In terms of its origin, this idea probably reflects the influence of Buddhism and Taoism, the first of which tended towards a purely negative definition of the first principle and the second of which allowed that there was such a principle but was always skeptical about defining it. In terms of its function in Zhu Xi's system, however, *li* plays a role rather more like the Platonic Good or the Aristotelian unmoved mover, as the end sought by all things, something that is reflected in his tendency to actually identify it with the *taiji* and with *tian* (Ching 2000: 27–29, 44). Ultimately the best way to understand Zhu Xi's position is this: the material universe is the drive of *qi* towards *li*. *Li* itself is one and indivisible, and identical with *tian*, but the myriad things embody it as they strive for and evolve towards it.

This interaction between *li* and *qi* within the universe is reflected in the tension between *dao xin* and *ren xin*, between the mind of the way of Heaven and our natural human mind, which has a limited grasp of the *dao* and thus narrow and selfish desires. Moral cultivation is a result of study (*xue*) but also of ritual, which forms human nature in conformity with heavenly principle.

Lined up in opposition to Zhu Xi was the *xin xue* associated with Lu Jiuyuan (1139–1193) and Wang Shouren (1472–1528). Where Zhu had emphasized investigation, this school focused on meditation on humanity's moral nature (Yao 2000: 105–15). Where Zhu said *xing ji li* (human nature is principle) this school said *xin ji li* (mind/heart is principle). *Xin* functions in this system as a monistic universal principle, the source of all things, in such a way that *li* and *qi* cannot really be differentiated. The *xin xue* school sharply attacked Zhu's emphasis on exegetical study and natural science as elitist, and argued that because everyone has *xin*, indeed *is xin*, that everyone can become a sage.

What was the political valence of these debates? This is a difficult question. There can be no doubt that *dao xue* generally was at once a product of, and played a critical role in shaping, the Song system. It is the ideology of a lay (nonmonastic, not primarily ritualist) intelligentsia deeply bound up with organizing and directing human affairs, and with rationalizing the imperial system and redirecting it towards human development and civilizational progress. We also know that many of the practitioners of *dao xue* sharply opposed the reforms of Wang An-shih, and were demoted and had their teachings banned as a result of this. Collins interprets this as a defense of the economic interests of the southern gentry, but this seems unlikely, given the historic Confucian emphasis on social justice. Rather, we know that they advocated instead a return to the archaic land tenure patterns codified in the Chou-li, under which land was divided into nine equal plots, eight private and one public, so that the peasants in effect contributed only one ninth of their total product to support political and religious functions. Their position should, therefore, not be regarded as a rejection of reform and a defense of gentry interests, but rather as a different strategy for reform, one which would have strengthened the links between local scholars and peasants, while limiting the level of surplus extraction, rather than creating a centralized state based on the direct taxation of small peasants and a somewhat reduced (and thus less independent) landlord class. The practitioners of *dao xue* also stressed the importance of ritual and moral reform against Wang An-shih, who had reduced the role of these disciplines in favor of practical training (Collins 1998: 302, 312–16).

Crisis and Decline

The crisis of this whole wave of civilizational development—of centralizing empires taxing the Silk Road trade and significantly rationalized by salvation religions and metaphysical systems originating in the Axial Age—came as a result of a long series of invasions. In Christian Europe these invasions were partly constitutive of the civilization in question, and expressed their full impact only gradually, with the formation of modern sovereign states as a result of the Norman Conquests (which completed the Germanic migrations), the Crusades, and the Reconquista. In India the invasions were carried out by the relatively mild Turks as opposed to the more ruthless Mongols and allowed traditional Indian civilization to largely persist under Islamic rule. But the two most advanced regions of the planet—*Dar-al-Islam* and China—felt the full force of the Mongol invasion and as a result found their global leadership significantly compromised to say the least. And when the underlying civilizational traditions eventually recovered—under Turkish rule in the Islamic world and under the native Ming Dynasty in China—what was restored was a formalized version of that tradition that had largely lost touch with its creative sources and that was not really prepared for the confrontation with European modernity.

While perhaps less destructive in China than in the Islamic world, the Mongols systematically exploited the wealth of the planet's richest and most developed country, imposing brutal new taxes and effectively preventing primitive accumulation at just precisely the time when it had become possible. They confiscated public lands, imposed summer taxes on grain and autumn taxes on cloth, and added onerous corvées to the burdens already carried by the oppressed peasantry. While trade continued to flourish, they favored Islamic merchants, who accumulated much of the wealth generated by China during this period. They also carried out systematic discrimination in the administration of the civil service examinations, reserving one fourth of the positions for Mongols, one fourth for other foreigners, and one fourth of the positions each for Chinese from the north and south of the country, in spite of the fact that most scholars came from the south (Gernet 1985: 368–72). While they continued state sponsorship for *dao xue*, and for Zhu Xi's *li xue* in particular, it lost its original meaning, becoming a form of legitimation for an oppressive regime rather than a strategy for rationalizing imperial rule.

The Ming Restoration represented, in many ways, a bold attempt at recovery. The new regime divided up the population into peasant, craft, and military families and guaranteed land for each (Gernet 1985: 392–93). An effort was made to make a transition from use of the old land routes to a sea-based trade, and Chinese treasure fleets sailed, during this period, at least as far as Malabar, Arabia, and the Swahili coast. In short, an effort was made to restore China's economic pre-eminence.

There were, however, serious difficulties with the Ming system from the very beginning. The first Ming emperor was profoundly distrustful of the literati and vested much of what had traditionally been their authority in court eunuchs. There was an active secret service and regular waves of repression directed above all at dissident literati (Gernet 1985: 393–97)

The later Ming period saw significant technological progress, including the introduction of American crops, especially peanuts, sweet potatoes, and later maize, all of which could be cultivated in less forgiving soils than rice, wheat, or soy and thus lead to rapid population growth (Frank 1998). There were significant improvements in textile and ceramic technology, making possible what amounted to mass production for international trade. Without the regulatory influence of the Confucian intelligentsia, latifundialization proceeded apace and large workshops emerged that employed craftsmen under what were, in effect, fully proletarianized conditions.

Both of the principal Confucian trends took a stand against the injustices of the Ming period. Under the circumstances it should not be surprising that the opposition *xin xue* school took the lead, with its emphasis on interiority and the underlying equality of all human beings. Wang yang-ming himself had a checkered political career, advocating decentralization of military campaigns and trying to limit the influence of the court eunuchs (Collins 1998: 314–15). Eventually, however, the *li xue* party began its own initiative and played a major role in the reforms of the Wan-li era (1573–1619) during which limits were placed on marriages by the nobility and on new patents of nobility, in order to slow the growth of unproductive claims on income. This reform movement was closely connected with Tung-lin academy at Wu-xi, which argued for a return to the tradition of Menzi with its historic focus on moral conduct and social reform, and for a rejection of philosophy of Wang yang-ming. The Tung-lin group was crushed during the repression of 1625, but briefly came back under last Ming emperor (1628–1644) under the name *fu-she*, the party of renewal (Gernet 1985: 432–34).

Ultimately, however, the authoritarian Ming system so weakened China that she fell to yet another wave of northern invaders, the Jurchen or Manchus. We will return briefly to the story of China in a later chapter, when we consider the role of traditional metaphysical systems in the resistance to European modernity.

CONCLUSION

We are now in a position to make some contribution to answering the principal questions posed in this work, at least with respect to the great age of metaphysics, the Silk Road Era or "long" Middle Ages:

1. Are humanity's great civilizational traditions locked in mortal combat with each other, founded on radically different and incommensurable civilizational ideals, or can we speak of a real dialogue, even one that progresses towards certain conclusions?

2. What was the social basis and political valence of "metaphysics," i.e., what social interests did it represent and what impact did it have on human development and civilizational progress during its great age?

Dialogue or Clash of Civilizations

With respect to the first question, it should be clear by this point that during the Silk Road Era the deepest contradictions were not between but rather within civilizations. Christendom, *Dar-al-Islam*, and China, all pursued civilizational ideals shaped by axial-age ideologies and more specifically by salvation religions at least partially rationalized by the metaphysical systems used to argue for them and to flesh out the implications of their founders' insights, and all were characterized by profound conflicts regarding the proper interpretation of that civilizational ideal. In the West, in both Christendom and *Dar-al-Islam*, the conflict was between a univocal and analogical metaphysics, the first driven by Christian, Islamic, and occasionally Jewish conceptions of God as a divine sovereign and the latter by a reflection, carried out by the dialectical tradition, on the original Jewish insight into God as Being as such, which turned out to complete the dialectical tradition's rational ascent to a first principle. In the East, in both India and China, the conflict was between the Buddhist doctrine of *pattica sammupada*, which denied any transcendental first principle, i.e., any principle independent of the flux of causality, especially as interpreted in the Madhyamika tradition as pointing to the emptiness (*sunyata*) of all things, and various Hindu, Confucian, and Taoist doctrines, which argued for such a first principle, nearly always understood in terms that in the West we would call analogical. All of these various metaphysical traditions, furthermore, including Buddhism, were arrayed against the full-blown nihilism of the Skeptics and Atomists (in the West), the Caravakas (in India), and the Legalists (in China).

Within each of these various civilizational traditions we also see a definite pattern of development. In the West, the line that leads from Socrates, Plato, and Aristotle through the Neo-Platonists, ibn Sina, ibn Rusd, and Moshe ben Maimon, up to Thomas Aquinas points towards a continuous clarification and elaboration of an analogical metaphysics of *Esse*, which in turn grounds not only a natural-law ethics that attempts to hold political authorities accountable before objective standards of justice, but also a soteriology that links wisdom and the just act in a reciprocal relationship, so that wisdom grounds natural justice and natural justice leads us into increasingly challenging situations that stretch our ability to act in a way that promotes the development of complex organization and thus our understanding of God beyond what is natural to us and towards authentic divinity. And it is above all the synthesis between dialectics and prophetic religion that at once yields the metaphysics of *Esse* as the solution to the contradictions of the Hellenic ideal while shielding the West (at least temporarily) from the full force of the univocal metaphysics implicit in the prophetic concept of a divine sovereign.

In the East, on the other hand, Buddhism challenges Brahminism and *ru xue* to develop a more subtle metaphysics capable of answering the claims made on behalf of *pattica sammupada* and *sunyata*, and then is both gradually displaced by the resulting Hindu and Confucian ideologies (especially *Vedanta* and *dao xue*) and internally transformed so that, by the time of the Tang dynasty, the originally soteriological principle of the *tathagatagarbha* has become an authentic creative ground for the universe—indeed an infinite complex of universes.

Over the course of the Silk Road Era, in other words, humanity gradually discovers a common concept of the first principle: Being, or creativity, albeit variously understood, and comes to understand its participation in this principle as embracing both the ordinary labor of civilization building and the drive to transcend mere humanity through specifically religious disciplines.

The Social Basis and Political Valence of Metaphysics During the Silk Road Era

What was the social basis of the incredible flourishing of metaphysics during the Silk Road Era? There is a tendency in the West (going back at least to Comte) to regard metaphysics as a kind of "halfway house" between religion and secularity (Collins 1998: 317). But this assumes that secularization is an inexorable process resulting from humanity's gradual mastery of the natural and social worlds. Metaphysics, according to this view, is what intellectuals do when they know that nature behaves in a lawlike manner, but have not yet unlocked the secret of those laws.

Our analysis has suggested a very different reality. Metaphysics in fact emerges out of the struggle to defend meaning against the nihilism and despair that accompanied the emergence of market relations during the Axial Era. In the Silk Road Era it continues this struggle but now on two fronts, combating both the atheistic nihilism of the Skeptics, Caravakas, and Legalists and the theistic nihilism characteristic of certain radical forms of Christianity and Islam, which regards meaning as something imposed from the outside—a reflex of the new waves of Germanic, Arabic, and later Turkic conquests.

What social interests are being defended when we defend meaning? In order to answer this we need only look at the way in which the various metaphysical systems we have analyzed understand the first principle: i.e., as creativity. Creativity is first and foremost the activity of the working classes. To the extent that creativity is identified with consciousness or reason (as in *Vedanta, xin xue*, or some forms of Neo-Platonism), the base is narrowed somewhat to the intelligentsia. But the intelligentsia is, after all, simply the most highly skilled section of the working classes, whatever privileges it may win for itself.

This said, we must acknowledge that the power exercised by intellectually motivated rational metaphysics during the Silk Road Era was due to an alliance with the military aristocracies who remained the core ruling class. What did the military aristocracies get from this exchange? They did, to be sure, benefit from the legitimation conferred by scholars who allowed them to represent themselves as sage kings, philosopher kings, and the like. But they also had to accept significant restraints on their conduct. A better clue comes from the strategy pursued by the Confucian scholars who eventually gained an element of hegemony over the Han monarchy—appealing to rulers on the basis of their knowledge of divination and practical disciplines that today we would regard as technical in nature. While sometimes the interest that scholars appealed to was quite narrow—how to win a battle or how to build better weapons—it often represented a much broader option for a strategy centered on the cultivation of human creativity, a "high road" in which the empire in question would become prosperous because it was more creative and produced more rather than simply because it had the power to tax desperately poor peasants and raid rich neighbors. The influence of metaphysics, in other words, restrained the rapacity of the neotributary empires that emerged during the Silk Road Era and redirected surplus in ways that promoted human development and civilizational progress.

This said, there were many different models of interaction. In general, after a first effort to rationalize the empires that emerged at the beginning of the Silk Road Era (Neoplatonic philosophers in the Hellenistic and Roman Empires, Ashoka in India, the Han Confucians in China) failed, the intellectual center of gravity shifted to monastic movements such as Christianity and Buddhism, which developed civilizational centers away from the major metropoles (which in the West especially, but to some extent in India and China as well, had actually declined) and in relative autonomy from the state. These monastic communities were initially radically otherworldly in their motivations, but grew into powerful economic actors capable of centralizing a vast surplus, which was invested not only in artistic, scientific, philosophical, and theological activity, but in almsgiving and economic development. Monasteries became, in Europe, India, and China, major engines of economic development, especially in frontier regions. In the process, however, they created a social context in which Christian and Buddhist otherworldliness made less and less sense, leading to both internal transformations in these ideologies and to the emergence of new or re-emergence of old innerworldly doctrines. Monocracy or bikkhuocracy was an option only in regions too poor for prosperity to extend much beyond the monastery walls—e.g., Tibet. The most important new doctrine was Islam, which was distinguished by its determination to actually vest authority in the intellectually and morally best individual and to effectively command right and forbid wrong, a determination preserved by the Sh'ia generally, and the Ismailis in particular, as well as by many Islamic Aristotelians, who argued that philosophers or religious scholars should exercise authority directly. Puranic Hinduism with its six acceptable *darshanas* and Neo-Confucianism (*dao xue*) represent the reassertion of older doctrines in radically new form. In both models intellectuals built and exercised power largely as advisors to monarchs, gaining more formal status than power in the Hindu model and more power than formal status in the Chinese. Medieval Europe and Southeast Asia represent intermediate realities in which an entire institution—the Catholic Church and the Theravadin Sangha—attempted to hegemonize and hold accountable the military aristocracy without, however, entirely displacing them.

The Crisis of Metaphysics

This process of development, which pointed towards an eventual engagement between the Thomistic metaphysics of *Esse, dao xue, Vedanta*, and something like a Hua-yen Buddhism was cut short by a series of conquests that at least temporarily displaced an only recently and partially hegemonic philosophic intelligentsia—the Mongol conquest in the East, which was followed in the Islamic world by that of the less destructive but still very martial Turks, and the Norman Conquests, the Crusades, the Reconquista, and the Conquest of Africa and the Americas in Europe, which led to the formation of sovereign states. In the West this process favored a univocal metaphysics of divine or human sovereignty; in the East it simply undercut the political authority of intelligentsia and thus led to stagnation, as philosophy became cut off from the real corridors of power. It is to this process that we must now turn.

4

Modernity and Metaphysics

INTRODUCTION

WE ARE NOW APPROACHING the crux of our argument. We began this work by proposing to investigate sociologically Heidegger's claim that metaphysics or ontotheology is somehow behind the horrors of the modern era—that the drive to rise rationally to a first principle in terms of which the universe can be explained and human action ordered is, in fact, simply the intellectual side of the drive towards total control which defines modernity. We have seen that this is not an adequate description of the rational metaphysics that emerged in the Axial Age and that dominated the long Middle Ages, the Silk Road Era, which was the great age of metaphysics. On the contrary, metaphysics emerged out of a movement of religious rationalization and democratization and was associated with a growing concern about the injustices associated with the emergence of petty commodity production. During the Silk Road Era philosophers engaged oppressive social structures in a number of ways—by withdrawing and forming monastic communities, by penetrating and trying to gain hegemony over the state. At no point, however, did they attempt anything remotely resembling a strategy of total control. Indeed, none of the principal metaphysical schools we have been analyzing would have sanctioned such a thing or even believed it to be possible. There was a growing consensus, to be sure, that human beings and indeed everything existing, precisely because it shares in Being (or in the *tathagatagarbha*, *Brahman*, or the *T'ai Chi*), was ordered to the first principle, and in that broad sense shared a common end. But this implied a respect for beings, not a warrant to organize and direct their development. Integral to what we have called an analogical metaphysics is the recognition of a first principle, which, while rationally knowable, is beyond our comprehension and thus beyond our control and of the fact that everything existing shares in that principle and is thus equally beyond our control.

During the modern era we will see something very different. As we analyze the emergence of modern civilization and look at the social basis and political valence of metaphysics during the modern era we will be able to see, quite clearly, the logic behind Heidegger's thesis. What passes for metaphysics in the modern era, both theistic and atheistic (as well as modern science, which *replaces* metaphysics as the architectonic discipline in the ideological field), does indeed serve to ground larger ideological structures that legitimate polities of total or near total control.

In analyzing this dynamic we will identify two distinct traditions or trajectories. On the one hand, the Augustinian Reaction continued, leading in the Reformation to the emergence of a full developed and internally consistent spirituality of authority and submission grounded in a univocal metaphysics. This metaphysics was, as we have seen, both a reflex and a form of legitimation for the emerging modern nation states. Parallel developments took place in those absolutist states that remained Catholic as well as outside of Christendom in *Dar-al-Islam*, India, and China. But the Augustinian Reaction, in condemning Aristotelian physics, with its focus on teleological explanation, which was seen to limit divine sovereignty, also set in motion a process that ultimately issued in the Scientific Revolution. And in the context of a univocal metaphysics in which God is simply the infinite, this opened up an exciting new possibility: transcending finitude, and thus achieving divinity, by means of scientific and technological progress. In the process, metaphysics is gradually displaced by "science," and specifically by mathematical physics, as the architectonic discipline, and philosophy is relegated to a disciplinary role, exposing as "misunderstandings" the questions that modern science cannot answer. But as we will see, there is indeed a metaphysics implicit here, univocal and centered on power, and it does indeed legitimate a strategy of total technological control.

On the other hand, the interests represented by the Averroist or Radical Aristotelian Counter-Reaction did not disappear. While *Latin* Averroism gradually died out as a leading philosophical trend, many of its concerns were translated into the Neo-Platonizing Humanism of the Renaissance. And we will show that there was, in fact, a direct line between the Jewish Aristotelianism of Moshe ben Maimon and the rationalism of

Benedict Spinoza, who conserves and advances the concerns of this trend in a new ideological context. Initially, in the early modern era, this trend tended simply to counterpoise to the Augustinian spirituality of authority and submission one of meaning and human self-cultivation without clearly defining the relationship between human self-cultivation and humanity's ultimate spiritual aims. Later, however, this trend was joined to the democratic and socialist revolutionary movements, leading to the emergence of a new ideal centered on transcending contingency (and thus achieving a kind of divinity) by means of political action, a tendency we will call *immanentism*. We see this expressed clearly in Hegel, for whom the French Revolution represents a watershed by means of which Spirit becomes fully conscious of itself and Reason is embodied in the concrete order of the State. We see it in Marx (his atheism notwithstanding), for whom communism is not only the "solution to the riddle of history" but also the "resolution of the contradiction between existence and essence" (Marx 1844/1978), and we see it in Lukacs for whom the proletariat is the "unique subject-object" of the historical process (Lukacs 1921/1971).

Far from representing an aspiration to total control, this tradition understands itself as moving humanity at long last from the realm of necessity to that of freedom. But as we will see, there are internal contradictions in the project, which make it unworkable. The kind of politics that allows humanity, through the medium of the state or the party, to become the subject of human history—much less of the whole cosmohistorical evolutionary process—turns out to be incompatible with rational autonomy.

These various strains of modernism are carried by various types of intellectuals. There is, first of all, a new clerical intelligentsia allied with the absolutist state that is the agent of the Augustinian reaction and that persists into the modern era. There are, also, however, various secular intelligentsias that emerge. There is, first of all, the scientific-technical intelligentsia, which responds to the Augustinian reaction by retreating into mathematical formalization only to emerge in the era of high modernity as a key participant in both capitalist and socialist civilization building and legitimation strategies. Second, there is a secular humanistic intelligentsia, which traces its roots back to the Radical Aristotelians and which stages what amounts to a counter-Augustinian reaction and becomes the principal carrier of ideologies of immanent divinity. Unlike the scientific-technical intelligentsia, which is content to occupy a privileged role in class coalitions led by other groups, the secular humanistic intelligentsia actually mounts a bid for power at the head of a coalition including various elements in the petty bourgeoisie, the proletariat, and the peasantry. In the process a division emerges between the humanistic intelligentsia proper and the political-organizational intelligentsia that emerges from it and that is uncomfortable, as we will see, with the claims made by the humanists for philosophy and thus for their own leadership. What attempts have been made to thematize and defend the ideal of the rational, autonomous human subject have largely been the work of humanistic intellectuals after their break with the political-organizational intellectuals leading the socialist movements, but before their final and radical disillusionment.[1]

Late modern and postmodern critiques of high modernism are, by contrast, rooted ultimately in the failure of the modern project to realize its aims. This has given rise to a number of tendencies that, however, share convergent concerns with the relationship between knowledge and power: Neo-Augustinians concerned with the impact of modernity on spirituality, dialecticians disillusioned by the authoritarianism of actually existing socialism, Romantics, vitalists, and Neo-Pagans concerned with the impact of modern technological discipline on the will to life and the will to power, and Jews working out of rabbinic and Kabalistic traditions anxious to explain modern totalitarianism generally and the Holocaust in particular. The result is a postmodern ideological field with three poles: one Neo-Augustinian and focused on a restored spirituality of authority and submission, one critical and deconstructionist and focused on exposing ideological strategies for power, and the third vitalist and focused on releasing life from the constraints of modern technological and bureaucratic discipline. In between lies an emerging postmodern center represented by John Caputo's "weak theology" and the late Derrida's "acts of religion," focused on a spirituality of difference and respect for the Other.

We will argue that all of these postmodern trends fundamentally misunderstand the problem with modernity. It is not metaphysics as such that is the problem, but *modern* metaphysics, which is either univocal and attempts divinization by means of total technological control, or endows innerworldly civilizational progress generally, and the political in particu-

---

1. I am thinking here especially of humanistic Marxists such as Lukacs, Fromm, and the Frankfort School.

lar, with a burden it cannot bear: that of elevating humanity to the status of Subject or Necessary Being.

Arguing these theses will require that we address some of the most profound and contested questions regarding the history of the modern era: Why and how did Europe, which in 1000 was a global backwater and in 1500 was still well behind China and *Dar-al Islam*, manage to become globally hegemonic? What can this process tell us about the development of capitalism and the emergence of the modern civilizational ideal? And what, precisely, is that ideal? Is capitalism really an optimum system for resource allocation, or was Marx correct in arguing that it contains irresolvable internal contradictions? Was socialism a mistake, as the neoliberals argue (Hayek 1988), was it the solution to the contradictions of capitalism as Marxists claim, or was it something else, more complex and ambiguous? And where do we stand now, after the crisis of socialism and the apparent global victory of capitalism? What is the significance of our postmodernity? Are we at the end of history? On the verge of a great clash of civilizations? Or do need other categories if we are to understand the present period.

We will begin by analyzing the origins of modernity and the basis for European global hegemony and will situate early modern metaphysics in this context. We will also consider the social basis and political valence of some nonmodern alternatives during this period, e.g., the Second Scholasticism that flourished in southern Europe, Neo-Confucian orthodoxy in China, Vedanta in India, and the theosophical tendencies that became prominent in *Dar-al-Islam*. From there we will go on to examine the two conflicting tendencies of high modernity, distinguishing between the Anglo-American and statist roads to modernization and state formation, and the resulting divergence between the anti-metaphysical tendency of most Anglo-American philosophy and the totalizing metaphysics of modern dialectics. This will be the occasion for an in-depth look at where dialectical materialism and other variants of modern dialectics stand with respect to the larger tradition. We will conclude with a look at the crisis of modernity, which we argue goes back to at least 1850, and analyze the social basis and political valence of the critique of metaphysics from Kierkegaard and Nietzsche through Heidegger, Levinas, and the postmodernists.

EARLY MODERNITY

The Origins of Modernity and the Rise of European Hegemony

The State of the Question

There are, broadly speaking, four principal theories that attempt to explain why Europe, which in 1500 was still well behind China and *Dar-al-Islam* both technologically and economically, was able to become, shortly after 1800, a global hegemon and, together with its offspring, the United States of America, to dominate the planet for over 200 years:

1. the interpretive sociological developmentalist theory, which traces its origins to Weber, and which ascribes the rise of Europe to cultural changes, and specifically to a new attitude towards work that derived ultimately from the Calvinist reformation;

2. the classical historical materialist theory, which attributes the rise of Europe to technological breakthroughs, which in turn led to the economic, political, and cultural changes associated with capitalist development, which in turn necessitated the colonization of Asia, Africa, and Latin America and the emergence of structures which held back their development;

3. dependency theory, which modified the original historical materialist position to stress the role of the European conquests in the primitive accumulation of capital; and

4. the ecological-demographic thesis advanced by Elvin (1973) and Lee (1986) and modified by Frank (1998), which attributes Europe's (temporary) surge ahead of Asia to ecological and demographic conditions that favored investment in labor saving technology.

Developmentalists argue that capitalist modernization was the product of a new attitude towards work that originated in the Calvinist reformation. The Calvinist doctrine of predestination, according to Weber, created profound anxiety for believers, who wanted desperately to be able to think about themselves as among the elect. Hard work and a judicious stewardship of resources were regarded as signs of election, something that encouraged the habits essential to the accumulation of capital. Other analysts in this tradition, such as Ho Ping-ti, have argued, conversely, that there were powerful cultural forces in places like China that militated against capitalist industrialization: a focus on scholarship rather than business and on philosophy rather than science and technology, the absence of primogeniture and an ethic that required resources be shared across broad family networks, and the excessive role of the state in regulating the economy, granting profitable and safe monopolies, etc.

Clearly Weber captures something distinctive about the modern—and especially the Calvinist—ethos. His explanatory strategy is, however, only one layer deep: he fails to explain where Calvinism came from. And there are powerful reasons to believe that Calvinism itself was a reflex of underlying economic and political processes. The correlation between Calvinism and capitalist development is not, furthermore, nearly as tight as Weber argues, something that has required the development of "epicycles" to explain, for example, Japanese industrialization. And many of the practices Ho Ping-ti identifies as holding back development in China, such as the sale of offices and the granting of monopolies, were, in fact, quite common in Europe.

According to the classical historical materialist approach, European dominance is first and foremost the result of distinctive technological developments—the technical division of labor and later the steam engine—which vastly increased productivity and which in turn broke the old feudal restrictions on production and ushered in the capitalist system. Marx and Engels themselves (Marx and Engels 1848/1978) are a bit ambiguous in places as to just how this worked. The *Manifesto*, for example, suggests that the European "discovery" of the Americas and improved sea routes to Asia played a critical role by expanding markets, but that it was above all the "cheap prices" of European commodities produced by the new industrial system that broke down all "Chinese walls." Colonization and primitive accumulation are not even mentioned. *Capital* suggests otherwise, acknowledging the necessity of primitive accumulation and the role of colonialism in that process, without, however, modifying the overall character of the theory.

This theory fails to actually answer the question posed—namely *why Europe underwent an industrial revolution and other, previously more advanced regions of the world, did not.* To suggest that the expanded markets made accessible by African and American gold and silver by the development of improved sea routes to Asia catalyzed development simply will not do. Asia already enjoyed access to an enormous world market. The truth is that Marx simply took European superiority for granted. The reasons for the rise of Europe did not become a real topic of investigation for Marxists until much later.

Dependency theory represented, in this sense, a real step forward, in that it acknowledged Chinese and Islamic superiority prior to 1800 and took the rise of Europe as something to be explained. The focus on the role of the conquests in the primitive accumulation of capital is clearly essential to any understanding of how European industrialization was possible. Even so, it leaves critical questions unanswered. First, it fails to explain *why* the Europeans conquered the planet when they did. Second, it fails to explain why the Chinese and the Moslems, who certainly *had* the capital necessary to industrialize, even without (further) conquests, did not do so.

Ecological-demographic theories focus on explaining just that phenomenon. China and India, it is argued, had lush environments, which, with wet rice agriculture, made it possible to produce up to four crops per year and thus to support a large population with relatively little labor, something that led to low wages. Europe, on the other hand, had a relatively thin population. Even with the vastly improved agricultural techniques developed during the Middle Ages, it could generate only one crop of grain per year. This helped keep wages high. At the same time, Europe had relatively abundant coal and metal ores, something China and India did not. The resulting complex of incentives made it worthwhile for the Europeans to invest in labor-saving devices, while in India or China it made more sense just to continue using abundant low-wage labor.

Like dependency theory, this approach clearly makes a contribution to the problem. Together they represent the most complete explanation advanced to date. There are, however, remaining gaps in the theory. First, like dependency theory, it does not explain why the Europeans moved to conquer the planet. Second, it is by no means clear that the industrial revolution can be characterized as simply "investing in labor saving devices." On the contrary, industrialization represents an entirely new way of relating to the physical, biological, and social universe, and is bound up with a whole complex of economic, political, and cultural changes that it certainly helped to shape but on which it also depended. More is at issue here than the rise of a new global hegemon. We are looking at the emergence of an entirely new civilization.

What follows is an attempt to answer these questions.

A Civilizational Approach

We have already noted in the previous chapter the role of the new wave of conquests that began in the eleventh century in catalyzing the Augustinian reaction and the emergence of a univocal metaphysics—and the role of that univocal metaphysics in catalyzing the Averroist counter-reaction that led ultimately to the emergence of modern dialectics. What we will do now will be to set that process in a larger context and show how it can be used to explain the global crisis of the civilization of the Silk Road Era and the emergence of modernity.

The Germanic migrations that brought medieval Europe into being were part of a much larger movement of peoples, which must be seen to include, in addition to the Germans, the Arabs, the Turks, and the Mongols at the very least. It may also have included the Athabascan peoples who, during this same period, harassed the advanced civilization of the Anasazi in the Red Rock valley. These migrations may well have been motivated in part by ecological and demographic pressures, but we do not need to postulate such pressures in order to explain them. Rather we are looking at peoples who were still wholly or partly nomadic and who lived by stockbreeding and raiding, moving to gain access to the riches of the developed civilizations of the Mediterranean Basin, Mesopotamia, Persia, India, China, and southeast Asia. Like many such conquerors they were at least partly absorbed and acculturated by those they conquered, but they also altered profoundly the course of civilizational development. Partly this was simply the result of the shocks they imposed. Rome never fully recovered from the Germanic invasions, nor did the Celtic fringes of northwestern Europe. The same may be said for Mesopotamia in the wake of the Mongol invasions. Ultimately, though, these invaders, precisely to the extent that they were not merely destructive, seeded a new cultural pattern deeply at odds with the Silk Road traditions. Specifically, they reasserted, in societies increasingly dominated by merchants and scholars, the role of coercive military power. This was especially true in two places. Europe generally, and Norman England in particular, gave birth to a new ideal of sovereignty deeply in conflict with the natural law polity favored by papalists and Radical Aristotelians alike. The Turks, meanwhile, put an effective end to the Islamic quest for a political system that vested effective power in the hands of the legitimate successors to that prophet and forced *Dar-al-Islam* to accept the reality of military dictatorship. We have

Modernity and Metaphysics

already seen that in both cases the effect was to support those elements in the Christian and Islamic traditions that favored a univocal metaphysics and a theology centered on the idea of divine sovereignty.

This said, we must still explain why it was Europe, and not the Ottoman Turks, who managed to achieve global hegemony, or at least pioneer the new cultural pattern. A number of factors were at work here. First, the forces for global conquest were stronger in Europe than they were in China or *Dar-al-Islam*. Once the Turks had taken control of the Islamic world and of India—and the Mongols of China—they had, in effect, access to the most powerful economic engines on the planet. This was not true of Germanic Europe, which remained, at best, a promising backwater. The gradual *Reconquista* of Iberia had given the Germans access to one of Islam's civilizational centers, but the real prizes were further east. European social structure, furthermore, and especially the institution of primogeniture, meant that younger sons of the aristocracy were often left landless. During the early Middle Ages, when much of Europe was still being cleared and put under cultivation, this was less of a problem. Younger sons of the nobility could expect to serve a period as "knights bachelor," but would eventually be granted land as it was cleared or conquered. But after about 1100, most of the arable land in Europe was already subject to feudal claims. Groups of armed young men accumulated in the castles of the elite with little prospect for land or marriage. The Crusades and the *Reconquista* represent an attempt, on the part of the European ruling classes, to find a solution to this problem.

This situation was only complicated by the Black Death, which cost Europe roughly one third of its population during the fourteenth century. On the one hand, the Black Death strengthened enormously the hand of the working classes, creating labor shortages and increasing the pressures to search out labor-saving devices. On the other hand, resolution of the crisis took vastly different forms in different parts of Europe. In northern and central Italy and the Low Countries, the peasants were effectively emancipated from feudal burdens. Some began producing wine and oil for the market; others took jobs in the flourishing woolen mills of the cities. The result was a period of prosperity based on large-scale handicrafts production, which provided the economic and social basis for the cultural movement we call the Renaissance. In England, on the other hand, an early victory by the peasants was met with effective countermeasures by the landowners, who began clearing the land of the peasants and replacing them with sheep, forcing millions into the cities where they provided the reserve army that made industrialization possible. In northern Spain the peasants formed an alliance with the monarchy in its struggle against the military orders and benefited from land reform, which bound it to the monarchy and Church for centuries. In the south (the Algarve, Andalusia, and the Two Sicilies) as well as the region east of the Elbe the peasants were put down and a long seigniorial reaction followed (Anderson 1974a).

It was in this context that a new civilizational ideal was born. In a very real sense the whole wave of Germanic conquests reaching back to Roman times had tended to undercut the integration of Europe into the Silk Road networks and to reassert the primacy of military might. This is, as we have seen, what created the social basis for the Augustinian trend within the Christian tradition, which remained a significant current throughout the Middle Ages. It is just that throughout most of the medieval period the Latin and Celtic patterns remained stronger than the Germanic and tended to absorb and overcome it. After about 1250 the balance shifted, and a new ideal of sovereignty emerged. Initially, this was just a matter of state formation. When the Normans succeeded in conquering Britain, they brought a compact and cohesive land mass together under the suerzerainity of a single king for the first time. They eliminated the older Saxon ruling class and began chipping away at the autonomy of their own aristocracy. Something similar happened a little bit later in Spain. The French and German monarchies were less successful—the French in part because they based their authority on a defense of the papacy, and the Germans because they were locked in a long frontal confrontation with it, but the underlying drive remained the same.

The gradual emergence of sovereign states had, in turn, a profound impact in the ideological arena. Partly this effect was spontaneous. Living under a sovereign king, people began to think of God in much the same way. Europe, which had long been only superficially Christianized and related to God only through the medium of the Blessed Virgin and locally important saints, found itself gradually beginning to understand cults such as that of Christ the King. But part of the change was conscious. As we saw in the last chapter, the emerging monarchies mounted a frontal assault on analogical metaphysics and natural law ethics, which tended to constrain their autonomy by subjecting them to the authority of clerics who claimed to be privileged interpreters of natural law. Intellectuals, as we have suggested above, responded in two ways: either by retreating in to mathematical formalization, a process that led to the scientific revolution, or by emancipating itself from the clergy entirely and elaborating a secular humanistic ideology that increasingly treated humanity itself as the center, or at least the cutting edge, of the universe.

Meanwhile, another dynamic was at work—a dynamic distinct from but which at once benefited from and encouraged the development of sovereign nation-states: the gradual emergence of capitalism or of a generalized commodity production. This process had its roots, to be sure, in the flourishing of crafts production in the high Middle Ages and in the incorporation of Europe into the Silk Road networks as an exporter of dyed wool cloth. Those who made a fortune in trade eventually turned to banking, creating concentrations of capital that could be used to finance larger enterprises, while the emancipation of the peasantry provided, in many places, a pool of free labor that could be employed in those enterprises.

These developments by themselves would not, however, have produced a structure radically different from what we see in China in the same period: large-scale handicrafts production carried out by a still skilled but increasingly proletarianized labor force in workshops that approach the scale, but not the productivity, of the modern factory. The full development of modern industry required, on the one hand, a vastly larger pool of capital, something that was acquired largely by means of conquest. The Crusades and the *Reconquista* represent simply the first stages in this process, which was then extended to Africa, the Americas, and eventually to Asia. This process would bear fruit only in the eighteenth century.

It was these two dynamics—the emergence of sovereign nation-states and the development of generalized commodity production—that were, in turn, responsible for the two great cultural developments that ushered in the modern world: the Reformation and the Scientific Revolution. The Reformation was, ultimately, simply an extension of the Augustinian reaction that began in the mid-thirteenth century. The Scientific Revolution was the result of a more complex process but can also trace its lineage to this same point of origin. Repression of Aristotelian science encouraged a shift from teleological explanation, which was regarded as theologically suspect, to mathematical model-building, and set in motion a flourishing of mathematical physics that ultimately bore fruit in the work of Kepler, Galileo, and Newton.

In both cases the impact of the underlying political economic dynamics are readily apparent. On the one hand, in a market society, people experience the world as a system of only externally related atoms—just precisely the universe of early modern mathematical physics. The ruthless competition that emerged as the guild system declined encouraged a perception of human nature as irreducibly selfish, while the inscrutable workings of the marketplace, which rewarded many a mediocre slacker and punished many who were talented and hard working, made people feel that they were at the mercy of forces beyond their control and created a basis in experience for the idea of God as an arbitrary divine sovereign who rewards people on some basis other than their works—i.e., the God of Luther and Calvin. The larger context of the absolutist state, meanwhile, meant that the interactions between individuals unfolded in the context of a fixed frame of reference established outside the market. This is the fixed frame of Newtonian physics, in which space and time are absolute, a kind of stage on which physical interactions take place. Indeed, just as in developing capitalism commodities retained relatively stable values, because market forces had not yet been fully unleashed, so too, in Newtonian physics the basic physical determinations of bodies—extension and mass, for example—are fixed and are not affected by their interactions with other bodies.

It is only one step from this point to the claim that if we understand the laws that govern the world we can, in effect, bring that world under our own rational control, putting ourselves in the place of God or at least making us his rational agents. Early modernity tends to stop just short of taking that step, leaving the sovereign (divine and human) in place and simply trying to understand and observe his laws.

Within this broader context of early modernity, the social forces that created and sustained the Averroist counter-reaction persist as a kind of under-current. On the one hand, the artisan-mercantile enclaves of northern and central Italy and the Low Countries created a context in which civilizational progress (which had been at the center of the Averroist program) could flourish without coming into conflict with either the Church or the emerging absolutist states. In the Protestant countries many thinkers tried to "read" the Reformation in a humanistic way as opening up the way towards Enlightenment. And something like a more traditional Averroism persisted in the Jewish communities that had fled *al-Andalus* after the *Reconquista*, constituting a kind of internal opposition to the whole trend towards a univocal metaphysics and a spirituality of authority and submission.

Metaphysics in the Early Modern Era

A Univocal Metaphysics

What impact did this all have on the development of rational metaphysics? And what was the political valence of the metaphysics that developed?

We should note, first of all, the well-documented philosophical roots of the Reformation in the philosophy of John Dun Scotus and William of Occam. Scotus's understanding of God as the *infinite* laid the groundwork for the emergence of a coherent doctrine of divine sovereignty among the Reformers. Luther, meanwhile, was profoundly influenced by the nominalism of William of Occam, which had the effect of making it impossible to rise rationally to a first principle in terms of which the universe can be explained and human action ordered—and thus setting the stage for Luther's claim that religious knowledge comes only from the scriptures, and thus for the displacement of metaphysics from its place as an architectonic discipline with regulating functions even with respect to theology (McGrath 1987, White 1994).

The most direct philosophical heirs of this nominalist trend are the empiricists, who join the philosophical concerns of the Reformation with those of the Scientific Revolution. Empiricism represents, by its very nature, a step away from metaphysics. This is because, by limiting what we can know to possible objects of sensation we push God into the realm of the unknowable, if not the nonexistent.

This said, both moderate and radical empiricists in the early modern era managed to sustain a metaphysics of sorts. The most common approach among the moderates was the use of the argument by design and more specifically the eutaxiological argument, which begins with the observation that things in the universe are well ordered and from the fact that in our experience generally is regarded as the product of rational design or conscious intention. The universe, therefore, must have an intelligent designer who endowed it with its magnificent, mathematically elegant structure and who brought into being the many things we see in nature that are clearly ordered to a purpose. This is the approach of John Locke and of William Paley, whose *Natural Theology* was long a required text in British universities. This approach draws out the metaphysical implications of Newtonian physics and, like the rationalist metaphysics of the same period, makes the line between creator and creature essentially quantitative.

Another approach entirely is represented by the radical empiricism or subjective idealism of George Berkeley (Berkeley 1710). Berkeley saw himself as vindicating religion against the attacks of the materialists. Berkeley says that we know *nothing* except what we experience. But experience occurs *inside*, not *outside* the mind. This led him to the conclusion that "to be is to be perceived." But what does this do to things that are not currently perceived—to the famous tree that falls in the forest with no one to hear it? Berkeley must resort to the idea of an Ultimate Observer—God—who guarantees the possible objects of sensation by perceiving them when we are not. Variations on this theme have been developed in the present period by information-theoretical "physical idealists" such as Frank Tipler, who attempt to resolve the dilemmas of quantum cosmology by reference to an ultimate observer.[2]

From here, a divine command theory follows necessarily. Indeed, in so far as everything is an idea in the mind of God, everything is, in effect, a result of divine action. Similar ideas can be found in Jonathan Edwards and other New Divinity men anxious to find a philosophical foundation for Reformed Theology. Not only is the Good a result of divine decree, but so is our response to it, for which we are nonetheless morally responsible because it is *also* what we will (Edwards 1754/1957–1989).

Ultimately, however, empiricism began to undercut metaphysics. We see this, for example, with the radical empiricism of David Hume (Hume 1777/1886). Humeans generally begin by granting that we can perceive "facts" and "events." But since such things as "structures" and "causal relationships" are not direct observables, they deny their objectivity. All we are really seeing is a "constant conjunction" of phenom-

---

2. According to quantum theory, subatomic particles (and by implication the universe, which is composed of such particles) cannot be described in terms of their position and momentum, but only by a wave function that describes the relative probability of various "quantum states." According to one interpretation (the so-called "Copenhagen interpretation") this wave function is "collapsed" when an observation is made and a definite value given to position, momentum, and so on. The alternate "many worlds" theory suggests that the wave function never collapses and that *all* possible values are in fact realized, so that the universe branches out into an infinite number of worlds, each corresponding to a specific quantum state of each particle. Tipler synthesizes these two approaches, arguing that all possible values of the quantum wave function describing the universe as a whole exist mathematically, but that only those which permit observers exist physically (the Berkeleyan criterion) and that all those which permit observers evolve necessarily to an "Omega point" which is, in effect, Berkeley's Ultimate Observer (Barrow and Tipler 1986, Tipler 1994).

ena. Assuming that all knowledge derives ultimately from the senses (and thus ruling out the ontological argument), and in the absence of an authentic doctrine of causality, it becomes quite impossible to argue for the existence of God. Indeed, the whole notion of truth and value becomes radically relativized. Some ways of organizing our experience are better than others only because they lead to practices that work. Ideas that work survive; those that don't die out. Survival value is not, however, the same thing as truth value.

Morality is, from this point of view, simply a way of talking about what pleases us. This notion can be developed in a number of different ways. Hume himself, and many thinkers of similar temperament, argued for the existence of a sort of moral sensibility, which led us to take pleasure in benevolent conduct. It is actions that are pleasing to this sort of preference in particular that we call moral. Later Humeans, such as F. A. Hayek (Hayek 1988), argue that there is a sort of natural selection for social practices that have survival value. It is these practices that are conserved and become part of a moral tradition. Religion, similarly, if it has a place at all, is simply a collection of practices with demonstrated survival value.

The traces of the Augustinian Reaction can, however, also be found in most forms of Enlightenment rationalism, both directly and by way of an attempt to apply to philosophy the mathematically formalizing methods of the Scientific Revolution. Descartes, for example, begins at exactly the same point as Augustine, with an immanent critique of skepticism, which, with some generosity, we might say he "borrowed" from the troubled African saint. Modern rationalism, however, has tended to pull away from the illumination theory advocated by Augustine (the idea that rational knowledge is the product of the illumination of our intellects by God's) in favor of an attempt to ground knowledge on what it claims are analytically self-evident first principles from which rational deductions can then be made. Thus Descartes, after proving his own existence and that of God, argues that a perfect being would not have created us with faulty senses, thus grounding the validity of sense data and evading the necessity of an appeal to divine illumination.

A word is in order regarding Descartes' concept of God. God, for Descartes, is defined simply as "a perfect being." We should note that the specification of God as *a being* rather than as *Being as such* already marks this metaphysics as univocal. This is further reflected in Descartes' use of the ontological argument, which, as we have demonstrated elsewhere, is essentially convertible with Zorn's Lemma (Mansueto 2002). According to Descartes we know that God exists because God is perfect and perfection includes existence. This is essentially the same thing as saying that any partially ordered set (i.e., any set with elements "greater than," "less than," or "equal to" others has a maximal element. Not only can this latter proposition not be demonstrated (Geroch 1985), it makes the difference between us and God essentially quantitative.

It is easy to see how such a metaphysics could lead *both* to an ethics and spirituality of submission and to the later "high modern" aspiration for human beings to actually *become* God. Like Duns Scotus, Descartes argues that morality is ultimately dependent on the divine will (Descartes 1641/1998). God could have created a universe governed by moral norms different from those that govern ours. That God created a universe ordered to the virtue and happiness of human beings is a result of a free act of grace. This virtue and happiness is furthered by means of knowledge of God, of the soul, and of the physical universe. Knowledge of God is knowledge of the principle that creates and governs all things. Knowledge of the soul is knowledge of our capacity to transcend the material world. Knowledge of the physical universe allows us to manipulate and control the world for our own benefit, while teaching us subordination to the divinely sanctioned laws by which it is governed. Similar reasoning can be found (in radicalized form) in Malebranche (Malebranche 1674/1980, 1684/1977, 1687/1980) and (in somewhat moderated form) in Rosmini (Rosmini 1841/1993). It should not surprise us to discover that Descartes was favored over Thomas in seminaries that operated under the *de facto* control of the French absolutist state, which was anxious to protect its autonomy from Rome (Thibault 1971). Descartes' divine sovereign looks far more like a heavenly monarch than like a spiritual father dedicated to the development of his children. What is demanded by his ethics is, quite simply, submission to the will of God on no ground other than His infinite power. That this power may endow us with certain rights, or manifest itself in a loving manner, does not alter the underlying dynamic, which is, in the final analysis, every bit as relativistic as the most extreme postmodernism. And it is far from clear why command by a powerful being, even a singularly powerful being, makes something obligatory. By this reasoning what Hitler commanded would at least have been *more* obligatory than the silent pleas of his victims.

Similar, if more moderate, tendencies are evident in Leibniz. Leibniz argues that the universe is composed of distinct monads, some rational and some not, which are maintained in a pre-existent harmony by the coordinating activity of God, who is at once the author and sovereign monarch of the universe. The Good consists first and foremost in this harmony, which produces pleasure for all rational creatures, and right action is action that is in accord with and helps to promote it. Humanity seems to play a critical role for Leibniz in God's plan for the perfection of the universe. We thus find here a more dynamic conception of both the universe and of humanity than we saw in Descartes. Indeed, Leibniz clearly aims at rebuilding something like the old Aristotelian teleology on the foundation of the new mathematical physics. This physics does not, however, allow such a conclusion. Rather than an organic conception of the universe as growing naturally towards God, Leibniz gives us a universe of monads directed externally by God towards a perfection in which they remain always and forever subjects. Leibniz is careful to avoid making explicit the voluntarist implications of his approach, but they are inevitable. Indeed, it is not difficult to see in Leibniz an implicit justification for royal regulatory power during the era of emerging capitalism (Leibniz 1714/1991).

Early Modern Dialectics

As we noted above, the concerns of the Averroist counter-reaction were, in significant measure, driven underground by the ascendancy of Augustinian philosophy and theology in the late Middle Ages. Latin Averroism persisted as an independent philosophical trend only at the University of Padova, in the work of thinkers such as Cesare Cremonini. But many of its broader themes were taken up by the Renaissance humanists. This is true first of all with respect to method. Like ibn Rusd, the humanists of the Renaissance devoted themselves to careful textual scholarship, and developed an "originalist hermeneutic," which privileged the author's meaning over that of commentators. On the one hand, this tended to diminish the importance of ibn Rusd himself, and of the other Islamic and Jewish Aristotelians, as a source for understanding Aristotle. But it represented the first step towards the development of the historical-critical method, which has dominated religious studies in the modern era and which has certainly favored rationalizing interpretations with a broadly Averroist flavor.

But the substantive concerns of the Averroists also found expression, albeit in a very different philosophical vernacular, within the context of Renaissance humanism. Specifically, Renaissance philosophers such as Pico della Mirandola and Giordano Bruno, translated the Averroist focus on human self-cultivation and civilizational progress into the language the Neo-Platonic revival. This represents, in many ways, a development parallel to the reorientation of scientific activity towards mathematical formalization following the Condemnations of 1270 and 1277, which set the stage, as we have argued, for the Scientific Revolution.

This survival of Averroist concerns was made possible, in large part, due to the unusual cluster of social conditions that existed in Renaissance Italy. The stalemate between the Papacy and the Empire had created a context in which networks of autonomous city-states could develop governed largely by powerful merchants and bankers but sometimes with significant participation of the artisan class. These cities were inserted into the Silk Road trade networks in a fairly privileged way. The papacy maintained its legitimacy in this context in large part by positioning itself as a patron of human self-cultivation and civilizational progress (especially when viewed against background the darker visions of Luther and Calvin). Renaissance humanism, furthermore, unlike Latin Averroism, did not propose a globally rationalizing hermeneutic that called into question the legitimacy of the Church or reduce it to a mechanism for social control in a system in which philosophers were the sole legitimate rulers. Even so, those Renaissance humanists who pressed Averroist themes most consistently—e.g., Giordano Bruno—did not fare well in spite of the support of powerful secular patrons.

The most direct line between Radical Aristotelianism and modern dialectics, however, bypasses *Christian* philosophy entirely. Idit Dobbs Weinstein (Dobbs Weinstein Forthcoming a, b) has traced out the lineage linking Spinoza to the Radical Aristotelians by way of Gersonides. Yirmiyahu Yovel (Yovel 2001), for his part, has stressed the *converso* milieu as the context that nurtured this tradition. It is not hard to see how the cross-fertilization of Jewish inner-worldliness and the Christian focus on divinization would trace a pathway from ibn Rusd through Spinoza to Hegel and beyond.

It is, furthermore, clear that Spinoza, despite his fascination with the results of the Scientific Revolution, had deep roots in the medieval Aristotelian and specifically Averroist tradition. Spinoza frames the question of God not quantitatively, as perfect being, in the manner of Descartes, but rather qualitatively, in terms of the problem of substance, which for Spinoza is that which can exist on its own—i.e., Necessary Being. At the same time, he makes a very subtle move that opens up the way for a modernist transformation of the Aristotelian tradition. Human beings are but modes of this one substance, the product of intersecting networks of relationships. Our only hope for beatitude consists in identification with the whole, i.e., with God. This can be read in the manner of a very sober philosophical spirituality in the manner of Maimonides or ibn Rusd, for whom human beings found fulfillment in identification with the Agent Intellect, simply adapted to the realities of a post-Copernican cosmology, in the context of which the idea of the Agent Intellect no longer made much literal sense. But it can also be read as a challenge: to develop to or at least towards the point at which we *are* in fact identical with the single substance.

What happens, in effect, is that for both an inner core of Radical Aristotelians (many of them Jews, *moriscos* or *conversos* operating in the shadows of a world in which they are no longer intellectually at home) and a broader periphery of thinkers working in other traditions (e.g., the Neo-Platonism that became prominent during the Renaissance) the developments of the late medieval and early modern era—the scientific revolution and later the democratic revolutions—are read as actually raising humanity to a higher ontological level. At first this is simply a new spin on the old Radical Aristotelian soteriology, which terminates (when we understand fully how the sublunar realm works) in identity with the Agent Intellect. But ultimately it pointed, by way of Spinoza's more ambiguous doctrine of the intellectual identification with Nature = Substance = God, toward the Hegelian doctrine of innerworldly divinization.

Let us see how this transformation plays itself out in Spinoza's metaphysics. Spinoza begins with a number of definitions and axioms and—skipping over the *cogito* entirely—proceeds through analysis of the idea of substance (something that can be conceived in and through itself, independently of any other conception) to a proof of the existence of God and of the identity between God and the universe. All particular systems are simply modifications of God; thought and extension are those two of the infinite divine attributes of which we are able to conceive (Spinoza 1675/1955). This is, in effect, an attempt to draw out fully the implications of the Avicennist and Thomistic distinction between Necessary and

Possible Being for the Aristotelian concept of substance. Ultimately only Necessary Being—i.e., God—exists in and through itself.

How do we know that "substance" exists at all? In one place (Proposition VII of Part One of the *Ethics*) Spinoza seems to depart from the Aristotelian tradition, which argues from existence and motion, and presents instead an analytic argument that reflects the spirit of modern rationalism—that existence belongs to the notion of substance. Later, however, in Part Two, Proposition XVIII, he acknowledges that *we* know that something exists because our bodies are modified in certain ways by other bodies. Our knowledge of the universe, in other words, derives from sensation of finite particulars, from which we *infer* the existence of God.

Though Spinoza sometimes uses mathematical language that conceals this fact, his metaphysics is analogical—i.e., the distinction between substance and modes, or God and universe, is qualitative and turns on the attribute of necessity.

Spinoza's Ethics is first and foremost an ethics of *seeking Being*:

> To act absolutely in obedience to virtue is in us the same thing as to act, to live, or preserve one's being (these terms are identical in meaning) in accordance with the dictates of reason on the basis of seeking what is useful to one's self. (Spinoza *Ethics*, Part IV, Proposition XXIV)

Lest we read this as a kind of hedonism or ethics of power, we should note that the highest expression of this drive is the intellectual love of God.

> The highest endeavor of the mind, and the highest virtue, is to understand things by virtue of the third kind of knowledge. (Spinoza *Ethics*, Part V, Proposition XXV)

By the "third kind of knowledge" Spinoza means an intellectual intuition in which we grasp the very essence of God.

> The intellectual love of the mind toward God is that very love of God whereby god loves himself. (Spinoza *Ethics*, Part V, Proposition XXXVI)

This is, of course, very close—at least in the language used—to the Thomistic concept of connatural knowledge of God. But for Spinoza this is possible on the base of natural reason alone. We will see that this sets the stage of a distinctive strategy for innerworldly divinization—one that bears fruit, ultimately in the modern communist movement.

A Note on Reactionary and Conservative Metaphysics

We have already noted that there were parts of Europe that underwent only some of the changes associated with the early modern era—they developed modern sovereign state structures, but neither emancipated nor liquidated their peasantries and they did not undergo capitalist development. This was true especially in the regions that, in the period after the Black Death and the peasant revolts of the late fourteenth century, underwent a seigniorial reaction: the Algarve and Andalusia, and the Kingdom of the Two Sicilies, which after having been conquered by the Normans eventually landed in the hands of the Spanish, which held it as a nominal papal fief, as well as the whole region East of the Elbe. Whatever progressive potential there had been in Northern Spain was, meanwhile, undercut by the expulsion of the Jews and then of the Moors, which effectively exported the country's wool textile industry and most of its bourgeoisie to the Ottoman Empire.

It was in these regions above all that we see the flourishing of the Second Scholasticism and more specifically of the Neo-Thomism of thinkers such as Cajetan, John of St. Thomas, Bañez, Suarez, Molina, etc. This Second Thomism had a social basis quite different from the first. The work of Thomas himself represented an organic expression of the most advanced tendencies in high medieval Europe. Specifically, his thematization of Being as such reflects the growing weight within the social structure of human creativity, as represented not only by the intelligentsia but also by the artisan class. The political valence of Thomism, furthermore, reflected this. Thomas was almost certainly the first thinker in the dialectical tradition to affirm that since political authority rests on the exercise of the intellect and since every human being has an intellect, political authority derives ultimately from the people—even if the people may choose to delegate all or some of that authority to those who are especially wise and prudent and just. Thomas is a papalist only in the sense of upholding the role of the papacy as guardian of natural law. Political authority in and of itself is autonomous and needs no ecclesiastical sanction.

The Second Thomism emerges out of a very different situation. On the one hand, Portugal, Spain, and the Two Sicilies were as advanced as any part of Europe in the area of state formation. These new states did, furthermore, already enjoy very substantial autonomy from the papacy. Spain had special privileges that it had acquired during the Reconquista and had its own Inquisition, which was both more brutal and more effective than anything the papacy could have devised. Indeed, by the middle of the sixteenth century the papacy had been reduced to a dependency of the remaining Catholic great powers in the struggle against the Reformation. It was above all in the economic realm that these regions were beginning to lag behind. Spain completed the Reconquista by expelling first its Jewish and later its Moorish population and in the process essentially exported its wool textile industry and much of its bourgeoisie and intelligentsia to the Ottoman Empire. This move affected the Two Sicilies as well, if less completely and effectively. Land reform in the north, meanwhile, and seigniorial reaction in the south, kept the peasantry on the land and undercut the development of a proletariat. The gold and silver that Spain and Portugal extracted from their new colonies, as well as the revenues from emerging plantation agriculture, were simply expended on luxury consumption, and especially on manufactured goods from northern Europe, where the capital was actually accumulated. In the south just as much as in the Protestant north, however, the Church gradually lost its autonomy and the means were much the same: the secularization and capitalization of church lands, the suppression of monasteries, the gradual erosion of ecclesiastical immunities and exemptions, of the right of sanctuary, etc. (Chadwick 1981).

In this context, Second Thomism functioned not as an organic expression of the underlying creativity of a rising civilization, but rather as a defensive form of legitimation for the Catholic monarchies and their papal allies. The result was a series of subtle changes in core doctrine. This is most apparent in the Jesuit Thomism of a thinker like Suarez, who all but abandons the Thomistic doctrine of *Esse* and opts for what looks suspiciously like a univocal metaphysics. He also introduced into Thomism an essentially Augustinian doctrine of the will (Treloar 1991: 387). The Dominican Thomists remained more nearly faithful to Thomas, but even their work reflects a very substantial admixture of Augustinianism, especially in their more negative anthropology and their more mechanical defense of ecclesiastical authority.

This transformation of Thomism from a creative and critical theology into a means of legitimation for conservative monarchic states is not too different from the fate of *dao xue* under the Yuan and Ming Dynasties, or later on in Korea or Japan. These states all served as bulwarks of meaning and order in a world that seemed to be tumbling out of control. But in the process of trying to conserve meaning they ceded more ground than they realized to their adversaries and the systems they upheld were subtly transformed in ways that gave far more scope to the role of brute power and under that of wisdom and creativity.

This "conservative" metaphysics must, however, be distinguished sharply from the "reactionary" metaphysics of traditionalist thinkers such as de Maistre and de Bonald, who wrote during the eighteenth century. If the Second Thomism represents the need of the monarchies of southern Europe to lean on the papacy for legitimation, and thus to at least *claim* to rule on the basis of natural law criteria, traditionalism represents just precisely an effort to emancipate the monarchies from such constraints.

Traditionalism emerged as a response to the rationalism of the Enlightenment. Against the claim of Descartes and his followers to derive all knowledge from analytically self-evident first principles, the traditionalists insisted that human knowledge was a social product, based on concepts embedded in language, which constitute a sort of primitive revelation shared by all human beings. This understanding of human civilization as the product of divine revelation extended to social institutions—including the economic privileges of the feudal or ex-feudal "nobility" and (not always consistently) the authority of both the absolutist monarchies that emerged at the end of the Middle Ages and the popes. The effect was to put the kings and the warlord "aristocracy" on a par with the clergy as agents of God. This was the ideology par excellence of the Restoration regimes that put themselves forward as defenders of the Church and especially of the popes, but did so only at a price. Specifically, they claimed for kings not only the direct mandate from God that the Imperialist philosophers of the Middle Ages had claimed for the Holy Roman Emperor, but also a radical permanence that those philosophers had not. The fact that the papacy was itself regarded as an institution established by divine revelation notwithstanding, this made traditionalism an unattractive option for the papacy, which had always claimed the right to depose unjust rulers, but it nonetheless had significant influence and probably a majority of the bishops present at the First Vatican Council had some traditionalist sympathies (Heyer 1969, Thibault 1972, Chadwick 1981). The doctrine of papal infallibility proclaimed by the Council can be read either as an attempt to construct a papal absolutism along traditionalist lines as a bulwark for the *ancien regime* (which is probably how most of its supporters understood it) or as an attempt on the part of the papacy to assert its authority vis-à-vis the traditionalists, which is how Pio IX understood it.[3] Ultimately, however, the Council condemned the principal traditionalist thesis—fideism—which holds that knowledge of God is possible only on the basis of faith (Vatican I 1990).

Another way of understanding the difference between the conservative metaphysics of the Neo-Thomists and the reactionary metaphysics of the traditionalists is by looking at the implications of these metaphysical doctrines for the modern ideal of the rationally autonomous individual. Even as Thomism was pressed into service as an instrument against Protestant and liberal dissent, it could not help but defend the priority of conscience, arguing not that Catholics were obliged to simply submit to the magisterium, but rather that they had an obligation to inform their consciences by listening openly and respectfully to the teachings of their bishops. If this is something short of a full embrace of the ideal of rational autonomy, it is certainly not incompatible with it. Indeed, one might argue (as we will in a later section) that Thomism provided a more adequate ground for this ideal than modernist metaphysics. This is because the analogical metaphysics of *Esse* locates the autonomy of the individual at the ontological level, and *defines* humanity as the capacity to rise rationally to knowledge of first principles—something that makes it possible for human beings to order themselves to the first principle *without* submission of the intellect or the will. Indeed, such ordering is the natural expression of the immanent teleology of the human will itself, which seeks ever fuller participation in the Being in which it already enjoys a created share. Traditionalist metaphysics, on the other hand, is the metaphysics of power and submission *par excellence* and seeks not merely to correct the individualism of the Enlightenment ideal, but rather rejects that ideal as such, arguing that social order is possible only on the basis of submission.

---

3. When the Dominican General Guidi offered the council a compromise text that recognized the infallibility of the pope's dogmatic definitions, rather than of his person, and under the condition that these definitions were consistent with the Catholic tradition, Pio IX responded by saying "La tradizione son'io!" (in Heyer 1963/1969: 191).

HIGH MODERNITY

Civilizational Patterns

Early modernity represents just the first stage in the development of a new civilizational ideal. The full development of that ideal involves movement from a spirituality of authority and submission to a sovereign God to one of human self-divinization. The high-modern ideal is, furthermore, understood in two very different ways. On the one hand the univocal metaphysics emerging out of the Augustinian Reaction and the Scientific Revolution, in which God is understood as *the Infinite*, gives birth to the notion that human beings might achieve what amounts to divinity by means of scientific and technological progress. On the other hand, the analogical metaphysics sustained by modern dialectics led ultimately to the hope that humanity, by becoming the *Subject* of human history, might overcome contingency and realize the freedom appropriate to Necessary Being.

In tracing out the development of these two variations of the high-modern ideal, we will begin by analyzing the common features of high modernity: industrialism, the commodification of labor power, the modern democratic state, and secularization. We will then examine why each variant prevailed when and where it did and what impact it had on human development and civilizational progress.

Common Structures

Industrial production has traditionally been defined as the application of non-human energy sources to the production process, coupled with a rationally developed social and technical division of labor that makes possible the mass production first of consumer goods, and later of the capital goods (the machines) used to produce those consumer goods. This definition does provide a more or less adequate *empirical* marker by which we can differentiate industrial from preindustrial production. But in order to grasp the *concept* of industry, we need to analyze the actual process of industrial production in the context of its impact on the qualitative complexity of the ecosystem.

Industry proceeds by breaking down the organization of both the natural and the social factors of production in order to release the energy that they contain, and then harnesses that energy to reorganize matter into more complex forms to serve human purposes. Industrial generation of energy, for example, breaks down the chemical (electromagnetic) bonds of various fossil fuels, or the nuclear bonds of certain heavy metals, and uses the resulting heat either directly to drive machinery, or to produce steam, and eventually electricity, which in turn drives machinery. These machines then combine various elements mechanically, chemically, or biologically to produce complex structures that serve human purposes. Similarly, industry breaks down pre-existing social organisms (family, clan, village) and harnesses the social capacities of the individuals through a complex social and technical division of labor, enabling them to create products more complex than any individual worker could alone.

This is in sharp distinction to the "hortic" modes of production that preceded the modern era, in which human beings tapped into and encouraged (which is the etymological meaning of hortic) the already existing dynamics of development and simply encouraged them. Thus the seed grows naturally when placed into the ground; it grows better when watered and weeded and manured. Medieval alchemy, whether based on Aristotelian, Taoist, or Ayurvedic categories, represented the highest development of this hortic technological regime, in that it proposed to tap into the creative dynamic present in nature in such a way as to produce results that in some way exceeded the purely natural, accelerating the cosmohistorical evolutionary process. Even so, it still depended on dynamics already at work in nature. Industry, on the other hand, presupposes dead or at least inert matter, and imposes order from the outside, using purely mechanical means.

There are several distinct stages in the development of industrial production. These stages are defined by progress in the development of new energy sources and in the organization of labor power. Let us consider each of these dimensions separately. The development of energy sources is fundamentally a matter of harnessing the four fundamental forces of the universe. The first steps in this process were taken prior to the industrial revolution: the discovery of air, water, and animal power, which, in effect, harness thermodynamic gradients, the force of gravity, and the complex organic capacities of other mammals to perform useful labor. With the scientific revolution, however, it became possible for humanity to begin to harness the electromagnetic force, at first indirectly through the oxidation of various compounds to produce heat and drive steam and internal combustion engines, and later directly with the development of the electric motor. Finally, during the middle of the last century, we learned how to harness (albeit only very imperfectly) the strong and weak nuclear forces. The logical conclusion of the replacement of human by nonhuman energy sources is, of course, the elimination of direct manual labor, or at least routine and uncreative direct manual labor, altogether through automation.

The organization of labor power has also proceeded through various stages. The first of these—the social division of labor or the development of specialists in various crafts—was largely completed within most advanced tributary social formations. The second stage consists in dividing the production of a particular object into a constantly increasing number of more or less routine tasks, which can be performed by relatively unskilled (and therefore relatively cheap) labor. This is what we call the technical division of labor. Integral to this stage is division between the mental and manual dimensions of the production process. One worker or team of workers (initially the inventor or entrepreneur, later a team of salaried engineers) designs the object and the production process; another team actually executes the process. Third, the individual tasks involved in production are subjected to detailed analysis (time motion studies, etc.), and the whole complex of bodily movements of the worker are subjected to a scientifically developed discipline designed to increase the efficiency of the production process, transforming the worker, in effect, into simply one part of a larger machine—and not, by any means, its most intelligent part.

Industry involves the vast majority of the population in the civilizational project in a way that was not previously possible. Much, though not all, of the industrial working class is involved in producing machines, building structures, etc., which become a semipermanent part of the human environment, and which contribute not simply to the *reproduction* of humanity, but to its actual *development*. And the high level of productivity characteristic of industry makes it possible to release an increasingly large part of the population from direct production altogether.

At the same time, industrial uses of energy and natural resources run up inevitably against certain definite ecological limits. It is not at all clear that industry really increases the overall complexity of the ecosystem, and if it does, there seems to be a real point of diminishing returns. There are, furthermore, serious limits to the ability of industrial production to tap fully the self-organizing potential inherent in matter itself. Rather than catalyzing the development of complexity that already exists in matter (physical, chemical, biological, social), industry breaks matter down into its component parts and reorganizes it in a way that serves human purposes. For the most part, it uses only the raw energy stored in material structures, not the organizing dynamic that created those structures. This is most apparent in the way industry uses human beings: i.e., as batteries. Industrial strategies for increasing productivity reduce the vast majority of workers (including, increasingly, intellectual workers) to mere cogs in a wheel, simply moving physical, chemical, biological (or, in the case of intellectual workers, social) matter from one place to another. Industry has no way to tap into the skill or creativity of workers, and no way to recover the waste that derives from all of the potential Mozarts and Einsteins who have passed their lives painting tail fins for Cadillac. Both of these limits are rooted in the "exploitative" character of industrial production, an exploitation that is prior to the marketplace or any other means of surplus extraction. In this sense, it is necessary to regard industrialization as at best a very ambiguous step forward in the antientropic vocation of the social form of matter—and at worst as a tragic detour.

Industrialization by its very nature presupposed the commodification of labor. Nearly all earlier ways of organizing labor left the worker in charge of the labor process and determined the division of the value added on an essentially political and cultural basis: the exploiter could take whatever he could force the worker to give him while maintaining sufficient legitimacy to prevent rebellion. Slavery afforded the master greater control over the labor process, but left him burdened with surplus labor during downturns in demand and with unproductive laborers who he was, under most systems, obliged to support, at least after a fashion, during old age.

Capitalism overcomes all these problems. The commodification of labor means that its price, like that of all other commodities, fluctuates around its value, which is determined by the average socially necessary labor time required for its (re)production (and for the production of the inputs necessary for its production). The capitalist pays the worker the value of his labor power and owns the product of the labor performed, which includes the surplus the worker is able to produce above and beyond what he needs to reimburse the capitalist for his wages. The market at once disciplines the capitalist to pay the worker what is necessary for his reproduction *and* disciplines the worker to consume no more than is strictly necessary, making the whole social surplus product available for reinvestment. The development of capital markets, meanwhile, disciplines the capitalist to actually reinvest the surplus he captures, rather than simply consuming it in the form of luxuries. Capitalists who fail to make rational investments will, quite simply, be driven out of business. The emergence of fully developed capital markets is, however, a phenomenon of what we will call late modernity and is completed only at the end of the twentieth century with the development of information technology, which makes possible the instantaneous reallocation of capital.

In this context, the debate between capitalism and socialism takes on a very different character. Early arguments for capitalism—or for free markets, since that is the way in which the arguments were cast— began from the premise that the aim of political economy is to maximize the generation of wealth. Wealth is produced by labor, and labor can produce only when it is set into motion by capital. The wealth of a country will thus be determined by its capital supply. Now the capital supply cannot be increased by regulation, because investors will naturally choose the most profitable allocation of their resources possible. Regulation could at best match this and is thus pointless (Smith 1776).

Marx's critique of capitalism is first and foremost a response to this claim that the market is an optimal economic regulator. An early form of this critique centered on the problem of underconsumption. As industrialization advances, the value of labor power declines since it takes less labor to produce the goods and services that workers need to reproduce themselves. This means declining wages and ultimately results in insufficient effective demand. Workers cannot buy what they produce, and the result is an ever-deepening cycle of crises (Marx and Engels 1848/1978). Later versions of the critique focused instead on the tendency of the rate of profit to fall as the economy became more technologically advanced. Value is produced by living labor. As more and more of the input into production takes the form of technologically sophisticated machinery, the rate of profit declines, leading to a tendency for capital to be redeployed to lower wage, lower technology activities in which the rate of profit is higher (Marx 1967/1978).

Socialism, understood as a real historical social structure rather than as the ideal of a social movement, never really transcended—indeed it never really made an effort to transcend— the commodification of labor. What it did, rather, was to replace the capital markets with the state as the principal resource allocator while reducing market discipline on labor by political means and for political reasons. In the classical Marxist vision, this would complete the transition to a fully rational model of resource allocation and unleash a rapid development in the productive forces that would, in relatively short order, lead to the mechanization of essentially all noncreative labor.

The democratic revolutions must be understood in the context of the defining technological and economic features of modernity. It is not so much democracy as the modern sovereign nation-state that is essential to realization of the modern ideal. The modern sovereign nation-state provides a unified national market in which mass production can develop, as well as the complex monetary and legal framework that capitalism requires. Where necessary the modern state can drive industrialization by means of state expenditures, generally on arms.

Democratic revolutions have engaged modernity in two very distinct ways. Where absolutist monarchies had build effective modern states and were leading the process of industrialization and capitalist development, democracy was primarily a means of *resisting modernity* and *limiting sovereignty*. Where, on the other hand, absolutist monarchies were unable to successfully modernize, democratic revolutions became the principal agents of modernization. As we will see below, this was one of the principal factors determining which variant of the high-modern ideal became dominant in a particular country.

Secularization, similarly, is a nearly universal characteristic of modern civilization, but like democracy its meaning is hotly contested. High modernity *is* secularization in the sense that the aim of deification, which earlier civilizations sought to realize by primarily spiritual means, and often only beyond this world, modernity seeks to realize by material means, in this world, by means of civilizational progress of some kind. This does not, however, mean that modernity, even high modernity, is characterized by a decline of religious interest or even of traditional religious belief and practice. On the one hand, high modernity is itself a kind of secret religion—rather two secret religions. On the other hand, traditional religion survives, in varying measures, in modern societies, as a form of refuge from or resistance to high-modern ideals that have never been entirely accepted by the people.

Like democracy, furthermore, the degree and form of secularization within modern societies depends in large measure on the process of modernization itself. Where traditional religious structures were able to

Modernity and Metaphysics

adapt to the demands of modernity, militant secularism has been rare, but where religious institutions have actively resisted modernity, it has been far more common.

Divergent Pathways of Modernization

All this suggests that we need to look very closely at the different ways in which societies have embraced and attempted to realize the high-modern ideal. Here we find two divergent pathways, with a number of tributary routes and detours around and between them. The development of capitalism in England and North America proceeded along what, from a global perspective, must be regarded as very unusual lines. Throughout most parts of Europe the peasant revolts of the late tributary period were put down, and a long period of feudal reaction ensued. Much the same was true throughout most of Asia, Africa, and the Americas, where European conquerors put down local revolts and strengthened indigenous tributary structures as a mechanism of surplus extraction and social control (Anderson 1974a). In England, on the other hand, the peasant revolts, particularly the revolt of 1381, led to a partial victory, and by the end of the fourteenth century, the peasants had succeeded in eliminating most strictly feudal obligations, and in significantly increasing their total share of the social product. In response to this situation, landowners began a long struggle to rationalize agricultural production. Many converted from grain production, which was relatively labor intensive, to wool production, which required fewer hands. Others began to implement new and more sophisticated techniques for cultivating grain. Implementation of these techniques required a smaller and more disciplined work force, with the result that, in grain growing areas as well, peasants were run off their land. Over a period lasting nearly four hundred years, the greater part of the English peasantry was gradually driven from the land and transformed into a massive agricultural and industrial proletariat.

When the English conquered North America, they continued this process. The indigenous peoples of the continent actively resisted the imposition of forced labor, and so they were driven off their land, pressed westward, and eventually exterminated, opening up the continent to capitalist development. In the southern part of the continent, they imported African slaves. The northern part of the continent, on the other hand, served as an outlet for English, and later European, peasants, displaced by the penetration of capitalist relations into the countryside.

The result was the famous "triangle trade," a powerful engine for the primitive accumulation of capital. English traders captured or purchased slaves from Africa, whom they sold to the sugar, tobacco, and later the cotton planters of the Caribbean basin. These planters in turn sold them agricultural raw materials, which the traders then carried to the industrial centers of England, or later the American northeast. The finished goods—rum, tobacco products, textiles, as well as guns and other manufactured goods—were then resold to African slave traders or Caribbean planters. Grain farmers in New England, and later in the Northwest Territories, kept workers and slaves alike supplied with cheap food, and provided a secondary but growing market for manufactured goods. Capital was accumulated primarily by the industrialists. This is because plantation agriculture, dependent as it was on slave labor, was resistant to rationalization. Planter culture was, furthermore, oriented towards high levels of luxury consumption, something which diverted surplus away from investment in new techniques or new economic activities.

It is in the context of this distinctively Anglo-American experience that liberal theorists are most likely to look for evidence to support their claim that capitalism was a spontaneous development. And it is true that the Anglo-American road created a powerful constituency for liberal economic policies and for a liberal understanding of democracy. England, as the global hegemon, was the principal advocate of free trade in the late eighteenth and early nineteenth century. In England, furthermore, the monarchy had been largely successful in building a modern sovereign nation-state. Building on the early advantage of the Norman Conquest, the English monarchy successfully won autonomy from Rome, built an independent gentry, which served, at least initially, as its social base, and subjected the entire territory to a common system of laws and courts, a common system of taxation, etc. The democratic revolutions in England always sought to resist or at least limit this dynamic. It was the Norman barons who led the resistance to absolutism, winning the Magna Carta in 1215; other social classes gradually demanded the same rights—i.e., the same protections against the exercise of royal sovereignty—as the barons had won for themselves. Popular participation in the affairs of state came about indirectly, as first the lords, then the gentry, and eventually the bourgeoisie and working classes demanded protection from the single most important exercise of royal sovereignty—taxation—without their consent. Once the Commons had established control over taxation, of course, it had effectively gained control over the state apparatus. It was the "progressive gentry" of England during the later seventeenth and eighteenth centuries who provided the principal constituency for liberal theories, such as that of Locke, who argued that the state existed only to protect the "natural rights" of life, liberty, and property, and that a right to property emerged spontaneously when human beings mixed their labor (or that of agricultural laborers or African slaves under their direction) with the land.

The United States followed a similar pathway, though northern industrialists, facing stiff competition from England, were less inclined to support free trade than their English counterparts. It was the planter elites of Virginia, the Carolinas, and Georgia who provided the single most consistent constituency for limited government during the first century of U.S. independence, arguing for low levels of taxation and state expenditure, low tariffs, and a minimum of state regulation of the economy. The United States also inherited the liberal understanding of democracy and radicalized it in the context of its successful struggle for independence from the British Crown. In both contexts it was able to survive in large part because it served as a means of defending vigorous, developing capitalist economies from the encroachment of the state, and led to the development of state structures that bring together the principal interests (mostly, but not exclusively capitalist) that must be accommodated in managing a modern capitalist economy.

Elsewhere in Europe the peasant uprisings of the late feudal period ended in defeat and were followed by a long period of feudal reaction. When commercial agriculture finally began to develop it took a very different form. In France for example, commercial agriculture was centered in the production of wine for export; in Eastern Europe it was centered on the production of grain to feed the workers of the emerging industrial region along the Rhine (Moore 1966: 48–54, 435). In this context, the industrial bourgeoisie remained very weak: dependent on state subsidies and state monopolies and focused on the production of arms and luxuries (Moore 1966: 56–57). Asia, Africa, and Latin America suffered an even more extreme reaction, with local tributary structures strengthened so as to facilitate these regions into agro-export platforms.

Within this context, two distinct alternatives were available. Where the state rationalized itself and became an engine of modernization (Prussia, Japan), democracy came late and only as a result of defeat in the Second World War. Where it did not (France, Russia, and much of the Third World), we see the emergence of a revolutionary democratic and even socialist path to modernity (Moore 1966: 57–58). Here an intelligentsia deeply formed by the tradition of modern dialectics was able to focus popular resistance to modernization on *capitalism*, and to cast themselves in the role of the organizers and directors of human history. In this context, democracy *means* popular sovereignty, not the defense of traditional or natural rights.

These divergent pathways of modernization essentially define the different meanings of secularization within the modern world. By the time of the Reformation and Counter-Reformation, the Christian churches were largely dependent on the emerging monarchic states. Where these states were able to modernize themselves, they protected their churches but in the process discredited them, so that religious dynamism became focused outside the established churches. This dissent flourished largely in places where liberal democratic revolutions had successfully limited sovereignty: England, but especially the United States. Indeed, a proposal to appoint an Anglican Bishop for the colonies was one of the principal motives for the American Revolution, one often neglected by secularizing historians (Heimart 1966). In countries that followed the revolutionary democratic or socialist roads to modernity, on the other hand, modernization came to be associated with a militant secularism that confined traditional religion to the private sphere, or else attempted to repress it altogether. This dynamic was avoided only in parts of Asia, Africa, and Latin America where local religious traditions allied themselves with struggles for national liberation.

High Modern Metaphysics

The divergent pathways of modernization, in defining the meaning of secularism, also determined which of the two variants of the high-modern ideal became dominant, with profound implications for the fate of metaphysics. In sectors and regions in which the Anglo-American (i.e., liberal, "spontaneous") pattern of capitalist development predominated, or which looked to these sectors or regions for leadership, rational metaphysics tended to decline, as the leading role in civilization building was taken by an alliance between the bourgeoisie and the scientific-technical intelligentsia. This was partly a spontaneous development. In a society that lacks a conscious, rational center, it becomes increasingly difficult for people to think a transcendent first principle, whether in univocal or analogical terms. The spontaneous metaphysics of a pure market society is univocal and atheistic. It is the universe of atomistic materialism that is ordered but not organized (i.e., lawlike but not purposeful) and in which individuals who understand the operation of the laws of nature can use them to their own advantage. This will be especially true where the state serves only to maintain the formal conditions for the operation of the marketplace, and does not intervene directly in outcomes, and where the Church has been tamed by the state, as is the case in most developed Protestant polities.[4] Partly, though, the eclipse of metaphysics is the result of conscious policy. In the absence of a rational metaphysics there is no way to ground a moral critique of the market order. Capitalists who do not need the state will generally favor intellectual currents that thus leave them free from moral scrutiny, a preference expressed increasingly in the nineteenth century. Philosophical critiques of metaphysics in these regions serve to "make the world safe for capitalism."

Elsewhere, where the state became the engine of modernization, we see a very different pattern. Here the leading role is undertaken by the intelligentsia itself, though as we will see sharp tensions emerge between the political-organizational, humanistic, and technical fractions of this "new class." Rational metaphysics of some kind remains necessary in order to legitimate the role of conscious rational leadership and to ground the moral norms that guide the allocation of resources. In so far as this metaphysics attempts to theorize the modern project, it tends to put humanity at the very center, explicitly or implicitly divinizing humanity or some element therein as the unique subject-object of the cosmohistorical evolutionary process. At the same time, the state—or the revolutionary party that controls the state—itself resists being held accountable for its decisions and advances increasingly radical claims to an ideological monopoly. This sets up a profound ambiguity regarding the whole enterprise of metaphysics, which often continues to be practiced under some other

4. The United States presents a rather unique situation. There, the individual churches remained autonomous and in many cases were quite powerful, attempting to affect the development of U.S. society in a way that reflected their particular political-theological agendas. The value-neutrality of the public arena was established only gradually, as the proliferation of sects created a situation of stalemate and as the disappointment that followed the failure of Radical Reconstruction after the Civil War pushed American Protestantism in an increasingly otherworldly and premillenial direction.

name, as the church/state struggles of early modernity are replayed inside the state or state-party apparatus itself.

In what follows we will analyze these two very different patterns and ask to what extent they suggest that rational metaphysics can actually be blamed for modern nihilism and state terror. But before we can do this we must look in some depth at the thinker who stands at the turning point between early and high modern philosophy and whose work has been interpreted in very different ways by the positivistic and dialectical traditions.

The Kantian Watershed

There are many ways to understand the significance of Kant. From a purely philosophical standpoint, he represents a very natural response to the philosophical impasse that had been reached by the end of the eighteenth century. Ultimately neither rationalist nor empiricist approaches to philosophy proved convincing. Having to prove the existence of God in order to validate the reliability of sensation seems to violate the principle of economy, while the empiricist insistence on beginning with sensation turns out yield conclusions no less exotic than those of the rationalists. By the end of the eighteenth century science, ethics, and religion all seemed to be in jeopardy. Kant's aim was to reground them. That he concluded this was impossible from the standpoint of pure or theoretical reason is merely a step in the development of modern dialectics, which turned instead to practical reason and ultimately to revolutionary practice to overcome the limits of pure theory.

But today Kant's philosophy is rarely invoked as a way of grounding science, ethics, or religion, but rather as a demonstration that rational metaphysics, whether in the older sense in which it had been practiced by the scholastics or early moderns, or in the sense in which it was revived by Hegel, is, quite simply, impossible.

Kant's argument is simple. He begins by making a distinction between two types of judgments: analytic and synthetic. In analytic propositions the predicate is already contained in the subject; analysis merely draws it out.

All triangles have three sides.

Synthetic propositions, on the other hand, join ideas that were previously separate.

The chair is red.

Prior to Kant, it was taken for granted that analytic arguments are *a priori*, and that synthetic arguments are *a posteriori*. The judgment that all triangles have three sides requires no observation; we conclude directly from the definition. The judgment that the chair is red, on the other hand, is possible only after we have observed the chair and determined its color. What Kant proposes is that there is another sort of synthetic argument, the synthetic *a priori*, which provides the solution to his problem. Synthetic *a priori* judgments join two ideas prior to any observation, by showing that they are the condition of any possible experience. Kant claims that we make this kind of judgment all the time in mathematics. The idea of "seven" is not, he claims, contained in the ideas of "three" and "four," nor is the idea "shortest distance between two points" (which is quantitative) contained in the idea "straight line" (which is qualitative). The same is true of physics. The conservation of matter, for example, involves not an analysis but rather a synthesis of ideas. But in none of these cases are the judgments based on observation. We make the judgment prior to any observation whatsoever.

What Kant concludes from this is that knowledge is not so much a matter of conforming our minds to objects as it is of conforming objects to our minds. He did not mean by this that the object is created by the mind, and therefore exists only within it, but rather that we know the object only as it is structured for us by the operation of the intellect. What the mind does is to take the manifold data of experience and impose on it a unified structure, which makes thought possible. The forms of intuition, space, and time, structure our actual sensory experience; the categories of the understanding—quantity, quality, relation, and mode—structure the way we relate experiences to each other and form them into a unified whole.

What this does for Kant is to establish a sort of foundation for mathematics and science. Universal and necessary knowledge is possible in these disciplines because everyone organizes and unifies the given data of the senses in the same way. The same is not, however, true for metaphysics. Because the intellect unifies rather than abstracts, we cannot conclude to anything supersensible. Concepts such as the self, the cosmos, and God, which Kant calls the transcendental ideals, reflect nothing more than the drive of the intellect to unify our experience perfectly. These ideas do not, however, correspond to any possible object of experience, and we thus have no basis on which to claim that they correspond to anything outside the mind. Indeed, when we try to treat the transcendental ideas as if they were objects of experience, reason runs into contradictions or antinomies from which it cannot extricate itself. Thus the interminable debates regarding freedom and necessity, the finitude or infinity of the universe and its infinite divisibility or reducibility to simple parts (atoms), and the existence or nonexistence of God.

It is on this basis that Kant rejects the historic arguments for the existence of God. The ontological proof he rejects out of hand. Being, he points out, is not a real predicate that can be deduced by analysis of some other predicate, such as "than which nothing greater can be thought" or "perfect." We know something actually exists only by observation. But he goes on to reject the cosmological and teleological arguments as well. The cosmological argument, he points out, turns on extending the category of causality, by which the understanding orders sensible experience, to the supersensible realm—a move he claims is illegitimate. Similarly, the teleological argument argues from the presence of cosmic order to the notion of an orderer who is, however, beyond any possible experience.

Unable to conclude to a first principle, Kant had to seek some other way in which to ground ethical judgments. Here, too, Kant turned to *a priori* reason. Like science, ethics is grounded in the *a priori* structure of human reason. Just as the mind unifies experience under the forms of the intuition and the certain definite categories of the understanding, so it seeks to unify our action under a single, internally consistent and universal principle, the categorical imperative: "Act only on that maxim whereby you can at the same time will that it should become a universal law." From here, Kant goes on to argue that in order to follow this principle through consistently, we must assume (though we cannot prove) freedom of the will, immortality, and the existence of God.

In itself, Kant's philosophy represents an attempt from within the dialectical tradition to realize the ideal of rational autonomy and democratic citizenship within the context of a capitalist social order. It also demonstrates clearly the impossibility of this project. In the absence of a rational metaphysics in the traditional sense it becomes impossible to make substantive judgments regarding questions of meaning and value and thus. Ethics becomes purely formal. This meets very precisely the ideological needs of the rising bourgeoisie. A formal ethics can ground such principles as property, contract, etc., but provides no basis on which to challenge the market allocation of resources. Religion, meanwhile, is respected but pushed to the background. There is no room here for interventions into the market order on the basis of revealed wisdom, but also no basis for the sort of radical secularism that attempts to replace God with humanity in the sense of investing humanity with fully divine prerogatives.

From here, two options were left open: a radical rejection of the whole enterprise of metaphysics, even in the very limited way in which Kant tried to practice it, and an attempt to work through the contradictions that Kant discovered in pure or theoretical reason by developing a fuller and more complete account of practical reason and the revolutionary political practice it grounds.

Positivism and the Analytic Tradition

The catalogue of high-modern schools that took the first path, and rejected the whole enterprise of rational metaphysics, understood very broadly as an attempt to resolve fundamental questions of meaning and value on the basis of reason alone, is quite long and we cannot possibly address them all here. Perhaps the most straightforward way of showing how this trend developed is to begin with Kant's claim that Being is not a proper predicate. This claim does two things. First, from a purely methodological standpoint, it points towards the focus on logical and linguistic analysis that has dominated high-modern philosophy in the English speaking world. Second, at the substantive level, it points towards the claim, formulated most clearly by Alfred Ayer (Ayer 1936), that most of the claims of what had hitherto passed for philosophy are meaningless.

Where logical positivism in the tradition of Ayer differs from Kant is in its rejection of the synthetic *a priori*. Ayer, for example, restricts meaningful sentences to those that are purely analytic (the realm of pure mathematics) and those that describe a verifiable empirical reality (the realm of the sciences). The role of philosophy, in this context, is not so much to engage questions of meaning and value as it is to exclude them from deliberation as meaningless and not subject to rational resolution.

Later analytic philosophy, following Wittgenstein, opted for a somewhat broader understanding of what is meaningful, allowing the existence of different types of "language games," including even religious language. Their legitimation of these differing forms of language, however, presupposes their exclusion from accountability before any higher rational criteria of the sort that philosophy generally, and metaphysics in particular, has generally upheld. Religious belief, in other words, might be reasonable, but not on the basis of evidence or argument, but rather because it is, as Alvin Plantinga has argued, "properly basic" in the same way as our belief that Friday follows Thursday (Plantinga 1983). This radically undercuts the authority of philosophy with respect to both ordinary discourse and the sciences.

High modernity in the positivistic tradition has, for the most part, *pretended* to have "gotten over" humanity's concern with fundamental questions such as "what, if anything, does it all mean?" But this is mere pretence. The capitalist high modernity that gave birth to positivism is, as we have argued above, every bit as much oriented towards the end of divinization as any other human society. It just pursues it differently, by means of scientific and technological progress. This is what we have called "the secret religion of high modernity."

From time to time this secret has gotten out. When it does, it usually takes the form of more or less explicit and transparent attempts to replace metaphysics or theology with modern mathematical physics, and to resolve questions of meaning "scientifically." Perhaps the most striking example of this phenomenon in recent years is the vast literature regarding Anthropic Cosmology (Barrow and Tipler 1986) and especially Frank Tipler's *Physics of Immortality*. It is worth looking at Tipler's approach in some depth, because it gives us a window on how a certain sector of capitalist high modernity engages the questions formerly dealt with by metaphysics.

Tipler takes as his starting point a high-technology variant of Berkeley's subjective idealism. The universe is a vast information processing system. Matter is the "hardware" component of the system, the laws of nature the "software." Drawing on the information theory developed by Shannon and Weaver (1949), Tipler argues that the organization of a system is its negative entropy, or the quantity of information encoded within it. "Life" is simply information encoded in such a way that it is conserved by natural selection. A system is intelligent if it meets the "Turing test," i.e., if a human operator interrogating it cannot distinguish its responses from those of a human being (Turing 1950). The mathematical physical reductionism of Tipler's model should be apparent.

What is distinctive about Tipler, however, is his technological triumphalism, which promises eternal life on a technological basis. Intelligent life continues forever, he argues, if:

1. information processing continues indefinitely along at least one worldline γ all the way to the future c-boundary of the universe; that is, until the end of time;

2. the amount of information processed between now and this future c-boundary is infinite in the region of spacetime with which the worldline γ can communicate; that is the region inside the past light cone of γ; and

3. the amount of information stored at any given time τ within this region diverges to infinity as τ approaches its future limit (this future limit of τ is finite in a closed universe, but infinite in an open one, if τ is measured in what physicists call "proper time"). (Tipler 1994: 132–33)

The first condition simply states that there must be one cosmic history in which information processing continues forever. The second condition states that it must be possible for the results of all information processing to be communicated to world-line γ. This means that the universe must be free of "event horizons," i.e., regions with which an observer on world line γ cannot communicate. It also means that since an infinite amount of information is processed along this world line, an observer on this line will experience what amounts subjectively to eternal life. The third condition avoids the problem of an eternal return, i.e., an endless repetition of events as memory becomes saturated and new experience thus impossible.

Tipler then goes on to describe the physical conditions under which "eternal life" is possible. In accord with the as yet incompletely unified state of physics, he presents separate "classical" or "global general relativistic" and "quantum mechanical" theories. We take his "classical" theory first. Information processing is constrained by the first and second laws of thermodynamics. Specifically, the storage and processing of information requires the expenditure of energy, the amount required being inversely proportional to the temperature.

> ...it is possible to process and store an infinite amount of information between now and the final state of the universe only if the time integral of P/T is infinite, where P is the power used in the computation and T is the temperature. (Tipler 1994: 135)

Eternal life thus becomes essentially a problem of finding an adequate energy source. Tipler proposes finding this source in the "gravitational shear" created as the universe collapses at different rates in different directions. This imposes a very specific set of constraints on the process of cosmic evolution. Only a very special type of universe, the so-called "Taub" universe, named after mathematician Abraham Taub, collapses in just precisely the way required. And even most Taub universes tend to "right" themselves, returning to more nearly spherical form. For information processing to continue forever, life must gain control of the entire universe, and force it to continue its Taub collapse in the same direction far longer than it would spontaneously (Tipler 1994: 137). Thus the requirement that intelligent life gain control of the universe as a whole, and control the rate and direction of its collapse, so as to create the enormous energies necessary to guarantee eternal life.

Meeting the second and third conditions outlined above requires, furthermore, that the universe be closed, because "open universes expand so fast in the far future that it becomes impossible for structures to form of sufficiently larger and larger size to store a diverging amount of information" (1994: 140). It also requires that "the future c-boundary of the universe consist of a single point ... the Omega Point" (1994: 142). Finally, in order to meet information storage requirements, "the density of particles must diverge to infinity as the energy goes to infinity, but nevertheless this density of states must diverge no faster than the cube of the energy" (1994: 146). Tipler identifies, in addition to these requirements, which he calls "weakly testable," a variety of other predictions that can be used to test his theory, including the requirement that the mass of the top quark be 185 +/- 20 GeV and that the mass of the Higgs boson must be 220 +/- 20GeV (1994: 146). Fermilab recently measured the top quark at just a little bit below this mass.

In order to understand Tipler's Quantum Omega Point Theory, it is necessary to understand some of the internal contradictions of current quantum cosmology. In general relativity the spatial metric h and the nongravitational fields F are taken as given on the underlying three-dimensional manifold S. Cosmologists then attempt to find a four-dimensional manifold M with a Lorentz metric g (the gravitational field) and nongravitational fields F such that M contains S as a submanifold, g restricted to S is the metric h, and K is the extrinsic curvature of S, or, to put the matter differently, K says how quickly h is changing along the fourth, "temporal" dimension (1994: 162). In quantum cosmology, on the other hand, the universe is represented by a wave function $\Psi(h,F,S)$, which determines the values of h and F on S (1994: 174–75). One feature of the system, however, remains arbitrary: the selection of the fixed three-dimensional manifold S. Hartle and Hawking have proposed to eliminate this contingency by allowing the wave function to be a function of any three-dimensional manifold. According to this view, the domain of Ψ includes all possible values of h, F, and S (1994: 178). The Hartle-Hawking formulation, however, still requires h to be spacelike on all three-dimensional manifolds S. This restriction brings the formulation into conflict with classical general relativity, which does not distinguish so sharply between space and time.

Tipler points out, however, that the requirement that h be spacelike derives from a subjectivist interpretation of quantum mechanics, which interprets the wave function as a probability amplitude at a given time. This, obviously, requires times to be sharply distinguished from space. Tipler, however, favors a Many-Worlds interpretation of quantum mechanics, according to which all possible values of the wave function exist mathematically, and all those which permit the existence of observers physically. This removes the need to distinguish between space and time, and thus the requirement that h be always spacelike. Tipler proposes instead to allow the domain of the wave function to include all four-dimensional manifolds that permit a Lorentz metric g. All such manifolds permit what is known as a foliation. They can, that is, be represented as a "stack" of three-dimensional manifolds S(t), each representing the topology of a possible universe at a different moment of time. Each foliation will have a metric h, which need not be space like, as well as nongravitational fields, induced by the enveloping spacetimes (M,g). Any (h,F,S) which cannot be represented this way has $\Psi=0$; it does not exist. Similarly, there will be many spacetimes that permit the same (h,F,S). Some of these may have a future c-boundary that is a single point—the Omega Point (1994: 174–81). Thus the Omega Point Boundary condition on the universal wave function:

> The wave function of the universe is that wave function for which all phase paths terminate in a (future) Omega Point, with life continuing into the future forever along every phase path in which it evolves all the way to the Omega Point. (1994: 181)

Now, the Four-Manifold Non-Classification Theorem states that there does not exist any algorithm that can list or classify all compact four-dimensional topological or differentiable manifolds without boundary, nor is it possible to tell if any two given manifolds are the same or different (1994: 190). This means that it is impossible to derive the system as a whole from any one of its elements—a situation which, following William James, Tipler identifies with radical, ontological indeterminism (1994: 187). This means that the existence of life and intelligence, and the *decision* on the part of intelligent life to guide the universe towards Omega, is in fact logically and ontologically prior to the universal wave function itself (1994: 183): "The wave function is generated by the self-consistency requirement that the laws of physics and the decisions of the living agents acting in the universe force the universe to evolve into the Omega Point" (1994: 203). Indeed, in so far as the equations of both general relativity and quantum mechanics are reversible, there is no scientific reason to assume that causality runs only in one direction: from the past, through the present, into the future. It might just as well be seen as running from the future, through the present, into the past. From this point of view, it is God, the Omega Point, which, existing necessarily, brings the entire universe into existence and draws it to himself.

> At the instant the Omega point is reached, life will have gained control of *all* matter and forces not only in a single universe, but in all universes whose existence is logically possible; life will have spread into *all* spatial regions in all universes which could logically exist, and will have stored an infinite amount of information, including *all* bits of knowledge which it is logically possible to know. And this is the end. (Barrow and Tipler 1986: 677)

The question arises, quite naturally, just how we are to reach Omega. The key link between actually existing carbon-based life, and this nonmolecular intelligent living system is a "race" of intelligent, self-reproducing, interstellar probes (the so-called von Neumann probes). Tipler proposes launching a series of such interstellar probes in the expectation that as they evolve they will grasp the conditions for the long-term survival of intelligent life in the cosmos, and eventually reorganize the universe on a cosmic scale in order to bring into being the nonmolecular life-form(s) that can survive into the final stages of cosmic evolution.

Such probes would, of course, be extremely expensive. It thus becomes necessary to identify an optimum path of economic development. It is interesting to note that both Barrow and Tipler make extensive reference to the neoliberal economist F. A. Hayek in their work. Hayek, like Barrow and Tipler, identifies complex organization with negative entropy, or with the quantity of information that a system can encode. An economy is simply an information processing system. No centralized planning agency or redistributional structure can grasp the complexity of a highly interdependent, rapidly developing human system, and any attempt on the part of such agencies to plan the society will inevitably result in a loss of complexity and will hold back growth and development.

> Certainly nobody has yet succeeded in deliberately arranging all the activities that go on in a complex society. If anyone did ever succeed in fully organizing such a society, it would no longer make use of many minds, but would be altogether dependent on one mind; it would certainly not be very complex but extremely primitive—and so would soon be the mind whose knowledge and will determined everything. The facts which could enter into the design of such an order could be only those which were known and digested by this mind; and as only he could decide on action and thus gain experience, there would be none of that interplay of many minds in which alone mind can grow. (Hayek 1973: 49)

What Hayek calls the "extended order" of the marketplace, on the other hand, is uniquely capable of accessing, processing, and communicating vast quantities of information.

> Much of the particular information which any individual possesses can be used only to the extent to which he himself can use it in his own decisions. Nobody can communicate to another all that he knows, because much of the information he can make use of he himself will elicit only in the process of making plans for action. Such information will be evoked as he works upon the particular task he has undertaken in the conditions in which he finds himself, such as the relative scarcity of various materials to which he has access. Only thus can the individual find out what to look for, and what helps him to do this in the market is the responses others make to what they find in their own environments. (Hayek 1988: 77)

> Information-gathering institutions such as the market enable us to use such dispersed and unsurveyable knowledge to form super-

individual patterns. After institutions and traditions based on such patterns evolved it was no longer necessary for people to strive for agreement on a unitary purpose (as in a small band), for widely dispersed knowledge and skills could now readily be brought into play for diverse ends. (Hayek 1988: 15)

The market thus takes on for Hayek what he acknowledges to be a transcendent character, organizing interactions of a scale beyond the capacity of any single mind or organization—beyond even the mind of God.

> There is no ready English or even German word that precisely characterizes an extended order, or how its way of functioning contrasts with the rationalists requirements. The only appropriate word, "transcendent," has been so misused that I hesitate to use it. In its literal meaning, however, it does concern that which *far surpasses the reach of our understanding, wishes and purposes, and our sense perceptions,* and that which incorporates and generates knowledge which no individual brain, or any single organization, could possess or invent. This is conspicuously so in its religious meaning, as we see, for example, in the Lord's Prayer, where it is asked that "*thy* will [i.e., not *mine*] be done on earth as it is in heaven . . ." But a more purely transcendent ordering, which also happens to be a purely naturalistic ordering (not derived from any supernatural power), as for example in evolution, abandons the animism still present in religion; the idea that a single brain or will (as for example that of an omniscient God) could control and order. (Hayek 1988: 72–73)

Barrow and Tipler draw on Hayek's reasoning to argue that in a market system the technological and economic development necessary to support the construction of interstellar von Neumann probes will take place spontaneously. They argue that insofar as

> the economic system is wholly concerned with generating and transferring information . . . the government should not interfere with the operation of the economic system . . . if it is argued . . . that the growth of scientific knowledge is maximized by information generation and flow being unimpeded by government intervention, does it not follow that the growth of economic services would be maximized if unimpeded by government intervention? (Barrow and Tipler 1986: 173)

Indeed, they argue that if the operation of the marketplace is left to run its course, the cost of energy and raw materials relative to wages will decline to the point that humanity will become capable not only of interstellar travel, but ultimately of reorganizing the structure of the cosmos on a macroscale—developments that are both critical for their meliorist physical eschatology.

> ... the price of raw materials and energy have, on the long term average, been decreasing exponentially over the past two centuries ... (Barrow and Tipler 1986: 172)

The sort of interstellar probes that Barrow and Tipler believe are necessary in order to secure the destiny of intelligent life in the cosmos would currently cost between $3x10^{10}$ and $2x10^{14}$, depending on their speed.

> These costs ... seem quite large to us, but there is evidence that they could not seem large to a member of a civilization greatly in advance of ours ... the cost relative to wages of raw materials, including fuel, has been dropping exponentially with a time constant of 50 years for the past 150 years. If we assume this trend continues for the next 400 years ... then to an inhabitant of our own civilization at this future date, the cost of a low velocity probe would be as difficult to raise as 10 million dollars today, and the cost of a high-velocity probe would be as difficult to raise as 70 billion dollars today. The former cost is easily within the ability of ... at least 100,000 Americans ... and the Space Telescope project budget exceeds $109. If the cost trend continues for the next 800 years, then the cost of a $3x1010 probe would be as difficult to raise as $4,000 today. An interstellar probe would appear to cost as much then as a home computer does now ... In such a society, someone would almost certainly build and launch a probe. (Barrow and Tipler 1986: 583)

Tipler's cosmology even has theological implications. Despite his frequent references to Aristotle and Aquinas, and his effort to show the compatibility of his theory with most of the principal religious traditions, these implications tend very clearly towards Calvinist Christianity. This is because of the centrality of what he calls "agent determinism." Realization of the Omega Point is, in one sense, inevitable; it is required by the very existence of the universe itself. But it presupposes the subordination of the interests of individual carbon-based organisms to a larger cosmic plan that involves the displacement of carbon-based organisms by machine, and eventually by nonmolecular intelligence. And in so far as this transition is best carried out through the unimpeded operation of rationally inscrutable market forces, it requires the submission of individual carbon-based organisms to cosmic imperatives that they cannot understand, with which, at the very least, they cannot fully identify. Eternal life, furthermore, is not something the soul achieves, by becoming actually capable of infinite self-organizing activity, but rather something bestowed on it by the nearly omnipotent and omniscient beings near Omega, simply because it is in *their* self-interest. Tipler makes a game-theoretical argument (1994: 245–59) that these beings will resurrect us, and will bestow eternal life upon us, and that this will be a life of potentially infinite richness and joy—but ultimately the decision is theirs. We have here, in effect, an anthropic cosmological argument not only for neoliberal economics but for a peculiar, high-tech Calvinism.

What are we to make of all this?

We have published detailed critiques of Tipler's *science* elsewhere (Mansueto 1995, 2002b, 2005). From the standpoint of this work, his project is interesting precisely because it shows that high modernity, and especially the high-modern project of (in this case quite literally) *universal* technological control, is in fact in no way dependent on anything like a traditional rational metaphysics. And indeed, it is due to his innocence of such metaphysics that Tipler is unable to understand the distinction between his Omega Point and the God of historical Judaism, Christianity, and Islam or why his vision, which is certainly *intended* to be hopeful, is nothing short of terrifying to most readers.

What Tipler proposes to build is, in effect, the God of univocal metaphysics: a being like us, but infinite in knowledge and power. This is quite different from *Esse* as such, which *is* in a qualitatively different way than we are, and which is defined not by sovereignty but rather by creativity.

This difference may, perhaps, be better illustrated at the imaginative level. The God of Judaism, Christianity, and Islam, the God understood by analogical metaphysics as *Esse* as such, appears to the prophet Elijah, for example, not in wind, earthquake, or fire, but rather in a gentle nurturing breeze (1 Kings 19:11). Attempts to illustrate something like Tipler's strategy of technological god building, on the other hand, have yielded such images as that of the Borg Collective in the *Star Trek* universe, which assimilates cultures and annihilates all difference, *The Matrix,* or the Replicators in *Stargate SG-1*, who consume everything around them in order to replicate and eventually take over the universe—i.e., exactly the economy of salvation that Tipler proposes for us.

High modernity, in other words, is quite possible without metaphysics. Indeed, in its capitalist form it works as hard as possible to drive metaphysics from the scene, declaring it not merely impossible but actually meaningless. In its place it proposes to solve all questions of meaning and value by means of mathematical physics. And the result of this antimetaphysical strategy of technological godbuilding is just precisely the nightmare of universal technological domination that the postmodernists attribute to metaphysics.

High-Modern Dialectics

There was, however, another way to read Kant—i.e., not as finally ruling out engagement with or even resolution of fundamental questions of meaning and value but, rather, as displacing that engagement from the realm of pure to that of practical reason, and from the realm of contemplation to that of action. This is, in effect, a radicalization of the dynamic already at work in the Averroist counter-reaction and Renaissance humanism, which focused humanity's attention on the task of civilizational progress as opposed to the pursuit of the beatific vision. Here, the analogical metaphysics of the dialectical tradition is saved, but with the—extraordinary—difference that the qualitative difference between contingent and necessary Being is overcome by means of revolutionary practice, which elevates humanity to the status of conscious subject of the cosmohistorical evolutionary process and confers on it what amounts to a divine status.

It is, of course, above all in Hegel that we find this agenda stated most clearly. Philosophically, Hegel represents an attempt to answer Kant's critique of pure reason by arguing—as Thomas had more than five centuries earlier—that there is a form of reason higher than the Kantian *Verstand*, what Hegel called *Vernunft* (Hegel 1830/1971) and what the scholastic tradition knew as the *separatio* (Aquinas, *In Boethius De Trinitate*). This higher form of reason goes beyond a formal description of the laws relating phenomena to each other—beyond even an analysis of underlying structures—to grasp the organizing principle of things and thus the reason for their existence. Hegel's rediscovery of this sort of reason (which, with an arrogance typical of the modern world, he took as an original discovery) enabled him to reconstruct rational metaphysics and, drawing on the extraordinary experience of the democratic revolutions, to enrich the *cosmic teleology* on which it had been based with a grasp of *historical teleology* and the ultimate meaningfulness of the human civilizational project. He even begins a critique of the market order, which, he argues, must be regulated and its contradictions ameliorated.

Many commentators have seen in Hegel's *Philosophy of Right* a profound accommodation with the Prussian state and even with the semi-feudal aristocracy and Evangelical (Lutheran) Christianity. Bhaskar (Bhaskar 1993), for example, argues that after an early infatuation with the democratic revolutions, Hegel resigned himself to the status quo and became a *de facto* apologist for Prussian absolutism, mapping out a strategy by means of which it might hegemonize the revolutionary intelligentsia. This verdict is not, however, really fair. His own pretensions to the contrary, Hegel was, after all, finite and a person of his time. The wave of democratic revolutions that began in France in 1789 crested and receded early in his career, and the next wave did not come until after his death. It was already becoming clear that the new world that these revolutions had ushered in was far from perfect—something that Hegel acknowledged implicitly in his critique of the limitations of the market order. It would be more accurate to say that Hegel sought an accommodation with the Prussian monarchy in order to leverage influence for the intelligentsia, which he called the universal class. Despairing of establishing the intelligentsia as the ruling class, he opted, in other words, for a classic Confucian solution. Hegel's position with respect to religion, furthermore, was hardly fideistic or irrationalist. On the contrary, he reproduces within a Protestant context what amounts to a moderate (Arab) Averroist position on the religious question, apparently without even being aware of it. Religion is, for Hegel, simply an imaginative statement of truths grasped more completely and more profoundly by philosophy and above all by his own system.

Hegel's standpoint was, in any case, fundamentally unstable. Hegelianism soon disintegrated into right and left wings. The right wing did devote itself to polemics on behalf of the Prussian state (Lukacs 1953/1980). The left wing, on the other hand, cultivated the revolutionary insight that human beings create their own institutions and ideas to mount an increasingly revolutionary critique of religion, the state, and eventually the market order.

Modernity and Metaphysics

The challenge, of course, was to find a strategy by means of which the secular humanistic intelligentsia could actually come to power. By the middle of the nineteenth century, the answer was becoming clear: the intelligentsia could rule only in alliance with the working classes and above all with the emerging proletariat, the size and potential power of which was rapidly increasing as Europe industrialized and which seemed to have nothing to bind it to the old order. Thus Marx's claim that "philosophy is the head of the revolution and the proletariat is its heart" (Marx 1843/1978: 65).

That the aims of communism are every bit as metaphysical as they are economic or political is apparent from Marx's formulation in the Paris Manuscripts, where he calls it:

> the definitive solution of the contradiction between man and nature and between man and man, the true solution of the contradiction between existence and essence, between objectification and self-realization, between freedom and necessity, between the individual and the species. Communism is the solution to the riddle of history and knows itself to be that solution. (Marx 1844/1978: 84)

Understood in the context of the larger history of the dialectical tradition, and the claims of Althusser (Althusser 1965/1977, 1968/1970) and his followers notwithstanding, there is no contradiction between this metaphysical and "humanistic" concern for transcending contingency and the focus in Marx's later works with the development of the productive forces. Like ibn Rush and Levi ben Gerson (and like Hegel), Marx regarded *all* knowledge and *all* mastery as contributing to a human self-realization that, even though the religious language has dropped away, still amounts to a kind of divinization. Indeed, communism can realize its metaphysical aims *only* if humanity masters cosmic history as well as its own.

This is the interest expressed in Engels' *Dialectics of Nature* (Engels 1880/1940), which is nothing if not an attempt to argue for the ultimate meaningfulness of the universe and thus to supply dialectical materialism with a more adequate cosmological foundation—a foundation that is "metaphysical" in the sense of being a universal explanatory deductive theory. Specifically, he argues that matter has within itself a principle of motion that leads to the development of ever more complex forms of organization. This motion is governed by the "three laws of the dialectic":

1. Quantitative changes in material systems eventually develop to the point where they lead to qualitative difference, and thus new forms of organization.

2. This process is driven by internal contradictions, such as those that Marx discovered between the forces and relations of production but which, not confined to the social form of matter, characterize physical and biological systems as well.

3. The contradictory character of material systems notwithstanding, the drive is always towards a higher synthesis, the "negation of the negation" of which Hegel had spoken, so that not only human history but the whole cosmic evolutionary process has a definite upward direction.

By understanding these laws, human beings can become the real subjects of the whole cosmohistorical evolutionary process. Indeed, we *are* that process become conscious of itself.

This ideal, unfortunately, began to fall apart very early on. This is because it was always internally contradictory. First, the development of science in the nineteenth century did not sustain Engels's teleological cosmology. Engels's vision foundered on the emerging pessimism of nineteenth-century science, something reflected most immediately in the somber predictions of cosmic heat death after the discovery of the Second Law of Thermodynamics. Second, the communist movement never really mounted a critique of *industrialism* or developed a strategy for transcending the *commodification of labor*. On the contrary, it actively celebrated the first and promoted the second by means of forced collectivizations and other policies that stripped peasants and artisans of direct control over the means of production. This is because both were necessary to the realization of the high-modern ideal of mastery over nature. Only industrial production and the wage relation could *generate* and *capture* the enormous surplus necessary if humanity was to develop technologically to the point that it became the subject rather than a mere product of cosmic evolution. But this meant that far from cultivating rational autonomy and creativity among the working classes, actually existing socialism was every bit as alienating as capitalism. Third, the kind of world-transforming politics, which was implicit in the communist ideal, was never really compatible with participatory democracy. This is already apparent in Marx himself:

it is philosophy, not the proletariat, which is the head of the revolution and thus the subject of the cosmohistorical evolutionary process. But this contradiction is reproduced, as it were, at a higher level within the revolutionary intelligentsia, which, if it is to be effective and not disintegrate into a bohemian subculture of warring ideological sects, must be disciplined into a compact vanguard, as Lenin suggested (Lenin 1905/1971). And yet the effect of this is to strip even most of the revolutionary intelligentsia of its role in organizing and directing human history. Indeed, the tendency has been towards the sometimes visionary but almost always brutal dictatorship of a single great leader, who becomes the real subject of the cosmohistorical evolutionary process, a god-emperor of a sort that would have made the Pharaohs envious, or else bureaucratic management by a collective of colorless technocrats. Finally, at the ideological level, modern dialectics suffers from a failure to complete its own metaphysics. We have already noted above that from the nineteenth century on modern science failed to sustain the teleological cosmology that dialectical materialism required. This was a problem not only from the standpoint of the aim of technological mastery, but also from the standpoint of intellectual coherence. A universe which, according to the very science that is to be the means of our mastery, ends inevitably in cosmic heat death, or an endless frigid expansion, or a "big crunch," does not really permit human self-divinization. This, in turn, creates a legitimation problem because it undercuts the rationale for the sacrifices demanded by industrialization, the commodification of labor, and revolutionary discipline.

It is as if high-modern dialectics was born crippled and already out of time.

We will explore the contradictions of actually existing socialism later in this chapter, as part of our analysis of late or "post" modernity and of the current situation. For now we need to ask how what we have said thus far about high-modern dialectics bears on the principal question of this work. We should note, first of all, that it is *only* with regard to the tradition of modern dialectics—which we have been tracing from the Averroist Counter-Reaction up through Hegel, Marx, Engels, and their interpreters—that the claims of Heidegger and the postmodernists regarding "metaphysics" really make any sense at all. Modern dialectics is the *only* totalizing metaphysics that can reasonably be connected with modern nihilism and state terror. *The political-theological critique of metaphysics is actually a form of disguised anticommunism.* But we have already demonstrated that there is nothing in metaphysics as such, or in the larger dialectical tradition, which leads to nihilism or state terror. Quite the contrary, we have shown that the analogical metaphysics of *Esse* and its analogues in other civilizational traditions have a long history of grounding efforts to advance human development and civilizational progress. It is, rather, specifically the innerworldly strategy of divinization, that, as in the case of positivistic modernity, leads to totalitarianism, albeit for slightly different reasons. Positivistic modernity seeks an unworthy goal—infinite power. Modern dialectics seeks a worthy goal by impossible and contradictory means.

This, in turn, raises an important question: why conceal a critique of *communism* in a broadside critique of rational metaphysics? The answer is actually rather simple. There is nothing in the contradictions that we noted in the communist project that condemns the broader aim of transcending the market order. On the contrary, this aspiration was shared by the larger dialectical tradition, which, as we have seen, came into being as part of an effort to reground a discourse around justice in the context of emerging petty commodity production, and which pursued the aim of either containing or transcending the market order without investing that aim with divinizing significance for over two millennia. It is, rather, the demand that in so doing we also transcend contingency, and that we thus gain total mastery over nature and history, which points towards a totalitarian practice. And yet it is just precisely the communist critique of the market order that Heidegger and the postmodernists seek to undermine. And there is no better way to undermine that critique than to disarm it metaphysically by undercutting the metaphysical framework in the context alone of which substantive judgments of value make sense.

We will analyze the social basis and political valence of postmodernism in the next section. For now, however, we need to look at least briefly at the actual record of high-modern dialectics as an ideological architectonic.

In tracing the subsequent development of high-modern dialectics, it is necessary to distinguish between the three geopolitical domains in which it has exercised influence: the Soviet bloc, the European (and to a far lesser extent North American) workers movements, and the national liberation movements of the Third World. It is also possible to identify trends within each of these domains that interpret the dialectic in ways that emphasize one or another of Engels's three laws. There are, in other words, dialecticians who see change primarily in terms of a gradual accumulation of forces, those who see change in terms of ongoing struggle and contradiction, and those who see change teleologically, as the working out of an immanent drive towards higher forms of organization.

From the standpoint of the analysis set forth here, it is hardly surprising that the Soviet tradition should have been more friendly to Engels's dialectics of nature than the European tradition. The attempt to find a cosmological ground for socialism and indeed a pull towards metaphysics makes sense in the context of a successful revolutionary struggle that provides a basis in experience for hope in the ultimate meaningfulness of the universe. This pull towards a resurgence of metaphysics has come from widely diverse directions within the Soviet tradition, including both the "tektology" of Bogdanov (Bogdanov 1928)[5] and his followers, which pretended to be a "universal science of organization" that replaced philosophy once and for all, but that, as a universal causal theory which claims to explain the universe and order action, qualifies as metaphysical from the standpoint of the political-theological critique, and the "dialectics" of Deborin and the "Menshevizing idealists," which represents a return, through Hegel, to positions not unlike those of the Arab and Latin Averroists (Wetter 1958, Joravsky 1961, Dahm 1988). Bogdanov in particular was associated politically with the "god-builders" Lunacharsky and Gorky, who argued that socialism, by expanding human creative potential to infinity, would eventually bring God into being, though he himself did not use that language.

We must note, however, that the pull back towards metaphysics was sharply resisted by elements within the Communist Party, and that the

---

5. The placement of Bogdanov within our typology is a somewhat difficult matter. Generally considered part of the "mechanistic" trend, Bogdanov shared with the other mechanists strong roots in positivism and the belief that science had superseded philosophy. And it was largely within mechanistic circles that his systems theory was conserved and developed after his death in 1928. The mechanistic trend generally acknowledged no teleology except a trend towards "stability," which they believed was characteristic of all systems. Bogdanov, on the other hand, clearly had a broader vision that stressed the gradual development of all systems towards ever higher degrees of organization, a claim carried further by his God-building comrades who saw the aim of the revolution as extending beyond socialism towards the creation of an infinite and perfect form of organization, i.e., God. It is interesting to see that the tradition of Soviet systems theory has given birth in the post-Soviet era to a new variety of teleological thinking that draws on the complex systems theory of Ilya Prigogine and others (Knyazeva and Kurdyumov 1996 and Knyazeva 1998).

ensuing conflict had a very specific political content. Both the "tektological" and the dialectical trends were based in the Communist Academy and the Institute of Red Professors, institutional predecessors of the Institute of Philosophy of the Soviet Academy of Sciences. Lenin, in spite of his emphasis on ideological discipline within the party, seemed willing to tolerate and even encourage a quasi-independent philosophical leadership based in these institutions—and this in spite of the fact that Bogdanov had been Lenin's chief competitor for leadership within the Bolshevik party during its early years, and Deborin a former Menshevik who joined the Communist Party only late in life. After Lenin's death, however, both trends were attacked for, among other things, conciliating religion, and for failing to "integrate theory and practice," or, as the Maoists would later say, to "put politics in command." Under the leadership of Deborin's former student Mitin, "dialectical materialism" was retheorized in such a way as to give priority to the principle of contradiction, rather than that of "the negation of the negation," as had been the case for both Bogdanov and Deborin, and ideological leadership was transferred to the Central Committee, with the Communist Academy and the Institute of Red Professors, now merged into the Academy of Sciences, reduced to the status of a support staff.

At issue here is a concern on the part of the party apparatus that both the resurgent metaphysical tendencies represented by Bogdanov and Deborin (which certainly differed very profoundly from each other), and the existence of a philosophical authority independent of the party, would ultimately constrain their political autonomy. Here the metaphysicians are cast in the role of a new clergy, with the party defending the autonomy of the lay sphere—or rather the sovereignty of the party and its General Secretary. The new theorization of dialectical materialism, in a way that gives priority to the principle of contradiction, had the effect of making organization and meaning purely and simply a product of power (here human rather than divine).

But the tektologists and the "Menshevizing idealists" both had a very serious problem. Their metaphysics really didn't allow for the existence of an autonomous philosophical authority—a philosophical "church" in tension with the political "state." If humanity is not merely a *participant* in God's creative power but is, rather, God himself, if we have not simply a created or emergent share in Being as such, but actually are or are becoming that power, then philosophy plays a secondary and subaltern role. It is scientific and technological progress and political organizing, not the dialectical ascent, which divinizes humanity. In the immanentist metaphysics of high modernity it is indeed the General Secretary, not the philosopher in the narrower sense, who is *dominus et deus*.

Given this situation, it should come as no surprise that the crisis of high modernity and the crisis of socialism so nearly coincided with each other. There were, to be sure, elements in Europe that rejected socialism and adopted a late or postmodern standpoint as early as the middle of the nineteenth century. We shall have more to say about them shortly. And the crisis of socialism was, to be sure, long and drawn out. As early as the late 1920s many in the Bolshevik camp were beginning to question the ability of the party-state to carry out its divinizing mission. By the time Stalin's crimes were revealed in the 1950s, it was difficult indeed to be a true believer. But it was not until the actual collapse of the Soviet bloc in the years between 1989 and 1991 that the fate of high modernism was finally sealed.

The reason for this crisis has already been identified. Actually existing socialism, like all historic forms, has both civilizationally progressive potential and potent internal contradictions. Socialism proved an effective way of industrializing countries that lacked colonies that could contribute to the primitive accumulation of capital. Strict restrictions on luxury consumption made it possible to simultaneously superexploit large sections of the population *and* to improve living standards in relatively short order, before superexploitation became a real legitimation problem. Socialism also made it possible to centralize resources for "big projects" such as space exploration and the creation of a world-class artistic, scientific, and cultural establishment.

So long as industrialization contributed to a rising standard of living, the party was able to maintain its legitimacy. Beginning in the 1950s, however, the party and the people began to part ways. Stalin's strategy called for investing most of the social surplus in civilization-building activities such as the arts, science, and culture and in increasing leisure time so that ordinary workers could gradually become participants in that civilizational building project, little by little fulfilling Marx's dream of a society in which everyone could be creative. Proletarianization, however, tends to strip people of their creativity and transform them into passive consumers. What the people wanted was to consume on a scale comparable to Europe or the United States. People had rising incomes, more leisure, and growing ruble bank accounts—but nothing to spend their money on. The result was a gradual decline in labor discipline and growth in productivity, a trend that became critical some time in the mid to late 1970s. Increasingly the party was seen as supporting only itself and a small elite of the culturally creative. When an attempt was made to resolve the crisis by imposing market norms and opening up the political system in order to allow more accountability, the people rebelled and the system collapsed.

In Europe, on the other hand, socialism was stillborn. More favorable economic conditions made it possible for the bourgeoisie to meet the demands put forward by the workers movement, undercutting the revolutionary impulse and defeating the strategy of the intelligentsia, which had been to leverage a proletarian revolution into a strategy for power.

In this context the principle of contradiction never completely overshadowed the other principles of the dialectic. Social democrats emphasized the slow, quantitative accumulation of forces in the hope that this would eventually lead to qualitative change. This trend reflected a kind of merging between the perspectives of the technical and humanistic intelligentsia. A diverse cluster of thinkers including Lukacs and the Frankfort School emphasized the search for wholeness and a higher synthesis—what Lukacs called "the standpoint of totality" (Lukacs 1922/1971). Only the Gramscian trend emphasized concrete political analysis, something that focused them on the identification of political contradictions. What all these trends had in common, however, was a rejection of the dialectics of nature and a tendency to transform Marxism into a purely sociological theory or into a philosophical anthropology ungrounded by any metaphysics.

This is, once again, hardly surprising given the situation of the left in Europe. Cosmological pessimism retained its hold over the defeated workers movements. But in Europe as in the Soviet Union, the conscious political strategies of the bourgeoisie also played a role. Even as Stalin and Mitin moved to constrain the resurgence of metaphysics in the Soviet Union, European Marxists rejected Soviet "diamat" and the dialectics of nature, which remained an integral part of Soviet doctrine even after Mitin, in large part because it seemed to chain them to a larger cosmo-historical process—and a central political authority legitimated by that process—which constrained their autonomy. The humanistic socialist defense of the rational subject, in other words, came at the expense of the ultimate meaningfulness of the universe. In spite of their frequent invocations of Hegel, humanistic socialists were actually closer to Kant, affirming an ungrounded ideal of humanity—understood as rational subject—as the creator of meaning in an otherwise meaningless universe.

Eventually, of course, the European left recognized this. The response, however, was not a turn towards metaphysics in search of a ground (and this in spite of the powerful opening by and to the Catholic Church during the 1960s and 1970s) but rather the "Althusserian reaction," which, even more so than Mitin's diamat, gave priority to the principle of contradiction and rejected the search for meaning and direction in even the limited arena of human history—and the ideal of the rational subject—in favor of concrete political analysis of "complex structured totalities." Marxism was reduced to an analytic tool for the workers movement in a desperate last effort to find a strategy for power. By the 1960s and 1970s, however, when this trend emerged it was already too late. Most humanistic intellectuals had already abandoned the modernist ideal.

Marxism in the Third World represents a more complex problem, one that reflects the situation of late modernity. Before we turn, therefore, to Third World Marxism, we must look at the conditions of late modernity itself.

LATE MODERNITY[6]

Social Structure

Contradictions of the Modern Project

What we are calling late modernity is, in effect, what happened to modern civilization as it became increasingly obvious that its ideal was unlikely to be realized. Late modernity thus includes both explicit rejections of the modern ideal as either unworkable or unworthy (what eventually became known as postmodernism) *and* adaptations of this ideal to changed conditions.

We have already suggested in the preceding section some of the contradictions of the modern ideal in both its positivistic and dialectical

---

6. I prefer this term to the more common "postmodernity" since it captures the sense in which the culture of this period represents at once a radicalization of certain elements of the modern reality (the groundlessness of principles and values) and a sense that the larger modern project is still dominant, but declining.

variants. Here we will merely restate these for clarity and then proceed to outline the complex process by which the modern project disintegrated.

For the positivistic variant of the modern ideal, the contradictions are fundamentally scientific and technological. Modern science and technology, for all their achievements, not only *have not* but *cannot* deliver us from finitude.

The limits of modern science and technology were already becoming apparent to some thinkers by the end of the eighteenth century. The first difficulty that came to light was demographic. Thomas Malthus, using reasoning that remains both influential and controversial to this day, claimed in 1798 that the planet would soon face unavoidable population pressures. This was because population grows geometrically and food production arithmetically. Efforts to ameliorate the situation of the poor, would, furthermore, only exacerbate the problem by allowing people who might otherwise have starved to survive and reproduce, leading eventually to a situation in which humanity exceeded the planet's carrying capacity. While many argued, and still argue, that Malthus's claims fail to taken into account the contribution of new technology, the actual experience of China and India in particular suggests that he was at least partly correct.

The limitation that Malthus identified was, in a certain sense, only a special case of the still broader limitation embodied in the Second Law of Thermodynamics—a result that, whatever one's position on the specifics of Malthus's argument and conclusions, suggests that there *are* limits to what industrial technology can do for us. Efforts to improve the heat engine, which was the driving force behind industrial production and thus humanity's campaign for mastery over nature, soon led to the conclusion that a perfect heat engine, one that recycles all of its energy and thus needs only a finite amount of fuel to do an infinite amount of work, was impossible. Stated more generally, the Second Law of Thermodynamics holds that in closed systems heat dissipates, or, to put the matter somewhat differently, closed systems tend towards entropy or disorder. In so far as current thinking held that the universe itself was such a closed system, the implications were especially somber. Not only does humanity face real limits to technological progress, but the universe itself is headed for a thermodynamic heat death. This result was problematic both for "early modern" natural theologies that argued for the existence of God based on the good order of the universe, and secular for humanists who had displaced hopes of individual immortality onto a future of infinite civilizational progress.

Other scientific results also raised questions about the high-modern ideal of unlimited progress. Attempts to bridge the theoretical gap between classical physics, which analyzed the movements of individual particles, and the new discipline of thermodynamics, which analyzed aggregate properties like heat, temperature, pressure, and entropy, led to the conclusion that, over an infinite period of time a closed system will return an infinite number of times to any arbitrary initial state. This result, known as the Poincaré Recurrence Theorem, seriously undercut the idea of infinite linear progress and reappeared in philosophical form in Nietzsche's doctrine of the eternal return.

Even Darwinian evolutionary theory, which seemed to be all about progress, had ambivalent implications. Thus Darwin's claim that evolution occurred through random variation and natural selection, while it allowed for at least local evolutionary progress, made progress the result not of conscious rational planning and cooperation but rather of spontaneous and rather ruthless natural forces. And in so far as the "value" implicit in Darwinian theory is survival and reproduction rather than complexity, it is possible to read the theory has having nothing to do with progress after all. Organisms evolve to fill niches and while some (such as human beings) do this by developing complex new capacities, the most successful (e.g., the insects) do it by sheer reproductive exuberance.

This situation was not, furthermore, remedied by the development in the twentieth century of relativity and quantum mechanics. On the one hand, from a purely scientific perspective these theories are mutually incompatible, based on fundamentally different mathematical infrastructures. Relativity assumes that reality is continuous; quantum theory that it is discrete. Relativity treats time as simply an additional dimension of a complex four-dimensional manifold; quantum theory retains the "classical" model of particles travelling through space "over" time. On the other hand, these theories have, for the most part, tended to produce very pessimistic cosmologies, predicting either that the universe will eventually collapse in a "big crunch" or, as is more common recently, that it will expand endlessly, with matter becoming more and more evenly distributed and complex organization rarer and rarer. While there certainly *are* scientists who have "kept the faith" with the secret religion of high modernity, as we saw in our consideration of Tipler in the previous section, this has become less and less common. Mature scientific rationality is increasingly associated with an abandonment of hope in redemption of any kind, material or spiritual. It has, in other words, become postmodern.

If these contradictions within the positivist variant of the high-modern project never quite became fully explicit, this is because the opposing, dialectical tradition instead focused attention on the structural contradictions of the capitalist system, which, for nearly 150 years, became a kind of lightening rod, attracting what was ultimately, at a deeper level, resistance to modernity as such.

We have already discussed the internal contradictions of capitalism that Marx identified: tendencies towards underconsumption and towards a declining rate of profit and thus disinvestment in just precisely the technologically most advanced sectors of the economy. The political-economic problems were, however, even deeper than Marx had realized. Capitalism, it turned out, had a way of coping with the underconsumption and with the tendency of the rate of profit to fall as the economy became technologically more advanced. By gaining hegemony over Asia, Africa, and the Americas, Europeans were able first to secure markets for goods they could not sell at home and then, as the rate of profit began to decline, to export capital to low-wage, low-technology enclaves abroad. Rather than investing in steel mills, machine tools, and railroads, in other words, capitalists in the late nineteenth century were investing in banana plantations. It is this phenomenon that Lenin called "imperialism." In reality empire building had always been part of the capitalist enterprise, as it was of many other earlier social structures. But Europeans during the early nineteenth century had regarded their own era as that of the nation-state, and even many Marxists did not expect capitalism to lead to a rebirth of empire. Instead, by the end of the nineteenth century, the great capitalist powers were engaged in a struggle to divide up among themselves not only Asia, Africa, and Latin America, but also the less developed (Celtic, Slavic, and Latin) fringes of Europe itself.

The result was a sharp polarization of the planet. Much of Europe, North America, and Japan had access to the imperialist superprofits necessary to ameliorate the internal contradictions of capitalism and make concessions to the working class sufficient to blunt the socialist challenge. Asia, Africa, and Latin America, on the other hand, descended ever deeper into poverty, as foreign investment distorted their economies, displacing subsistence with plantation agriculture and focusing development on low wage, low-technology activities. In between were a group of "weak links" in the imperialist chain that either broke with capitalism altogether (Russia) or militarized their societies in order to gain or keep the colonies they needed to resolve the internal contradictions of capitalism (the fascist states, especially Germany, Italy, Japan, Spain, and Portugal).

This phenomenon was accompanied by radical changes in the internal organization of capitalist economies. Lenin's *Imperialism* captured only part of the phenomenon: the concentration of capital and the merging of banking and industrial capital into what he called "finance capital," coupled with the emergence of large international monopolistic groupings. What was happening was, more precisely, the gradual emergence of authentic capital markets. While many enterprises well into the nineteenth century, including the most important, were privately held, the massive undertakings made technologically possible by the second industrial revolution required more capital than even the wealthiest individuals could accumulate. Increasingly the publicly held corporation, with shares traded on the stock markets, became the norm. This led to the emergence of a large class of investors who were not directly involved in the management of their corporations and to the reduction of entrepreneurs and managers to subaltern strata dependent on *rentiers* and on the capital markets.

The political implications of these developments were two-fold. First, the enormous concentrations of wealth that they implied seriously undercut the whole democratic project. Universal suffrage no longer meant universal participation—even indirect—in governance. The vast sums of wealth mobilized by large capitalist groupings gave them effective control over the state, except where the working classes were able to respond with equally vast mass organizations. But effective political action required an almost military degree of discipline. The members of mass working class organizations were either passive supporters who were mobilized on election day or else cadre who followed the directives of a small number leaders. The old autodidact tradition of the skilled trades that had played such a role in both the democratic revolutions and the early stages of the socialist movement began to gradually die. Second, the nation-state itself gradually began to lose its significance as a form of political organization. This pattern became fully apparent only in the second half of the twentieth century, and is still far from complete, but it presented a still greater challenge for those who still upheld the democratic ideal: how to have real participatory democracy in a globalized civilization dominated by large corporations and/or mass movements?

The contradictions of modern science and technology that undermined the positivistic variant of the high-modern ideal also affected modern dialectics. Becoming the subject of the cosmohistorical evolutionary process, after all, presupposed scientific and technological mastery of nature every bit as much as achieving infinite power. For the dialectical tradition, however, these contradictions were set within a context that was determined by the dynamics of revolutionary practice. We have already noted above that there was, from the very beginning, a real tension between rational autonomy and democratic participation, on the one hand, and the kind of world-transforming politics to which modern dialectics aspired. This contradiction was, furthermore, reproduced in the economic realm. To the extent that modern dialectics aspired to organize and direct not just human but cosmic history it became wedded to an industrialism that degraded and dehumanized workers and stripped them of even the ordinary subjecthood and personhood enjoyed by peasants and artisans in earlier societies. But if it abandoned its cosmic aims—as it was increasingly forced to do anyway, as modern science yielded increasingly pessimistic results—it ceased to offer real redemption. It remained humanistic but became postmodern.

The Unfolding Crisis of Modernity

The contradictions inherent in the modern project have unfolded over a very protracted period, which, as we have already suggested, reaches back to the end of the eighteenth and the beginning of the nineteenth century. It is, however, possible to identify several discrete stages in this crisis.

First, beginning in the late eighteenth and early nineteenth century, we see an early recognition of the profound tension between the dialectical ideal of rational autonomy on the one hand and the realities of industrialization and revolutionary politics on the other hand. Industrialization, as we noted, instrumentalized human beings in the name of a future in which everyone would be liberated from toil in order to engage in creative work and to participate fully in the life of the city. Revolutionary politics require that principled difference be submerged in favor of organizational discipline and effective mass action. First the Terror and then the dictatorship of Napoleon established a pattern that has been re-enacted with more or less rigor by essentially every modern revolution since then: attempts to reorganize human society in such a way as to liberate humanity from the bonds of necessity disintegrate ineluctably into terror and repression and yield not utopias of creativity and participation but rather dictatorships that retreat from repression only in ultimately compromising with the very traditional institutions (private enterprise, the church) that they sought to overthrow. And what is more, this revolutionary repression is directed first and foremost at the revolutionary intelligentsia itself, whose exercise of rational autonomy comes almost by necessity into contradiction with revolutionary *raison d'état*.

The first symptoms of this crisis appear in the arts. Theodor Adorno, for example, argued that the abandonment of the sonata-allegro form,[7] which he reads as the musical trace of the ideal of the self-unfolding of a rational, autonomous subject, in Beethoven's late style, in favor of the external form of the Catholic mass or the more static theme and variations, reflects a double disillusionment, first with the Revolution, as a result of its termination in Napoleon's dictatorship, and second with the Restoration, which followed his defeat (Subotnik 1976). Lukacs has made a similar point about the modern novel, which reflects the struggles of the critical modern subject in a world in which meaning has become radically problematic (Lukacs 1916/1974). But the whole of the Romantic movement with its celebration of the passions over the intellect and its furtive glances backwards towards the Middle Ages can be regarded as a sign that the modern ideal was already in trouble as early as 1815.

The philosophy of Hegel and Marx represents, in many ways, an attempt to come to terms with these first signs of crisis, either by reconciling reason to reality or reality to reason. Soon, however, even deeper contradictions began to emerge. We have already noted that Capital responded to its own internal contradictions by seeking colonies from which it could extract superprofits to compensate for the declining rate of profit in high-technology sectors at home. This in turn led to the division of the world

---

7. Sonata-allegro form, characteristic especially of the music of Haydn, Mozart, and Beethoven, begins with one or two initial themes or musical subjects, which it then modulates to a different key (usually one fifth higher, or in minor key compositions one fourth lower) and then develops extensively, driving towards a recapitulation in which the original subjects are reinstated in the original key but in more complex form. Adorno reads this as a metaphor for the self-unfolding of the rational, autonomous subject, which derives its content from itself and grows in complexity without dependence on anything outside itself.

by competing imperial powers and to "a long war" for global domination that the United States finally won only in 1989.

Integral to this war was the emergence of fascism as political and ideological movement and strategy. Fascism was, at the political-economic level, an adaptation on the part of those more or less industrially developed capitalist countries (Germany, Italy, Japan) that lacked colonies from which they could extract the surplus necessary to ameliorate contradictions back at home. These countries needed to mobilize and militarize their populations in an effort to conquer colonial empires that England, France, and Great Britain had simply occupied. In this sense, fascism was a political strategy fully in the modern tradition.

At the political-ideological level, on the other hand, fascism tapped into the growing disenchantment with modernity that had been growing ever since the late eighteenth century. Romantic themes of land, people, blood, nation, and even religion were woven into a complex discourse to mobilize peasants, workers, and especially the dispossessed petty bourgeoisie in a struggle for empire designed to save the very modern order they believed themselves to be rejecting. Meanwhile, at a psychological level, fascist ideologies spoke to deeply felt anxieties generated, in part, by the failure of modern philosophy, positivistic or dialectical, to adequately address fundamental questions of meaning and value (Gramsci 1948, Laclau 1974, Fromm 1941).

What is less widely acknowledged, but hardly cause for surprise, is the fact that a similar dynamic operated within the anti-colonial and anti-imperialist movements in Asia, Africa, and Latin America. From a purely ethical standpoint, to be sure, the situation of these movements is quite different. It is one thing to mobilize the people to build an empire and quite another to mobilize them to resist one or to recover from the damage empire has done. But the method of mobilization bears a frightening resemblance to that employed by fascism: national, popular, and religious themes that tap into a deep-seated resistance to modernity and the disruption of traditional ways of life serve to motivate struggles against imperial powers and to discipline the population for the long years of sacrifice that follow. At the same time, with a very few exceptions, the *aim* remains modernization (industrialization, the commodification of labor, a modern sovereign state, and the displacement of traditional religious leaders by a modern intelligentsia). One thinks here of the various Third World Socialisms (Arab/Islamic, African, Buddhist) that emerged in the postwar period as well as the implementation of dialectical materialism in the Third World.

Ultimately the displacement of popular resistance from *modernity* to *capitalism* began to unravel. Partly this was due to the internal contradictions of the socialist project itself. Where capitalism is characterized by tendencies towards underconsumption and decapitalization of high-technology sectors, socialism is characterized by what has come to be known as a "scissors crisis." This term derives from the agrarian struggles of the 1920s in which Soviet peasants, enjoying the results of land reform and lacking outlets for their increased incomes, reduced production to subsistence levels, nearly starving the cities and creating the pretext for the forced collectivization that followed (Bettelheim 1976). More generally, a scissors crisis occurs when a socialist economy, following its internal logic, both substantially frees workers and enterprises from market pressures and invests surplus rationally in civilization-building activities. Workers and enterprises do not need to produce in order to survive, have no outlets for their increased incomes, and so reduce their activity or investment levels, resulting in economic stagnation. Thus the slow collapse of the Soviet system; thus the ability of the Chinese to avoid a similar collapse only by fully exposing workers to global market pressures and entering the world market as a low-wage entrepot—i.e., just specifically the fate socialism was to help them escape.

More broadly, however, the crisis of socialism is the crisis of the modern project itself. Nearly everywhere mass socialist movements reflected an alliance between an intelligentsia driven by the dialectical variant of the high-modern ideal of divinization by means of innerworldly civilizational progress and peasants, artisans, and workers whose resistance to capitalism was really a resistance to modernity, at least as it actually developed. In Europe—and to a lesser extent in the United States—this alliance was able to force a "social democratic" accommodation within a still basically capitalist modernity that allowed the working classes to share in many of the benefits of modernity while protecting them from many of its contradictions—an accommodation which is now beginning to break down under the pressures of globalization. In the Soviet bloc and those parts of the Third World that followed an essentially Soviet model of socialist construction, the alliance brought to power regimes that modernized rapidly, resulting in higher standards of living during the first generation, but also led to the scissors crisis noted above. As socialist economies began to stagnate after the late 1970s, and the aspirations of the postrevolutionary generation for higher levels of private consumption came into conflict with socialist goals of civilizational progress, support for these regimes waned rapidly. Finally, in some parts of the Third World, usually where a strong peasant base dominated the revolutionary alliance, the aim of modernization was abandoned entirely—e.g., China during the Cultural Revolution and Cambodia under the *Khmer Rouge*, but also the Tanzania of Julius Nyere and Burma before the coup of the early 1960s. These regimes all lacked a credible alternative to the modern ideal. At their best they traded inequality for a shared poverty; at their worst they became frankly anticivilizational.

Metaphysics and Late Modernity

The implications of these developments for the whole project of rational metaphysics were, of course, devastating. If the Silk Road Era was the Great Age of Metaphysics, Late Modernity is the Great Age of Anti-Metaphysics. In this section we will first sketch out the complex lineage of this anti-metaphysical trend. We will then specify what we call the "postmodern spectrum" of philosophical tendencies that extend from the radically secular project of the (early) deconstructionists through the "weak theological" center occupied by the late Derrida and Caputo up to such openly theological thinkers as Jean Luc Marion, specifying the social basis and political valence of each position in turn. We will conclude by considering briefly movements that rejected the anti-metaphysical turn of late modernity such as Neo-Thomism before moving to address the current situation for philosophy in the next chapter.

Lineages of Postmodernism

There are, broadly speaking, two separate streams, each with its own tributaries, which have flowed into what has come to be known as postmodernism. On the one hand, with the eclipse of the positivistic and dialectical variants of the high-modern ideal, older and deeper currents in the Germanic culture that lies behind the modern West have resurfaced. Within this broad stream we can distinguish a religious current—essentially the Augustinian tradition—and a current that, while not secular in the modern sense, has little use for piety as it has come to be understood in the post-axial religious traditions. It might be best to call this the warlord tradition. Nietzsche, of course, is its greatest exponent. On the other hand, the dialectical tradition itself underwent a profound transformation under the conditions of late modernity, which increasingly emphasized the negative, critical dimension of dialectics at the expense of the synthetic, metaphysical dimension. This stream includes much critical theory after Lukacs, including most of the humanistic "Frankfort" School *and* the structuralist/poststructuralist Althusserian school, as well as older dialectical currents such as Kaballah that flowed underground, as it were, through the period of modernist ascendancy, only to resurface in the work of deconstructionists such as Derrida.

It is difficult to pinpoint precisely the point at which Augustinianism ceases to be "early modern" and becomes "postmodern," but if we define as postmodern any thought that aims the main blow at (and thus presupposes) high-modern rather than medieval metaphysics, then the first major postmodern Augustinian is without question Kierkegaard (Kierkegaard 1840/1941). Where earlier Augustinians simply restricted the scope of human reason, Kierkegaard actually argues that the *via dialectica* is itself a path to perdition. For Kierkegaard, the very attempt to construct a system excludes the possibility of discovering God, because in rendering the universe intelligible it rules out in advance the encounter with another free personality—human or divine. God is known only in the radical inwardness of human subjectivity, only after we have despaired of the effort to comprehend and organize the world on the basis of some principle accessible to reason.

The warlord tradition, on the other hand, is represented first and foremost by Nietzsche (Nietzsche 1889/1968). At first, no two figures could seem more different: the radical Christian and the prophet of the anti-Christ. And certainly their reasons for rejecting metaphysics are nothing if not diametrically opposed. Kierkegaard (who continues in the tradition of the Augustinian reaction) rejects metaphysics as a manifestation of human pride and the will to power; Nietzsche rejects it precisely because it represents a retreat from the raw struggle for power that, in his mind, is the only real principle that governs the universe—an attempt on the part of the weak-spirited to hide from "the world as it is" in the name of "the world as it should be," a search for some pre-existing pattern of organization on which to depend rather than a bold struggle to organize the universe ourselves, as best we can, in full knowledge that our efforts will, in time, be swept away.

What is rejected by Kierkegaard and Nietzsche both is the presence of a meaning immanent in human activity and in the universe generally, which, however, points beyond itself to an intrinsically meaningful ground. Both ultimately regard meaning as a function of power. For Kierkegaard, this power is always and only the power of God before which the only proper human response is one of radical submission. Nietzsche, on the other hand, scorns such submission and counsels us to join the eternal struggle in which meanings are created and destroyed.

These two strains flow together in the work of Martin Heidegger, where we find the first really complete and rigorous statement of the political-theological critique of metaphysics. We have already stated the main elements of this critique above. Here we merely summarize.

Heidegger's work is notoriously complex and obscure and has been buried in layer upon layer of commentary, so that it becomes difficult to say anything about him without risking exposure for some scholarly *faux pas*. This complex of defensive ramparts, however, in fact conceals a cluster of relatively simple claims. Heidegger's early critique of metaphysics, set forth in *Problems of Phenomenology* (Heidegger 1927) and *Being and Time* (1928), focuses on the failure of thinkers, beginning with Plato, to grasp the distinction between Being and beings, and instead attempts to theorize Being as the beingness of beings—i.e., it thinks Being in entitative terms. Where the pre-Socratics, according to Heidegger, were able to think the self-manifestation of Being, something he associates with the term *physis* or nature, Plato and Aristotle increasingly use the language of *morphe* (form) and *energeia* (actuality). Form, and especially the Good or the "form of forms" is, for Plato, what really is and that in terms of which this world of appearance must be explained and judged. Aristotle goes even further down this road, arguing that it is form that actualizes matter, bringing things into being. Rather than simply allowing Being to manifest itself, to present itself as a question, it is reduced to something other than Being, something that can be comprehended—and once comprehended, used to ground our own process of making, our own process of bringing into being. Indeed, as Heidegger points out, the very notion of *morphe* derives from the language of the craftsman: it is the look or appearance given to something by its producer. *Energeia*, similarly, is rendered in German as *Wirklicheit*, from the root for work. Metaphysics thus grounds technology, and the larger technological mode of relating to the world.

Later Heidegger (Heidegger 1941) modified both his historical analysis and his philosophical position. Increasingly identifying ancient Greek and German romantic thought, he claimed to hear in Plato and Aristotle echoes of the earlier Greek *aletheia* or unconcealment of Being and located the crystallization of metaphysics in the "translation" of Greek thought into Latin, the language of road builders and empire makers, a crystallization completed in the Middle Ages when Being is identified with the supreme maker, the Christian Creator God. This process culminates, of course, in Thomas, who is the supreme philosopher of the "ontotheologic," the universal causal-explanatory system in which Being is simply an instrument for explaining and ultimately manipulating entities. Modern metaphysical theories, such as those of Descartes and Hegel—or for that matter Marx—differ only in giving human rather than divine subjectivity or labor pride of place. Nietzsche's claim that the world is just the "will to power" is simply the culmination of this long metaphysical tradition, and offers just one more formulation of the first principle.

Being, for the later Heidegger, manifests itself in a people only through the voice of the few who help it to discover its "god," a sort of mythos under which Being is revealed.

> ... the essence of the people is its "voice." This voice does not, however, speak in a so-called immediate flood of the common, natural, undistorted and uneducated "person." The voice speaks seldom and only in the few, if it can be brought to sound ... (Heidegger 1934/1989: 319)

> A *Volk* is only a *Volk* if it receives its history through the discovery of its god, through the god, which through history compels it in a direction and so places it back in being. Only then does it avoid the danger of turning only on its own axis ... (Heidegger 1934/1989: 398–399)

In this regard Heidegger remains close to Kierkegaard, seeing humanity as a passive instrument of Being rather than an active creator of meaning. After the "turn" in his thought, however, Heidegger also becomes more interested in analyzing the historical process by which Being is unconcealed—or by which it "withdraws," leaving the world subject to *techne* and to the will to power—than he is in the existential analysis of *Dasein* (human being or literally "being-there") as an opening to Being. While the historical process is treated here simply as a product of Being's unconcealments and withdrawals, the effect is, nonetheless, to reinstate the Nietzschean focus on the nexus between power and meaning, while endowing this nexus with an ontological legitimation that makes the forcible irruption of meaning in history no longer the product of finite human organizing activity, but rather an epiphany of Being itself.

The political valence of Heidegger's synthesis of the Augustinian and warlord traditions remains a subject of considerable controversy, largely because many of his ideas have been taken up by the postmodern thinkers who understand themselves as part of a New Left. This controversy is, however, not really justified. Whatever nuances continued research may add to judgments regarding Heidegger's personal responsibility and guilt for his association with the Nazi Party, it should be apparent that his philosophy is organically fascist. This is true in the technical sense that it provides a philosophical framework in which the fascist strategy of tapping into premodern ideological currents to legitimate the mobilization and militarization of the population in service of a project of empire building makes sense. Specifically, the notion of the historical destiny of the people as an unconcealment of Being, by Being, accessible only through a kind of foundational *mythos* and not subject to rational criticism and comprehension, provides a possible grounding for the Nazi project, even if it is not the grounding that the Nazi Party, much to Heidegger's disappointment, ultimately chose.

After its first complete formulation in the work of Heidegger, the political-theological critique of metaphysics developed in a number of apparently very different directions. Levinas (Levinas 1965) argued that Heidegger's continued use of the language of Being perpetuated the effacement of the Other in the interests of power and domination that had characterized the whole Greek philosophical tradition, which he refers to as "ontology," and advocated a new "metaphysics" rooted in confrontation with the radically Other, the victim, in which alone we can discover—but never conceptually possess—God. This line of reasoning has been taken up by Latin American liberationists, explicitly by Miranda (Miranda 1972, 1973) and Dussel (Dussel 1998), and more loosely and eclectically by others, for whom the encounter with the poor and oppressed becomes the unique privileged hermeneutic key for reading the Scriptures—and reality in general.[8]

8. It is often supposed that this hermeneutic is compatible with or even builds on the sociological reading of the Scriptures advanced by Gottwald, Pixley, and others,

The "democrat" Hannah Arendt does not frame her argument in terms of a critique of metaphysics, but the link to the thought of her fascist lover (Heidegger) is readily apparent. At the very core of Arendt's political theory is a sharp distinction between labor, work, and action. By labor she means the physical, biological, and economic processes necessary to sustain life. Labor leaves nothing behind except life itself, and perhaps the freedom of another (the master) to engage in work or action. By work she means the process of producing objects that possess some permanence, serve some purpose beyond themselves, and which are executed in accord with some pre-conceived plan. Work is an intrinsically teleological process. By action she means the disclosure of the subject in relationship with other subjects—a process which, unlike labor or work, directly presupposes the presence of others, and, consequently has a characteristic frailty, and the outcome of which is always uncertain (Ardent 1958). Arendt criticizes the entire tradition of Western political philosophy from Plato though Marx, which, she says, understands politics as a form of fabrication or work rather than as the quintessential form of action.

> Plato and Aristotle elevated lawmaking and city building to the highest rank in political life... because they wished to turn against politics and against action. To them, legislating and the execution of decisions by vote are the most legitimate political activities because in them men "act like craftsmen": the results of their action is a tangible product, and its process has a clearly recognizable end. This is no longer, or rather, not yet action (praxis) properly speaking, but making (poesis) which they prefer because of its greater reliability. It is as though they had said that if men only renounce their capacity for action, with its futility, boundlessness, and uncertainty of outcome, there could be a remedy for the frailty of human affairs. (195)

---

which points out the origins of many strains in the Jewish and Christian traditions in the struggles of the oppressed. Actually, however, the two hermeneutics are quite opposed. According to the sociological reading proposed by Gottwald, for example, the cult of YHWH emerged not out of some "encounter with the oppressed," but rather out of an encounter by the oppressed with their own historical power, a power which, if we accept the theological reading proposed by Judaism and Christianity, was a real participation in the power of the living God. Gottwald's reading is a reading from the standpoint of the oppressed, or at least one that attempts to recover something of this standpoint; the readings proposed by the Latin American disciples of Levinas are readings from the standpoint of a guilt-ridden elite.

The tradition that Arendt criticizes, of course, reaches its consummation in the work of Marx, for whom the transformation of the working class from mere makers of physical objects into the conscious makers of history constitutes the highest possible level of human development.

The link between making and metaphysics is located for Arendt as for Heidegger in the Platonic doctrine of forms or ideas, though Arendt focuses on the term *eidos* rather than *morphe*. She notes that according to Aristotle, Plato himself was the one to introduce this term into philosophical usage and that Plato (Republic X) explicitly uses an analogy with craftsmanship to explain the doctrine.

Is there any difference between the critiques of metaphysics advanced by Heidegger and Arendt? Absolutely. For Heidegger the critique of metaphysics makes way for the disclosure of Being, something he makes quite clear takes place first and foremost in the historical destiny of peoples. This is especially true after the "turn" in his thinking, when he becomes less and less concerned with the existential analysis of *Dasein* and more and more concerned with the historical conditions for a new unconcealment of Being. For Arendt, on the other hand, the critique of metaphysics clears the way for a disclosure of the subject in action, to other like subjects, from whom there is some possibility of recognition. Thus the pull in Arendt's theory towards a broadly "democratic" politics. Note, however, that both share a common rejection of work, and of the historical movements that have regarded work or creativity as a privileged opening to understanding Being itself: i.e., Catholicism and dialectical materialism. We should note as well that Arendt's "democratic" politics is fully as elitist as Heidegger's fascism: it is only those who have been freed from the necessity of labor and from the obsession with work who are really capable of public life.

Deconstructionist postmodernism (Derrida 1967/1978) can be understood as standing within this same tradition. In "Violence and Metaphysics," for example, Derrida develops his position dialectically, accepting the Heideggerian critique of all earlier metaphysics and Levinas's critique of Heidegger. But he then goes on to point out that Levinas, as well, is unable to escape the "violence" of metaphysics. In finding God in the face of the Other, do we not efface the *differance* and specificity of the Other as surely as if the Other (and his suffering) were reduced to a necessary expression of the divine first principle, an object of divine providence, of a vanishing moment of the human historical process?

What Derrida suggests is that violence is unavoidable: there is no escape. The best that we can do is to unmask the violence embedded in our own discourse and that of others in an effort to contain the damage.

But it is also possible to read deconstructionism as the product of a protracted disintegration of high-modern dialectics from within. Here the critical events are fascism, Stalinism, the Twentieth Congress of the Communist Party of the Soviet Union, the Sino-Soviet split, and the advent of new communisms in the Third World, and most especially of Maoism.

Fascism represented a fundamental challenge for Marxism generally, but this was especially true for humanistic Marxism in the tradition of Lukacs, for whom the proletariat enjoyed an epistemologically and ontologically privileged position. The task of explaining how and why millions of workers were hegemonized by fascism proved daunting. Lukacs's own *Assault on Reason* (Lukacs 1953/1980) provides a powerful critique of what we have called the Augustinian and warlord traditions in German philosophy, and does so within a still broadly high-modern framework, but it does not address directly the question of the hegemonization of the proletariat.

It was above all an engagement with that question that pushed much of the Frankfort School towards growing pessimism. Erich Fromm (Fromm 1941) is really the only thinker in this tradition who advances a theory that focuses on the contradictions of *capitalism*. According to Fromm, while capitalism liberated humanity from millennia of external constraint, it failed to give most people the tools they needed in order to realize their latent potential for wisdom, creativity, and relationality and left them at the mercy of forces beyond their control. The result was the emergence of a "sado-masochistic" personality structure that seeks meaning and belonging by means of submission to an external authority.

This theory was powerful enough to explain not only fascism, but also Stalinism, and, with some revisions (Fromm 1947), the conformism that Fromm saw in liberal democratic societies during the postwar period, while still suggesting that a humanistic socialism would be able to transcend these contradictions and unleash the full development of human capacities. But it did not take into account the fact that many of the factors leading to alienation—industrial production, bureaucracy, the triumph of instrumental reason—were characteristic of actually existing socialism as well as of capitalism, a point emphasized by the later Frankfort School, including Horkheimer, Adorno, and Marcuse, something that made the hope of "true socialism" seem more and more Utopian.

Meanwhile, humanistic Marxism itself came under attack from a new quarter. When Khrushchev finally acknowledged Stalin's crimes publically at the Twentieth Congress of the Communist Party of the Soviet Union in 1956 and committed the party to reform, he also broke sharply with what many regarded as fundamental principles of the communist tradition. On the economic front he moved to give enterprise managers far more authority and to partially restore the operation of market forces, and on the political front he broke with the Leninist principles of the dictatorship of the proletariat and of anti-imperialist struggle, declaring that the CPSU would henceforth be a "party of the whole people" and the Soviet Union a "state of the whole people" that would pursue the goal of communism through peaceful cooperation and peaceful competition with the West, in the hopes of achieving a peaceful transition both there and in the Third World. Louis Althusser (Althusser 1965/1977, 1967/1970, 1966–1969/1971) linked this new political line with the humanistic Marxist tradition with its emphasis on "expressive totalities" and argued that it led to a fundamental departure from the historic aims of the communist movement. In its place he argued for a new "structural" Marxism that treated human societies as "complex structured totalities" that could be analyzed only through empirical social-scientific investigation, effectively purging the last residues of metaphysics from dialectical materialism. Critics from within the Soviet bloc, on the other hand (Konrad and Szelenyi 1967), while recognizing the self-conscious dissent of humanistic Marxism from the policies of the Soviet bloc states, argued that these "teleological intellectuals," with their focus on transcending market norms, constituted a kind of strategic reserve for Stalinist restorationism. The first trend gravitated increasingly towards Maoism and other Third World Marxisms; the latter ultimately offered support, however critical, to the developments that led eventually to a capitalist restoration in the Soviet Bloc.

These Third World Marxisms themselves reflected two tendencies that, while not absolutely incompatible, were fundamentally in tension with each other. On the one hand, they upheld, against Soviet Marxism after 1956, the aim of achieving not just socialism (a society in which the state has replaced the market as the principal resource allocator) but *communism*, a society that is classless and communal and in which all social contradictions have been radically transcended. Also against the

Communist Party of the Soviet Union, they upheld the necessity of armed struggle and of continuing class struggle after the revolution if the bourgeoisie was to be definitively defeated. The purest expression of this tendency was undoubtedly Maoism, which gave it a rigorous philosophical formulation. For Mao, dialectics is *defined* by the principle of contradiction. Both the role of the quantitative accumulation of forces and the goal of achieving a higher synthesis are eclipsed by a focus on identifying and "playing" the principal contradiction during any period or conjunction. Reality is essentially a complex of contradictions, and politics the science of contradiction.

In terms of political analysis, this focus allowed Mao and his followers to perceive clearly one of the principal dangers of the whole process of socialist construction: the contradiction between socialist property forms and the residues of commodity production, which reproduce bourgeois ideology and consumerist values and can lead to a capitalist restoration—something that did indeed eventually take place in the Soviet Union, even if one is skeptical about the claim that the restoration occurred under Khrushchev rather than Gorbachev. At the same time, the Maoist focus on contradiction tended to obscure the real achievements of the Soviet system in the areas of technological, economic, political, artistic, scientific, and philosophical development—i.e., the enormous contribution of the Soviet system to the human civilizational project, which is after all the whole point of socialism. More broadly, the Maoist focus on the principle of contradiction carries even further than Soviet diamat the transformation of Marxism in a Nietzschean direction—into a theory in which power grounds meaning rather than meaning power. And it is unclear that the restoration of capitalism in the Soviet Union was a result of tendencies rooted in residual *petty* commodity production, as Lenin feared and his Maoist interpreters argued (Yao Wen-yuan 1968), as opposed to the privatization of state enterprises based on an at least partially *generalized* commodity production (the wage relation).

Maoism has, based on its analysis of the "principal contradiction" of the imperialist system, argued that the progressive bloc should be based on alliance between not only the working class and the peasantry, but also the national bourgeoisie, which produces domestically for domestic consumption in the countries of the Third World. This alliance was reflected in the generous terms of compensation for "patriotic" businessmen whose enterprises were nationalized early in the revolution, in the strategy of delinking from the global market coupled with radical land reform and rural demand-led industrialization during the peak years of Maoist dominance, and in the turn towards privatization within the context of a still carefully regulated and protected market economy in the past twenty years. At the same time Maoism, especially in its leftist forms, has been ruthless in its attacks against the tradition of the old Mandarin intelligentsia, mobilizing a series of campaigns against Confucianism and "self-cultivation" that led eventually to the Cultural Revolution. The bearers of these attacks on the intelligentsia were, however, themselves intellectuals—generally students whose prospects for intellectual employment were poor under the rather spartan Chinese regime—acting in conjunction with the Red Army, with its poor peasant base, against the principal organization of the secular intelligentsia, i.e., the Communist Party. As late as the 1970s it would have been easy to regard the political significance of this movement as more or less transparent: an "ultra-left" movement of marginalized intellectuals and poor peasants frustrated by the ability of the socialist system to meet their demands, and determined to break the alliance with the national bourgeoisie and accelerate the pace of socialist transformation. Their defeat could, similarly, have been read as the triumph of national bourgeois elements within the anti-imperialist bloc. This analysis, however, fails to comprehend the real political valence of the Cultural Revolution. By liquidating the older gentry intelligentsia, especially its partially modernized section that was organized in the Communist Party apparatus, the Gang of Four and their allies removed or at least weakened one of the principal obstacles to marketization in China. They acted, in other words, as agents of the bourgeoisie in its struggle against what Samir Amin calls the "statist" (i.e., civilization building) tendency that gained the upper hand in the USSR.

This analysis is strengthened if we examine the ideological itinerary of Amin, one of the leading theoreticians of the national liberation movements and one who has historically identified himself with the Maoist trend. Amin contributed significantly to the analysis of unequal development and unequal exchange and has consistently argued, against both the hegemonic neoliberal trend, but also against the dominant tendencies on the left, in favor of a radical delinking from the world market and a broadly Maoist approach to the problems of socialist construction (Amin 1976, 1977, 1978, 1980, 1982, 1985). While not a philosopher, he has shown increasing interest in recent years in ideological questions.

In the 1970s Amin was an apologist for the Khmer Rouge; by the early 1980s he was defending Maoism in terms of its contributions to economic growth—i.e., in distinctively "national bourgeois" terms. In the later 1980s he took up the critique of metaphysics, an indirect blow at the religious left, which by that point was practically the only left that remained, in favor of a universal culture based on the struggles of the poor and oppressed. Amin's comments on metaphysics are contained in a short book published in 1988 entitled *Eurocentrism* (1988/1989). The book is part of his larger polemic against the dominant social democratic and pro-Soviet "revisionist" tendencies in the international communist movement which, he says, have erred in a number of related ways:

1. stressing the leading role of the development of the productive forces rather than the class struggle in the historical process;

2. focusing on the leadership of the industrial working class rather than on the alliance of the working class and the peasantry; and

3. situating the center of the world revolutionary movement in the advanced capitalist centers (especially Europe) rather than in the national liberation movements of the Third World.

At the same time, with the crisis of socialism and the rise of various nationalist and religious trends within the national liberation movements, especially in the Islamic world, the critique of Eurocentrism has come increasingly to mean the critique of Marxism, which is increasingly understood as just another European import. Amin's book is an attempt to reframe the critique of Eurocentrism in a way that does not give aid and comfort to Islamic fundamentalism and that leaves open room for a "truly universal culture" based on the common experience of the revolutionary struggle against imperialism.

Amin situates "metaphysics" in the context of the emergence of what he calls tributary social formations. In communal societies, where there was little or no systematic exploitation, the social structure did not require any special legitimation; the religion of communal societies was first and foremost an expression of humanity's dependence on the natural world. As warfare and conquest became strategies for economic growth and development, the need arose to legitimate what would otherwise have been transparently exploitative social relationships. Furthermore, as empires grew, so too did the need for ideologies that transcended the religious particularism of the individual city or region. Rational metaphysics, of the kind developed independently in Greece, China, and India, and brought to perfection in the various scholasticisms of the long "medieval period," (which begins for Amin with the Hellenistic era and not after the collapse of Rome), presented the universe as a vast hierarchical system in which all finite systems derive from a supreme first principle—a sort of abstract, cosmic reflex of the tributary imperial structure itself. It is only the advent of capitalism, in which the relations of exploitation are opaque, which eliminated the need for metaphysical reflection and legitimation.

It is interesting to note that Amin regards Soviet dialectical materialism, and indeed the entire tradition springing from Engels's *Dialectics of Nature*, as itself quasi-metaphysical. Indeed, in so far as it is both a universal causal theory, and centered on grounding human *techne*, it would also count as metaphysical from the standpoint of the other thinkers we have been considering, even though it has no recourse to immaterial principles. Elsewhere (Amin 1979/1980, 1981/1982) Amin has argued that the Soviet Union, far from being socialist was in fact a "statist" society, something that he describes in terms that suggest a sort of industrialized version of the tributary state. And the political expression of Soviet "diamat" is, of course, the "workerism," the privileging of productivity over revolutionary struggle, which is the principal object of Amin's polemics.

In a recent paper that appears in *Dialectic, Cosmos, and Society*, Amin nuances his critique of metaphysics slightly, acknowledging that human beings are "metaphysical animals" that by their very nature pose fundamental questions of meaning and value. At the same time, he develops an even more radical critique of metaphysics as an obstacle to the democratic revolutions. Judaism and Islam, he notes, are both oriented fundamentally towards the establishment of a society in which the divine will is fully accomplished, through the medium of a revealed law. For Judaism the complete realization of this project remains in the future, in the messianic age. For Islam the messiah has, in a sense, already come, in the form of the Prophet, whose law Islam seeks to extend by conquest or conversion throughout earth. In both cases, however, the ideal remains a society in which the revealed law is actually realized. This has made it difficult for Judaism and Islam to accommodate themselves to democracy, the essence of which for Amin is the right of the people to make their own laws and their own history, without reference to either a revealed or a rational metaphysics. Christianity, on the other hand, while it has often succumbed to the theocratic temptation, has an easier time accommodating itself to democracy because of its insistence that the kingdom of God is not of this world and that the people are free to work out their historical destiny under the guidance of only the broadest moral principles. Metaphysical systems, in other words, in order to be compatible with democracy, must not ground a revealed or natural law that stands in the way of the free legislative activity of the people themselves by setting up principles of which human positive laws are regarded as mere applications.

Amin's position has merit as an analysis of the difficulties of democracy in the Islamic world. What it misses, of course, is that any system that leaves moral norms ungrounded and a matter of negotiation will also make it impossible to ground a critique of the market order. Amin seems not to recognize the possibility of democracy understood as a public debate around the interpretation and application of natural law—as a real dialogue around fundamental questions of meaning and value.

The other tendency in Third World Marxism has been an engagement with, or even an embrace of, popular religious traditions and other forms of resistance to modernity as a means of mobilizing the people for resistance to Empire. In some cases (Asian/Buddhist, Arab/Islamic, and African Socialism) the contribution of Marxism to the ideological mix has been rather small—little more than a vague impetus towards socialism—while in other cases (Cuba) it is Marxism rather than the indigenous tradition that has dominated. Perhaps the most important example of this phenomenon, however, is liberation theology.

It is interesting to note, in this regard, that liberation theology for the most part eschews the Thomistic dialectics characteristic of earlier Catholic theology in favor of a largely biblicist social ethics. The appeal here is to the authority of revelation even if the Scriptures are interpreted according to what Cardinal Ratzinger and the Congregation for the Doctrine of the Faith call a "rationalist hermeneutic," e.g., some sort of sociological reductionism. Liberation theology for the most part has remained within the framework of a "left-wing Augustinianism" that grounds the preferential option for the poor (not, mind you, the working classes) not on their creative participation in the life of God but rather precisely in their suffering and their poverty, which through an intellectual sleight of hand is confused with the voluntary poverty of the religious and taken as a sign of the ordering of the will to God. The struggle within the Catholic Church over liberation theology is really just a struggle within its Augustinian wing between these leftist forces and more traditional Augustinians who insist on an actual scrutiny of the will before rendering judgment on the spiritual state of the individual. It is, in other words, Ratzinger's Bonaventure against Boff's Angelo Clareno. Both parties reject the ultimate meaningfulness of the human civilizational project. Thomas is nowhere to be found.

What liberation theology does is to link the peasant communities, and working class communities that conserve a memory of the village community, and thus a spontaneous ability to understand the universe as ultimately meaningful and ordered to God, to the national liberation movements, via their organic intellectuals, e.g., catechists and other subaltern "pastoral agents." At the same time, the biblicist ethics and the underlying Augustinian theology actually subverts the spontaneous teleology of the indigenous wisdoms in favor of a doctrine that makes meaning and value a function of power: ultimately that of God, and immediately that of the revolutionary *commandantes*, who play a role in the scheme not unlike that of the Emperor Frederick in radical Joachite doctrine. The people and their "pastoral agents" don't notice that this is happening. Their most pressing demands are, after all, being prosecuted and their "faith" is being respected. But when the *commandantes* abandon the people, either after a successful revolution or after a negotiated settlement, the people are ideologically disarmed. Nothing in the liberationist political culture, in either its secular or religious dimensions, allows them to ground specifically anticapitalist demands—the only demands that will really improve their situation in the long run.[9]

In this sense, liberation theology—and the engagement of Third World Marxisms with popular religious traditions generally—represents a phenomenon that, while ethically very different from fascism (because it represents resistance to rather than militarization on behalf of Empire) is strategically very similar, a point noted by Ernesto Laclau (not with respect to liberation theology but with respect to populist movements

---

9. It must be noted that there are tendencies that are often grouped together with liberation theology—e.g., the perspective represented by someone like Ernesto Cardenal—that do not reflect this Augustinian dynamic and that have, in fact, served as centers of resistance to the treason of the *commandantes*. It should also be noted that Cuba represents, both in its fidelity to the socialist project and in its gradual opening to religion, in spite of the fact that popular religious movements played no real role in the genesis of the regime, a real exception to the patterns noted here.

generally (Laclau 1974). Indeed, Laclau's work represents a critical intersection between an evolving European "structural" Marxism and Third World Marxisms engaged with popular religious traditions. Drawing on Gramsci as well as Althusser (or on Gramsci read through an Althusserian lens) Laclau argues that fascism was a strategy for hegemony centered on the appropriation of national, popular, and democratic traditions in order to reinforce capitalism and imperialism. The appropriate strategy for the Left is an appeal to these same traditions on behalf of socialism.

But if such different political forms can be constructed in such similar ways—indeed, if political forms are ultimately *constructed*, rather than being expressions of an underlying class standpoint, as they were for Lukacs and his interpreters, then Marxist class essentialism has already been abandoned (Laclau and Mouffe 1985). And this, indeed, is the long term tendency of both European structural Marxism and Third World Marxisms generally. Maoism, to be sure, retains the language of class, but is ultimately an open-ended politics without ground and without *telos*, which exploits contradictions for the sake of building power and effecting change. The more populist trend in Third World Marxisms exchanges the language of class for that of "the people" or an "oppressed" that includes the whole Third World, and not only workers and peasants, as well as women, the young, the disabled, etc., for whom a fundamental "option" is made on the grounds of faith—or even groundlessly—rather than on the basis of reason.

And here, of course, we arrive at deconstruction by an entirely different route. Late-modern dialectics, disillusioned by the experience of fascism, Stalinism, and the "revisionist" turn in European and Soviet Marxism, alternately inspired and horrified by Maoism and other Third World revolutionary upheavals, turns in on itself and rejects the foundational claim of modern dialectics: that "philosophy is the head of the revolution and the proletariat its heart," that by linking itself to the aspirations of the working classes the modern revolutionary intelligentsia can not only realize its millennial dream of a society ruled by philosopher kings, but actually elevate itself to a kind of collective divinity or quasi-divinity, establishing itself as the subject of the cosmohistorical revolutionary project. Chastened, this intelligentsia instead adopts a purely critical posture, and a purely negative dialectics, or what Derrida calls "an Hegelianism without reserve" (Derrida 1967/1978), i.e., one that does not aim at resolving contradiction but only at exposing them.

At the same time, largely by way of its experience with Third World struggles, late-modern dialectics has become as fully engaged with the religious question and the religious tradition as the Augustinian tradition. It is now all but taken for granted that religion represents one of the principal ways in which social contradictions are articulated and engaged and liberatory or emancipatory projects constructed.

If the Germanic Augustinian-warlord lineage of postmodernism represents at the very least a flirtation of intellectuals disillusioned with modernity with the fascist project, then late-modern dialectics represents the gradual demobilization of the humanistic intelligentsia that emerged out of the Averroist counter-Reaction of the late medieval era. Stripped of their base in the working classes, they have disavowed any attempt to build a new base—and to ever again speak in the name of or as God—in return for comfortable sinecures in the academy. They comfort themselves with the thought of their continued critical stance *vis-à-vis* oppression and injustice; but without either a political base or metaphysical authority, their "critique" is impotent.

The result of these developments has been the emergence of a postmodern spectrum defined by a shared rejection of the whole project of rational metaphysics but which is by no means united in its position on the religious question. At one end of this spectrum, we find those whose rejection of high modernity has led them to an essentially fideist position, embracing philosophically ungrounded theologies, accepted largely through faith and on the authority of revelation. The clearest example of such theologies are Protestant and Islamic fundamentalisms, which invoke religious traditions that never had much use for reason to begin with and that, internally to their theologies, make truth a function of power, i.e., through the medium of a strong Augustinian/Calvinist or Asharite doctrine of divine sovereignty. These traditions represent the permanent latent danger of a resurgent fascism of political formations as declining and defeated empires (the United States and Europe, separately or together, but also *Dar-al-Islam*, which we must remember *was* an empire, however benign, and still sometimes sees itself as such) struggle to hold on or rebuild.

At the other end of the spectrum, we find those determined to adhere to the original deconstructionist project in its radically secular form, without any "acts of religion" or concessions to theology, however "weak." This position is becoming increasingly unpopular at the highest levels of discourse (perhaps simply because it is now old, and no longer provides much of a basis for novelty and invention, and thus for academic careers), but it retains widespread influence among the humanistic intelligentsia, for whom it has developed into what amounts to an alternative reading of modernity. Rather than discovering how the world works, and thus the secret to realizing through innerworldly civilizational progress the ideals that earlier civilizations sought through spiritual discipline, a process in which the critique of religion and analogical metaphysics were necessary but subordinate moments, modernity becomes one long process of critical disillusionment, first with religion, then with metaphysics, and finally with science and with postmetaphysical philosophy, all of which are reduced to language games or discourse communities in which meanings are constructed and deconstructed in what amounts to an endless play of signification.

The most interesting point in the postmodern spectrum is, however, the middle. This point has always been there, represented by religious thinkers such as Kierkegaard and Levinas, who sought to counter the religious metaphysics of Being and Presence with a spirituality of intersubjective relationship and respect for the Other. In recent years, however, this trend has grown, being joined by Derrida in the years leading up to his death, and by such critical interpreters of the postmodern tradition as John Caputo. Derrida's "acts of religion" mount a traditional deconstructionist account of religion as "globolatinity."

> According to Derrida the "Latin" is the word for the West. The Latin is what overreaches with its sumptuous signatures of power and meaning; it is a perfection of the organizational, a vast economy of coding as well as a "reterritorialized" ... system of administration necessary for the expansion of a planetary sociopolitical apparatus.
>
> As in Old Rome, the notion of "religion" functions as an aggregate signifier for the "re-binding" (*re-ligio*) together of previously profuse and dissociated particularities of faith and devotion with their own indigenous or "territorial" characteristics into a grand ideology of unity in diversity. (Raschke 2005)

At the same time, it joins to this deconstruction of religion an identification of certain religious terms as not simply undeconstructible, but as *the* undeconstructible. These are justice and the messianicity that invokes justice to deconstruct law and other crystallized forms of injustice. The result is a "messianicity without messianism," a religion without religion, which attempts to capture the fact that in the present period the most effective struggle for justice is religiously motivated, even as religion continues to function as one of the principal structures of oppression.

Caputo, who is one of Derrida's principal interpreters, takes a similar approach, arguing that images of God as omnipotent, omniscient, etc. have served to legitimate oppressive social structures *even when they have aimed at legitimating resistance*. Instead, he (with Catherine Keller) proposes a "weak theology" centered on what he regards as the constitutive element of Christian revelation.

> The dangerous memory of the crucified body of Jesus poses a threat to a world organized around the disastrous concept of power, something that is reflected today in the widespread critique of the concept of "sovereignty"—of the sovereignty of autonomous subjects and the sovereignty of nations powerful enough to get away with acting unilaterally and in their own self-interests. The call that issues from the Cross threatens what Derrida calls the "unavowed theologism" of the political concept of sovereignty by returning to its root, to its understanding of God, to its underlying or archi-theology. The crucified body of Jesus proposes not that we keep theology out of politics, but that we think theology otherwise, by way of another paradigm, another theology, requiring us to think of God otherwise, as an unconditional claim or solicitation without power, as a weak force or power of powerlessness, as opposed to the theology of omnipotence which underlies sovereignty. (Caputo and Keller 2006:3)

Caputo and Keller's position illustrates what we have said about postmodernism generally: i.e., that it represents the resignation of the modern humanistic intelligentsia from the struggle for class power, but also from *effective* struggle on behalf of justice. As Barrington Moore demonstrated nearly a half-century ago in his analysis of the Indian national liberation movement (Moore 1966), nonviolent struggle and ideologies of the power of powerlessness not only leave the peasantry and the working classes disarmed, they condemn them to the secular violence of gradual modernization, which inevitably claims as many lives, if not more, than the bloodiest of revolutions.

What the late Derrida and Caputo miss, of course, is that it is possible to reject the claims to innerworldly divinization mounted by modern univocal and immanentist metaphysics without abandoning metaphysics—

and power—altogether. More specifically, in the context of a traditional analogical metaphysics of *Esse*, we ground our moral claims in an appeal to a power that is absolute, but not our own, and thus render those claims authoritative without becoming authoritarian.

Just how this works is the topic of the next chapter. Before we proceed, however, we need to address briefly attempts to restore an analogical metaphysics from outside the stream of late modernity and explain why those attempts failed.

Conservative Metaphysics

In our discussion of early modernity, we distinguished sharply between the *reactionary* metaphysics of traditionalist thinkers such as de Maistre and de Bonald and the *conservative* metaphysics represented by the Second Thomism. This same distinction obtains in late modernity. Indeed, it is marked sharply by the fact that during the crisis of the mid-twentieth century, the Augustinian progenitors of postmodernism leaned towards or actively supported fascism, while Thomists and representatives of analogous tendencies in other traditions formed part of the Resistance.

The Third Thomism must be understood in the context of the Second. Central to the Church's strategy (and especially the strategy developed by the Society of Jesus) for coming to terms with the Reformation, and with capitalist modernization generally, was the creation of a powerful papacy, autonomous with respect to the Absolutist States and sovereign, in a way it never had been historically, within the Church itself. The idea was, simply, that only a global institution like the papacy could stand up effectively to the Absolutist state and, later on, to global capital. It is this strategic commitment to the papacy that has led the Society of Jesus to submit to the popes even when they have acted against the Society's interests, as has not infrequently been the case.

This proved to be a difficult task. The autonomy of the popes was insured in large part by means of their temporal power over the Papal States. This meant that the papacy was an Italian state on the modern absolutist model as well as if not more so than a universal ecclesial institution. But the papacy was, like all of the other Italian states (with the partial exception of Piemonte, which enjoyed a favorable position because of the international balance of power), a *dependent* state subject to the "protection" of the other Catholic powers. Recovering its prophetic office required the papacy to come to terms not only with modernity in general, but with "the Italian question" in particular. To put matters differently, like the Italic peoples themselves, the papacy had to liberate itself from the political-economic tutelage of the great powers.

This lead some thinkers—the so-called Neo-Guelphs—to imagine that the papacy might lead the Italian national liberation struggle at the head of a confederation of the already existing Italian states. This strategy suffered from two serious flaws. First, it was incompatible with the prophetic vocation of the papacy, which required it to become less rather than more identified with specifically Italian interests. Second, it failed to take into account the underlying dynamic behind the Risorgimento, which was first and foremost a conquest of the south by the north (Zitara 1971) and of the countryside by the city (Sereni 1968), in the interests of the primitive accumulation of capital and the commodification of social relationships. As elsewhere, these processes proceeded at the expense of the peasantry and at the expense of the Church. For both reasons, the Church could not but oppose unification.[10]

On the one hand, the Third Thomism offered the papacy a way of recovering its prophetic office even as it was losing the last residue of its temporal power. Thomism had never favored the direct temporal power of the popes, but rather what it called the "indirect power." Political

---

10. Recent "revisionist" approaches to the Risorgimento, while they suggest numerous ways in which the work of Sereni and Zitara might need to be refined, especially by incorporating some consideration of global-economic and geopolitical factors, do not really call into question the main points of their arguments: that both the southern peasantry and the clergy were subjected to brutal repression during the so-called "brigand war" that followed unification, that the tax burden after unification fell heavily on the south while expenditures (except for the costs of repression) were directed primarily to the north, to Tuscany, and the former Legations, that unification undermined what little industry there was in the south (especially silk and sulphur), and that the capitalization of demesne and church lands almost everywhere worked to the advantage of large capitalist landowners and to the disadvantage of the peasantry and the church.

This is not precisely the "Gramscian" thesis, at least as it has usually been understood. It is not so much that the leaders of the Risorgimento failed to appeal effectively to the peasantry when they could have, or even that because of the underlying social conditions they could not make that sort of appeal, but rather that the Risorgimento project was, fundamentally, one of violence towards the people and their institutions. According to this view fascism is not so much the result of a flawed or incomplete bourgeois revolution, but rather a potential latent in capitalism itself, which is realized under very specific conditions: i.e., in countries that need colonies in order to resolve internal economic contradictions but lack them. Fascism draws on popular, religious, and even democratic traditions in order to mobilize the population and discipline them for imperialist wars of conquest.

authority is based on the exercise of reason in interpreting the natural law—something in which every human being can participate, if not in equal degrees. Political authority thus needs no blessing from the Church to be legitimate. What the Church does is, on the one hand, to serve as a channel of the grace that creates in us supernatural capacities—the ability to love God and neighbor for their own sake and not only for what they contribute to our development—and to serve as a guardian of natural law. Thus Thomists historically taught that the pope, or even the local ordinary, could declare particular laws invalid because they violated natural law, and dissolve the bonds between an unjust ruler and his subjects. This is quite different from actually exercising "state power" or using the modern state to enforce religious norms.

Thomism's competitors all tended to weaken the distinction between the natural and supernatural in a way that at once undermined the prophetic vocation of the Church and liquidated the distinction between clergy and laity. Traditionalism, for example, regarded all social institutions—including the absolutist monarchies and the economic privileges of the feudal or ex-feudal "nobility"—as the product of a "primitive revelation" that was only very vaguely distinct from the salvific revelation made through the prophets. The effect was to put the kings and the warlord "aristocracy" on a par with the clergy as agents of God. This was the ideology *par excellence* of the Restoration regimes. Ontologism, on the other hand, by claiming for reason a direct vision of God, seemed to liquidate the role of revelation—and thus of the clergy—altogether. This was the ideology of the Catholic bourgeoisie, anxious to free itself and its state from clerical supervision that might get in the way of modernization and capitalist development and to gain within the Church something like the democratic "citizenship" they enjoyed in the state.

Thomism, in other words, offered something both to those anxious to strengthen the prophetic vocation of the Church and to those anxious to reinforce clerical authority, and did so in a way that, particularly when the doctrine is viewed against the background of its competitors, and particularly in the light of the Jesuit commitment to the papacy as the principal instrument of the Church's prophetic office, made it difficult to distinguish between these two functions. Like earlier Thomisms, it upheld and, with *Rerum Novarum* and eventually with the development of Social Catholicism and Christian Democracy, began to exercise in an entirely new way, the "indirect authority" of the pope over political communities.

The popes learned to discipline governments by appealing directly to the people, who in turn bore the responsibility for acting to promote justice. Like the Second Thomism of the Counter-Reformation era, the Third Thomism of the Counter-Risorgimento (and unlike the original Thomism of Thomas himself) was bound up with a strategic decision in favor of the leading role of the papacy and the hierarchy generally as the cutting edge of the struggle against capitalist modernization. This meant that it was deformed philosophically and especially theologically in such a way as to legitimate this option. Specifically, it remained more Augustinian in its anthropology and soteriology, more christological in its theology, and thus more papalist, clerical, and disciplinarian in its ecclesiology than had been the case with original Thomism, which was closely aligned with democratizing movements such as the mendicant orders and the Beguines. (This is because the doctrinal basis for the authority of the ministerial priesthood is in the sacrificial high priesthood of Jesus himself. In order to guarantee clerical authority, the role of Jesus cannot be nearly so diminished as it was in original Thomism.)

The Third Thomism can claim for itself notable successes. Thomists combined ethical critiques of capitalism that focused on the inability of the market, because of its agnosticism regarding values and its irreducible individualism, to promote the full development of human capacities, with a critique of the whole concept of "sovereignty" shared by capitalists and socialists alike, and defended the principle of subsidiarity against the hegemonic claims of the state, be it liberal or socialist. Social Catholics played an important role in the labor movement, can take credit for the greater protections that artisans, shopkeepers, and peasants enjoy in Europe by comparison with the United States, and played the leading role in the constitution of the first really effective international political authority—the European Union.

This said, there were also some real failures. The Church was slow in supporting the development of Catholic lay movements and Christian Democratic parties, insisted on clerical control of those movements, and always gave first priority to defending clerical interests. The Church's record during World War II was nothing short of scandalous. It was only after the Second World War that Social Catholicism became politically effective, and even then the promise of a "third way" between capitalism and socialism was never realized, or rather tended to be reduced to a moderate social democracy friendly to Church interests on questions of education and family law. Christian Democratic parties, rather than representing the authentic alternative to both capitalism and socialism that they imagined themselves to be, became instead an instrument of U.S. anticommunist strategy in the postwar period. Within the Church the Thomists did little or nothing to advance the position of women or to come to terms with an increasingly literate laity anxious to participate more actively in the internal life of the Church as well as to engage in the "social apostolate" assigned to them by Neo-Thomistic ecclesiology.

Ultimately, however, the failure of the Third Thomism was a failure to fully engage modernity. It is one thing to regard modern univocal and immanentist metaphysics as mistaken; it is quite another to understand fully why they emerged in the first place—i.e., as a product of and counter-reaction, respectively, to the Augustinian ascendancy. Only once this is understood can the legitimate aspirations of modernity be separated from their idolatrous deformations and an alternative crafted, which, while acknowledging the historic role of the Church as a conservator of the analogical metaphysics of *Esse*, looks forward rather than backwards and which is prepared to engage all of humanity's wisdom traditions.

The Third Thomism, in other words, failed because it proposed a revived Christendom (precisely the structure that had given birth to modernity) rather than an extended *Convivencia*.

Let us turn, now to a metaphysics that can ground such a *Convivencia* and thus help chart the next steps in the human civilizational project.

5

Towards a New Dialectical Metaphysics

INTRODUCTION

In the preceding chapters we have demonstrated that rational metaphysics, far from being responsible for modern nihilism and state terror, is, in fact, a necessary precondition for a just social order, in that it grounds claims regarding justice and thus makes rational discourse in the public arena possible. It is rational metaphysics that at once opens up for public participation the discourse around first principles that was originally the preserve of hereditary priesthoods, while holding accountable before the court of natural law the activities of the public authorities and the operation of the market order. A question remains, however: *Which Metaphysics?*

There are, broadly speaking, two dimensions to this problem. There are, first of all, a number of "half-steps" back towards metaphysics that have gained currency in recent years. These can, broadly speaking, be divided between those that attempt to reinstate a religious metaphysics, such as the Radical Orthodoxy of John Milbank and his associates or the Reformed Liberalism of Franklin Gamwell, and emerging tendencies in the dialectical tradition, such as the work of Badiou and Bhaskar, which claim to break explicitly with postmodernism while explicitly rejecting a metaphysics of *Esse* or presence. Before we proceed to a make a proposal of our own, we need to show why these alternatives are inadequate.

Once this is done, we will argue, there remain two sharply divergent alternatives: the metaphysics of *Esse* that emerged out of the Socratic tradition and its interaction with the Semitic prophetic tradition, and the metaphysics of *pattica samupada* advanced by the Buddhists. The reason for this is simple. Once we have rejected the univocal metaphysics that emerged out of the Asharite and Augustinian traditions, and that is encoded in the ontological argument for the existence of God, we are left with a metaphysics that proceeds along the lines of Thomas's first three *ways*: i.e., either by causation or by the distinction between necessary and contingent being. And ultimately these three ways are one: what must be explained by causation is contingent being. Either we can conclude to a first principle that, unlike all of the phenomena of the empirical world, is its own cause, and thus the power of Being as such, or not. If we can, we have a metaphysics of *Esse*; if we cannot, we have a metaphysics of dependent origination.

This said, I would like to argue that there is more room for *rapprochement* between these two perspectives than might at first meet the eye. On the one hand, the development of mathematical physics has tended to gradually erode if not the concept of Being then at least the concept of essence that was traditionally associated with it. It is more and more difficult to claim that the things we encounter in the empirical world have a substantial form that gives them being and that makes them radically different from accidents such as "red" or "tasty," which exist only in other things. Rather, mathematical physics points to a radically relational universe in which the empirical properties of things are determined by an underlying but by no means substantial or unchanging structure. While these underlying structures may not be subject to the sort of global technical manipulation to which modern civilization has aspired, they are, nonetheless, undergoing constant evolutionary transformation according to an internal logic that we are still very far from comprehending.

At the same time, we saw that the larger trend in the development of Buddhist metaphysics was away from a focus on radical emptiness or *sunyata* towards the idea of some sort of underlying first principle such as the *tathagatagarbha*, which is obscured by the illusion of self or inherent existence but which is nonetheless real and the ground of the empirical personality and indeed the whole empirical universe. We also showed that to the extent that Buddhist metaphysical systems adhered to the idea of emptiness or *sunyata* they had great difficulty explaining why the empirical universe appears at all—i.e., why there is a falling away from the intrinsic enlightenment of the *tathagatagarbha*.

This chapter that will suggest a synthesis that leans rather unabashedly in the direction of the metaphysics of *Esse* but which learns nonetheless profoundly from Buddhism. Specifically, the metaphysics of dependent origination will be adopted, with some modifications, as a theory of contingent being. The principal modification will be in recognizing in contingent being an evolutionary drive towards Being as such. As contingent beings move up the dialectical scale, however, they gradually discover that Being is not so much having as it is giving and creating. Thus the profound convergence between the Buddhist ideal of the *bodhisattva* and the Jewish, Christian, and Islamic concept of the *tzadik* or saint, the metaphysical differences notwithstanding. The concept of *Esse* will, furthermore, be analyzed in a way that emphasizes its generativity as opposed to its impassibility. The result will be a metaphysics of *Esse* that is radically historicized and profoundly dynamic and that will ground an ethics and spirituality focused on meaning, creativity, and self-cultivation at both the individual and civilizational level.

We will begin by analyzing the current situation and situating the enterprise of rational metaphysics politically in the context of that situation. We will then explain why the principal contemporary alternatives to our position are inadequate and will summarize briefly arguments made in previous works regarding the possibility of knowing first principles and regarding the foundations of metaphysics in philosophical cosmology. From there we will elaborate the synthesis we have outlined above, drawing out the implications for our understanding of human nature and the human civilizational project.

AN ERA OF CIVILIZATIONAL CRISIS

The Dominant Paradigms

Geopolitical analysis in recent years has been dominated by two conflicting readings of the underlying dynamics of the world in the period after the collapse of the Soviet bloc. According to the first, advanced in 1989 by Francis Fukuyama, the crisis of socialism represents the definitive victory of capitalism, democracy, and secularism, and the end of the age of global ideological conflict—the end, in fact of "history" as we know it. Any remaining conflicts, such as the intense ethnoreligious conflict in the Balkans that dominated the 1990s or the still more intense conflict with Islamic fundamentalism that has come to dominate the present decade, are nothing more than rear-guard actions and while they may require "mopping up operations," they do not represent a fundamental threat to the way of life represented pre-eminently by the United States. The alternative theory, advanced in 1993 by Samuel Huntington, argues instead that we face a "Clash of Civilizations" rooted in fundamentally different approaches to the most fundamental questions of meaning and value, a conflict at present that pits "the West" against "the rest," and especially against *Dar-al Islam* and what he regards as the Confucian civilization of East Asia.

A similar pair of paradigms has, over the course of the past decade, come to be used in analyzing U.S. domestic politics as well. The first paradigm, which reflects assumptions similar to the "end of history thesis" and which enjoyed popularity during roughly the same period, might be referred to as the technocratic paradigm. It was summed up accurately by the 1992 Democratic Party slogan: "it's the economy stupid." According to this view, elections are fundamentally about economics—not so much in the Marxist sense of being about class struggle, but in the neoliberal sense of being about the stewardship of the economy. Incumbents will be evaluated based first and foremost on their handling of the economy; challengers will have to show that they can do better in this arena. The opposing scenario, which dominated most analysis of the November 2004 U.S. general election, is generally referred to as the "culture wars" paradigm and puts "blue states" against "red states" and "seculars" against conservative religious voters.

I would like to suggest that both pairs of paradigms are fundamentally mistaken and misunderstand both the complex cultural dynamics of the present period, domestically and globally, and the way in which these dynamics articulate and impinge on economic contradictions. More specifically, I will argue that that we are entering the early stages of a civilizational crisis in which the secret religion of high modernity—the ideal of divinization by means of innerworldly civilizational progress—has been called into question, but nothing else has as yet emerged to replace it.

First, however, let me explain why the dominant paradigms are inadequate. The "end of history" thesis is the weaker of the two. This view is essentially just a restatement of the principal claims of modernist social theory: that as humanity matures and understands better how the world works it will give up its religious illusions and instead focus on scientific and technical control of the physical, biological, and social environment. It differs from earlier variants of the thesis simply in regarding as "religious" certain nontheistic modern ideologies, such as Marxism, which regard matter rather than "spirit" as the first principle, but are no less metaphysical as a result. As such it shares all the problems of modern social theory. On the one hand, it fails to recognize the accumulating contradictions of the modern project: a building ecological crisis, the failure of both capitalism and socialism to deliver on the modern ideal, the disintegration of the social fabric, a loss of a sense of meaning and value, etc. On the other hand, it also ignores the persistence of both religion generally and of religious conflicts in particular. One need only consider the prominent role of popular religious ideologies in the mass movements for socialism and national liberation throughout the nineteenth and twentieth centuries or the persistence of religious belief and practice in what is arguably the very homeland of modernity—the United States of America—a phenomenon that continues to drive political discourse here. The ethnoreligious conflicts in the Balkans and Islamic fundamentalism are but recent examples of a long series of phenomena that modernist social theory cannot really accommodate.

This does not, however, mean, that what we are facing is a "clash of civilizations" in the sense understood by Samuel Huntington—much less his looser interpreters in the neoconservative camp. First, the whole idea of a "Western Civilization" stretching from Ancient Israel and Ancient Greece up through the present is highly problematic. Even if one allows that a diverse complex of cultural traditions, mostly Indo-European and Semitic, flowed together to form an at least partially unified civilization during the Middle Ages, this cultural sphere must be understood to include *both* Christendom *and Dar-al-Islam* as well as a distinct Jewish minority culture. And *modernity* was constituted first and foremost by a *rupture* with this civilizational complex, which had been unified by a common Aristotelian philosophical language in which disputed questions of meaning and value were hashed out. Neither modern Europe and North America nor the modern Islamic world can really be regarded as faithful to this heritage. Second, the thesis fails to even describe correctly, much less really explain, the main lines of global conflict in the present period. The Jews and Christians who are most committed to sustained conflict with *Dar-al-Islam* are not, for example, secularized liberal interpreters of their tradition, but fundamentalists who actually *agree* with the fundamentalist Muslims with whom they are at war on a broad range of cultural questions, from the proper approach to the interpretation of the sacred Scriptures (literal inerrancy) through the nature of God (absolutely transcendent and sovereign) to church/state relations and the role of women in society. At even a rudimentary level of abstraction, in other words, this supposed *clash of civilizations* turns into a cultural convergence among groups who are, nonetheless, really and truly in conflict with each other on the geopolitical stage. East Asia, meanwhile, has embraced capitalism in a way that is hardly coherent with a traditional Confucian worldview and must be read either as representing a rupture towards modernity or a mobilization of other elements in their cultural heritage—e.g., a long-standing mercantile tradition and a statist authoritarianism associated more closely with Buddhism and Legalism respectively than with anything even remotely resembling a Confucian *ru xue*.

Finally, both the *end of history* thesis and the *clash of civilizations* thesis miss the emergence of an increasingly powerful third force that is present in the cultural dynamics of the present period: a pluralistic, tolerant, and eclectic spiritual culture characterized by dialogue and seeking rather than dogmatism and certainty. This third force had its antecedents in the powerful religious movements for social justice that characterized the postwar period: the movements around Gandhi in India and Buddhadasa in Thailand, Buddhist Socialism in Burma, certain strains of Islamic socialism, the civil rights movement in the United States, and liberation theology in Latin America and other parts of the Third World. While, after the collapse of the Soviet Union, these trends became less attached to the ideals of historic socialism, anyone familiar with the left today knows that, at least at the grass roots, it remains very largely a religious movement. Even such "moral issues" as gay marriage do not pit "seculars" against "religious" so much as people with conflicting religious commitments against each other. We must remember that the conflict over gay marriage, at least in the U.S., was a conflict within the *churches* before it became a conflict within the *state*. Many gay couples are deeply religious and seek formal recognition not only of various legal rights but also of the sacred character of the bond that unites them.

An Alternative Framework

In view of these criticisms, I would like to suggest an alternative analysis of the current situation and of the role of religion therein. Modern social theory, whether capitalist or socialist in its leanings, has tended to negate the role of both properly material factors outside human control—the ecosystem—and of transcendental principles in shaping human action and human social life, and has focused instead on things subject to human control: technology, economics, politics, and sometimes culture (though not the principles about which cultures speak). Historical materialism treats the ecosystem as essentially raw material and ideas as merely a superstructure that can serve to legitimate or contest the existing order. Weberian interpretive sociology, on the other had, seems to *talk* a lot about ideas but ultimately treats them as tools in an ongoing power struggle—a kind of "war of the gods," as Weber put it in *Science as a Vocation*.

In order to understand the current situation, we need a more subtle theory, which without negating structural factors (technology, economics, politics, culture) takes seriously *both* the fact that human beings pursue transcendental aims—aims which are understood differently by different cultures (Being, Sunyata, Progress, etc.)—*and* that they do so under definite material conditions—in a definite ecosystem, with particular technologies at their disposal, etc. Human civilizations, in other words, pursue transcendental aims that they understand in a particular way (what we will call their civilizational ideal). They do this using definite structures (capitalism, socialism) and under definite material conditions.

This framework allows us to distinguish between three very different types of crisis: a *crisis of regime*, a *structural* crisis, and a *civilizational* crisis. The first sort of crisis occurs when a long-established way of managing a given society no longer allows people to realize their aspirations, but where the contradictions are not so profound as to require a change in social structure. The economic crisis of the 1930s and the advent of the New Deal and European social democracy would be an example of such a crisis, as would the end of that regime and its replacement by neoliberalism between 1973 and 1989. A structural crisis occurs when it is no longer possible for a society to pursue its civilizational ideal within the context of the existing structure. The option for socialism in countries that were experiencing difficulty modernizing under capitalism, and the transition back when they had exhausted the limits of statist accumulation strategies, represent responses to crises of this sort.

A *civilizational crisis*, on the other hand, takes place when, generally after a succession of structural crises, people actually lose faith in a civilizational ideal and stop pursuing it. Such a civilizational crisis seems to have occurred at the end of the Bronze Age, at which point humanity seems to have lost faith in the god-kings who were the principal focal points for surplus centralization and civilizational development and in some cases—Israel and China—seem actually to have overthrown them. The crisis of Roman civilization shows how a structural crisis can lead ultimately to civilizational transformation. The Roman Empire ran into a structural crisis because its basic strategy—using the surplus generated by chattel slavery to buy into the Silk Road trade network—ran into insuperable limits. Logistic and ecological factors made further expansion impossible, bringing an end to the wars of conquest, which provided a steady supply of slaves. The empire was forced to settle slaves on the land with families (so they could reproduce and ensure a steady supply of labor) and to bind hitherto free tenants to their farms, while drastically increasing the burdens of taxation and civic service on the middle and upper middle strata. This undermined the radical distinction between free citizens and slaves that had been central to the whole fabric and self-understanding of Hellenistic-Roman Civilization. Christianity assisted with this transition because (at least in the forms in which it was adopted) it at once legitimated the continued existence of class differences, making it palatable to the ruling classes, but also insisted on the underlying humanity of the slaves and *coloni*, disciplining the ruling classes and forcing them to stop working their slaves to death and thus undercutting the long-term supply of labor. All were, furthermore, engaged by an ethos of "service" that legitimated both what was left of the empire in the East and the emerging feudal order in the West. Ultimately, however, the adoption of Christianity ordered Europe towards a radically different civilizational ideal, one that was no longer recognizably "Roman." Structural crises can, in other words, but need not, lead to civilizational crises.

It is just such a civilizational crisis that, I would like to argue, we are beginning to face, and that is a key to understanding the complex cultural dynamics of the present period. The collapse of socialism represented not the triumph of the positivistic variant of the modern ideal and of capitalism as a strategy for realizing it, but rather the collapse of the dialectical variant of that ideal in a context in which the positivistic variant had already been abandoned by the majority of humanity long ago. The deepest cultural cleavages on the planet are between those who continue to embrace variants of the high-modern ideal (neoliberals and neosocialists), those who are attempting to reinstate an early modern ideal (most fundamentalists, who are Augustinian or Asharite restorationists), deconstructionist postmodernists who regard modernity as the last ideal, after which there will be no others, and an emerging "fifth force": those who are engaged in an open, pluralistic, and tolerant search for a new ideal that is both more respectful of the material conditions under which we live (i.e., the ecosystem) and that, without negating the real possibilities of scientific and technological progress, orders humanity to a higher spiritual end. It is this latter group that represents the new and true opposition—the party of meaning and hope in a world that, at present, knows little of either.

Given this analysis, it should be clearer now why we believe rational metaphysics not only can, but must, have a future. Rational metaphysics represents a sharp alternative to both the vain pretensions of the high-modernist intelligentsia, which claimed that either science and technology or dialectics and revolutionary politics would liberate humanity from finitude and contingency, and its principal competitors: early-modern fundamentalists who preach submission to a sovereign God and postmodern nihilists who argue that freedom can be bought only at the cost of meaning. Rational metaphysics offers us a way to reground a meaning and a hope that at once includes but also transcends the human civilizational project and that conserves—indeed regrounds—the autonomy of the human subject while situating that subject in the context of a larger framework of meaning.

This said, we need to address directly the political valence of any possible revitalized rational metaphysics. We demonstrated in the last chapter the peculiar irony in the humanistic intelligentsia's bid for power. In order to ground its claims for autonomy from the clergy, that intelligentsia elaborated an ideology that vested ultimate meaning in the human civilizational project itself, and pitted this meaning sharply against any transcendent human destiny. The result, however, was to elevate the authority of the actual civilization-builders—scientists and engineers and political organizers—above their own, to transform themselves into, in effect, legitimators of a new secularist clergy and a new aristocracy.

The sort of rational metaphysics we are suggesting has a very different political valence. On the one hand, it safeguards the leading role of the philosopher and theologian. By suggesting that human beings participate in but are not identical with the creative power of God, we preserve a role for those who keep humanity ordered to that higher end, without in any way demeaning those whose work consists in creating. At the same time, what the philosopher excels in is not something radically different from what every human being does. As Antonio Gramsci pointed out, everyone is an intellectual, everyone a philosopher. The philosopher leads the community in reflecting on fundamental questions of meaning and value and guards the sanctity of natural law against the usurpations of tyrants and mobs. But it is the people as a whole who actually do the reflecting and who bear ordinary responsibility for interpreting and implementing natural law. In this sense, the rational metaphysics we are proposing is more compatible with democracy than modernist univocity and immanentism or rejections of metaphysics that vest unique authority in specialized knowledge.

THE STATE OF THE QUESTION

Rational metaphysics, it seems, is making a modest comeback. This change of fortune is due to a complex conjunction of factors. On the one hand, with the collapse of the high-modern ideal, humanity is engaged in a new search for meaning. On the other hand, as John Milbank puts it, "Since 9/11 we have been confronted with the apparent displacement of ideological terror by religious terror, whether perpetrated by small groups or by nation-states" (Milbank 2006b). This has begun to call into question the explicitly antimetaphysical spirituality that emerged out of the disintegration of deconstructionist postmodernism. Even secular thinkers such as Alain Badiou have begun to question the antimetaphysical tenor of philosophy in the past century, arguing that it creates space for religious fanaticism (Badiou 1988, 2005).

This said, the space being accorded a rational metaphysics is very limited indeed. What is very emphatically *not* granted, by either the dialectical left or the Radical Orthodox right, is the full *autonomy* and indeed *primacy* that metaphysics enjoyed in premodern philosophy. For Milbank and Radical Orthodoxy, an authentic metaphysics is possible only as a reflection on faith, and is complete only in theology. As Milbank puts it, "the *destiny* of metaphysics without theology is to be reduced to speculative materialism" (Milbank 2006b). For Badiou (Badiou 1988, 2006), it is not really metaphysics at all, but rather mathematics that constitutes the first philosophy, and that tells us what is really real; metaphysics merely validates that mathematics can actually do this, and thus re-grounds what amounts to a modest nuancing of the modern scientific worldview.

There are far too many philosophical tendencies that in one degree or another re-engage metaphysics for us to consider them all here. Rather we will consider four: two that attempt to reinstate a secular and two that attempt to reinstate a religious metaphysics.

Restoring Modern Dialectics

The crisis of socialism presented the dialectical tradition with a fundamental challenge. Humanistic and structural dialecticians alike regarded the Soviet Union with some disdain and assumed that its collapse would yield a more authentic socialism, even if they understood this differently as one that affirmed the rational autonomy of the human subject and recognized the liberal and democratic rights that go along with it, or as one that returned to the revolutionary ideal of creating a classless and communal society. When instead the crisis led to capitalist restoration, and dissident socialists on both the right and left were marginalized, it catalyzed a fundamental rethinking on the part of partisans of dialectical materialism. What, specifically, in the dialectical tradition had led to the deformations of the socialist project, not only in the Soviet Union but elsewhere? Was it possible to affirm enough of the historic claims of the dialectical tradition regarding the objectivity of knowledge and values to reground that project while avoiding the errors that had led to totalitarian deformations?

Most attempts to answer this question from within the dialectical tradition have shared a common point of departure: a sharp rejection of the "metaphysics of presence"—i.e., the appeal to some higher principle, whether transcendent or immanent (God, History), which in turn grounds the moral claims of socialism—and which is shared by both premodern and high modern philosophy. We will see that this approach is ultimately unviable, because apart from such a principle there simply isn't any way to ground substantive moral claims of the kind that socialism makes in contesting the market allocation of resources.

Critical Dialectical Realism

Roy Bhaskar (Bhaskar 1989, 1993) is, to be sure, well aware of just precisely this problem, and has been one of the most vocal critics of the philosophical foundations of neoliberalism. Bhaskar begins by mounting a systematic critique of positivist epistemology and metaphysics. He makes what amounts to a transcendental argument for the reality of those objects of scientific knowledge historically affirmed by the dialectical tradition, but denied by the positivists ("society," "social structures"). Specifically, he argues that structures are, in fact, the condition of possibility of the "facts" and "events" to which Humeans would reduce reality

(Bhaskar 1989: 62–65). He does not, however, then argue for an ascent through knowledge of these structures to a positive doctrine of Being. On the contrary, he argues that the difficulty with all hitherto existing dialectics, including those of Hegel and, to some extent, Marx, has been an insistence on the positivity of Being—i.e., on the priority of Being over Non-Being. Even where the category of contradiction is introduced as a determination of being itself, as it is in Hegel and Marx, the priority of the positive leads inevitably to closure of the cosmohistorical process and the collapse of Being into an undifferentiated expressive unity. In the case of Hegel, because of his idealism and spiritual monism, this lead to a reconciliation with the status quo of a still semifeudal Germany. In the case of Marx it led to the claim that history terminates (or, what is the same thing, that prehistory terminates and history begins) with the achievement of communism, a doctrine easily mobilized by the Stalinist state to close-off further progress not only beyond, but actually towards, communism. Bhaskar proposes instead to give priority to the category of *absence*, which he claims is the condition for the possibility of physical systems of any kind, being implied by spatio-temporal extension, physical interaction, and thus motion, and which is the driving force of human society from the demanding cry of an infant distressed at the absence of the mother, through the most sophisticated demand for the "absenting of constraints on the absenting of constraints" and thus for the full development of human capacities (Bhaskar 1993).

Bhaskar gives this notion of "absenting constraints" concrete content through his proposal for an "explanatory-critical social science." He begins by pointing out that the subject matter of the social sciences includes not just social objects, but also beliefs about those objects. Some of those beliefs, he argues, are false, and if one can explain the falsity then, other things being equal, one can move to "a negative evaluation of the *explanans* and a positive evaluation of any action rationally designed to absent it" (Bhaskar 1993: 261–62).

What Bhaskar is doing here, of course, is to make explicit and rigorous the ethics that are implicit (and not always consistent) in Marx's social-scientific and ideological-critical work, while extending it beyond the scope of Marx's specific analyses, which were confined to a study of the capitalist system. Thus Marx's critique of political economy, as a critique of beliefs about capitalism, not only shows those beliefs to be flawed, but shows them to be rooted in the capitalist order itself, of which it is an ideological reflex. The critique of political economy thus becomes a critique of capitalism and a mandate for social transformation. Similarly, he suggests, critiques of sexist and racist ideology imply critiques of women's oppression and imperialism, and provide a mandate for emancipation.

Bhaskar's approach is, to be sure, a real step up from neoliberalism. Grounded in a solid epistemological realism, it provides a basis for distinguishing between true and false and from there going on to criticize structures that give rise to false judgments and thus stand in the way of effective action on behalf of human development. Bhaskar's position is, furthermore, self-correcting. He is able to do for aspects of Marx's theory, and certain claims of later Marxists, what Marx himself did for bourgeois political economy, thus limiting the tendency toward dogmatism and ideological legitimation of structures which once promoted social progress but which may have outlived their usefulness.

Implicit in Bhaskar's ethics, however, is the assumption that effective action on behalf of human development is somehow a moral imperative. But this, precisely, is to assume what must be demonstrated. Bhaskar does take some tentative steps towards showing that human beings have a drive towards such development, arguing that the drive towards universal human autonomy is implicit in the infant's "primal scream" (Bhaskar 1993: 264) and that it becomes explicit through hard experience of what Freud called the "reality principle," which teaches us the extent to which and the real conditions under which our desires can actually be realized. What this does not do, however, is tell us just what a fully developed human being *is*. Indeed, Bhaskar seems to remain scrupulously agnostic on this question. He gives us no basis, for example, on which to prefer investment in liberal arts education over the production of luxury automobiles, except, perhaps, the claim that the latter is not sustainable or doesn't work in the long run due to economic or ecological limitations. But this is quite different from showing that the former is intrinsically preferable. Desire remains the watchword of Bhaskar's ethics, standing in for the absent Good, just as absence stands in for Being itself.

The symptom that allows us to diagnose Bhaskar's disorder is an ambiguity in his language. While he often uses the language of human development or human flourishing, in his more rigorous formulations he always reverts to the term "autonomy" or "freedom." And it is indeed this latter value to which his argument actually concludes. Bhaskar abbreviates his ascent to first principles intentionally, precisely because a more substantive doctrine of the Good would undermine his ultimately libertarian agenda. His whole enterprise, in fact, can be read as an attempt to show that contrary to the claims of Hayek and his camp, the market order neither advances human freedom nor promotes the long-term survival of the species. Neither, in other words, answers the primal scream schooled by the reality principle.

This approach reflects, fundamentally, the vantage point of the humanistic intelligentsia in the present period, for whom capitalism generally and neoliberalism in particular have proven themselves ultimately inadequate, but who are hesitant about any restored metaphysics that might ground a critique of their own practice—which might, even noncoercively, call into question their exercise of their freedom. In the process, though, they accept the principles fixed by the bourgeoisie—freedom and survival value—and agree to contest capitalism on its own terrain.

This said, we should note that Bhaskar does not actually *ground* the values of freedom and autonomy, but rather simply presupposes them as a criterion of judgment. It is not at all clear from his argument why freedom is important, or indeed the most important value. The result is a certain arbitrariness in his argument.

Even so, might not Bhaskar win on bourgeois terrain? Not with the weapons currently at his disposal. The judgment of the peoples of the former Soviet bloc against socialism was first and foremost a judgment against the fact that it did not allow them to freely pursue their own self-interests, which they had come to understand in narrowly consumerist terms. The judgment against the new market order is, rather, a judgment against the failure of the market to support certain higher-order aspirations that were well-funded under socialism—the desire to dance, to paint, to teach, or to engage in research. While these aspirations can be recast in terms of freedom, it remains necessary to show that the freedoms or aspirations that socialism makes possible or fulfills are higher than those made possible or fulfilled by capitalism. And for this we need a principle of value higher than freedom.

Dialectical Formalism

Our second dialectical alternative takes a very different approach to transcending postmodernism. Alain Badiou looks not to an immanent critique of Hegelian and Marxist dialectics, but rather to the epistemic ideal of modernity itself—mathematics—to re-ground the objectivity of knowledge, a doctrine of the subject, and a sort of ethics. Specifically, Badiou argues that mathematics—and more specifically set theory—*is* ontology. This immediately generates severe constraints on what kind of metaphysics is possible. On the one hand, the Russell paradox and the axiom of foundation imply that a set can neither contain nor belong to itself. This means that there is no "set of all sets," whether we call that set Nature, History, or God, but only what Badiou calls "multiplicities." On the other hand, precisely because of this, sets are defined disjunctively and in relation to one another. This means that they are defined by something outside themselves and thus indiscernible by ontology. This void is the site of what Badiou calls the "event."

Badiou identifies four distinct types of events: art, science, politics, and love. In each case, the event involves naming the indiscernible and thus the term in terms of which all sets are defined. The event is, in effect, a kind of ontological revolution. The subject is constituted in and through this process, by the naming of and fidelity to the event (Badiou 1988/2006).

It is only when we reach this point that the relationship between Badiou and his mentor Sartre becomes apparent. As for Sartre (Sartre 1973), Badiou understands human beings as constituted by the desire to be God, and as fully human only when they are engaged in metaphysical revolution.

Badiou's political roots are in the Maoist tradition, and his philosophy is, in a very real sense, the first fully developed and explicitly philosophical groundwork for what is often called "Western Maoism." As we noted in the previous chapter, Third World Maoism represented a complex coalition between marginalized humanistic intellectuals anxious to make their mark by breaking with every tradition and poor peasants who regarded civilization itself as an unwarranted burden. Western Maoism severs these humanistic intellectuals from their peasant base, creating a politics in which revolution becomes, in effect, an end in itself, the process by which the subject effaced by capitalist high modernity is reconstituted.

Like most philosophical products of the New Left, however, Badiou's philosophy is not simply wrong; it is founded on a fundamental misunderstanding. We have already shown that attempts to demonstrate the existence of God within the context of a purely formal reason—i.e., the ontological argument—inevitably fail for the simple reason that they are based on bad mathematics. Thus the ontological argument—the claim that God exists because "that than which nothing greater can be thought"— would not meet the terms of its definition if it *didn't* exist, is convertible with Zorn's Lemma, which claims that a partial ordered set with an upper bound must have a maximal element. This lemma, while intuitively obvious, cannot be proven. Badiou, similarly, sets up a set theoretical definition of and argument for the existence of God, which he then knocks down. But this argument is based on a confusion between the numerical and the transcendental One. The numerical One—the One that can be defined set-theoretically—is simply a function of the ordering of sets by inclusion and has none of the properties historically associated with the divine. The transcendental One, on the other hand, is One in the sense of being integral: it cannot be divided without ceasing to exist, and is thus convertible with Being. It cannot be defined set-theoretically. The "god" whose existence Badiou disproves, in other words, is not God at all, but merely a number.

Some thinkers have charged that Badiou arbitrarily excludes the religious from his typology of events (Dews 2004, Zupanic 2004). Might not God be defined here, *outside* ontology, as the "event of events" (Dews 2004)? But such complaints misunderstand Badiou, whose atheism is, ultimately, not of the intellect but rather of the will.

Both dialectical critical realism *and* the dialectical formalism of Badiou are, we should note, still "late-modern" or "postmodern" in the sense that they *deny* the existence of a first principle, understood as either the Infinite or as *Esse*, which is prior to or immanent in the universe. They simply return to the *agon* from which deconstructionist postmodernists had retired. In the case of Bhaskar, this *agon* is still the struggle for liberation and justice. It is just that it is inadequately grounded. But for Badiou it is an authentic theomachy or struggle among the gods or would-be gods. In this sense, he reaches back behind the deconstructionists and Heidegger to Nietzsche and makes (almost) explicit what Nietzsche did not: that the will to power is the will to the divine.

This makes the political valence of Badiou's work profoundly ambiguous. His option for an emancipatory politics is, in the end *worse than arbitrary*. It is a function of the fact that he, and the humanistic intelligentsia to whom he appeals, stand outside the current bloc in power and outside the ontology they have defined. But if the motivation behind politics is the self-constitution of the subject through an act of ontological revolution, it is unclear why such a revolution might not be carried out, as it was for Heidegger, by and on behalf of a fascist movement. Third World Maoism was held back from this danger by its peasant base; Western Maoism is not. It is in the end an ideology of pure terror, the nightmare nihilism against which Dostoevsky warned us in *The Possessed*.

THE NEW RELIGIOUS METAPHYSICS

What this means, of course, is that any metaphysics that is going to transcend both modernity and postmodernity—which is going to ground judgments regarding meaning and value without reverting to godbuilding or immanentism—will have to be religious in the sense of recognizing a reality or process that, while present in contingent being, also transcends it.

Attempts at such a metaphysics are still rare. Here we consider two of the most important: Franklin Gamwell's Reformed Liberalism and John Milbank's Radical Orthodoxy.

Reformed Liberalism

Gamwell's position is, in many ways, close to our own, precisely because he argues for both a teleological approach to ethics and for the necessity of grounding ethics in a theistic metaphysics. His metaphysics itself, however, is quite different, and we need to consider its merits.

Gamwell approaches the problem of metaphysics from within the transcendental tradition that traces its lineage to Kant. By a transcendental approach to metaphysics, we mean any approach that argues by means of an analysis of the conditions or presuppositions of human subjectivity. Thus Kant, for example, argued that human subjectivity was inconceivable apart from what he called the "forms of intuition"—space and time—and the "categories of the understanding"—quality, quantity, relation, and mode. Kant, however, regarded the idea of God along with the ideas of the self and the world as what he called transcendental ideals—ideas we naturally use to organize our experience of the world, but which are not actually preconditions of any possible experience. For this reason he ruled out rational metaphysics in the traditional sense of the word.

Transcendental theism accepts Kant's basic approach, but argues against him that the idea of God is, in fact, a precondition of or implicit in all acts of human subjectivity. There are many different types of transcendental theism. The most important is undoubtedly the Transcendental Thomism represented by Karl Rahner and Bernard Lonergan. According to Rahner, for example, every existential judgment we make—every judgment that some particular thing exists, contains a "nonthematic preapprehension" of *Esse* as such and thus of God (Rahner 1957). Lonergan (Lonergan 1957), similarly, argues that God as Being is the object of our constitutively human unrestricted desire to know.

Gamwell, while he occasionally makes gestures in the direction of the ontological argument and Thomas's third way (Gamwell 1990: 165–68, 176–78), is actually closer to Kant than most transcendental theists, in that he looks for the foundation of his argument in an analysis of practical reason. He begins from the fact that every human choice, simply because it involves a judgment of better or worse, makes implicit reference to some "comprehensive variable in accord with which all actualities may be compared" (Gamwell 1990: 168), or some principle against which their relative worth can be measured (Gamwell 2000: 13–58). Such a comprehensive variable, in turn, "implies a comprehensive actuality of which all other things are parts" (Gamwell 1990: 168). Following Hartshorne (Hartshorne 1949) he calls this actuality the "divine relativity," a term which, he shows, is convertible with creativity (Gamwell 1990: 169, 178ff., 2000: 122–31, 139–49).

Where Gamwell differs from the Transcendental Thomists is in his characterization of the nature of God. While his argument closely tracks Thomas's fourth way and while he makes some reference to the Thomistic principle of the convertibility of the transcendentals, he rejects the idea that God is outside of space and time on the grounds that this is a purely negative determination and thus not, strictly speaking, comprehensible (Gamwell 1990: 175–76, 2000: 107–22). For Gamwell, as for Hartshorne, God is the supremely temporal individual.

On the basis of this metaphysics, Gamwell is able to derive a well-defined moral imperative: act in such a way as to promote the divine good, understood as maximum future creativity. He follows the Platonic and Aristotelian tradition in tracing wrong action to the limited character of human knowledge, which means that lesser goods are sometimes known more vividly than higher goods, but he rejects the Aristotelian identification of virtue and happiness, arguing that there may well be a contradiction between our own future creativity and that of others and ultimately the maximal future creativity of the universe (Gamwell 2000: 59–104, 131–39).

There are a number of difficulties with this approach. First, transcendental arguments for the existence of God are not really decisive. The fact that the idea of God (whether understood as the Thomistic *Esse* or as Hartshorne's divine creativity) is in fact a condition of any possible knowledge or subjectivity and is implicit in each and every human choice, does not necessarily imply that God in fact exists. Rather, knowledge, choice, or other observable attributes of subjectivity may themselves be illusions. Second, attempts to rise to the idea of God that, like the transcendental argument, evade rather than pass through cosmology, are inevitably religiously unsatisfying and lead to otherworldliness of a sort that leaves them open to the critiques of Feuerbach, Marx, Nietzsche, and Freud (Mansueto 2005). Third, in spite of its otherworldliness, the transcendental approach fails to challenge fundamentally what is arguably one of the principal characteristics of modernity: the notion that human subjectivity is the proper point of departure for all philosophical reflection. By taking subjectivity as its starting point, transcendental theism (classical or neoclassical) implicitly imports into its system the whole complex of principles and values that constitute modern liberalism. To put this another way, by using subjectivity as the foundation for theology and ethics, transcendental theism rules out in advance the possibility that subjectivity might be called into question, while at the same time leaving it radically ungrounded.[1]

Finally, Gamwell's concept of God as "supremely temporal" reflects a similar failure to subject modernity to serious criticism. Gamwell's failure to engage the issue of analogical predication means that he not only fails to understand what is meant by the claim that God is eternal, but also and more seriously that he (perhaps accidentally) falls into the trap of a univocal metaphysics. This is reflected above all in his claim that virtue and happiness are not the same in human beings. This is because a univocal metaphysics implies, more or less necessarily, a "zero-sum"

---

1. For a detailed consideration of this problem, see Hans Urs von Balthazar's *Love Alone* (von Balthazar 1968) or John Milbank's work (Milbank 1990, 1999). Von Balthazar makes the same criticism, to be sure, of the cosmological approach favored in this work. The criticism applies, however, if and only if the God to which such a cosmological argument points exists in the same way as the world She explains, i.e., if the resulting metaphysics is univocal, and cannot therefore call our assumptions about that world radically into question. This need not be the case.

view of the world in which the maximal future creativity of one person or system may detract from that of others or even of God. It is just precisely this zero-sum worldview that is shared by both the liberal and the Augustinian traditions constitutive of modernity. As we will see, if God, and thus "Being" or "creativity," is understood analogically, then the moral imperative is not so much to maximize creativity or Being (our own or others) but rather to maximize our *participation* in an indivisible and uncreated power of creativity of Being. Our own authentic participation in this power is never in contradiction with the similar power of others nor does it take away from the power of God who draws all things to Herself. There is thus no possible contradiction between the Good and our own happiness properly understood.

This brings us to the problem of the social basis and political valence of "transcendental" theism. What this trend does is recognize the fundamental necessity of an ontological ground to any coherent science, ethics, or religion—and thus to the full development of human capacities. They argue further that, *contra* Kant, God is a condition for any possible experience and for any act of human choice, and not merely, as Kant claimed, a moral postulate. But they fail to transcend the realm of the subject that is first and foremost the realm of the marketplace and the bourgeoisie.[2] It is little wonder that at the political level the resulting theologies tend, on the one hand, to legitimate action to restrict and modify the operation of market forces in accord with general moral principles, without, however, advocating a real break with the market order. For this reason it is legitimate to speak of "liberal" Protestantism and "liberal" Catholicism. Put differently, transcendental theism makes room for God in bourgeois society, on the condition that God not call the basic structure of that society into question. This is reflected in Gamwell's political theory, which opens up the possibility of democratically-directed state intervention in the market, but which also makes agnosticism about fundamental questions of value the cornerstone of the political order, providing effective constitutional protection for bourgeois right.

---

2. The standpoint of subjectivity is the standpoint of the bourgeoisie because for the bourgeoisie meaning and value are constituted by the individual human subject: they are ultimately grounded in individual preference.

Radical Orthodoxy

Radical Orthodoxy is, first and foremost, an attempt to respond from within the Christian tradition to the critique of "ontotheology" mounted by Heidegger and his followers. In his early work, Milbank largely accepts the Heideggerian critique and argues, in effect, that the whole dialectical tradition is ultimately grounded in an ontology of violence in which will is pitted against will. This is illustrated for him not only in modern theories of class struggle, but also in the older dialectical ethics of Socrates, Plato, and Aristotle. Even Plato's ideal state, he claims, is an "armed camp," and Aristotle's whole concept of virtue is really just transformation of a fundamentally military ethic of heroism. Indeed, Aristotle counsels his students to be haughty to those beneath them in station and to make sure that others depend on them (Milbank 1991).

Against this ontology of violence, Milbank proposes an ontology of peace, the carrier of which is the Christian Church, which, following Augustine, he calls the "Other City," founded on different loves. Milbank argues that when we recognize Being as difference, we learn a nonpossessive love that at once cancels and preserves the distance between persons. This is the creative love of God, who brings into Being creatures different from Himself and authentically free, and who calls us to love each other in the same way. There is, Milbank argues, no way to ground this ontology dialectically; indeed to try to do so is to yield to the very ontology of violence that seeks truth through struggle and contradiction.

Gradually, Milbank has pulled back from this position, and granted greater space for metaphysics. Even in *Theology and Social Theory* we find the seeds of an alternative critique of philosophical modernity, one that locates its point of origin not in Plato and Aristotle, or even in the Latin Middle Ages generally, but rather in John Duns Scotus, whose doctrine of the univocity of Being laid the groundwork for both the Reformation and secular modernity. As we have noted, this doctrine makes the difference between God and human beings quantitative rather than qualitative. On the one hand, this approach grounds divine authority in power rather than love; on the other hand, it opens up the possibility that defines humanity—that human beings, by building power (through, for example, scientific and technological progress) might be able to transcend finitude and achieve divinity.

In a recent paper (Milbank 2006b) Milbank further develops this thesis, dating the "ontotheological lapse" clearly to around 1300.

> During the course of the Middle Ages however, beginning back in the 12thC but then dominantly from 1300 onwards, most theologians indeed lapsed into "onto-theology" by making being the prime object of metaphysics and God in some sense an object of study within the field of being. Rather like modern analytic philosophers, they tended to regard being as a surd propertyless transcendental presupposition of all of reality, such that being *as such* had and required *no cause*. Only finite being as created required a cause. Of course infinite being as uncreated did not require a cause and this might be seen (as by Scotus) as the most primary and paradigmatic instance of being, but the further and subtle point being made here is that for the dominant later medieval viewpoint it was also true that "transcendental being" in itself, neutral as between infinite and finite, did not require a cause. So God created all finite "thereness," but there was a kind of residue of "thereness" which God did not create and which even his own infinite existence in some sense presupposed. This was primarily a logical presupposition, but also one given a certain ontological valency to the extent that infinite and finite started to be seen as both "equally" and univocally existing: that is to say as both occupying a "transcendental" space of being that exceeds the space of formal logic. It was rather (in Scotus, who is the clearest here), a "formal" space, hovering between the sheerly real and the merely logically modal (meaning here the *modus* in which we must perforce conceive things).
>
> It was especially in terms of this new concept of the transcendentality of being that metaphysics became independent of theology and transcendentally prior to it, in the course of a long process that culminated with Suarez in the early 17thC. (Milbank 2006b)

Following Benedict XVI, furthermore, Milbank attributes this ontotheological lapse to the growing influence of Islam, which, together with Judaism, because of the primacy that they both give to the law over the image as disclosing the divine, he deems resistant to an analogical metaphysics of participation. Thomas, along with Nicholas Cusanus and a few others, is deemed uniquely resistant to this lapse.

What Milbank proposes instead of an independent metaphysics is not entirely clear. He does not, for example, define specifically the boundary between philosophy and theology, but rather gives examples:

Augustine, of course, and Bonaventure and Thomas. He also speaks well of traditions that recognize essentially no boundary at all between these two disciplines, and in which dialectical ascent merges seamlessly into mystical speculation: Sufism, Mystical Judaism, and (with some misunderstanding and oversimplification, I think) Hinduism and Buddhism.

I would like to suggest that Milbank's approach to the problem of ontotheology is flawed, both in its historical analysis and in its treatment of substantive philosophical and theological issues.

First, as we have already suggested, his understanding of the history of metaphysics reflects fundamental confusions. He seems, on the one hand, to want to *keep* the Heideggerian critique of ontotheology (which has gradually shaded into a critique of an *autonomous* rational metaphysics) while at the same time *recovering* Thomas, and perhaps Plato and Aristotle as well. And he associates the birth of ontotheology with Islam (and by extension, though less explicitly, the medieval Jewish subculture within *Dar-al-Islam*). Let us look at each of these problems in turn.

It is, first of all, quite impossible to reject ontotheology, in the sense that Heidegger and his followers understood the term, and still have Thomas. By ontotheology Heidegger meant a rational ascent to first principles in terms of which the universe can be understood and human action ordered—a unitary explanatory deductive system that used Being to explain the world and then derived from this explanation certain ethical, political, and even soteriological conclusions. This, precisely, is the enterprise that Socrates, Plato, and Aristotle begin, as an attempt to reground meaning and value in response to the sophistic critique. And it is the enterprise that the fusion of dialectical philosophy with prophetic religion, beginning with Philo of Alexandria and culminating in the work of Thomas, completes (Mansueto 2005). It does this by identifying the God of Abraham, Jesus, and Mohammed, the God whose name is YHWH (the causative form of the verb "to be") with the Platonic Good and the Aristotelian Unmoved Mover. This metaphysics remains autonomous, in spite of its obvious dependence on the historic engagement with Judaism, Christianity, and Islam, because it upheld the capacity of human reason to rise to the first principle, understood as *Esse* (Thomas) or Necessary Being (for Ibn Sina), *prior to and apart from* revelation.

Where the Heideggerians go wrong is in regarding this "ontotheology" as the philosophical foundation for modern nihilism and state terror. As we have seen, the record of rational metaphysics in the premodern world is one of holding the great empires accountable to higher standards of justice, containing exploitation and encouraging the investment of surplus in activities that promote human development, but without attempting utopia. Modernity derives, rather (and thus far the later Milbank is correct), from the turn towards a univocal or immanentist metaphysics. Classic "ontotheology," Jewish, Christian, and Islamic, concludes to a first principle that is understood first and foremost as necessary, as opposed to contingent being. It is *Esse* as opposed to *ens commune*. From this point of view, every thing in the universe seeks and participates in Being, in proportion to its nature: minerals by conserving form, plants by nutrition, growth, and reproduction, animals by sensation and locomotion, and human beings by the exercise of the intellect and will, which allow us to actually *create*. But the ontological boundary between God and universe is impermeable. One cannot, simply by extending one's capacities, become God. With a univocal metaphysics, on the other hand, the difference between God and universe is merely quantitative. It is that between infinite and finite. Initially this takes the form of spiritualities of authority and submission, which diminish humanity's role in the face of an arbitrary divine sovereign, heavenly reflex of the emerging absolutist monarchies. Eventually, however, the idea develops that human beings can, by means of scientific understanding and technological manipulation, gain control of the universe and develop potentially infinite powers—actually becoming God. Immanentism, by the same token, posits the possibility of humanity rising to divinity by means of a revolutionary transformation that makes it the real subject of nature and history.

The Heideggerian misunderstanding of the relationship between ontotheology and modernity is not, furthermore, simply an intellectual error. It has a definite social basis and political valence. As Georg Lukacs has pointed out (Lukacs 1953/1980), it forms an integral part of an indirect apologetic for capitalism. Specifically, in attacking ontotheology as a "road-builder's ideology," Heidegger attacks the ontological primacy of labor and of human creativity, something that Marx carried over, if perhaps in distorted form,[3] from the earlier dialectical tradition. Heidegger's

---

3. I say that Marx's appropriation of the ontological primacy of creation is distorted because, being an atheist, he does not distinguish between the autonomously creative power which characterizes *Esse* as such and the participation in that power which we humans enjoy on the basis of our intellect and will.

"mistake" is also organically anti-Latin and anti-Semitic—something that should not surprise us given his Nazi sympathies.

Milbank, by failing to fully unravel this knot, becomes complicit in Heidegger's errors, and he does so in a way that has particularly dangerous consequences in the current situation: by means of a kind of soft endorsement of Benedict XVI's anti-Semitism and anti-Islamicism. It is certainly true that much *modern* Islam, especially of the Wahabi variety, reflects a univocal metaphysics. It is a mistake, however, to regard the turn towards a univocal metaphysics as a product of Islamic influence on the West in the high Middle Ages. Rather, the turn towards a univocal doctrine of Being was something that happened *within* both Christendom and *Dar-al-Islam*, probably as a reflex of the emergence of absolutist political structures and market economies. The analogical metaphysics of thinkers like Moshe ben Maimon, ibn Sina, and Thomas Aquinas grounded a rich and complex natural law ethics. If every thing seeks Being in proportion to its nature, then the moral imperative consists in cultivating those capacities that enable us to *be* and to be most fully. A just society is one that cultivates these capacities. Neither absolute monarchs nor the emerging bourgeoisie wanted to be held accountable before the court of this often demanding natural law and thus favored theologies that reduced law to a matter of divine command and restricted the capacity of philosophers and the religious authorities to argue that their actions were unjust on the basis of reason alone. In Islam, this process is reflected in the rise of Asharism—of which al-Ghazali, who Milbank favors, was a moderate advocate. The great Islamic Aristotelians, however—and most especially ibn Sina, whose *Danish* defines God as Necessary Being, and who is usually misread in the West by philosophers and theologians who rely too heavily on Etienne Gilson—were clearly advocates of an analogical metaphysics. In Christendom, the rise of a univocal doctrine of Being was associated with the Augustinian reaction that gained force in the 1270s with the condemnations of Averroism by Peter Tempier. Scotus certainly carries this doctrine to new extremes, but earlier Augustinians, such as Anselm (who defined God in quantitative terms as "that than which nothing greater can be thought"), also upheld a univocal metaphysics.

What difference do these errors in historical analysis make at the substantive philosophical and theological level? First, they blind Milbank to the fact that *only* an autonomous metaphysics can defend effectively against both atheistic nihilism and religious fanaticism. The reasons for this are rather starkly simple, and may not appeal to those inclined to accept only arguments that require great subtlety to comprehend, but they are valid nonetheless. On the one hand, only an autonomous metaphysics, which begins with the facts of ordinary experience and/or the results of the special sciences, can convince skeptics of the reasonableness of belief and the possibility of revelation. Milbank's claim that such an autonomous metaphysics can, furthermore, ground only a bare procedural liberalism, which formally excludes religion from the public arena but leaves what he calls "plural fideism" to compete without any basis for adjudicating their competing claims, is simply not fair. As we have already suggested, the autonomous metaphysics of thinkers such as ibn Sina, Moshe ben Maimon, and Thomas Aquinas grounded a rich and complex natural law theory, which *both* acknowledges and respects a realm of revealed truth that (being indemonstrable) cannot be made the object of compulsion *and* provides a set of universal principles governing the way people from competing traditions engage each other in the public arena. It is possible, for example, to argue on the basis of natural law not only for certain liberal rights, or for the full equality of men and women (based on the fact that both share common intellectual capacities) but also for public policies that restrict exploitation and encourage investment in activities that promote human development, while at the same time recognizing that many questions (e.g., the Incarnation and any imperatives regarding spiritual development that flow from the Incarnation) transcend rational demonstration and cannot be made the object of public policy. Indeed, it would not be too much to say that an autonomous rational metaphysics of *Esse* grounds a public arena *constituted* by dialogue around fundamental questions of meaning and value.

Second, Milbank's attack on the autonomy of metaphysics is also an attack on the autonomy of theology as an intellectual discipline. This is apparent from his tendency to blur the boundary between theology and speculative mysticism of the sort represented by Russian Orthodox sophiology, the Kaballah, and the illuminist or *israqi* school in Islam. This is dangerous because theology has a definite social function within the community of the Church. Just as philosophy governs the shared space of civil society, a space in which authority rests on arguments accessible to anyone capable of reason, theology governs the shared public space of the Church, in which authority rests on arguments accessible to reason as it has been completed and extended by a body of revealed wisdom regarding the extent and status of which members of the community more or less agree. Mystical union may well represent a higher wisdom still, but it is nondiscursive and thus cannot be shared and public and thus cannot form the basis for the exercise of authority *in foro externo*. Speculative mysticism of the sort represented by Russian sophiology, Kaballah, and the *israqi* school of Islam blur these lines, making discursive, cognitive claims on the basis of fundamentally private experiences.

Finally, and most seriously, Milbank's historical errors lead him into what can only be called a soft anti-Semitism, denying the compatibility of a spirituality centered on fulfillment of the Law (such as we have seen in Judaism and Islam) with an analogical metaphysics of participation and associating it instead with the univocal metaphysics that (we agree) tends to promote state terror. Here I quote Milbank at some length:

> ... Judaism and still more Islam tend to be suspicious of the capacity of image to disclose God, whereas they both consider law to be supremely disclosive of God. But Christianity is somewhat suspicious of law as the prime disclosure of God (Paul declared that it is 'preceded' by faith) and testifies that one supreme image (Christ) fully manifests God, such that all other images are in some degree sanctified.
>
> Now law prescribes in advance. While it would be utterly crass to say that premodern law wholly favoured possibility over actuality (since it relied greatly upon precedent, narrative and legal fiction) nonetheless law as a category in general does so more than image as a category in general. The primacy of image also entails the primacy of actuality (*this* realised picture beyond any pre-given formula rather than another), whereas any shift towards making law and will the most central considerations will tend also to favour the priority of the possible.
>
> ... to deny the primacy of the actual is to deny the primacy of the image and the exceeding of the law by the incarnate Christ. (Milbank 2006a)

What Milbank is missing here is the long tradition, reaching back to the prophets, and extending into Christianity as well as Judaism and Islam, which identifies *doing justice* and *knowing God*. Thus when the prophets speak of *da'ath 'elohim* (knowledge of God) they are not speaking of something theoretical, but rather an experiential and nonconceptual knowledge that we gain in actually realizing the divine will.

> Hear the word of YHWH, O Israel;
> for YHWH has a charge to bring against the people of the land;
> There is no faith or mutual trust,
> no knowledge of God [*da'ath 'elohim*] in the land,
> oaths are imposed and broken, they kill and rob;
> there is nothing but adultery and license,
> one deed of blood after another. (Hos 4:1–2 NEB)

> Let us humble ourselves, let us strive to know YHWH,
> whose justice dawns like morning light,
> and its dawning is as sure as the sunrise.
> It will come to us like a shower,
> like spring rains that water the earth. (Hos 6:3 NEB)

Da'ath 'elohim was rooted for Israel in the revolutionary struggle that brought it into being as a people—a struggle against the warlords of Canaan and their Egyptian overlords, which led eventually to the establishment of a new kind of society characterized by at least a rough social justice (Gottwald 1979). At first Israel understood its God in this context—as *el yahwi sabaoth yisrael*, El who brings into being the armies of Israel. Gradually, however, by living in a just society that promoted human creativity, this understanding deepened, and Israel began to understand that its revolutionary warrior God brought into being not only the armies of Israel, but in fact the cosmos as a whole, and did so in a single unified movement, so that creation and redemption were not radically distinguished. And in this insight Israel achieves an insight into the divine nature—that is, Being Itself. Thus the name "YHWH" is the causative form of the Hebrew verb "to be." In this sense one could argue, using the language of later dialectics, that the judgment of justice and thus of the Good led ineluctably to the judgment of Being with which it is convertible. This is true in spite of the fact that Israel remained skeptical about elaborate cognitive claims regarding God, rejecting not only representations of the divine nature, but even pronunciation of the divine name outside of the most solemn context of the cult.

This knowledge rooted in the just act came, in the context of the Catholic tradition, to be understood to represent a real participation in the life of God (and thus something that can be understood only on the basis of an analogical metaphysics). This understanding was based on the Aristotelian concepts of connatural knowledge and intentional being. According to Aristotle, "like knows like." Thomas in particular developed this idea into a complex doctrine of connatural knowledge—the sort of knowledge we have of cold, for example, by being cold—or of justice, by being just, which is quite different from the knowledge we have of "cold" from thermodynamic theory or of "justice" from a theoretical ethics. Also according to Aristotle, when we know something, our intellect takes on its form, and we become that thing, if only in a limited intentional way. Thus when we know God, *either* theoretically or connaturally (by engaging in "Godly" or right action) we experience some measure of divinization.

Different degrees of justice, and thus of knowledge, furthermore, represent different degrees of participation in the life of God. The ordinary knowledge we have of God through an autonomous metaphysics is only of God in relation to the universe, not of God in Herself. We know God in the mirror of natural beauty, not as Beauty itself, as a principle that helps us to explain the universe, not as the Truth itself, as our supreme good and not as the Good itself. And the divine *Esse* and unity seem merely requirements of logic, themselves forever shrouded in darkness. Because of this our natural love of God is, in a certain sense, love of God as a means. We love God because She is our creator, the principle of our existence, and the condition for the full development and exercise of our capacities. This kind of love is not to be disparaged. It is not sinful or even selfish. It is, on the contrary, right and just—the part of justice that Thomas calls the virtue of religion. But it is not love of God for Her own sake, and it will not satisfy us. This is because, however noble the human condition, it is ordered to higher ends, and those who love it as the highest good will inevitably be frustrated when they learn, as we all inevitably do, that the universe is not in fact structured to serve us. Only a knowledge of God in Her essence, and a love that loves the highest Good for its own sake, will leave us at peace with a universe ordered to that Good and with our place therein.

We achieve this supernatural knowledge and this supernatural love precisely by running up against the limits of natural knowledge and natural love. Consider, for example, the case of Israel. At first the people are struggling merely for their own liberation and their own justice. On the basis of this struggle they develop a new understanding of God—first as *el yahwi sabaoth yisrael*, and eventually as YHWH, the causative power of Being as such. Gradually, however, it becomes clear that liberation and justice are not the final *telos*, that the universe is not built around the human person or human civilization—even the just person or the just society. No sooner had the people of Israel recognized the hand of God in their amazing victories over enemies that far outmatched them in terms of military might, than that hand was withdrawn, or extended in ways that seemed directed to some end other than their own temporal well-being. It is at this point that one realizes that the struggle isn't about me, that it isn't even about us, if indeed it is about anything at all, and that any attempt to name what it is about, while necessary and even, within limits, satisfying, risks limiting its scope in a way that will inevitably lead to idolatry and disappointment. The struggle is about this great Unnameable-Bringing-Into-Being that we experience in being called each and every day to become more than we are and that we learn to discover as much in the disappointments as in the successes, as these point us towards an ever deeper appreciation of divine nature. This gradual revelation of the divine nature through struggle and contradiction is what Juan de la Cruz called the dark night of the soul.

If Judaism and Islam have been more reluctant than Christianity to see in the fulfillment of the law a real participation in the life of God, this is not because such an understanding of the Law is impossible, or because these traditions are wed ineluctably to the univocal metaphysics that lies at the root of modern nihilism and state terror, but rather because of their caution about the idea of divinization as such, which seem to them to violate the strictures against idolatry or *shirk* (the crime of associating something with God). Thus Jewish and Islamic Aristotelians regarded the very pinnacle of human spiritual achievement as the identification with the Agent Intellect achieved by the greatest of the prophets: Moses, Jesus, and Mohammed (Nasr 1964: 43–44), rather than as a beatific intentional union with God of the sort theorized by Thomas and represented imaginatively by Dante.

On the other hand, Judaism and Islam have historically been more optimistic than Christianity about the possibility of realizing the Law, and thus creating a just social order. In the case of rabbinic Judaism, this optimism was balanced by the fact that Jews have rarely had the political power to govern themselves in accord with the Law, much less to engage in a process of global social transformation. Islam, on the other hand, is *constituted* by the principle of *al-amr bi'l-ma'ruf wa'nahy 'an al-munkar*: commanding right and forbidding wrong. The result is a tendency in Islamic Aristotelianism generally, and in Averroism in particular, to regard the *human civilizational project* as the principal field of spiritual progress, while remaining circumspect about the possibilities for the individual.

Rather than administering to Judaism and Islam what amounts (for all its grounding in a philosophical discourse about possibility and actuality) to a standard Christian (especially Protestant) scolding for their "legalism," we ought to be engaging in a dialogue that, while acknowledging and engaging differences, also allows the possibility of a higher synthesis. Such an extended *Convivencia* might open up the prospect of a civilizational progress completed in full and complete enjoyment of God: the very divinization of humanity. Such a synthesis already has precedent in the poetry of Dante Alighieri. Trained in and deeply attracted to Radical (Islamic) Aristotelianism, Dante sought a middle position between the party in whose philosophy he had been nurtured and the teachings of St. Thomas. Dante (Alighieri, *De Monarchia*), who had been influenced by the Latin Averroists but rejected metaphysical monopsychism, stressed that it took humanity as a whole, collectively, to realize the full potential of the human intellect. He thus implicitly recognized knowledge as a social reality that develops over time and that is bound up both with the structures that organize human civilizations and with the larger struggle for a just social order that makes possible the full development of human capacities (Gilson 1968: 167). It was the function of the Empire to guarantee the conditions for human development and civilizational progress. At the same time, he upheld the possibilities of a higher knowledge and a higher love—indeed a higher destiny and a higher civilization— to which humanity was called by the "love which moved the sun and all the other stars." Setting out on the path of self-cultivation and civilizational progress, we found ourselves called to transcend the limits of the natural and challenged to become more than we are—more than human. This is symbolized in Dante's ascent into the heavens accompanied by Beatrice, lured by physical beauty to pursue a beauty that transcends even the intellect.

What is the social basis and political valence of Milbank's position? It represents, I would like to suggest, a distinctively European response to the current situation. Europe has been postmodern, in the sense of continuing to live the modern ideal without actually believing in it, since at least the end of the Second World War. This was a profoundly secular postmodernity, in that even the innerworldly, secret religion of high modernity had been largely abandoned. It was made tolerable by the extraordinarily high quality of life that Europeans secured for themselves by integrating a high-end export economy with social-democratic reforms that guaranteed not only basic necessities but also access to education and cultured leisure to the entire population.

As European social democracy has begun to erode under pressure from the global market, Europeans have become increasingly dissatisfied with this settlement—a tendency that is evident in the turn of even radical deconstructionists such as Derrida to a sort of religion. At the same time, Europe is deeply threatened—in a way the United States, for example, is not—by its growing internal diversity, and specifically by its growing Islamic population. The United States, after all, is a country of immigrants, and while more radically disestablishmentarian than most European states, it is far less secular. "America," much as it may struggle with this, can and will redefine itself by its pluralism; Europe cannot. Thus the search for a European identity, a search in which a renewed Catholicity is an obvious option.

This is, however, only a part of the identity of even the oldest Old Europe: the countries that once comprised the Holy Roman Empire and the Papal States. It will never be a credible identity for Milbank's own Protestant Great Britain. And it would be a very bad way to define the identity, and with a very different political valence than I think Milbank intends, for a still deeply Arabized and Islamicized *al-Andalus* and Two Sicilies,[4] as well as for every part of Europe that ever persecuted its Jews (and is there one that did not?). It is certainly not a solution for the Balkans or Turkey—or the world.

A REVITALIZED DIALECTICAL METAPHYSICS

We are now in a position to lay out our own alternative. We remind readers that the epistemological and cosmological foundations of this metaphysics have already been set out in earlier works (Mansueto 2002b, 2005). Here we focus specifically on core metaphysical issues and on showing how our approach answers the political-theological critique.

---

4. I am referring here not to the presence of new immigrants from the Maghreb but rather to the longstanding secularism of these regions which, as I have argued elsewhere, is ultimately an expression of a different, Jewish and Islamic religiosity. (Mansueto 2002a).

Being as Organization

We have already advanced and briefly argued for the claim that, once modernist univocity and immanentism are set aside, there are, broadly speaking, two metaphysical alternatives: a metaphysics of *Esse* or of Being as such and a metaphysics of *pattica sammupada* or dependent origination. This claim is further sustained by recent developments in the sciences (Bohm 1980, Gal-Or 1986, Prigogine et al. 1977, 1979, 1984, 1989; Lerner 1991, Sheldrake 1981; Margulis and Fester 1991), the philosophical significance of which we and others have analyzed elsewhere (Harris 1965, 1991, 1992; Mansueto 2005). Specifically, these results point to the *relational* and the *teleological* character of the universe. A radically *relational* cosmology, such as that advocated by David Bohm, would seem to provide warrant for the metaphysics of *pattica sammupada* developed by the Buddhists. Indeed, the debate between the more realist interpretations of quantum mechanics, the subjectivist Copenhagen interpretation, and anthropic interpretations can be seen as a kind of unconscious replay of the debates between the Madhyamika school, the Yogacara School, and some of the more synthetic schools that developed in China and Tibet. Scientific results that point to an underlying teleological dynamic, on the other hand, seem to provide support for the metaphysics of the unmoved mover developed by Aristotle and his followers (or, what is really the same thing, the Confucian metaphysics of the Great Ultimate). The first approach accepts the infinite regress of causes, which, to the Aristotelians, seems so abhorrent and a conclusion that, because everything is ultimately dependent on everything else, nothing has *inherent* existence in the sense that ibn Sina and Thomas, for example, assign to God. The second approach, rejecting such a regress, argues for a first principle that is its own ground, a project completed in the identification by ibn Sina and Thomas of the Aristotelian unmoved mover with the God revealed in Exodus. These are, taken at face value, two incompatible doctrines that cannot and ought not to be harmonized.

But matters look rather different if we focus on *Thomas* rather than Aristotle and the fully developed Mahayana Buddhism of The T'ien Tai or Hua-yen schools rather than the early doctrines of Nagarjuna. From this point of view, both doctrines look rather like competing ways of coming to terms with a *common* reality: the fact that what Thomists call *contingent* being is always and only dependent on and ordered to something outside itself, and that the ground of things consists not in self-possession but in a radical generativity. Put differently, we might say that being, in the sense of contingent being, means *being related*, which is essentially the same thing as *being dependent*, though it puts the matter in a rather more positive light. And once we have recognized this, we also recognize that the Thomistic metaphysics of *Esse* is quite incompatible with any notion that form or structure gives things being. Rather, each of the various grades of being—mineral, vegetable, animal, rational—and each of the specific forms of these grades of being are merely *ways of being related*, ways of seeking Being as such.

This leaves, of course, what looks like a more fundamental difference and one not so easily susceptible to resolution, between the Thomistic claim that Being *Is*, and the Madhyamika claim that *nothing has inherent existence*—a difference that would seem to entail a whole complex of practical differences, between, for example, an ethics centered on the cultivation of virtue and an ethics of detachment. But here too matters are more complex. In fact the whole Socratic tradition up until ibn Sina was quite reluctant to identify the first principle with Being. Thus Plato speaks of the first principle as "the Good," which he says is "beyond Being." Aristotle, while he sometimes falls into the trap of saying that it is form that gives contingent things their being, does not even really attempt to define the Unmoved Mover. Later Neo-Platonists speak of the first principle as the One, again "beyond being." The Christian Neo-Platonist Dionysus the Areopagite went even further, stressing the need to complement the *via positiva* that ascends to God rationally by means of affirming things of Him, with a *via negativa* that ascends by means of denying things of God. This reluctance to characterize the first principle as Being may well be the result of the fact that these thinkers all understood being as substance or self-possession and recognized that such a principle could not, in fact, be the source of all that is. Ibn Sina and Thomas, on the other hand, put forward a doctrine that is, in fact, radically different from any notion of Being as substance or self-possession. *Esse* as such is first and foremost a radical creativity that lives by sharing itself. Thomas's most common image of God is that of a craftsman. Much the same is true of the image we find of the Buddha in later Mahayana texts, such as the *Saddharmapundarika* (Lotus) Sutra. Here Buddhas do not pass over into *paranirvana* or complete extinction, but rather generate *Buddhaksetras* or Buddha-fields—what amount to entire cosmic regions, the quality of which is dependent on their level of merit they have accumulated. We live in *Saha*, the Buddha-field of Sakyamuni, which is not an especially pure place, largely due to his limitations by comparison with other Buddhas, such as Amitayus. What Buddhas do, according to these later Mahayana schools, is to create and teach, ripening beings who will themselves eventually become creators and teachers (Williams 1989: 224–25).

But a Buddha, of course, is not a first principle. One can, however, find hints of something like a doctrine of the first principle as creativity in Nagarjuna himself.

> The *prajnaparamita*
> Is a real dharma, not an inverted view...
> The Buddhas as well as the Bodhisattvas
> Are able to bring benefit to all.
> *Prajna* serves as mother to them.
> It is able to give birth to and raise them.
> The Buddha serves as father of beings.
> *Prajna* is able to give birth to the Buddha.
> This being so, it serves for all
> As the grandmother of beings...
>
> The *prajnaparamita*
> Is comparable to a great fiery blaze.
> It cannot be grasped from any of four sides.
> There is neither grasping nor not grasping.
> All grasping has already been relinquished.
> This is what is meant by being ungraspable.
> It is ungraspable and yet one grasps it.
> It is just this which is meant by "grasping."
> *Prajna* is characterized by indestructibility.
> It goes beyond all words and speech.
> Fittingly, it has nothing upon which it depends. (Nagarjuna *Treatise on the Great Perfection of Wisdom Sutra*)

It is not surprising that *prajnaparamita*, personified as a sort of wisdom goddess, became the center of powerful popular cults in Nepal and Kampuchea!

What all this suggests is that there is more common ground between the fully developed forms of these two great metaphysical traditions than has generally been allowed. What follows is an attempt at synthesis that incorporates insights from the Buddhist tradition generally and the Madhyamika tradition in particular—especially a focus on the relational character of Being—into the framework of a dialectical metaphysics of *Esse*, while building on recent scientific results that point to the relational and teleological character of the universe.

We consider first the shift from a metaphysics of substance to a metaphysics of relation. It is one of the ironies of history that an economic system marked by the most rapacious egoism should teach us about the radical interdependence of all things, but this, precisely, is the great lesson of the capitalist era. Markets emerged spontaneously as a result of the development of new specialized technologies, first in agriculture and later in handicrafts; ancient slavery and later capitalism developed when those who were profiting in the marketplace used coercion to try to liberate themselves from the imperative of serving the Common Good, something that, Marx demonstrated, is quite impossible in the long run. As first goods and services, then labor-power, and finally capital have become commodified, humanity has been forced to recognize the principle (which certainly holds with equal force in nonmarket societies) that everything depends on everything else. Petty commodity production, under which goods and services that would have been produced anyway were brought into relation to each other, created the basis in experience for the recognition of the *external relatedness* of all things—that everything depends on everything else for its behavior. Generalized commodity production, under which market forces determine what commodities are produced, created a basis in experience for the recognition of *internal relationality* (Harris 1987), the fact that the cosmos is a system not only in the sense that the behavior of its constitutive elements is radically dependent on the behavior of all the other elements in the system, but also in the sense that the essential nature, indeed the very existence, of these elements is determined by their interrelationships with each other, so that they are best conceived not as elements at all, but rather as relations. Being is, at the most fundamental level, a *system of relationships*, from which it is possible to abstract certain *nodes* that therefore *appear* particular, but which exist, and can thus be comprehended, only as part of the general system.

But recognition of the teleological character of being also undercuts traditional ideas of substance. In seeking Being, we seek to be other than we are. Traditional Aristotelian metaphysics recognized this dynamic but assumed it was confined within certain limits. Everything seeks being in proportion to its nature. Minerals conserve their form. Plants engage in nutrition, growth, and reproduction. Animals engage in sensation and locomotion. Human beings use intellect and will to create new forms of organization. But it is that essential nature which gives us our being. If an orange or a date palm ceases to be an orange or a date palm it ceases to be. If a donkey or an elephant ceases to be a donkey or an elephant, then it simply ceases to be.

Both the teleological cosmology we see emerging and the highest spiritual wisdom of both East and West suggest that this may not be true. In a dynamic, evolutionary universe, death ceases to be a mere mark of finitude. What is cancelled is also transcended. Death clears the way for new forms of organization, as do civilizational crisis and revolutionary transformation for the social form of matter. Similarly, Hindu and Buddhist notions of *samsara* suggest that as the wheel of rebirth turns we become something different than we were—more or less depending on the way we have lived. And the Christian ideal of the beatific vision is definitively *not* simply a continuation of our current finite existence under more enjoyable circumstances, but rather a real, if accidental (in the philosophical sense), divinization, a transformation that alone makes possible eternal life.

In this sense, it is the Buddhist metaphysics of *pattica samupada* that makes the point more clearly. This craving we have to persist in being by holding on to our present form of existence—that is the only existence which is really us—is futile and rooted in a profound illusion. "We" are not anything at all except a specific way of seeking to be ontologically more than we are. And authentic wisdom begins with this realization.

There *is*, at the same time, *something* that we seek and that is the ground of all our activity, enlightened or deluded. We have noted above that even the most complex and developed forms of Buddhist metaphysics, such as that of the Hua-yen school, have great difficulty explaining how the "fall" into delusion happened in the first place. This is simply a special case of their larger difficulty in meeting the principle of sufficient reason. Why is there anything rather than nothing, if *nothing* has inherent existence?

But what if there was no *fall* into delusion? What if, rather, delusion is simply a lower degree of development from which we gradually emerge, just as, every morning when we wake up, things appear at first one way—fuzzy and difficult to make out—and only gradually present themselves clearly, as our eyes become accustomed to seeing and to light? What if the craving to hold onto finite existence is simply an undeveloped way of seeking Being as such—a *something* that turns out to be very different from pure self-existence, but which, rather, turns out to be a supremely relational generativity?

It is here that the Western dialectical tradition sees more clearly, but only when we reach ibn Sina and Thomas Aquinas. There is, to be sure, the earlier Platonic idea of the Good that is beyond being—an attempt to convey the idea that the first principle is more than simple self-existence. But it is only in the fusion between dialectics and prophetic religion that humanity realizes that the first principle consists first and foremost in creating and that it is this that we seek, ignorantly, when we crave and take and consume. The Buddhist tradition captures the same idea in the ideal of the Bodhisattva, whose compassion brings into being and nurtures entire worlds. But this does not really rise above the level of image, and the underlying *concept* of Being is not adequately thematized.

It may seem strange that up until now we have stressed the dialogue between the traditions of India and those of the West, and said relatively little about those of China, and especially the fully developed synthesis represented by *dao xue*, the so-called Neo-Confucianism of the Sung dynasty. This is not, however, because we think that synthesis unimportant. Rather, in a very real sense, it represents just precisely an early attempt at the doctrine we are now trying to spell out systematically. *Dao xue* engaged the Buddhist challenge, absorbing much of the subtle metaphysical insights of the T'ien tai and Hua yen schools, while reinterpreting them in such a way as to emphasizes creativity and generativity rather than withdrawal. Thus the first principle is both *wu chi* and *t'ai chi*. And what this first principles does is to generate—not by external fiat, but rather by acting as a lure. And contingent beings—the myriad things which are generated—themselves gradually give birth to humanity, that is perfected by the five virtues that, it turns out, are all about generativity.

Thus a gloss on such classical texts and the Diagram of the Great Ultimate, reworked in the light of the forgoing analysis, might read something like this:

> The sage perfects the five virtues.
> The five Virtues perfect humanity.
> Humanity perfects the myriad things.
> The myriad things perfect the five agents.
> The five agents perfect heaven and earth.
> Heaven and earth perfect the yin and the yang.

The yang is just motion towards the Great Ultimate.
The yin is just the stillness which lies beyond.

How can these ideas be pulled together into a systematic metaphysics? The alternative that we propose builds on the insights of Errol Harris (Harris 1965, 1987, 1991, 1992) on the Hegelian side and Georgi Lukacs (Lukacs 1921/1971) and A. M. Deborin and Alexandr Bogdanov (Bogdanov 1928/1980) on the Marxist side, while insisting with traditional Thomism (Garrigou-Lagrange 1938) that the category of finality be given pride of place. Being, I would like to suggest, is organization. Imagine for a minute something that is stripped of all organization: it has no purpose, no structure, and no relation, either internally or externally. If this is the case, the thing, quite simply, doesn't exist.

In order to illustrate the usefulness of this idea, we begin with some distinctions. First, we should note that both "being" and "organization" are used in a variety of different ways. It is important, on the one hand, to distinguish between mere existence (what Thomas calls possible being and most modern philosophers contingent being) and *Esse* as such, the actual power of Being, which no finite system has in itself. On the other hand, it is important to distinguish between the various dimensions of the concept of organization:

1. relation;
2. form, order, or structure; and
3. purpose, end, or telos.

Drawing on this set of distinctions, we can say that *to be* in the sense of contingent being is *to be related*, i.e., to be an element of a larger whole. Any system that has a definite structure, however, can be said to have its own distinctive identity, and thus to exist in the much stronger sense of being something of which other things can be predicated. For a system to be organized, however, the structure must be ordered to some end or purpose. "Organization," finally, may mean.

1. being organized, in the sense of being ordered to an end;
2. having the capacity to organize, and thus create; or
3. being the end to which things are ordered, either relatively or absolutely and finally.

With these distinctions in place, it is easy to show the power of our approach. Relationship implies both unity and difference. Being realized as relationship consists neither in simple, undifferentiated unity nor in pure difference. Without difference there is nothing in particular, but only a One that is at the same time Nothing. Without a prior, underlying unity, difference is mere disintegration: the absence of any capacity to connect, to relate, and therefore potentially to act, have properties, etc. Being consists precisely in the capacity to unite things that differ—in the self-differentiating unity that we call "system." The word "system" comes from the Hellenic roots *sys-* and *histanai* meaning "to put together." At the very simplest level, therefore, system refers to the radical interconnectedness of all things, an interconnectedness so profound that the existence of the tiniest subsystem abstracted from the whole implies the system in its entirety. The most minute alteration at any point in the system affects the system as a whole. The fact that I am sitting here at my computer, thinking and writing, requires and implies, with iron-clad logical necessity, everything else in the universe—not only the existence, but the precise disposition of every particular system along every possible world trajectory in the cosmos, from the most intimate thoughts of a young woman on a corner in Bukhara or Bangkok waiting for her lover, to the precise disposition of the atoms and molecules in some remote nebula in a galaxy far too distant for its light to ever reach me during my lifetime.

Some important conclusions follow from this analysis. First, it should be clear that it is not really possible, given our scheme, to conceive of being as substance—as something that exists in itself. Finite systems clearly derive their being from each other; the first principle, on the other hand, while it clearly is the Power of Being, exists precisely in drawing others into being. Because of this both Aristotelian pluralism and Spinozist monism (while each grasping a part of the truth) are fundamentally inadequate. Neither really understands that Being is quite the opposite of self-possession.

Nor should we really think of being as subject. Subjectivity, as a way of being ordered to others and to the infinite, is incipient and emerging in contingent being, but it hardly makes sense to regard merely physical systems as subjective. But clearly such systems exist and thus share in being. Necessary being, on the other hand, while it can be shown to exercise an unlimited subjectivity and inwardness,[5] does not exist in this subjectivity but rather precisely in its creative power, which is always and only directed outward, as the power of teleological attraction. Rising to subjectivity—even becoming the unique subject-object of the cosmohistorical evolutionary process, in other words, is *not* an authentic divinization.

Being realized as relationship, on the other hand, has the merit, first of all, of grasping the interconnectedness of being without negating difference. Indeed, it makes it fully possible for us to meet the objection of existentialists and postmodernists who are concerned that any philosophical doctrine of God—or indeed any other totalizing metanarrative that attempts to describe or explain the universe as a whole—inevitably submerges difference into identity. And this is, indeed, a danger for both Spinozist and Hegelian monisms. When being is conceived as substance, and we assert (as we must, once we have taken this first step) that there is only one substance, one system that exists in and through itself, and that that is the whole, we are, in effect, saying that particular systems don't exist and that the rich difference which makes life interesting is, in fact, a mere difference of location in a single system—in effect, an illusion. When being is conceived as subject, similarly, one ends up reducing individuals to mere vanishing moments of the One subject, Absolute Spirit, which develops itself and becomes conscious of itself through them—and then casts them aside. Aristotelian pluralism—and more especially Thomism—avoids this problem only at the price of a certain inconsistency, arguing on the one hand that there are many substances, and that difference is therefore real, while at the same time arguing their dependence on the teleological attraction of the Unmoved Mover (for Aristotle), and on the Single Pure Act of Being that is God (for Aquinas), an argument that is tantamount to admitting that they are not really substances at all. By conceiving being as relationship we unify in a way that not only conserves, but in fact presupposes difference. One cannot, after all, be meaningfully ordered to something, in the sense we have defined it, without being different from it.

---

5. This can be demonstrated quite easily. Personality or subjectivity consists in the full possession of one's faculties. This requires intellect. Now intellect consists in taking on the form of the things known, including things that are purely intelligible, such as intelligible essences or even Being itself. But Necessary Being *is* those forms—it is the form of forms—and thus knows all and is therefore pure subjectivity. To put the matter in another way, Necessary Being knows things because it creates them and thus has infinite subjectivity.

At the same time, we avoid the fall into an infinite expanse of difference, without horizon or point of reference, which the "postmodern" philosophy of difference celebrates but which in fact is nothing less than a willful option for death and loss. The difference of being is always and only a difference of relationship, a difference of being ordered to, a difference of sensing and imagining, of knowing and judging, of desiring and hoping and willing, which are never possible for the same, but which nonetheless make difference a principle of unity rather than of division. And this series of differences, even if it is itself infinite in the sense of extending without limit through space and time (and there are good reasons, both scientific and philosophical, to believe this), nonetheless terminates in a principle that unifies (because it is the common *telos*) but does so precisely by creating "infinite diversity in infinite combinations."[6]

Thinking of being as relationship has profound implications for the way that we think about essence. It is no longer possible to understand the universe as a composite of immaterial forms and a passive material substrate, or as a set of interacting atoms that sometimes come together to constitute systems. On the one hand, *essence*, which Aristotle understood as form imposed on passive matter, and in some places as what gives things their being, must be radically re-theorized. At the same time, the atomism dominant since the eighteenth century, for which *what* things are is purely accidental, the product of random interaction and natural selection, must also be rejected. The universe generally, and its various subsystems, *appear* to us as things possessing various properties. The underlying essence or nature of a system or subsystem, however (what it is), is determined by its internal and external relationships, of which its appearance is merely the expression. *Essence*, in other words, is nothing other than *structure*, both a system's internal structure and its place in the larger structure of the cosmos as a whole, which defines both its own trajectory of development, and its contribution to the development of the cosmos generally.

Understanding essence in this way allows us at once to acknowledge the relative and partial meaningfulness of the world we know by means of the senses and the lower or analytic intellect, without assigning to it any absolute or autonomous existence. This is what the Hua-yen

---

6. This phrase is put in quotations because it is a favorite slogan of Star Trek fandom. I am unsure of the origin. It does, however, speak of just what sort of popular ontology underlies this uniquely hopeful vision of humanity's future.

doctrine of the three natures is intended to capture. The discriminated nature (*parikalpita-svabhava*) consists in the way things appear to us, i.e., as really existing independent things. The dependent nature (*paratantra-svabhava*) is the underlying nature of the thing as merely a node in a network of relationships and thus lacking any inherent existence. Finally, the perfected nature (*parinispanna-svabhava*) is "the real nature of this object as it is apart from our suppositions. We may say that this is its Suchness (*tathata*) divorced from concepts superimposed on it ..." (Cook 1977: 57). But what is Suchness if not Being as such, or at least the share or participation that a thing has in Being?

Now the structures of various subsystems of the cosmos do not merely differ from each other. They are arranged in a kind of hierarchy or dialectical scale. We already know from the results of the special sciences the characteristics of at least several different levels on this scale. Specifically, it is possible to identify physical, biological, and social degrees of organization. Physical systems are not themselves organized in the full sense of possessing differentiated structures of the sort that we find in living organisms that carry out definite functions in the service of some global purpose. They are, however, structured, and in fact structured in just precisely the way necessary to make possible the emergence of complex organization, life, and intelligence. In this sense, the physical universe as a whole can be said to be ordered to the higher end of complex organization, life, and intelligence. Even physical laws, such as entropy, which seem to work against the survival of particular complex systems, ultimately serve the cause of progressive cosmohistorical evolution by making room for new forms. Some physical systems are, furthermore, structured in ways that permit them to conserve their form, which constitutes the higher degree of participation in being that Aristotle called the mineral soul. Such systems are also characterized by a chemical holism, which means that they have distinctive properties that make them more than the sum of their parts in a way that is not true of mere mechanical ensembles. Biological systems, on the other hand, are actually organized, i.e., structured in such a way as to promote an end, namely their own survival and reproduction. In maintaining themselves in hostile environments that would undermine many mineral species, and in reproducing themselves, living organisms achieve a higher degree of participation in being than mere physical or mineral systems. Social systems, finally, are not only organized but also have the capacity to organize, i.e., through labor to contribute to the creation of new and more complex forms of organization.

All of these various and sundry forms of organization are ordered to a common end, namely Being, which, however, they pursue in ways appropriate to their structure and under the form of specific goods accessible to them. For mineral species, and indeed physical systems in general, this good is the thermodynamic stability, that allows them to persist in being. For living organisms, the good is nutrition and reproduction—in the case of animals in the form of food and mates actively pursued and enjoyed. In the case of the social form of matter this good is creativity as such, which is known indirectly in the form of ordinary manual and intellectual labor, and directly when the intellect rises by transcendental abstraction or caritative wisdom to the knowledge of God.

This approach to understanding being grasps not only internal relationality, but also the real participation of finite systems in the process of cosmogenesis and does so without violating the principle of sufficient reason. Everything, however humble, that participates in Being is, furthermore, itself a participation in the end or *telos* and thus in a very real sense a natural sacrament in which God is really present, and an authentic way to the divine. In this sense people in tribal and communitarian societies were not wrong to offer worship to animals, plants, and even minerals, even if in the light of philosophy and of the revelation of the divine name YHWH we recognize that what is actually to be worshipped is the power of Being in which these finite systems have a share.

Thus, when we say that "something exists" or that "the universe exists," we in fact mean that it is a real participation in Being as such, to the knowledge of which we have already risen, if perhaps without fully realizing it, in traveling the road of the special sciences.

With this said, the outlines of a unified cosmoteleological argument for the existence of God, an argument that simultaneously proves the ultimate meaningfulness of the universe, emerges quite naturally. Not surprisingly, the argument ends up looking quite a bit like a radically historicized version of Aristotle's argument in *Metaphysics* 12.7. What a teleological science shows, even in its present undeveloped form, is an ascending scale of progressively higher forms of organization—higher in the sense that they constitute progressively superior forms of organization. Each of these forms of organization is, in a very real sense, a distinct form of the motion of matter, which is only potential being, towards Being as such (a way of putting things that also connects our formulation back to Engels's language and that of dialectical materialism). Their organization and their motion and their participation in Being are all one and the same. Now in the case of each individual system, this organization, motion, and participation in being can be explained proximately in terms of the particular end to which the system is ordered: the possibility of there being any structure at all, varying types and degrees of thermodynamic stability, nutrition, growth, and reproduction, sensation and locomotion, or any of the myriad forms of organization that human beings and human societies labor to bring into being. But each of these particular ends or movers must (and in principle can) be explained in terms of further finite ends or movers at which they, in turn, aim. The whole ordered series, however, even if it is infinite in space and time, must itself be explained. There cannot, in other words, be an infinite logical regress even if there is an infinite physical regress and/or progress in space and time. The series and each of its elements can, furthermore, be shown to aim, albeit mediately, through the particular finite movers, at a common end that is *Esse* as such. What each and every form of matter seeks, each in its own way, and except at the highest levels of human development without knowing it, is Being as such. This is the great Unmoved Mover that draws all things to itself.

When we have risen to this point, it furthermore becomes apparent that not only God, but also the universe itself, exists necessarily. That God exists necessarily is apparent. Being as such has within itself the power to be and thus depends on nothing outside itself for its existence. In this sense a sort of *a posteriori* version of the ontological argument becomes possible. The universe, as the ascending scale of different forms of organization that moves towards God, is not to be identified with God and is not a "necessary being." Given that God exists, however, the existence of the universe follows necessarily. This is because it is the attractive power of God, that draws the universe into Being. God cannot cease to be God, and thus cannot help being attractive and drawing the universe into Being.

This, in turn, imposes definite constraints on physical cosmology. In order for the universe to exist at all, it must in *some sense* always exist, because God brings it into being necessarily. This does not necessarily rule out cosmologies that, like the Big Bang, may imply the finitude of the region of space-time that we now identify with the universe, but it does imply that motion towards God is without beginning and without end and is globally, at least over the long run, progressive in character.

Organization, Teleology, and Value

The analysis we have developed provides us with definite principles of value. If all things seek Being, and if Being is organization, then organization is the principle of value for which we have been searching. Indeed, it is possible to derive a both a qualitative and a quantitative scale of value from this principle. There, are, first of all, qualitative ontological differences between the various grades of being identified above:

1. being structured in such a way as to make organization possible;
2. having chemical holism and thus the capacity to retain form;
3. having the capacity for nutrition, growth, and reproduction;
4. having the capacity for sensation and locomotion;
5. having the capacity for intellectual knowledge and will and thus ability to organize and create;
6. being the End towards which things are ordered.

Within each of these fundamental ontological grades, the value of a system is determined by its level of organization, or its capacity to unite, under a common structure, a complex diversity of elements. The greater the number and diversity of elements united, and the greater the level of unity, the more organized, and thus the more valuable, the system.

This means that "value" in the ethical sense and value in the economic sense are no different from each other. What human beings do when they labor is to increase the level of organization of their raw material. The "average socially necessary labor time" contained in a product, which both Marx and his classical predecessors regarded as the measure of value, is simply a way of quantifying its level of organization. There are, however, products of nature that are highly organized, and thus exceedingly rare, which possess great value in and of themselves, apart from any human intervention. Our theory, unlike Marx's, allows us to capture this reality while still recognizing that it is *ordinarily* human labor that confers economic value on products.

The concept of value takes on various notes in virtue of the principle of the convertibility of the transcendentals—the Beautiful, the True, the Good, and the One—with Being as such. By convertibility we mean that these terms refer to the same thing as Being, though they add some relation (Thomas, *Summa Theologiae*, I, 5.1, 9.1, 16.3). Consider, for example, the nature of Beauty. By the beauty of a system, we mean simply its level of organization, understood as the object of (sensory or intellectual) perception. The greater the diversity of the elements organized, and the more perfect the harmony in which they are united, the more beautiful the system. This is true throughout the natural world, from the simple harmonies of the night sky, through the more complex forms of the crystalline structures and living organisms, to the rich, lush diversity of complex ecosystems and human societies. And it is true as well of great works of art, which are nothing if not a complex manifold of relations harmoniously arranged. Thus, we find a landscape, natural or painted, beautiful to the extent that it integrates a diversity of elements into a harmonious and purposeful whole. Not too many people are attracted by scenes of pure, undifferentiated gray. Things of great beauty have, furthermore, the capacity to harmonize and integrate those that perceive them, and thus draw them closer to God. Thus the centrality of beauty in religious experience, in liturgy, and so on. Beauty itself, as Albertus Magnus and Thomas Aquinas taught long ago, is the capacity to bring things into being, and is thus convertible with Being itself, or God (Eco 1970/1988).

Now because Beauty integrates diverse elements into a harmonious whole it also possesses *claritas*—it constitutes a window on the Truth. When we are in the process of forming an idea, what we see first is a pattern, a harmonious integration of elements in our experience. The truth value of a statement, a concept, or theory, is its capacity to organize large quantities of qualitatively diverse, and therefore highly complex, experience. The concept or theory in question does this by explaining the experience in terms of a principle or principles. It is necessary in this connection to focus equal attention on the complexity of the experience organized and on the level of organization of the experience in question. Our experience is most highly organized when we identify highly compact "organizing principles," knowledge of which permits us to derive logically all the rich particularity of the experience on which the principle was based. It is this organizing capacity of theories that leads us to speak analogously of their "power." The most powerful theories are those that comprehend the widest range of experience in unique compact statements that are themselves pregnant with rich experiential content. The Truth itself is, as we have seen, the infinite, necessary, and perfect Being that alone completes our explanation of the universe and that grounds all other partial explanations.

The Good, finally, is an end desired or willed or pursued. It is at once the object of our desire or appetite, whether sensual or intellectual, and the actual capacity to organize, to draw things into being. While everything existing is good, in so far as it is capable both of being ordered to the End and of being an (intermediate) end itself, there is a clearly defined hierarchy of goods, measured by the degree to which the system in question is ordered to God and can itself therefore participate in the divine organizing activity. The Good itself is the infinite, necessary and perfect End that alone has the capacity to draw something out of nothing.

It is interesting to note the intrusion of quantitative language into our account of the transcendentals. This is unavoidable, but it is a bit deceptive. One may attempt to quantify value, by means of a return from transcendental abstraction to formalism, and this move is often quite useful. We have already seen this in the case of Marx's labor theory of value. Charles Bennet's "logical depth" approach to the organization of information systems, which quantifies organization in terms of the number of logical steps necessary to derive a system from its principle (Bennet 1988), is similar in many ways. Other approaches to quantifying organization (and thus value) that focus exclusively on the number of different elements (for example, information content) are more problematic. But no quantification of value actually comprehends the fundamentally teleological character of the concept and thus the radical simplicity of the union effected among the complex elements of organized systems. And no quantification of value can comprehend the fact that the telos, the End itself, far from negating difference when it unites, in fact multiplies it infinitely as it draws ever new and more diverse forms of organization into being.

This is the significance of the fourth and last transcendental: the transcendental One. While the numerical one derives *from* difference (as the "ratio" of "similar differences" and "different similarities" which defines the unit of a formal system) and serves as a principle of identity, the transcendental One, in uniting all things to itself, in fact distinguishes them from the infinite sameness of mere possibility and draws them, in all their individual uniqueness, into the divine light of Being itself. It is, in other words, the transcendental principle of difference.

We are now in a position to derive specifically ethical principles. We should begin by clarifying the nature of the moral question. A certain prejudice has developed in the field of ethics against what, following the analytic philosopher G. E. Moore, is called "ethical naturalism," and "metaphysical ethics," which attempt to reduce the good to some single property accessible either to the natural sciences or to metaphysics, or to both. The result is, devotees of this approach argue, a confusion of fact and value, "is" and "ought." They argue instead that the predicate "good" is simple and unanalysable, and in fact is applied to many different kinds of things. Clearly, it is just precisely the kind of approach to ethics we are proposing that is the intended object of this attack. The criticism, however, is self-contradictory, for it takes as its canon "ordinary language," the usage of which it claims merely to clarify. But what is this if not to confuse "is" and "ought"? The way people use a certain language, in this case English, is without any further justification made into the standard by which ethics is grounded, and so on.

At the same time, to say that "good" is a simple and unanalysable predicate is to leave ethical judgment ungrounded and to transform it into nothing more than a peculiar use of language. What transcendental abstraction reveals is not a particular class of things or properties that are good, but rather a transcendental property of everything that *is*, to the extent that it *is*. The moral imperative is nothing other than the imperative of Being itself understood as that which is desired and aimed for. The Good is what draws finite systems into being in the first place; finite goods are secondary, intermediate ends that possess a participating power to draw into being.

Our analysis of the transcendentals allows us, furthermore, to give this principle some very definite content. We have seen that being is organization. Necessary Being is the End that organizes, contingent being is both that which is organized or "ordered to" and that which, in varying degrees, acts as a secondary ordering end. To be good, therefore, is at once to be organized and to participate in the divine creative power of organization. Concretely this means a drive upwards along the ontological hierarchy of being, a drive to grow and develop, to evolve, and to bring into being ever more complex and integrated systems. It means the move from the pure potency of nonbeing to the act of existence, the move from physical to biological and from biological to social organization. It means the development of human creative powers and of humanity's capacity to participate in the self-organizing activity of the universe and thus to share in God's work of creation.

The moral imperative or principle of right can, therefore, be stated, in its most abstract and general form, in the following manner:

> Act in such a manner as to promote the self-organizing activity of the universe, that is, to promote the development of ever more complex forms of organization.

By analyzing the way in which self-organization actually takes place we can, in turn, derive more specific principles of right. In this sense ethics is indeed informed by science not only indirectly, through the mediation of the doctrine of first principles that completes scientific inquiry, but directly, by recourse to investigations that clarify the means to the End. Thus, for example, the fact that organization is indeed a kind of order, and is characterized by at least a relative and temporary stability, allows us to derive the *principle of public order*:

> Act in such a way as to conserve the existing forms of organization unless acting otherwise can reasonably be expected to yield a higher level of organization.

As the same time, however, we know that the universe and its various subsystems grow and develop. This means that one form of organization yields to another, something that by its very nature involves qualitative differentiation, symmetry breaking, and an element of instability. This means that the structure of any give system ought not to be so rigid as to undermine these processes and the innovation they make possible. One way to insure this is to have multiple and diverse centers of power, each of which seeks the telos in its own way and on its own terms. Thus the *principle of subsidiarity*:

> Power and decision making should be as decentralized as is compatible with the ordering of the system generally to the common good.

This can be understood to apply not only within human societies, but in the relationship between human civilizations and the ecosystems they inhabit, as cautioning, for example, against an "industrial" mentality that seeks not only to cultivate higher forms of organization, but to bring the whole evolutionary process under rational human control.

Finally, we know that organization is an ordering to and is, therefore, fundamentally hierarchical in character. The *principle of hierarchy* states that:

> Lower order activities must serve higher order activities and all must serve the telos.

This is *not* an argument for unequal access to resources for consumption. On the contrary, it is precisely the ability to use resources productively, to order them to a higher end and thus bring into being new and more complex forms of organization which marks a system as "higher order." Unproductive consumption (luxury) is a mark of disorganization and disintegration. What it does mean, however, is that the cultivation of sensual goods, while in itself to be recommended, must serve the cultivation of intellectual goods, and the cultivation of lower intellectual goods (e.g., science and technology) the cultivation of higher intellectual goods (e.g., wisdom).

Being and Samsara

What does this metaphysics imply for the ultimate meaningfulness of individual, finite, contingent existence? We can, on the one hand, offer very little solace for those who remain attached to preserving their current form. But then common sense should have told them that their attachment was hopeless to begin with. This is true even if they hide from the inevitability of death. A child growing and developing ceases to be what it was and becomes something else. Indeed, from a more rigorously analytic standpoint, we die and are reborn in each and every instant. Contingent being withers like the autumn leaves and is no more.

But this is not the whole story. This particular structure, existing at this particular instant, is not our real nature. Rather, to the extent that our individual, contingent existence has any reality at all, we are simply a particular way of participating in Being and, as we mature and our capacities develop, we become a particular way of Bringing into Being. And our particular way of Bringing into Being is just that—a way, the conditions for the possibility of which do not disappear as we mature, age, and die. Rather, that pattern of action—that *karma*—remains as a kind of teleological attractor. And it is not just that—indeed it is emphatically not that "someone else," an entirely new being separate from us, takes up our way of bringing into being. What makes us who we are is nothing other than that *way*. Indeed, our memories and our knowledge and all our accumulated virtues are embedded in it. From this point of view, the Buddhist doctrine of rebirth, while perhaps not strictly demonstrable, nonetheless seems entirely credible.

What is different, of course, is that in our view the aim is not release from rebirth, but rather an endless succession of increasingly more capable lives in which we little by little outgrow our grasping and contingency and live to ripen Being. The Bodhisattva path—the way of the saint and the *tzadik*—is, in other words, the universal way of humanity and not merely a specialized calling for beings of great compassion. To put the matter differently, finite, contingent beings are not and cannot be saved *in* their contingency and finitude. There is no way that we can live forever in our present form. We can, however, discover in our finitude the principle and end that we seek and, along an infinite trajectory, grow towards that end in a way that conserves and gives meaning to what we were and what we have done while radically transforming it into something infinitely greater.

What this does, of course, is to at once ground and relativize the ideals of the rational, autonomous subject and innerworldly civilizational progress. The cultivation of rational autonomy, of the ability to make independent decisions regarding fundamental questions of meaning and value, and to participate in public deliberations regarding the common good, and to do so on a rational basis, clearly represents an important degree of achievement in our growth towards Being. But it is neither the beginning (in the sense of representing the motive force of a universe that finds its only true meaning in human subjectivity) nor the end (in the sense of representing the highest value). It is, rather, like all else, a stage along the way.

And what is true of individual beings is also true of civilizations and other higher order communities that are, after all, simply larger networks of relationships. There is no last empire, no solution to the riddle of history. Civilizations will continue to rise and fall, at least until humanity grows to the point where its form of organization has so utterly changed that it no longer makes sense to call it civilization. At no point will we pass through a threshold at which our knowledge effectively relieves us of the burdens of finitude, as the modernists imagined. But the achievements of past civilizations will live on in future ones, and the human civilizational project, without ever redeeming humanity from finitude, will open up into something still greater.

In this sense the postmodernists are quite correct in arguing that both premodern and modern "metanarratives" are corrupted by troubling illusions. There is no way out of contingency and finitude and difference. But this does *not* imply that there is no meaning. Rather, meaning lies *in* finitude as we struggle to grow and become, to give and to create, realizing ever more fully a principle that is always and forever beyond our grasp.

Such a metaphysics cannot be attacked as a legitimation for totalitarian rule, literal or figurative. It preserves the best of "premodern" systems—the great metaphysical systems of the Silk Road Era that grounded disciplines of individual spiritual perfection while ordering the human civilizational project to higher ends. It conserves the best of modernity—that dizzying discovery that we humans really are active participants in the cosmohistorical evolutionary process, co-creators with God. But it overcomes the limitations of both.

I cannot claim to have paved a road to the future. The road, after all, is already there; we have only to find it. Perhaps, however, I have cleared away some of the underbrush that has grown up during this pause in humanity's long march towards God, revealing a path still dimly lit in the twilight of a dying age and shown that, however difficult that path, it constitutes for us an inescapable lure.

Bibliography

Abu-Lughod, Janet. 1989. *Before European Hegemony: The World System AD 125–1350*. New York: Oxford University Press.

Aeschylus. 458 BCE/1952. *The Eumenides*, in *Aeschylus, Sophocles, Euripides, Aristophanes*. Chicago: Encyclopaiedia Britannica.

Alighieri, Dante. 1300–1318/1969. *De Monarchia*. Indianapolis: Bobbs-Merrill.

———. 1300–1318/1969. *Commedia*. Translated as *The Divine Comedy* and with commentary by John D. Sinclair. New York: Oxford University Press.

Althusser, Louis. 1965/1977. *For Marx*. London: Lane.

———. 1968/1970. *Reading Capital*. London: New Left.

———. 1966–1969/1971. *Lenin and Philosophy*. New York: Monthly Review.

Amin, Samir. 1978. *The Law of Value and Historical Materialism*. New York: Monthly Review.

———. 1979/1980. *Class and Nation, Historically and in the Current Crisis*. New York: Monthly Review.

———. 1988/1989. *Eurocentrism*. New York: Monthly Review.

Anaxagoras. c. 450 BCE/1996. *On Nature*. In *Classical Greek Reader*, edited by Kenneth Atchity and Rosemary McKenna. New York: Holt.

Anaximander. c. 560 BCE/1996. *On Nature*. In *Classical Greek Reader*, edited by Kenneth Atchity and Rosemary McKenna. New York: Holt.

Anaximenes. c. 545 BCE/1996. *Air*. In *Classical Greek Reader*, edited by Kenneth Atchity and Rosemary McKenna. New York: Holt.

Anderson, Perry. 1974a. *Passages from Antiquity to Feudalism*. London: New Left Review.

———. 1974b. *Lineages of the Absolutist State*. London: New Left Review.

Aristotle. c. 350 BCE/1946. *Politics*. Translated by Ernest Barker. Oxford: Clarendon.

———. c. 350 BCE/1952. *Metaphysics*. Translated by Richard Hope. New York: Columbia University Press.

———. c. 350 BCE/1973. *Physics*. In *Introduction to Aristotle*, translated by Richard McKeon. Chicago: University of Chicago Press.

———. c. 350 BCE/1973. *De Anima*. In *Introduction to Aristotle*, translated by Richard McKeon. Chicago: University of Chicago Press.

———. c. 350 BCE/1973. *Ethics*. In *Introduction to Aristotle*, translated by Richard McKeon. Chicago: University of Chicago Press.

Aquinas, Thomas. c. 1260/1963. "Commentary on Boethius' *De Trinitate*." In *The Division and Methods of the Sciences: Questions V and VI of his Commentary on the* De Trinitate *of Boethius*, translated by Armand Maurer. Toronto: Pontifical Institute of Medieval Studies.

———. 1272/1952. *Summa Theologiae*. Chicago: Encyclopaedia Britannica.

Athanasius. 325. *On the Incarnation of the Word of God.* Online: http://www.spurgeon .org/~phil/history/ath-inc.htm.
Asvaghosha. 2nd C CE/1964. *The Awakening of Faith in the Mahayana.* Translated by the editors of the Shrine of Wisdom. Brook, UK: The Shrine of Wisdom.
Augustine. 426/1972. *The City of God.* Translated by Henry Bettenson. New York: Penguin.
———. c. 386/1969. *Contra Academicos.* In *Medieval Philosophy: From St. Augustine to Nicholas of Cusa*, edited by John Wippel and Alan Wolter. New York: Free.
———. c. 395/1969. *De libero arbitrio.* In *Medieval Philosophy: From St. Augustine to Nicholas of Cusa* In *Medieval Philosophy: From St. Augustine to Nicholas of Cusa*, edited by John Wippel and Alan Wolter. New York: Free.
Arendt, Hannah. 1958. *The Human Condition.* Chicago: University of Chicago Press.
Avatamsaka sutra. 2nd–4th C CE/1993. In *The Flower Ornament Scripture*, translated by Thomas Cleary. Boston: Shambala.
Ayer, Alfred. 1937. *Language, Truth and Logic.* London: Penguin.
Badiou, Alain. 1988. *L'Etre et l'événement.* Paris: Seuil.
———. 2006. *Logiques de mondes.* Paris: Seuil.
Barrow, John, and Frank Tipler. 1986. *Anthropic Cosmological Principle.* Oxford: Oxford University Press.
Bellah, Robert. 1973. "Introduction." In Emile Durkheim, *On Morality and Society.* Chicago: University of Chicago Press.
———. 1991. *The Good Society.* New York: Knopf.
Belo, Fernando1975/1981. *A Materialist Reading of the Gospel of Mark.* Maryknoll, NY: Orbis.
Bennett, Charles. 1987. "Dissipation, Information, Complexity, and Organization." In *Emerging Syntheses in Science*, edited by David Pines. New York: Addison Wesley.
Bentley, Jerry. 1993. *Old World Encounters: Cross Cultural Contacts and Exchanges in Pre-Modern Times.* New York: Oxford University Press.
Berkeley, George. 1710. *Three Dialogues between Hylas and Philnous.* London.
Bettelheim, Charles. 1976–1978. *Class Struggles in the USSR.* 2 vols. Translated by Brian Pearce. New York: Monthly Review.
Beyer, S. 1977. "Notes on the Vision Question in Early Mahayana." In *Prajnamaramita and Related Systems*, edited by L. Lancaster. Berkeley: University of California Press.
Bhagavad Gita. Translated by S. Rhadhakrishnan. New York: Harper, 1948.
Bhaskar, Roy. 1989. *Reclaiming Reality: A Critical Introduction to Contemporary Philosophy.* New York: Verso.
———. 1993. *Dialectic: The Pulse of Freedom.* New York: Verso.
Bogdanov, Alexander. 1928/1980. *Tektology.* Seaside, CA: Intersystems.
Bohm, David. 1980. *Wholeness and the Implicate Order.* Boston: Routledge & Kegan Paul.
Bonaventura. c. 1274/1970. *Quaestiones disputate de Scientia Christi.* In *A Scholastic Miscellany: Anselm to Ockham*, edited by Eugene R. Fairweather. New York: Macmillan.
Boler, John. 1993. "Transcending the Natural: Duns Scotus on the Two Affections of the Will." *American Catholic Philosophical Quarterly* 67:1.
Bonald, Louis de. 1965. *Théorie du pouvoir, politique et religieuse.* Paris: Union générale d'éditions.
Brahma-sutra-bhasya. No Pages. Online: http://www.bharatadesam.com/spiritual/brahma _sutra/brahma_sutra_sankara_index.php.

Brundage, John. 1985. *The Fifth Sun*. Austin: University of Texas Press.
Buddhaghosa. c. 410–431/1920–1921. *Visuddhimagga*. Edited by C. A. F. Rhys Davids. London: Published for the Pali Text Society by H. Milford.
Caputo, John. 1982. *Heidegger and Aquinas: An Essay on Overcoming Metaphysics*. New York: Fordham.
———. 2006. *The Weakness of God*. Bloomington: Indiana University Press.
Caputo, John, and Catherine Keller. 2007. "Theopoetic/Theopolitic." *Crosscurrents*. No pages. Online: www.crosscurents.org/Caputo0406.pdf.
Chadwick, Owen. 1981. *The Popes and the European Revolution*. Oxford: Clarendon.
Chaney, Marvin. 1986. "Systemic Study of the Israelite Monarchy." *Semeia* 37:53–76.
———. 1993. "Bitter Bounty: the Dynamics of Political Economy Critiqued by the Eighth-century Prophets." In *The Bible and Liberation: Political and Social Hermeneutics*, edited by Norman K. Gottwald and Richard A. Horsley, 250–63. Maryknoll, NY: Orbis.
Chaterjee, Satischandra, and Dhirendramohan Datta. 1954. *An Introduction to Indian Philosophy*. Calcutta: University of Calcutta.
Childe, V. Gordon. 1951. *Man Makes Himself*. New York: Mentor.
Ching, Julia. 2002. *The Religious Thought of Chu Hsi*. Oxford: Oxford University Press.
Cleary, Thomas. 1990. *The Tao of Politics*. Boston: Shambala.
Collins, Randall. 1998. *The Sociology of Philosophies*. Cambridge, MA: Belknap.
Confucius. c. 500 BCE/1963. *Chung Yung (The Doctrine of the Mean)*. In *A Sourcebook in Chinese Philosophy*, edited by Wing-Tsi Chan. Princeton, NJ: Princeton University Press.
———. c. 500 BCE/1979. *Lun-yu (Analects)*, translated by D. C. Lau. New York: Dorset.
Cook, Francis. 1977. *Hua-yen Buddhism: The Jewel Net of Indra*. University Park: Pennsylvania State University Press.
Cook, Michael, and Patricia Crone. 1977. *Hagarism: The Making of the Islamic World*. Cambridge: Cambridge University Press.
Cornford, Francis Macdonald. 1952. *Principium Sapientiae: The Origins of Greek Philosophical Thought*. Cambridge: Cambridge University Press.
Crone, Patricia. 2004. *God's Rule: Government and Islam*. New York: Columbia University Press.
Cunningham, Agnes, editor and translator. 1982. *The Early Church and the State*. Philadelphia: Fortress.
Cusanus, Nicholas. 1440/1960. "On the Superiority of General Councils in Church and Empire." In *Readings in Church History*, vol. 1, edited by Colman Barry. New York: Newman.
Confucius. c. 500 BCE/1963. *Chung Yung (The Doctrine of the Mean)*. In *A Source Book in Chinese Philosophy*, translated and compiled by Wing-Tsit Chan. Princeton, NJ: Princeton University Press.
———. c. 500 BCE/1979. *Lun-yu (Analects)*. Translated by D. C. Lau. New York: Dorset.
Daly, James. 2000. *Marx and the Natural Law Tradition*. London: Greenwich Square.
Daly, Mary. 1984. *Pure Lust: Elemental Feminist Philosophy*. Boston: Beacon.
———. 1998. *Quintessence—Realizing the Archaic Future: A Radical Elemental Feminist Manifesto*. Boston: Beacon.
Dahm, Helmut. 1988. *Philosophical Sovietology: The Pursuit of A Science*. Dordrecht: Reidel.

Damasio, Antonio R. 1994. *Descartes' Error: Emotion, Reason, and the Human Brain.* New York: Putnam.

Darwin, Charles. 1859/1970. *The Origin of the Species.* In *Darwin: A Norton Critical Edition*, edited by Philip Appleman. New York: Norton.

Davies, Paul. 1988. *The Cosmic Blueprint: New Discoveries in Nature's Creative Ability to Order the Universe.* New York: Simon & Schuster.

———. 1994. *The Last Three Minutes: Conjectures about the Ultimate Fate of the Universe.* New York: Basic.

Deborin, A. M. 1916. *Introduction to the Philosophy of Dialectical Materialism.* Petrograd.

———. 1930. *Dialectics and Natural Science.* Moscow.

Deng Ming-Dao. 1990. *Scholar Warrior.* San Francisco: HarperSanFranscisco.

Denton, Michael. 1985. *Evolution: A Theory in Crisis.* New York: Burnett.

Derrida, Jacques. 1967/1978. "Violence and Metaphysics," and "From a Restricted to a General Economy: For an Hegelianism Without Reserve." In *Writing and Difference*, translated by Alan Bass. Chicago: University of Chicago Press.

———. 2001. *Acts of Religion.* London: Routledge.

Descartes, Rene. 1637/1975 *Discourse on Method*, Translated by Laurence J. Lafleur. Cambridge, UK: Cambridge University Press.

———. 1641/1975. *Meditations.* Translated by Laurence J. Lafleur. Cambridge, UK: Cambridge University Press.

Detienne, Marcel. 1967/1996. *Masters of Truth in Archaic Greece.* Translated by Janet Lloyd. New York: Zone.

Dews, Peter. 2008. "Alain Badiou, *Being and Event.*" *Notre Dame Philosophical Reviews.* Online: http://ndpr.nd.edu/review.cfm?id=12406.

Dharmakirti. C. 650 CE/1962. *Nyayabindhu-tika.* In *Buddhist Logic.* Vol. 2. Translated by F. Stcherbatsky. New York: Dover.

Dignāga. c. 480–540/1968. *Pramanasamuccaya.* In *Dignāga, On Perception; Being the Pratyak aparichheda of Dignāga's Pramā asamuccaya from the Sanskrit Fragments and the Tibetan Versions*, translated and annotated by Masaaki Hattori. Cambridge: Harvard University Press.

Dobbs-Weinstein, Idit. Forthcoming a. "Gersonides: The Supercommenator on Aristotle: The Decisive Forgotten Link Between Averroes and Spinoza." In *Problems in Arabic Philosophy*, edited by Miklós Maróth. Piliscsaba: Avicenna Institute of Middle Eastern Studies, 2003.

———. Forthcoming b. "Necessity Revisted: Spinoza as a Radical Aristotelian." Spinoza by 2000 series, vol. 5, edited by Yirmiyahu Yovel.

Duhem, Pierre. 1909. *Etudes sur Léonard de Vinci.* Paris: Hermann.

Dunn, James D. G. 2005. *The New Perspective on Paul: Collected Essays.* Tubingen: Mohr/Siebeck.

Duns Scotus, John. 1301/1965. *A Treatise on God as First Principle (De Primo Principio).* Translated by Allan Wolter. Chicago: Franciscan Herald.

Dumenzil, Georges. 1952. *Les Dieux des Indo-Europeans.* Paris: Presses Universitaires de France.

Durkheim, Emile. 1912. *Les formes élémentaires de la vie religieuse.* Paris: Alcan.

Dussel, Enrique. 1998. *Etica de la liberación en la edad de globaización y exclusión.* México: Editorial Trotta.

Eamon, William. 1994. *Science and the Secrets of Nature: Books of Secrets in Medieval and Early Modern Culture.* Princeton, NJ: Princeton University Press.

Eco, Umberto. 1970/1988. *The Aesthetics of Thomas Aquinas*. Translated by Hugh Bredin. Cambridge: Harvard University Press.

Edwards, Jonathan. 1746/1957. *A Treatise Concerning Religious Affections*. In *The Works of Jonathan Edwards*, vol. 2, *Religious Affections*. New Haven: Yale University Press.

———. *Treatise on the Will*. In *The Works of Jonathan Edwards*, vol. 1, *Freedom of the Will*. New Haven, CT: Yale University Press.

Eggan, Fred. 1973. *The Social Organization of the Western Pueblos*. Chicago: University of Chicago.

Eisenman, Robert. 1997. *James, The Brother of Jesus*. New York: Viking.

Eliade, Mircea. 1964. *Shamanism: Archaic Techniques of Ecstasy*. Translated by Willard R. Trask. Bollingen 76. Princeton: Princeton University Press.

Emmanuel, Arghiri. 1969/1971. *Unequal Exchange: A Study of the Imperialism of Trade*. Translated by Brian Pearce. New York: Monthly Review.

Empedocles. c. 500 BCE/1996. *On Nature*. In *The Classical Greek Reader*, edited by Kenneth Atchity and Rosemary McKenna. New York: Holt.

Engels, Frederick. 1880/1940. *Dialectics of Nature*. Translated by Clemens Dutt. New York: International.

Fang, Thomé H. 1981. *Chinese Philosophy: Its Spirit and Its Development*. Taipei: Linking.

Feuerbach, Ludwig. 1841/1957. *The Essence of Christianity*. Translated by George Eliot. New York: Harper.

Foucault, Michel. 1966. *Les mots et les choses*. Paris: Gallimard.

Frank, Andre Gunder. 1998. *ReOrient: Global Economy in the Asian Age*. Berkeley: University of California Press.

Frank, Andre Gunder, and Barrt Gills. 1992. "The Five Thousand Year World System: An Introduction." *Humboldt Journal of Social Relations* 18:1.

Frank, Andre Gunder, and Barrt Gills, editors. 1993. *The World System: Five Hundred Years or Five Thousand?* London: Routledge.

Fa-tsang. *Hua-yen I ch'eng chiao I fen-ch'I chang*. Al-Farabi. 10th C CE/1983. *Tahsil al-sa'ada*, edited by Ja'afar al-Yasin. Beirut: Dar al-Andalus.

Farella, John R. 1984. *The Main Stalk: A Synthesis of Navajo Philosophy*. Tucson: University of Arizona Press.

Freyne, Seán. 1980. *Galilee, from Alexander the Great to Hadrian, 323 B.C.E. to 135 C.E.: A Study of Second Temple Judaism*. Notre Dame, IN: University of Notre Dame Press.

Fromm, Erich. 1941. *Escape from Freedom*, New York: Holt, Reinhart & Winston.

———. 1947. *Man For Himself*. New York: Holt, Reinhart & Winston.

Fukuyama, Francis. 1989. "The End of History." *The National Interest* (Summer).

Gal-Or, Benjamin. 1987. *Cosmology: Physics and Philosophy: Including a New Theory of Aesthetics*. 2nd ed. New York: Springer.

Gamwell, Franklin I. 1989. *The Divine Good: Modern Moral Theory and the Necessity of God*. New York: Harper.

———. 2000. *Democracy On Purpose: Justice and the Reality of God*. Washington, DC: Georgetown University Press.

Garrigou-Lagrange, Réginald. 1932. *Le réalisme du principe de finalité*. Paris: Descleé.

———. 1938. *Les trois ages de la vie intérieure: prélude de celle du ciel*. Paris: Cerf.

Gautama. ?/1930. *Nyaya Sutra*. Translated by S. C. Vidyabhusana. Allahabad: The Panini Office.

Gilson, Étienne. 1968. *Dante and Philosophy*. Translated by David Moore. Gloucester, MA: Peter Smith.

———. 1936. *The Spirit of Medieval Philosophy*. Translated by A. H. C. Downes. New York: Scribners.

———. 1952. *Being and Some Philosophers*. 2nd ed. Toronto: Pontifical Institute of Medieval Studies.

Gernet, Jacques. 1985. *A History of Chinese Civilization*. Translated by J. R. Foster. New York: Cambridge University Press.

Geroch, Robert. 1985. *Mathematical Physics*. Chicago Lectures in Physics. Chicago: University of Chicago Press.

al-Ghazali. 10th C CE/2001. *The Incoherence of the Philosophers*. Translated by Michael Marmura. Salt Lake City: Bringham Young Univeristy.

Giambutas, Marija. 1991. *Civilization of the Goddess: The World of Old Europe*. Edited by Joan Marler. San Francisco: HarperSanFrancisco.

Gibbon, Edward. 1776–1788/2003. *The Decline and Fall of the Roman Empire*. New York: Modern Library.

Gilead, I. 1995 "The Foragers of the Upper Paleolithic." In *Archeology and Society in the Holy Land*, edited by T. E. Levy. New York: Facts-on-File Press.

Gleason, Sarell Everett. 1936. *An Ecclesiastical Barony of the Middle Ages: The Bishopric of Bayeux, 1066–1204*. Cambridge: Harvard University Press.

Gomez, L.O. 1967. "Selected Verses from the Gandavyuha." PhD diss., Yale University.

Gottwald, Norman. 1979. *The Tribes of Yahweh: A Sociology of the Religion of Liberated Israel, 1250–1050 B.C.E.* Maryknoll, NY: Orbis.

Gramsci, Antonio. 1948. *Il materialismo storico e la filosofia di Benedetto Croce*. Torino: Einaudi.

———. 1949a. *Il Risorgimento*. Torino: Einaudi.

———. 1949b. *Note sul Macchiavelli, sulla politica, e sullo Stato Moderno*. Torino: Einaudi.

———. 1949c. *Gli intelletualli e l'organizzazione di cultura*. Torino: Einaudi.

———. 1950. *Letteratura e vita nazionale*. Torino: Einaudi.

———. 1951. *Passato e presente*. Torino: Einaudi.

———. 1954. *L'Ordine Nuovo*. Torino: Einaudi.

———. 1966. *La questione meridionale*. Roma: Riuniti.

Gryson, R. 1982. "The Authority of the Teacher in the Ancient and Medieval Church." *Journal of Ecumenical Studies* 19.

Gutierrez, Ramon. 1991. *When Jesus Came the Corn Mothers Went Away*. Palo Alto, CA: Stanford University Press.

Hall, John. 1995. "Studies in the Rise of the West." *Metu Studies in Development* 22:3.

Harris, Errol E. 1965. *The Foundations of Metaphysics in Science*. London: Allen & Unwin.

———. 1987. *Formal, Transcendental, and Dialectical Thinking*. Albany: State University of New York Press.

———. 1991. *Cosmos and Anthropos*. Atlantic Highlands, NJ: Humanities.

———. 1992. *Cosmos and Theos*. Atlantic Highlands, NJ: Humanities.

Hartshorne, Charles. 1948. *The Divine Relativity: A Social Conception of God*. New Haven, CT: Yale University Press.

———. 1967. *A Natural Theology for Our Time*. LaSalle, IL: Open Court.

Hatab, Lawrence J. 1990. *Myth and Philosophy: A Contest of Truths*. LaSalle, IL: Open Court.

Hauerwas, Stanley. 1981. *A Community of Character: Toward a Constructive Christian Social Ethic*. Notre Dame, IN: University of Notre Dame Press.

Hayek, Friedrich A. von. 1973. *Law, Liberty, and Legislation.* Vol 1., *Rules and Order.* Chicago: University of Chicago Press.
———. 1989. *The Fatal Conceit: The Errors of Socialism.* Edited by W. W. Bartley III. Chicago: University of Chicago Press.
Hayden, Brian. 1986. "Old Europe: Sacred Matriarchy or Complementary Opposition?" In *Archaeology and fertility cult in the ancient Mediterranean,* edited by A. Bonanno, 17–30. Amsterdam: Gruner.
———. 1998. "An Archaeological Evaluation of the Gimbutas Paradigm." In *The Pomegranate* 6:35–46.
Hegel, G. W. F. 1807/1967. *Phenomenology of Mind.* Translated by J. B. Baillie. New York: Harper.
———. 1817/1990. *Encyclopaedia of the Philosophical Sciences (Outline).* Translated by Steven Taubeneck. New York: Continuum.
———. 1830/1971. *Encyclopaedia of the Philosophical Sciences.* Translated by William Wallace. Oxford: Oxford University Press.
Heidegger, Martin. 1928/1962. *Being and Time.* Translated by John Macquarrie and Edward Robinson. New York: Harper & Row.
———. 1934/1989. *Beitrage sur Philosophie* ("Contributions to Philosophy"). Frankfurt: Klosterman.
———. 1941/1979–1987. *Nietzsche.* 4 vols. Translated by David Farrell Krell. San Francisco: Harper & Row.
Heimart, Alan. 1966. *Religion and the American Mind: From the Great Awakening to the Revolution.* Cambridge: Harvard University Press.
Heraclitus. c. 500 BCE/1996. *On Nature.* In *The Classical Greek Reader,* edited by Kenneth Atchity and Rosemary McKenna. New York: Holt.
Hesiod. c. 750 BCE/1988. *Theogony.* Translated by M. L. West. Oxford: Oxford University Press.
Heyer, Friedrich. 1969. *The Catholic Church: 1648–1870.* London: Adam & Charles Beck.
Heyd, Thomas, and John Clegg, editors. 2005. *Aesthetics and Rock Art.* Aldershot, UK: Ashgate.
Hobsbawm, Eric. 1959. *Primitive rebels: Studies in Archaic Forms of Social Movements in the 19th and 20th Centuries.* New York: Norton.
Homer. c. 750 BCE/1961. *The Illiad.* Translated by Richard Lattimore. Chicago: University of Chicago Press.
———. 750/1965. *The Odyssey.* Translated by Richard Lattimore. New York: Harper.
Horsely, Richard, and Paul Hanson. 1985. *Bandits, Prophets, and Messiahs.* Maryknoll, NY: Orbis.
Hume, David. 1777/1886. *Enquiry Concerning Human Understanding.* London: Longmans, Green.
———. 1779. *Dialogues Concerning Natural Religion.* London: Longmans, Green.
Huntington, Samuel. 1993. "The Clash of Civilizations." *Foreign Affairs* (Summer).
Ingham, Mary Elisabeth. 1993. "Scotus and the Moral Order." *American Catholic Philosophical Quarterly* 62:1.
Isvara Krsna. 3rd C CE/1935. *The Sankhya-karika.* Edited and translated by S. S. Suryanarayana Sastri. Madras: University of Madras.
Jaimini. C. 400 BCE/1933–1936. Translated by Ganganatha Jha. Gaekwad's Oriental Series LXVI, LXX, LXXIII. Baroda: Oriental Institute.

Jaspers, Karl. 1953. *The Origin and Goal of History*. Translated by Michael Bullock. New Haven: Yale University Press.

Jayarasi Bhatta. 7th C CE/1940. *Tattopaplavasimha*. Translated by S. N. Shastri and S. K. Sakesena, revised by S.C. Chatterjee, edited by Pandit Sukhlalji Sanghavi and Rasiklal C Parikh. Gaekwad's Orietnal Series, LXXXVII. Baroda: Oriental Institute.

Jones, A. H. M. 1974. *The Roman Economy*. Oxford: Blackwell.

Joravsky, David. 1961. *Soviet Marxism and Natural Science, 1917–1932*. New York: Columbia University Press.

Kalupahana, David. 1992. *A History of Buddhist Philosophy*. Honolulu: University of Hawaii Press.

Kananda. 300 BCE/1923. *Vaisesika Sutras*. Translated by Nandalal Sinha. In *Sacred Books of the Hindus* VI. Allahaba: The Panini Office.

Kant, Immanuel. 1755/1968. *Universal Natural History and Theory of the Heavens*. Translated by W. Hastie. Ann Arbor: University of Michigan Press.

———. 1781/1969a. *Foundations of the Metaphysics of Morals*. Translated by Lewis White Beck. Indianapolis: Bobbs-Merrill.

———. 1781/1969b. *Critique of Pure Reason*. Translated by Lewis White Beck. Indianapolis: Bobbs-Merrill.

Kautilya. 321–296 BCE/1923. *Artha-sastra*. Translated by R. Shamasastry. In *Kautilya's Arthasastra*. Mysore: Weslyan Mission.

Lao Tzu. c. 500/1972. The Tao Te Ching. Translated by Gia-fu Feng and Jane English. New York: Vintage.

Kierkegaard, Soren. 1846/1941. *A Concluding Unscientific Postscript*. Translated by Walter Lowrie. Princeton, NJ: Princeton University Press.

Kingsley, Peter. 1995. *Ancient Philosophy, Mystery, and Magic: Empedocles and Pythagorean Tradition*. Oxford: Oxford University Press.

Konrad, Gyrogy, and Ivan Szelenyi. 1967. *Intellectuals on the Road to Class Power*. Translated by Andrew Arato and Richard E. Allen. New York: Harcourt Brace Jovanovich.

Kramer, Samuel Noah. 1963. *The Sumerians: Their History, Culture, and Character*. Chicago: University of Chicago Press.

Krauss, Lawrence, and Glenn Starkman. 1999. "The Fate of Life in the Universe." In *Scientific American* (November).

———. Forthcoming. "Life, the Universe, and Nothing: Life and Death in an Ever-Expanding Universe." *Astrophysical Journal*. No Pages. Online: xxx.lanl.gov/abs/astro-ph/9902189.

Kyrtatas, Dimitris J. 1987. *The Social Structure of the Early Christian Communities*. London: Verso.

Laclau, Ernesto. 1977. *Politics and Ideology in Marxist Theory: Capitalism, Fascism, Populism*. London: Verso.

Laclau, Ernesto, and Chantal Mouffe. 1985. *Hegemony and Socialist Strategy*. Translated by Winston Moore and Paul Cammack. London: Verso.

Lancaster, Roger. 1988. *Thanks to God and the Revolution: Popular Religion and Class Consciousness in the New Nicaragua*. New York: Columbia University Press.

Leaman, Olivier. 1988. *Averroes and his Philosophy*. New York: Oxford University Press.

Leibniz, Gottfried von. 1713/1992. *Discourse on Metaphysics; and The Monadology*. Buffalo, NY: Prometheus.

Lenin, V. I. 1902/1929. *What is to Be Done?* New York: International.

---. 1908/1970. *Materialism and Empirio-criticism: Critical Comments on a Reactionary Philosophy*. Moscow: Progress.

---. 1916/1976. *Philosophical Notebooks*. Collected Works 38. Moscow: Progress.

Lenski, Gerhard and Jean. 1982. *Human Societies: An Introduction to Macrosociology*. 4th ed. New York: McGraw Hill.

Lerner, Eric J. 1991. *The Big Bang Never Happened*. New York: Random House.

Li Ki. 1967. Translated by James Legge. Edited with an introduction and study guide by Ch'u Chai and Winberg Chai. New Hyde Park, NY: University.

Lukács, Georg. 1922/1971. *History and Class Consciousness: Studies in Marxist Dialectics*. Translated by Rodney Livingstone. Cambridge: MIT Press.

---. 1953/1980. *The Destruction of Reason*. Translated by Peter Palmer. London: Merlin.

Luria, Aleksandr. 1973. *The Working Brain: An Introduction to Neuropsychology*. Translated by Basil Haigh. New York: Basic.

---. 1974/1976. *Cognitive Development: Its Cultural and Social Foundations*. Translated by Martin Lopez-Morillas and Lynn Solotaroff. Edited by Michael Cole. Cambridge: Harvard University Press.

Lyotard, Jean François. 1979/1984. *The Postmodern Condition: A Report on Knowledge*. Translated by Geoff Bennington and Brian Massumi. Foreword by Fredric Jameson. Minneapolis: University of Minnesota Press.

MacAleer, Graham. 1996. "Saint Anselm: An Ethics of *Caritas* for a Relativist Agent." *American Catholic Philosophical Quarterly* 70.

MacIntyre, Alisdair. 1981. *After Virtue: A Study in Moral Theory*. Notre Dame, IN: University of Notre Dame Press.

Mahdva. 14th C CE/1940. *Sarvadarsanasamgraha*. Translated by E. B. Cowell and A.E. Gough. London: Kegan Paul.

---. 14th C CE/1936. *Brahma-sutra.bhasya*. Translated by S. Subba Rao. Tirupati: Sri Vyasa.

Maistre, Joseph de. 1965. *Works*. Translated by Jack Lively. New York: Macmillan.

Makdisi, George. 1989. "Scholasticism and Humanism in Classical Islam and the Christian West." *Journal of the American Oriental Society* 109:2.

Malebranche, Nicolas. 1674/1980. *The Search after Truth*. Translated by Thomas M. Lennon and Paul J. Olscamp. Columbus: Ohio State University.

---. 1684/1977. *A Treatise of Morality*. Translated by James Shipton. Ann Arbor,: University Microfilms International.

---. 1687/ 1980. *Dialogues on Metaphysics*. Translated by Willis Doney. New York: Abaris.

Mallory, J. P. 1989. *In Search of the Indo-Europeans: Language, Archaeology, and Myth*. New York: Thames & Hudson.

Mandel, Ernest. 1968. *Marxist Economic Theory*. Translated by Brian Pearce. New York: Monthly Review.

Mansueto, Anthony. 1995. *Towards Synergism: The Cosmic Significance of the Human Civilizational Project*. Lanham, MD: University Press of America.

---. 2002a. *Religion and Dialectics*. Lanham, MD: University Press of America.

---. 2002b. *Knowing God: Restoring Reason in an Age of Doubt*. Aldershot, UK: Ashgate.

Mansueto, Anthony, and Maggie Mansueto. 2005. *Spirituality and Dialectics*. Lanham, MD: Lex-ington.

Mao Zedong. 1937/1971. "On Contradiction." In *Selected Works*. Peking: Foreign Languages.

Margulis, Lynn, and René Fester, editors. 1991. *Symbiosis as a Source of Evolutionary Innovation: Speciation and Morphogenesis*. Cambridge, MA: MIT Press.

Maritain, Jacques. 1937. *The Degrees of Knowledge*. Translated by Bernard Wall and Margot R. Adamson. London: Bles.

———. 1951. *Man and the State*. Charles R. Walgreen Foundation Lectures. Chicago: University of Chicago Press.

Marx, Karl. 1843/1978. "Contribution to the Critique of Hegel's Philosophy of Right: Introduction." In *The Marx-Engels Reader*, edited by Robert C. Tucker. New York: Norton.

———. 1844/1978. *Economic and Philosophical Manuscripts*. New York: Norton.

———. 1846/1978. "The German Ideology." In *The Marx-Engels Reader*, edited by Robert C. Tucker. New York: Norton.

———. 1848/1978. "The Communist Manifesto." In *The Marx-Engels Reader*, edited by Robert C. Tucker. New York: Norton.

———. 1849/1978. "Wage Labor and Capital." In *The Marx-Engels Reader*, edited by Robert C. Tucker. New York: Norton.

———. 1859/1961. *Contribution to the Critique of Political Economy: Preface*. In Erich Fromm, *Marx's Concept of Man*. New York: Continuum.

———. 1867/1977. *Capital*. Vol 1. New York: Vintage.

———. 1881/1978. "Letter to Vera Zasulich." In *The Marx-Engels Reader*, edited by Robert C. Tucker. New York: Norton.

———. 1863/1963. *Theories of Surplus Value: Part One*. Moscow: Progress.

———. 1863/1971. *Theories of Surplus Value: Part Two*. Moscow: Progress.

Meikle, Scott. 1985. *Essentialism in the Thought of Karl Marx*. London: Duckworth.

Mellars, P. A. 1995. *The Neanderthal Legacy: An Archaeological Perspective from Western Europe*. Princeton, NJ: Princeton University Press.

Milbank, John. 1990. *Theology and Social Theory*. London: Blackwell.

———. 1999. "The Theological Critique of Philosophy in Hamman and Jacobi." In *Radical Orthodoxy: A New Theology*, edited by John Milbank, Catherine Pickstock, and Graham Ward. London: Routledge.

———. 2006a. "Geopolitical Theology." Unpublished paper. No pages. Online: http://www.theologyphilosophycentre.co.uk/papers.php.

———. 2006b. "Only Theology saves Metaphysics: on the Modalities of Terror." Unpublished paper. No Pages. Online: http://www.theologyphilosophycentre.co.uk/papers.php.

Miranda, José Porfirio. 1972. *Marx y la Biblia*. Salamanca: Sigueme.

———. 1973. *El se y el mesias*. Salamanca: Sigueme.

Moggaliputta-tisa. c. 250 BCE/1979. *Points of Controversy; Or, Subjects of Discourse Being a Translation of the Kathā-vatthu from the Abhidhamma-pi aka*. Translated by Shwe Zan Aung and Rhys Davids. London: Pali Text Society.

Moore, Barrington. 1966. *Social Origins of Dictatorship and Democracy: Lord and Peasant in the Making of the Modern World*. Boston: Beacon.

Nagarjuna, Siddha. c. 200/1970. *Madhyamakakarika*. Tokyo: Hokuseido.

Nasr, Seyyed Hussein. 1964. *Three Muslim Sages: Avicenna, Suhrawardi, Ibn-'Arabi*. Harvard Studies in World Religions. Cambridge: Harvard University Press.

Neusner, Jacob. 1975/1998. *Invitation to the Talmud*. Rev. ed. Atlanta: Scholars.

Bibliography

Nietzsche, Friedreich. 1889/1968. *The Will to Power*. Translated by Walter Kaufmann and R. J. Hollingdale. Edited by Walter Kaufmann. New York: Random House.

Owens, Joseph. 1980. *St. Thomas Aquinas on the Existence of God: Collected Papers of Joseph Owens*. Edited by John R. Catan. Albany: State University of New York Press.

Paley, William. 1802/1986. *Natural Theology*. Charlottesville, VA: Ibis.

Pawlikowski, John. 1982. *Christ in the Light of Jewish-Christian Dialogue*. New York: Paulist.

Peifer, John Frederick. 1964. *The Mystery of Knowledge*. New York: Magi.

Plantinga, Alvin. 1993. *Warrant: the Current Debate*. New York: Oxford University Press.

Plato. c. 385 BCE/1968. *Republic*. Translated by Alan Bloom. New York: Basic.

———. c. 385 BCE/1960. *Timaeus*. Translated by H. D. P. Lee. New York: Penguin.

Prajnaparamita-Hrdaya Sutra. 1st C BCE. No pages. Online: http://kr.buddhism.org/zen/sutras/conze.htm.

Prigogine, Ilya. 1977. *Self-Organization in Non-Equilibrium Systems*. New York: Wiley.

———. 1979. *From Being to Becoming: Time and Complexity in the Physical Sciences*. New York: Freeman.

———. 1984. *Order Out of Chaos*. With I. Stengers. New York: Basic.

———. 1988. "An Alternative to Quantum Theory." With Tomio Petrosky. In *Physica* 147A:461–86.

Pythagoras. c. 530 BCE/1996. *The Golden Verses*. In *The Classical Greek Reader*, edited by Kenneth Atchity and Rosemary McKenna. New York: Holt.

Rahner, Karl. 1957/1968. *Spirit in the World*. Translated by William V. Dych. New York: Herder & Herder.

———. 1976/1978. *Foundations of Christian Faith: An Introduction to the Idea of Christianity*. Translated by William V. Dych. New York: Seabury.

Ramanuja. 11th C CE/1904. *Sribhasya*. Translated by Beorge Thibault. Oxford: Clarendon.

Raschke, Carl. 2005. "Derrida and the Return of Religion: Religious Theory after Postmodernism." *Journal of Religious and Cultural Theory* 6:2:1–2.

Renfrew, Colin. 1989. *Archeology and Language: The Puzzle of Indo-European Origins*. London: Penguin.

Radhakrishnan, Sarvepalli, and Charles A. Moore. 1957. *A Sourcebook in Indian Philosophy*. Princeton, NJ: Princeton University Press.

Rig Veda, The. ?/1981. Translated by Wendy Doniger O'Flaherty. New York: Penguin.

Rosmini, Antonio. 1842–1845. *Opere*. 17 vols. Napoli: Batelli.

———. 1859–1874. *Teosofia: Opere Posthume*. 5 vols. Turin: Presso la Società Editrice di Libri di Filosofia.

Rostovzeff, M. 1960. *Rome*. Translated by J. D. Duff. New York: Oxford University Press, 1960.

Rubenstein, Richard E. 1999. *When Jesus Became God: The Epic Fight over Christ's Divinity in the Last Days of Rome*. New York: Harcourt Brace.

Ruether, Rosemary Radford. 1974. *Faith and Fratricide: The Theological Roots of Anti-Semitism*. New York: Harper.

ibn Rusd. 12th C CE/1979. *Tahafut al-tahafut*. Translated by Simon Van Den Bergh. Gibbs Memorial Trust.

———. 12th C CE/2002. *The Decisive Treatise*. Translated by Charles Butterworth. Salt Lake City: Bringham Young University.

———. 12th C CE/2005. *Averroes on Plato's Republic*. Translated by Ralph Lerner. Ithaca, NY: Cornell University Press.

Saddharmapundarkia Sutra. 1st C CE/1993. Translated by Burton Watson. *The Lotus Sutra*. New York: Columbia University Press.

Ste. Croix, C. E. M de. 1982. *The Class Struggle in the Ancient Greek World: From the Archaic Age to the Arab Conquests*. London: Duckworth.

Sanders, E. P. 1977. *Paul and Palestinian Judaism: A Comparison of Patterns of Religion*. London: SCM.

Sankara Acarya. 8th C CE/1890. *Vedanta Sutras with Commentary*. Translated by George Thibaut. In *Sacred Books of the East* XXXIV and XXXVIII. Oxford: Clarendon.

———. 8th C CE/1929. *Sarvasiddhantasamgraha*. Translated by Prem Sundar Bose. Calcutta.

———. 8th C CE/2004. *Viveka-chudamani*. *Scriptures of the World's Religions*, edited by James Fieser and John Powers. New York: McGraw-Hill.

Sarkisyanz, E. 1965. *Buddhist Backgrounds of the Burmese Revolution*. The Hague: Nijhoff.

Sartre, Jean-Paul. 1943. *L'être et le néant, essai d'ontologie phénoménologique*. Bibliothèque des idées. Paris: Gallimard, 1943.

———. 1960. *Critique de la raison dialectique: précédé de question de méthode*. Paris: Gallimard.

Sereni, E. 1968. *Capitalismo nelle campagne*. Torino: Einaudi.

Scheler, Max. c. 1928/1961. *Man's Place in Nature*. Translated by Hans Meyerhoff. New York: Noonday.

Shannon, Claude, and Warren Weaver. 1949. *The Mathematical Theory of Communication*. Urbana: University of Illinois Press.

Seifert, Josef. 1981. *Back To Things in Themselves: A Phenomenological Foundation for Classical Realism: A Thematic Study into the Epistemological-metaphysical Foundations of Phenomenological Realism, a Reformulation of the Method of Phenomenology as Noumenology, a Critique of Subjectivist Transcendental Philosophy and Phenomenology*. Studies in Phenomenological and Classical Realism. London: Routledge & Kegan Paul.

Sheldrake, Rupert. 1981. *A New Science of Life: The Hypothesis of Formative Causation*. Los Angeles: Tarcher.

———. 1989. *The Presence of the Past: Morphic Resonance and the Habits of Nature* London: Fontana.

Siddhartha, Gautama (The Buddha). 6th C BCE/1915. *Anguttara-nikaya, Samyutta-nikaya, Visuddhi-maggi*. In *Buddhism in Translations*, edited by H. C. Warren. Harvard Oriental Series 3, sixth issue. Cambridge: Harvard University Press.

Silberman, Neil Asher. 1998. *Heavenly powers: Unraveling the Secret History of the Kabbalah*. New York: Grosset/Putnam.

ibn Sina. 11th C CE/2001. *Danishnamah*. In Parwiz Morewedge, *The Metaphysica of Avicenna (ibn Sīnā); a critical translation-commentary and analysis of the fundamental arguments in Avicenna's Metaphysica in the Dānish nāma-i Alā i (The book of scientific knowledge) The Metaphysica of Avicenna*. Binghampton: Global.

———. 11th C CE/1996. *Isharat*. In Shams Inati, *Ibn Sīnā and Mysticism: Remarks and Admonitions, Part Four*. New York: Kegan Paul.

———. 11th C CE/2005. *al-Shifa'*. In *The Metaphysics of the Healing*, translated by Michael Marmura. Salt Lake City: Brigham Young University.

Skocpol, Theda. 1979. *States and Social Revolutions: A Comparative Analysis of France, Russia, and China.* New York: Cambridge University Press.
Smith, Adam. 1776. *The Wealth of Nations.* No pages. Online: http://www.econlib.org/LIBRARY/Smith/smWN.html.
Snodgrass, Anthony. 1980. *Archaic Greece: An Age of Experiment.* London: Dent.
Soloviev, Vladimir. 1878/1995. *Lectures on Divine Humanity.* Edited by Boris Jakim. Hudson, NY: Lindisfarne.
Spinoza, Baruch. 1677/1955. *Ethics.* New York: Dover.
Stone, Merlin. 1976. *When God Was A Woman.* London: Dorset.
Subotnik, Rose Rosengard. 1976. "Adorno's Diagnosis of Beethoven's Late Style: Early Symptom of a Fatal Condition." *Journal of the American Musicological Society* 29:242–75.
Summer, J. D. 1999. "The Shandiar IV Flower Burial." *Cambridge Archeological Journal* 9.
Tabor, James. 2006. *The Jesus Dynasty: The Hidden History of Jesus, His Royal Family, and the Birth of Christianity.* New York: Simon & Schuster.
Tathagatabargha Sutra.
Thales of Miletus. c. 575 BCE/1996. *Water.* In *The Classical Greek Reader,* edited by Kenneth Atchity and Rosemary McKenna. New York: Holt.
Thapar, Romila. 2002. *Early India: From the Origins to 1300.* Berkeley: University of California Press.
Theissen, Gerd. 1982. *The Social Setting of Pauline Christianity: Essays on Corinth.* Edited and translated by John H. Schütz. Philadelphia: Fortress.
Thibault, Paul. 1972. *Savoir et pouvoir: philosophie thomiste et politique cléricale au XIXme siècle.* Quebec: Université de Laval.
Tipler, Frank. 1994. *The Physics of Immortality: Modern Cosmology, God, and the Resurrection of the Dead.* New York: Doubleday.
Treloar, John L., S.J. 1991. "Moral Virtue and the Demise of Prudence in the Thought of Francis Suárez." *American Catholic Philosophical Quarterly* 65:387–400.
Tsung-mi. 828–835/1995. *Yuan jen lun.* In *Inquiry in to the Origin of Humanity,* edited and translated by Peter Gregory. Honolulu: Kuroda Institute, University of Hawaii Press.
Turing, Alan. 1950/1981 "Mind." in *The Mind's I,* edited by D. R. Hofstadter, and D. C. Dennett. New York: Basic.
Turnbull, Herbert Westren. 1956. "The Great Mathematicians." In *The World of Mathematics, Volume One,* edited by James R. Newman. New York: Simon & Schuster.
Umasvati Acarya. 3rd C CE/1920. *Tatvarthadhigama Sutra.* In *Sacred Books of the Jainas, II,* translated by J. L. Jaini. Arrah: The Central Jaina Publishing House.
Upanishads. ?/1953. Edited and translated by S. Radhakrishnan. New York: Harper.
van Zantwijk, Rudholph. 1985. *The Aztec Arrangement.* Norman, OK: University of Oklahoma Press.
Vajracchedika-prajnaparamita. 2nd C BCE–2nd C CE/1957. Translated by Edward Conze. Serie Orientale Roma 13. Rome: Instuto italiano per il medio ed Estremo Oriente.
Vasubhadhu. 4th C CE/1938. *Vimsatika.* Translated by Clarence Hamilton. New Haven, CT: American Oriental Society.
Vatican I. 1870/1990. *Dei Filius.* In *Decrees of the Ecumenical Councils,* edited by Norman P. Tanner. Washington, DC: Georgetown University Press.
Vernant, Jean Pierre. 1962/1982. *The Origins of Greek Thought.* Ithaca, NY: Cornell University Press.

Wallerstein, Immanuel. 1974. *The Modern World System*. Vol. 1, *Capitalist Agriculture and the Origins of the European World Economy in the Sixteenth Century*. New York: Academic.

———. 1980. *The Modern World System*. Vol. 2, *1600–1750: Mercantilism and the Consolidation of the European World Economy*. New York: Academic.

———. 1989. *The Modern World System*. Vol. 2, *The Second Era of Great Expansion of the Capitalist World Economy, 1730–1840s*. New York: Academic.

Wansbrough, John. 2004. *Quranic Studies*. New York: Prometheus.

Ware, Timothy. 1993. *The Orthodox Church*. New York: Penguin.

Waters, Frank. 1963. *The Book of the Hopi*. New York: Viking Penguin.

Weber, Max. 1920/1958. *The Protestant Ethic and the Spirit of Capitalism*. Translated by Talcott Parsons. New York: Scribners.

———. 1921/1968. *Economy and Society: An Outline of Interpretive Sociology*. Edited by Guenther Roth and Claus Wittich. Translated by Ephraim Fischoff et al. New York: Bedminster.

Wetter, Gustav. 1952/1958. *Dialectical Materialism: A Historical and Systematic Survey of Philosophy in the Soviet Union*. Translated by Peter Heath. New York: Praeger.

Whitehead, Alfred North. 1929. *Process and Reality: An Essay in Cosmology*. New York: Macmillan.

Wilhelm, Richard and Cary F. Baynes, translators. 1967. *The I Ching or Book of Changes*. 3rd ed. Princeton, NJ: Princeton University Press.

Williams. Paul. 1989. *Mahayana Buddhism*. New York: Routledge.

Wood, Ellen Meiksins, and Neal Wood. 1978. *Class Ideology and Ancient Political Theory: Socrates, Plato, and Aristotle in Social Context*. Blackwell's Classical Studies. Oxford: Basil Blackwell.

Wright, N. T. 2004. "Paul's Gospel and Caesar's Empire." No pages. Online: www.ctinquiry.org/publications/wright.htm.

Xenophanes. c. 500/1996. *On Nature*. In *The Classical Greek Reader*, edited by Kenneth Atchity and Rosemary McKenna. New York: Holt.

Yao Xinzhong. 2000. *An Introduction to Confucianism*. Cambridge: Cambridge University Press.

Yao Wen yuan. 1975. "The Social Basis of the Lin Biao Anti Party Clique." *Peking Review* 7 (March).

Yovel, Yirmiyahu. 2001. *Spinoza and Other Heretics*. Princeton, NJ: Princeton University Press.

Zhou Dunyi. 1017–1073 CE/2004. *T'ai-chi t'u shuo* or *Explanation of the Diagram of the Great Ultimate*. In *Scriptures of the World's Religions*, edited by James Fieser and John Powers, translated by Kurt Vall. New York: McGraw-Hill.

Zhu Xi. 12th C CE/2004. *Xing qing xin yi deng mingyi*. In *Scriptures of the World's Religions*, edited by James Fieser and John Powers, translated by Kurt Vall. New York: McGraw-Hill.

Zitara, Nicola. 1971. *L'unita d'Italia, Nascita di una colonia*. Milan: Jaca.

Znamenski, Andrei. 2003. *Shamanism in Siberia*. Dordrecht: Kluwer.

Zupanic, Alenka. 2004. "The Fifth Condition." In *Think Again: Alain Badiou and the Future of Phlosophy*, edited by Peter Hallward. London: Continuum.